RIGHTS, RESISTANCE AND CRITIQUE

This is the first edited volume on the work of essential critical legal theorist Costas Douzinas. It brings together his collaborators, students and contemporaries in legal critique to reflect on different aspects of his oeuvre and to celebrate his significant contribution to legal scholarship over the last 40 years.

From the inauguration of a distinctly critical legal project in the UK in the mid-1980s, Costas Douzinas has been at the forefront of a number of its key theoretical, legal and political debates. With key interventions in deconstructive and postmodern legal theory, legal aesthetics, psychoanalysis and law, the radical critique of human rights and, most recently, in the critical legal theorisation of social movement, protest, sovereign power, the state of exception and non-human rights, Douzinas's influence has been widely felt. This book provides a key overview of some key aspects of his oeuvre, uncovering fresh resources and new directions of analysis.

The book is aimed at students and researchers who share an interest in the politics and aesthetics of law. It refuses the easy critical equation of law and politics, and produces a more radical account of law, politics, resistance and social change.

Alexis Alvarez-Nakagawa is a Senior Lecturer in Law and a Fellow at the Institute for the Humanities and Social Sciences at Queen Mary University of London. His research interests range from the globalisation of Western legal forms and the colonial history of international law to emerging developments in human rights and environmental law, including transitional justice in South America and the growing recognition of legal personhood and rights for non-human beings. His work draws on philosophy, critical theory, anthropology and jurisprudence to explore these themes from an interdisciplinary and critical perspective. He is the founding Co-Director of the Forum on Decentering the Human, Co-Director of the Queen Mary Centre for International Law (CeILa) and founding Co-Director of the Group of Critical Studies in Politics, Law, and Society (PoDeS).

Illan rua Wall is a Lecturer at the Irish Centre for Human Rights and the University of Galway, School of Law. Until 2023, he was Professor of Law at the University of Warwick, and Director of the Centre for Critical Legal Studies. He is an editor of the blog criticallegalthinking.com, the open-access publisher Counterpress and a managing editor of the journal *Law & Critique*. He works on questions of protest and disorder, using contemporary critical legal theory.

RIGHTS, RESISTANCE AND CRITIQUE

The Legal Theory of Costas Douzinas

Edited by Alexis Alvarez-Nakagawa and Illan rua Wall

Routledge
Taylor & Francis Group
a GlassHouse Book

Designed Cover Image: Getty Images

First published 2026
by Routledge
4 Park Square, Milton Park, Abingdon, Oxon OX14 4RN

and by Routledge
605 Third Avenue, New York, NY 10158

Routledge is an imprint of the Taylor & Francis Group, an informa business

A GlassHouse book

British Library Cataloguing-in-Publication Data
A catalogue record for this book is available from the British Library

ISBN: 978-1-032-62218-7 (hbk)
ISBN: 978-1-032-62224-8 (pbk)
ISBN: 978-1-032-62222-4 (ebk)

DOI: 10.4324/9781032622224

Typeset in Sabon
by Deanta Global Publishing Services, Chennai, India

CONTENTS

LIST OF CONTRIBUTORS

Alexis Alvarez-Nakagawa
Queen Mary University of London
Law Department
London, UK

Joanna Bourke
Birkbeck College
University of London
Department of History
London, UK

Julia Chryssostalis
Westminster University
Law School
London, UK

Cormac Deane
Institute of Art, Design & Technology
Dun Laoghaire
Dublin, Ireland

Marcus V. A. B. De Matos
Brunel University
Law School
London, UK

Adam D. Gearey
Birkbeck College, University of London
Law Department
London, UK

Peter Goodrich
Yeshiva University
Benjamin N. Cardozo School of Law
New York, US

Oscar Guardiola-Rivera
Birkbeck College, University of London
Law Department
London, UK

Patrick Hanafin
Birkbeck College, University of London
Law Department
London, UK

Ozan Kamiloglu
London South Bank University
Division of Law
London, UK

Gilbert Leung
Max Planck Law
Frankfurt, Germany

Elena Loizidou
Birkbeck College, University of London
Law Department
London, UK

Daniel Matthews
University of Warwick
Law School
Coventry, UK

Andreas Philippopoulos-Mihalopoulos
Westminster University
Law School
London, UK

Moniza Rizzini Ansari
Federal University of Rio de Janeiro
Law School
Rio de Janeiro, Brazil

Illan rua Wall
University of Galway
School of Law
Galway, Ireland

Ceylan Begüm Yıldız
University of Greenwich
School of Law and Criminology
London, UK

1

INTRODUCTION

Thinking (Critically) as Friends and Neighbours

Alexis Alvarez-Nakagawa and Illan rua Wall

Few figures have left as deep and transformative a mark on the critical legal movement as Costas Douzinas. One of the key voices of the BritCrits—the distinctly UK iteration of critical legal studies that took shape in the 1980s—Douzinas has also crafted a bold and expansive philosophical project whose influence resonates far beyond the bounds of legal scholarship. Douzinas' books have been translated into 13 languages; his ideas are studied and debated in universities from Latin America to China; and his philosophy has informed political discourse and shaped events both in the UK and, most significantly, in his native Greece. This book began to take shape as Costas stepped down from his chair at Birkbeck Law Department—which he co-founded in the early 1990s. We see this as a timely opportunity not only to celebrate his intellectual contributions but also to reflect on their continuing significance today.

This volume will explore Douzinas' work, situating it within the broader intellectual and institutional landscape from which it took shape and evolved. These ideas and their context are brought to life through the voices of those who were present—friends, colleagues, and former students. Their reflections provide not only personal memories but also a unique and fragmentary account of one of the most significant legal-intellectual movements in recent decades across the UK and Europe. This volume is a collective endeavour—not merely because Costas was a prolific initiator of collaborative projects, whether editorial or institutional, but because the celebration of a life's intellectual labour is best rendered through a multiplicity of voices. Indeed, the collective assembled here is one that Costas himself helped to nurture over the years. Yet this volume does not aim to offer hagiography; it emerges instead from collegiality and friendship. It hardly needs saying

DOI: 10.4324/9781032622224-1

that colleagues and friends can be loving, but they are also among the most capable and staunch critics. In psychoanalysis, the neighbour, and in deconstruction, the friend, play vital roles in revealing both the joyous possibilities and the paradoxes, aporias, and limits of theory and relationships. It is also worth recalling—as one chapter in this volume does—that in the imaginary of the ancient city, particularly the Greek polis, the line between neighbour and stranger, friend and foe, was always blurred. Who better, then, than a collective of colleagues, comrades, and friends to assemble a volume grounded in camaraderie but addressed to a critical readership?

This is not a book about legacy in the traditional sense—Costas' work remains very much alive and evolving. In the past three years alone, he has published several books and edited multiple volumes on a wide range of topics, from the state of exception to the extension of rights to non-humans. This collection is best understood as an entry point into Douzinas' body of work, rather than a comprehensive examination or descriptive catalogue of his ideas. Inevitably, some aspects of his thinking are left out, not due to lack of importance, but because his thought has been expansive and continues to evolve and provoke. We hope this volume opens the door for future engagement and deeper exploration of his contributions. The gaps here should be seen as an invitation for ongoing dialogue and further volumes that will build upon and enrich Costas' oeuvre. We are confident this will be just the first of many publications to come, addressing the inevitable gaps left in this imperfect yet heartfelt initial effort.

If there is one thread that runs through all the chapters, it is the experience of re-reading Douzinas. For most of us, Costas' work has been familiar for some time, and taking on this project meant returning to articles and books we first encountered years ago. This volume, then, is about reencounter, reinterpretation, re-evaluation, and reappropriation. In this process, we discovered new insights hidden in earlier readings and, at times, found ourselves distancing from previous interpretations and encounters with his texts. Re-reading always brings something new to the old, unsettling certainties and established understandings. This kind of openness to the new—as Costas emphasized in his early work on deconstruction—is a defining feature of the written word.

The Book

This volume brings together 17 leading voices from the global critical legal collective, featuring both longer and shorter contributions that explore various facets of Douzinas' work. Throughout, the book situates his ideas alongside those of key figures in critical legal, feminist, and socio-legal theory, while also pointing to potential lines of flight as well as the challenges and impasses his work may provoke. The volume charts the coordinates of historical disagreements and traces the genealogy of contemporary debates, all while opening new conversations both in alignment with and in critique of Douzinas' thought. Some chapters revisit and revise his ideas, while others build upon or draw inspiration from him to move beyond the 'Douzinas toolbox'.

When we planned the book, it had three distinct sections: the first section, 'Traversing the Postmodern Moment', was to explore the significance of postmodern jurisprudence both in its rejection of legal formalism and in the new possibilities it opens for understanding legal relations. The second section, 'The Critique of Rights', was to engage with, expand upon, and sometimes critically diverge from Douzinas' perspective on rights. We hoped that the final section, 'Crisis, Resistance and Politics', would centre Douzinas' recent work on protest, resistance, and (il)legality. While the book still broadly accords to this delineation, as often occurs, the actual writing of the book has made things a little messier. So rather than artificially reassert our preconceived structure, we have left it fade into the background, gently guiding our authors, without constraining them unnecessarily.

The book begins with two chapters that aim to introduce Douzinas in different ways. In Chapter 2, Joanna Bourke begins the collection with a brief biography. With a historian's incision and brevity, she explores Costas' critical praxis, both in the institutions of academia (the creation of Birkbeck Law School, the journal *Law and Critique*, the Birkbeck Institute for the Humanities, and the blog criticallegalthinking.com) and in the political sphere (in the Greek parliament, the media). What emerges from this brief chapter is a sense of vibrancy and creation, where theoretical novelty is matched with radical institution-building. She writes: 'Without the materiality of institutions, it is impossible to build traditions of critical theory and practice or to reproduce ideas and values across generations'.

In Chapter 3, Illan rua Wall seeks to read across the Douzinas' oeuvre to uncover a critical praxis. He explores three moments in Douzinas' oeuvre, the article 'OUBLIEZ CRITIQUE', the critique of human rights and the claim in *States of Emergency* that critique is oriented around truth and the drive to change. He argues that despite being full of critical legal *theories*, Douzinas' work does not provide a singular critical legal theory. Instead, he identifies a threefold critical (legal) praxis of 'traversal, exhaustion and overcoming'. Human rights or jurisprudence are to be traversed. 'We must go *through* these forms, exhausting the affective pull of their imperial hegemonies. And in this traversal, we begin to find the resources to overcome their gravitational pull'.

In Chapter 4, Peter Goodrich traces the figure of the early Douzinas within the British legal academic scene of the late 1980s—a context marked by what he calls 'the asphyxiating walls of the epistemic prison house of the law faculty', a time when the jurisprudence curriculum had been reduced to analytical philosophy and black-letter law. Goodrich remembers—or perhaps envisions (it's difficult to be sure which)—a Douzinas reborn: a kind of 'superfetation of Costas D.', emerging after a difficult viva examination and a transformative encounter with deconstruction. Goodrich analyzes in some detail the Douzinas of *Postmodern Jurisprudence*, particularly the seminal essay *Fin(n)is Philosophiae* (written with Ronnie Warrington), an Oedipal attack on Oxbridge jurisprudence and its theological grip on the reproduction of the legal academy and profession. For Goodrich, *Fin(n)is Philosophiae* can be seen as an expression of a 'minor jurisprudence'—a different, deterritorialized, subaltern language that challenges the hegemony of analytic legal philosophy and the imperialism of legal method. As Goodrich recalls, *Postmodern Jurisprudence* was also born of irreverent and playful methods—recall the *whiskoletterosmotron*, a writing apparatus designed 'for the osmosis of graphic characters representing sounds used in speech with spirits distilled from grains'. In contrast to the closures fostered by the Oxford-style legal education, the book sought to open legal discourse to everyone. This subaltern, irreverent, open, and playful vision would soon crystallize in what Goodrich calls the 'Birkbeck non-School'.

In Chapter 5, Gilbert Leung draws on Douzinas' notion of the priority of injustice (*adikia*) over justice (*dike*) to develop a meditation on what he terms 'just listening'. Theories of justice inevitably fail because they enclose, limit, and hypostatize, offering only incomplete and provisional frameworks that cannot capture the full complexity of experience. As Douzinas provocatively puts it, 'the theory of justice is the oldest failure of human thought'. Rather than continuing to pursue elusive theories of justice, Douzinas suggests we turn our attention to the *sense* of injustice. While the idea of justice remains clouded in abstraction and controversy, injustice is immediately and viscerally felt. Importantly, the 'sense' of injustice is not about 'making sense' of it through conceptual frameworks. Rather, sense refers to materiality and corporeality—justice as felt through the body. Resistance, then, becomes a bodily response to harm, hunger, despair—an overwhelming sense of injustice. Across the many instances of resistance lies a shared, irrepressible desire to alter the prevailing order, a 'righting' that emerges not from theory but from the embodied sense of injustice. But what if we approached justice in a similar way? What would a non-theoretical, material *sense* of justice look—or rather, sound—like? If, as Leung suggests, listening is the material precondition of thought, and thought precedes theory, then perhaps the sense of justice is best understood as a mode of listening. What might justice sound like? Given its elusiveness, perhaps the answer lies in speculative metaphors. Drawing from the experience of music, Leung invites us to imagine justice as a cadence or even as silence.

In Chapter 6, Adam Gearey, Costas' co-author in *Critical Jurisprudence*, writes a wild and mercurial response, adopting the radical edge of the playful methodology developed in *Postmodern Jurisprudence*, as well as the feminist critique of that text, to stage theoretical conversations and readings which never took place. But it also develops something like a method: 'Like the feminist strategy, this method of reading *Deontology* does not seek a pre-existing position from which to speak. Rather, and again like the feminist strategy, it tried to locate an 'inter textual space' or 'gap' where meanings circulate and 'renewal' and 'transformation' might be possible'. Exploring Bentham's *Deontology*, Gearey finds an abject *embodied* training of the body in order to improve the economy of happiness. This allows him to double back to think of the *corpus* of law. A body that needs to be trained and habituated. Following this seam, Gearey suggests a lost thread of critique from Bentham through the Owenites, and on to Engels. This seam, he hints, might allow a recovery of a certain radical Bentham—against the hegemonic liberal re-readings: 'it might be that the legacy of our authors is to appreciate the labour of bodies whose work is the source of wealth: a sacrifice that makes ill-being the hidden foundation of Bentham's commerce of happiness'.

Elena Loizidou draws on the early Douzinas in Chapter 7 to analyze the concept of postmodern truth (as articulated in *Postmodern Jurisprudence*) in relation to the contemporary phenomenon of 'post-truth'. She examines the extent to which postmodern ideas of truth align with, or diverge from, those of post-truth. Her analysis focuses particularly on Chapter 2 of the volume—'From the Book to the Text: Hermeneutics, Critique, Deconstruction'—where Douzinas, Warrington, and McVeigh develop a postmodern critique of modern jurisprudence's understanding of legal truth as the product of a conscious and rational subject free from prejudice. For *Postmodern Jurisprudence*, the truth of a legal text is neither universal nor mechanically produced; it is instead shaped by history and language. Drawing on Derrida's deconstructive theory, the authors invite us to view the legal text as a play of signs—never fixed nor fully present, but rather 'a trace of presence and absence', 'temporarily deferred', and 'repeatable'. While this may suggest that there is no single, universal truth to a text, Loizidou stresses that this does not imply that 'we do not need truths'. Postmodern critiques never argue for the abandonment of truth, nor do they promote the kind of *confirmation bias* associated with post-truth thinking—where individuals follow only those opinions, texts, or media that affirm their existing views. On the contrary, *Postmodern Jurisprudence* warns against the dangers of universalizing and naturalizing one's own perspective. Unlike post-truth discourse, which rejects the very existence of truth, *Postmodern Jurisprudence* calls on us to remain vigilant toward all claims that seek to naturalize the world we inhabit and, in doing so, enact violent exclusions.

In Chapter 8, Ozan Kamiloglu writes a short intervention, exploring Douzinas' shifting analysis of law and the image. Law, he shows us, both loves and fears images. They are 'too worldly, too sensual and potentially corrupt, too contingent and transient' and so they must be replaced by the word which is malleable and more readily subdued. Kamiloglu maps Douzinas' thinking of the image against the three distinct phases of critical legal scholarship. In each phase, the image presents a dangerous supplement for law, opening horizons and generating a utopian field beyond the everyday of legal relations.

In Chapter 9, Julia Chryssostalis takes these analyses of the image and re-imagines them for the question of sound. She writes: 'by shifting from image to sound in his legal phenomenology, this contribution experiments with iteration'. This re-writing weaves 'a new text, that explores an aspect of the sensible... that Douzinas has written little about'. With immense care and wit, Chryssostalis experiments with Douzinas' analyses of the image to produce an entirely new but familiar analysis of sound. The result is both a new and compelling development of Douzinas' aesthetics, but also an 'irreverent, playful and joyous deconstructive corps-à-corps with the canon' that comes directly from the tradition of *Postmodern Jurisprudence.*

In Chapter 10, Andreas Philippopoulos-Mihalopoulos seeks to bring forth what he calls 'the material Douzinas'—a figure not explicitly articulated, but folded into the very fabric of Douzinas' work. This chapter focuses on Douzinas' writings on law and aesthetics as a gateway to the 'material Douzinas who is folded in Douzinas' material'. Douzinas' aesthetics, Philippopoulos-Mihalopoulos argues, dwell in a chiaroscuro of absence: something withdrawn, concealed, and beyond phenomenological reach. This, he contends, is the locus of materiality itself—because materiality is revealed through absence; the material becomes significant precisely when it gestures toward its own immateriality. In Douzinas' aesthetic theory, when the image is phenomenologically present, its material dimension—its production, substance, and *thingness*—withdraws. Visuality, for Douzinas, is rooted in the desire to perceive the invisible and ineffable, the radical otherness that always recedes. His aesthetic project, then, is to demonstrate how law and the image—and art more broadly—are not only historically and conceptually compatible, but also constitute one of the last social spaces in which radical otherness can appear. The project of new materialism stands to learn from Douzinas' oeuvre. For what is the ultimate aim of the material turn in law, asks Philippopoulos-Mihalopoulos, if not to move beyond identity politics and toward a planetary materiality, where ethical flows and affective encounters make bodies visible, legible, and politically significant?

In Chapter 11, Alexis Alvarez-Nakagawa draws on Douzinas' work to shed light on the contradictory logic underpinning the emerging discourse of 'non-human rights'. Indeed, if paradox has long been the 'organizing principle' of human rights, as Douzinas argues, how can we be sure that paradox is not also underpinning the emerging discourse of non-human rights? Alvarez-Nakagawa interrogates the ontological and anthropological grounds upon which rights—both human and non-human—are granted, using this as a lens to further unpack the paradoxes of extending rights beyond the human. What appears to be a progressive move within non-human rights toward 'decentring' the human often ends up reinforcing a more insidious form of 'recentring'. When non-human beings are recognized as subjects of rights on the basis of their similarity—or identity—to humans, as is often the case in the rights granted to animals, rivers, or machines, the human becomes the benchmark for the moral worth of non-humans. Rather than promoting an openness to the alterity of non-humans, non-human rights risk assimilating them into familiar legal and moral categories, thereby masking ontological difference. The chapter situates non-human rights within a broader movement that spans contemporary philosophical, economic, scientific, and technical discourses and practices, revealing a metaphysics obsessed with overcoming otherness and reasserting a disembodied, abstract model of the human as the ultimate standard of value, agency, and existence. Rights are indeed the 'ideology of the end'—not because they signify the end of ideologies, but because they mark the gradual assimilation of everything that exists into the horizon of the human's end.

In Chapter 12, Patrick Hanafin argues that Costas Douzinas' work exemplifies what he terms the 'errancy of rights'. Drawing on Jacques Rancière's notion of the orphan letter and Maurice Blanchot's reflections on refusal and insubordination, Hanafin suggests that this errancy refers to the capacity of rights to drift from their sanctioned, inert form—as 'dead letters' in biocratic constitutional documents—toward becoming tools of political subjectivation for the oppressed. In this errant form, rights no longer function as binding instruments within the normative order but instead open space for radical politics. Their unexpected and improper use disrupts their original function, allowing us to reimagine rights not merely as dispositifs of control and exclusion but as insurgent practices of resistance. This offers an agonistic understanding of the law and a counterpoint to the appropriation of rights by institutional power. In Douzinas' work, rights become something other than rights: they serve as vehicles of resistance against the hegemony of neoliberal legal discourse. His writing brings to the surface the repressed 'insurrectionary element' at the core of rights, unsettling their domestication and pointing toward a politics of emancipation yet to come.

In Chapter 13, 'The Electrical Dialectic', Cormac Deane explores the question of political entanglement as theorized by Douzinas by examining the *techne* of infrastructures, and of electricity in particular. Electricity is a disruptive, contorting force, which is also (infra)structured and determined. Drawing on media archaeology and infrastructure studies, Deane argues that it is important to parse 'entanglements in such a way that the interconnectedness of the technological and the political becomes hard to ignore'.

To do this, he focuses on political interpretations of electricity by Edmund Burke, Vladimir Lenin and Carl Schmitt. Deane explores how their thinking about electricity can be considered in terms of dialectics. Ultimately this takes him back to Douzinas' problem of *adikia*. The issue is that it is never static. Its dialectical energy promises 'a never-ending churn of attempts to achieve justice in the face of injustice, which itself is always in a state of becoming'.

In Chapter 14, Ceylan Begüm Yıldız revisits the notion of the 'right to resistance' in Douzinas' work, focusing on its relevance amid the tightening legal constraints on protest across the globe—recent examples include the prosecution of climate activists and university students demonstrating against the war in Gaza. The chapter opens with an analysis of resistance through the lens of anomie. For Douzinas, anomie emerges when there is a rupture between the social ethos and the legal order—when the values of a community are no longer reflected in state law. In such moments, the social ethos itself becomes a source of resistance against the law. While Douzinas' effort to ground the legitimacy of resistance outside the framework of positive law is compelling, Yıldız raises important questions about the concept of social ethos: who has the authority to invoke it? What happens when multiple, conflicting claims to ethos arise? The chapter concludes by turning to the figure of the resisting subject, focusing on Douzinas' reading of Antigone as a paradigmatic example of resistance to the law in the name of a higher, transcendental command. According to Yıldız, the figure of the resisting subject often carries a sacrificial undertone—one she argues must be challenged in favour of a conception of resistance that foregrounds life as both its source and its end.

Oscar Guardiola-Rivera begins Chapter 15 with an extraordinary story of Douzinas' visit to Colombia in the early 2000s, with the stage stormed by the Revolutionary Armed Forces of Colombia. The story, which is given a mythic treatment, gives way to a complex philosophical reflection on uses of Bloch and utopian analysis. Restaging Douzinas' reading of Bloch, Guardiola-Rivera pits a left- and right-Aristotelianism against one another within the human rights canon, and the result is a fresh opening of closed horizons. The article is a tour-de-force which winds together decolonial and critical reflection, so that a different kind of critique begins to emerge. Guardiola-Rivera explains this as:

> Investigative, detective-like, less indeterminate, associated with a general jurisprudence that exercises not only the power of forensic judgment but also a hopeful, projective, aesthetic, or fantastic judgment capable of mobilising the force of a new beginning from the interrupted orientations of the past into the future.... This is a view of the not-yet. Not only what just is, but also justice.

Chapter 16 situates Douzinas' work within the context of the Brazilian human rights movement that emerged from the street protests of the 2010s. Monica Rizzini Ansari describes how in moments of intense political repression—when protesters faced the overwhelming force of militarized police—networks of human rights defenders played a crucial role in documenting abuses and supporting protesters. Rather than institutionalized organizations, these were loosely formed collectives of volunteer lawyers and activists who operated during demonstrations to provide legal aid, monitor police misconduct, and ensure visibility of state violence. These defenders, often occupied hybrid roles—as protesters, observers, and advocates—armed with legal knowledge, access to reporting mechanisms, and ties to national and international institutions. A key feature of these human rights movements was their critical orientation. Rather than naively upholding universalist ideals, they approached human rights with reflexive scepticism, aware of its Eurocentric foundations and its complicity in global biopolitical governance. The critique of human rights was not an obstacle but a resource—fuelling efforts to re-politicize rights and align them with radical, emancipatory demands and new resisting subjectivities. In doing so, these movements blurred the boundaries between legal activism and social struggle, transforming human rights from tools of control into instruments of solidarity, resistance, and collective agency. What ultimately stands out from this engagement between the critique of human rights and social mobilization is that critical legal theory thrives not in abstraction but as praxis—when it is mobilized in pursuit of radical transformation.

In Chapter 17, Marcus de Matos addresses Douzinas and Warrington's work on the aesthetics of justice, looking to explore the right to reclaim lost bodies. The chapter focuses on an incredibly fraught case in Brazil that de Matos was involved in. In 2011, police invaded a poor neighbourhood in Rio de Janeiro and opened fire. They injured a number of people but killed one 11-year-old boy. Juan de Moraes' body was taken away by police, who tried to destroy the evidence. The chapter traces the right to recover lost bodies across history, finding religious and philosophical traces. De Matos explains: 'Losing the body, in Walter Benjamin's words, is also losing the memory of history. Resisting this loss is an act of resistance to claim memory over tradition: an act not to conform to defeat when the victory of the enemy will threaten the very existence of the dead'.

The final chapter of the volume features an unpublished interview between Daniel Matthews and Costas Douzinas, conducted on 28 March 2013. In this wide-ranging and insightful conversation, Douzinas revisits the origins of the critical legal movement in the 1980s, tracing the distinctions between American Critical Legal Studies and the British 'BritCrit' tradition. He discusses the strategic use of deconstruction as a means to move beyond both legal positivism and interpretivism, the founding of the Critical Legal

Conference in 1984 and the launch of the journal *Law and Critique*. The interview moves through key moments in Douzinas' intellectual and political trajectory: the ethical turn in critical theory, the global rise of human rights discourse, and the political upheavals of the 2010s—from Tunisia and Athens to the Occupy movements and the so-called age of resistance. He reflects on the (de)subjectification produced by financial capitalism and consumerism, and on the potential for political (re)subjectification in moments of collective mobilization—particularly in light of the then-possible electoral victory of Syriza in Greece. The interview closes with a short addendum written by Douzinas 13 years later, offering reflections on what came after: Syriza's electoral victory, the realities of governance, and the ongoing role of critical legal theory in an era marked by both hope and disillusionment. Together, the interview and its coda encapsulate some of Douzinas' most enduring ideas on law, politics, resistance, and praxis.

2

COSTAS DOUZINAS

Critical, Political, Institutional

Joanna Bourke

Costas Douzinas: dazzling intellectual, ebullient orator, political maverick. Imagine my dismay at being asked to condense his virtuosity into a few pages about the 'Institutional Douzinas'! Other chapters in this book attempt to do justice to his intellectual and political ideas, uncovering the genealogy of his thoughts, and often transforming them into something as precious and sparkling as the original. It is my fate, as Costas' partner for nearly three decades, to sift through the rubble and provide readers with something more prosaic: a simple, chronological narrative of place, publication, and institutional purpose.

Let me start by turning back in time when, almost fifty years ago, Costas was appointed to his first teaching post at a British university. It was a one-year lectureship at Middlesex Polytechnic. The Head of the Law Department at Middlesex was Alan Hunt, the great Marxist legal sociologist. One day, Alan took Costas aside and warned him: 'you're a lefty, you do legal *theory*, you have a strong accent: you won't go far in the English legal academy'. He offered to pay for Costas to take elocution lessons, adding that Costas might want to abandon his dreams of an academic life in Britain for a career in Greek politics.

Costas shrugged off the criticisms and rejected the advice. After all, he had been engaged in the Greek resistance since a young man but, as the Colonels' dictatorship came to an end in 1974, had left Greece in pursuit of a PhD at the London School of Economics. For Costas, the UK offered an opportunity to combine radical politics with his intellectual passions, which at that time included Marx, Marcuse, Foucault, Freud, and Habermas. He put this learning to good use in a PhD on the First Amendment of the American Constitution. It was to prove a risky choice: his PhD examiner

DOI: 10.4324/9781032622224-2

was John Finnis, a conservative philosopher of law who followed Thomas Aquinas and disapproved of anyone who quarrelled with Catholic theology.

Thankfully, neither Hunt's acerbic advice nor Finnis' reactionary admonitions discouraged him. Costas was offered the lectureship at Middlesex, where he taught until 1989 when he moved to Lancaster University. Intellectually, Middlesex and Lancaster provided the foundations for what were to become his lifelong passion for the fusion of radical thought with legal education. It was during this period that Costas, Alan Hunt, Paul Hirst, Peter Fitzpatrick, Peter Goodrich, Ronnie Warrington, and Alan Norrie founded the Critical Legal Conference. At their first conference, which took place in 1985, Costas and his closest friend and colleague Ronnie Warrington presented a talk entitled 'Fin(n)nis Philosophiae: On the Deconstruction of Jurisprudence' (the title was an ironic reference to John Finnis), signalling their interest in the scholarship of Derrida.[1] Goodrich ruminates about this talk in his contribution to this volume. This was also the period when Costas published (along with numerous articles) *Constitutionalism and Critical Theory* (1986) as well as *Postmodern Jurisprudence* (1991) and *Justice Miscarried* (1992), both with Warrington. In 1989, the journal *Law and Critique* was established with Costas as one of the founding managing editors, and in 1999, Birkbeck Law Press committed to the publication of theoretical legal scholarship.

These early, scholarly contributions to critical legal studies were to prove important when, in 1992, he was informed that Birkbeck, University of London, was advertising for three legal scholars to establish a new Law School. Costas and Goodrich (also at Lancaster University at that time) had less than forty-eight hours to meet the application deadline. They worked late into the night, submitting their applications with minutes to spare.

Establishing a totally new academic Department of Law was an unusual proposition in the early 1990s. There were already five Law Departments in London, the youngest of which had been created in the 1950s. As was to be expected, these established Departments were less than enthusiastic about the prospect of competition. Furthermore, there were serious questions about whether Birkbeck would even be *allowed* to set up a new Law Department. Admittedly, Law had been taught in the College until 1937. When the college was founded in 1823, it was regarded as an important subject of instruction. However, all legal classes were removed from the curriculum as a condition of Birkbeck becoming a full member of the University of London. By the late 1980s and early 1990s, however, the College was in financial crisis. In 1986, the University Grants Committee, which was then

1 Costas Douzinas and Ronnie Warrington, 'On the Deconstruction of Jurisprudence: Fin(n) is Philosophiae' (1987) 14(1) *Journal of Law and Society* 33

responsible for the public funding of universities, decreed that a part-time student was equivalent to 0.5 of a full-time one, reducing it from 0.8. This bureaucratic decision, which was made without serious consideration of the consequences for a unique college such as Birkbeck, would slash £2.5 million off Birkbeck's budget of £10 million. The person responsible for dragging Birkbeck out of crisis was the new Master, Baroness Tessa Blackstone. She instigated a massive restructuring plan and threw her energies into a series of strategic initiatives that would attract students and thus meet the shortfall of funds. One of these initiatives was a proposal to establish a new Department of Law.[2] Blackstone first had to win the support of the College governors, some of whom were not convinced that the proposal would be financially viable. She then had to persuade the *other* Colleges in the University of London to allow this initiative to go forward. After all, they were anxious that the establishment of a Birkbeck Law Department would threaten their recruitment of students. Blackstone promised that the Department would offer limited options: an undergraduate, *part-time* law degree together with a small number of research students studying for PhDs. The Department pledged not to introduce a new Master's degree (LLM), which was already being taught by the existing five London Law Schools as an intercollegiate degree.

Perhaps surprisingly, the job was unattractive to many legal scholars. The prestige of building a Law Department from scratch was offset by the fact that this had to be done within a daunting timeframe: the academic appointments were to be made in May, with students admitted to classes in September of the same year. Costas was interviewed by Blackstone, Goodrich, jurisprudence scholar William Twining, and legal semiotician Bernard Jackson. He was duly appointed the Rudolph Palumbo Charitable Foundation Lecturer in Law, then rapidly promoted to Senior Lecturer, then Reader, and, finally, Professor. Costas joined his friend Goodrich (appointed earlier the same year as the Corporation London Chair of Law and Head of Department) and Matthew Weait (City Solicitors' Lecturer in Law). Along with Valerie Hoare (the indispensable administrator), they set about setting up a Department that would provide a distinctive, scholarly Bachelor of Laws (LLB) programme for part-time, mature students in London. They also pledged that their Department's identity would represent a radical break from the rather conservative and staid legal establishment. At the time, Costas' philosophy of teaching can be deftly summarised by a statement in his *The End of Human Rights* (2000), where he contended that

2 See my *Birkbeck: 200 Years of Radical Learning for Working People* (OUP 2022) for a more complete history.

> For me, the greatest achievement of critical lawyers is that they teach, research and write under the guiding principle that a law without justice is a body without a soul and a legal education that teaches rules without spirit is intellectually barren and morally bankrupt.[3]

However, the first year was challenging. The four appointees found themselves saddled with heavy teaching (which, for Costas, meant lecturing on his less-than-favourite subject of Constitutional Law) and administrative responsibilities. But the main dilemma was that the newly born Department had to start admitting students before obtaining professional accreditation from the Law Society and the Bar Council. Without accreditation, the Department's graduates would be denied entry to the profession. A phenomenal number of hours were spent drafting the relevant and very lengthy documentation that would persuade the legal establishment to recognise the degree. By May 1993, the hard work was rewarded. The Department of Law at Birkbeck College was awarded 'Law Qualifying Degree status', meaning that the Birkbeck LLM was now recognised as a Senior Status Law Degree.[4] Within three years, they were also offering Master's degree course by dissertation.

From the start, the new School positioned itself as offering comparative and interdisciplinary approaches to the law in ways that were not offered elsewhere in London. This required a delicate balance between the research, teaching, and clinical training aspects of the programme. The programme undertook to provide 'high quality legal education for individuals who had not previously had the opportunity of studying law'. This commitment required the Department to pay particular attention to the needs of minoritised students, ensuring that both the content and form of classes were accessible to people with different working and cultural experiences.[5] In their inaugural year, the Department received over 850 applications. 200 applicants were interviewed in person and 75 were offered places. 60 per cent of the successful candidates were women and 39 per cent were from ethnic-minoritised communities.[6]

From the start, Goodrich and Costas were conscious of the ambivalence, even suspicion, in which they were held by mainstream legal academics. For

3 Costas Douzinas, *The End of Human Rights* (Hart Publishing 2000) vii.

4 'Department of Law. Progress Report 1993/94' (Birkbeck College 1994) np.

5 'Department of Law. Birkbeck College. University of London. Continuing Vocational Education. Development Funding Application for a Law Centre at Birkbeck College' (Birkbeck College, c. 1993–94) np

6 'Department of Law. Birkbeck College. University of London. Continuing Vocational Education. Development Funding Application for a Law Centre at Birkbeck College' (Birkbeck College, c. 1993–94) np.

Costas, this was a proverbial problem, given his 'outsider' status as a Greek-born, radical Leftist. But at this stage in his career, the challenge was also institutional. Historically, Law Schools in the UK tended to be *either* vocational *or* academic. Outside of Oxbridge and London, legal education was the preserve of professional bodies; it was not fully integrated into university communities. As the Birkbeck legal academics admitted in an annual report published three years after opening, the tradition of legal education in the UK was 'peculiar to the common law', which has made law schools in general 'fit uneasily within the University', thus creating 'a tension between the professional and the scholarly'.[7] In the 1970s, this tension was exacerbated by the establishment of vocational legal training courses in what were then called the 'polytechnics'. Even Oxbridge and older London universities emphasised editing treatises, providing short courses for professionals, and offering consultancy advice, rather than engaging in high quality and original scholarly research. Costas, Goodrich, and Weait (who were joined in their second year by Patrick McAuslan, Lindsay Farmer, and Emily Jackson) were determined to combine 'black letter law' (doctrinal legal education) with rigorous research. This did not mean that they abandoned clinical legal training – indeed, they recognised its centrality in the context of the conservatism of the profession and cuts in legal services. From the first year of the programme, the Department invited members of local firms and chambers to co-run courses in professional communication skills, interviewing, and case presentation.[8] Their European legal education style fitted well with their already expansive internationalist and research-based vision.[9] The Department's national and international success in comparative, interdisciplinary and theoretically informed legal research, over vocational and professionally-orientated teaching, distinguished them from their competitors.[10] The strategy paid off in 1996 when the Department was awarded the highest ranking in the Research Assessment Exercise.

It was a strategy that earned them strong opposition from certain sections of the legal establishment. In early 1993, Clive Blackwood, the Secretary of Conservative Lawyers (which describes itself as the 'home of the legal profession within the Conservative Party') launched an official complaint with

7 'Department of Law. Birkbeck College. Academic Plan' (Birkbeck College, 15 May 1995) np.

8 'Department of Law. Birkbeck College. University of London. Continuing Vocational Education. Development Funding Application for a Law Centre at Birkbeck College' (Birkbeck College, c. 1993–94) np.

9 'Department of Law. Birkbeck College. Academic Plan' (Birkbeck College, 15 May 1995) np.

10 'Department of Law. Birkbeck College. Academic Plan' (Birkbeck College, 15 May 1995) np.

the Law Society and the Bar Council. The chief objection was that Costas and Peter were 'immersed' in poststructuralism: 'real' legal cases were being replaced with 'literature', 'image', and 'signs'. He was especially incensed by Costas' and Ronnie Warrington's statement that 'postmodern jurisprudence' is 'an end [i.e., the purpose] to jurisprudence'.[11] Blackwood accused them of teaching that British judges were 'inflexible dogmatists, habitual crushers of liberty'. Indeed, Blackwood insinuated that Peter, Costas, and Matthew had conspired to create a 'nest of legal semioticists in the university'. By teaching the law in a politicised manner, Blackwood believed that the course should be listed as an Arts Degree or a Bachelor of Arts in 'Semiotics of Law', rather than a Law Degree proper. He bitterly concluded, however, that 'If the course had been billed as such, it is doubtful that the college would have needed a new department and library, and doubtful that 1,000 people would have applied'.[12]

Costas, Goodrich, and Weait responded to the attack. Their lengthy rebuttal of the criticisms was accepted by the Law Society and the Bar Council, both of whom 'commended the syllabuses and teaching techniques' in 'the context of mature students'.[13] By 1995, they had successfully established and validated two LLB programmes.[14] Retention rates of 85 per cent or above were also indicative of the success of the programmes. The Department grew rapidly from three academic members of staff in 1992, to six the following year, and seventeen by 2000. By 1998, Costas was a full Professor and, due to the departure of Goodrich, also found himself the Head of Department. On 9 December 1999, Costas gave his inaugural address. Entitled 'The Legality of the Image', his lecture was an expansive theoretical and political exposition of the links between political power, law, and images. In the one-hour-long lecture, he stunned his audience by drawing on thinkers as diverse as Plato, Tertullian, Artemidorus of Daldis, Pseudo-Dionysius, Nikephoros, Theodore Synkellos, George the Pisidian, Immanuel Kant, Gotthold Lessing, Edmund Burke, Arthur Schopenhauer, Jacques Lacan, Jean-François Lyotard, Jacques Derrida, and Pierre Legendre.

Pedagogic practices in the new Department were deliberately informal. Members sought to create a radical breathing space amidst the dusty, conservative lecture halls of legal education. Along with other members of staff,

11 This is a quotation from Costas Douzinas, Ronnie Warrington and Shaun McVeigh, *Postmodern Jurisprudence. The Law of Text in the Texts of Law* (Routledge 1991) 135.

12 Letter from Clive Blackwood, the Secretary of Conservative Lawyers (1993), in the Birkbeck Archive.

13 'Department of Law. Birkbeck College. Academic Plan' (Birkbeck College, 15 May 1995) np.

14 'Department of Law. Birkbeck College. Academic Plan' (Birkbeck College, 15 May 1995) np.

Costas had a distinctive style of teaching: open doors, high levels of sociability, and an emphasis on dialogic exchange both between and among staff and students. Key words were 'experiment' and 'excitement', along with 'reflexivity' and 'critical'.

Costas proved himself to be a prodigious organiser of scholarly events and intellectual programmes, while continuing to publish an extraordinary number of books and articles. The vast range of these intellectual pursuits is discussed in other chapters in this volume, but it is worth mentioning a few of his administrative initiatives. These include becoming one of the organisers of the University of London Legal Research and Theory Seminar series, a fortnightly event that encouraged people from different disciplines to reflect on their research. It brought to the London legal community luminaries such as Jacques Derrida, Niklas Luhmann, Ernesto Laclau, Georges Didi-Huberman, and Jurgen Habermas amongst many others. The seminar was followed by academics from all law schools and established Birkbeck as the prominent theoretical hub in London. With the Department of English, Costas co-organised an annual Law and Literature Conference. His passion for theorising art, law, and politics was demonstrated by books on art theory (including *Law and the Image*, with Lynda Nead) and their conference entitled 'The Art of Justice', held at the Tate Gallery in February 1996. The book and the conference launched the field of legal aesthetics with emphasis on painting and the plastic arts. Costas followed it with his book *Nomos and Aesthetics* (Athens, Papazissis, 2007), an early instance of a now burgeoning field. In 2009, Costas, Illan Rua Wall, Matt Stone, and Gilbert Leung imagined and then developed 'CLT' or the Critical Legal Thinking website; today, the largest critical theory website in the world. In its inaugural statement, CLT states that

> Critical (legal) theory must be re-linked with emancipatory and radical politics. We need to imagine or dream a law or society in which people are no longer despised or degraded, oppressed or dominated and from that impossible but necessary standpoint to judge the here and now. (Legal) critique is the companion and guide of radical change.[15]

Costas' efforts within the Department were matched by his involvement in the College more broadly. He was appointed Dean of the Resource Centre (later, School) of Arts and Social Sciences in 2000. He actively campaigned to have a senior administrative position dedicated to the College's international profile and when a Pro Vice Master of International Relations post was created, he was its first incumbent, travelling globally to spread the

15 Critical Legal Thinking <https://criticallegalthinking.com/purpose/>.

Birkbeck mission. In 2004, Costas established The Birkbeck Institute for the Humanities to stimulate research, public debate, and collaboration among academics and intellectuals on important public issues. Every year, they organised a two-week summer school where exchanges between renowned philosophers, critical scholars, students, and wider publics were encouraged. One of the most influential of these events occurred on 13–5 March 2009 when Costas, Slavoj Žižek, and Alain Badiou organised 'On the Idea of Communism'. 1,200 people turned up to engage in spirited debates with twelve invited speakers. These included Toni Negri, Terry Eagleton, Alain Badiou, Michael Hardt, Gianni Vattimo, Bruno Bosteels, Jacques Rancière, Alessandro Russo, Alberto Toscano, and (shamefully) the only female keynote, Judith Balso. They addressed the question of how communism as a philosophical concept could be made relevant in a century scarred by the 2008 financial crisis, climate change, and global struggles against neoliberal capitalism. Although the speakers differed in numerous ways, they shared the belief that 'from Plato onwards, Communism is the only political idea worthy of a philosopher'. Coinciding with a concert by Michael Jackson, *The Guardian* publicised the conference with a headline stating 'Move Over Jacko, Idea of Communism is Hottest Ticket in Town this Weekend'. They claimed that 'the hottest ticket in London this weekend is not for a pop singer or a football match but for a conference on communism which brings together some of the world's leading Marxist academics'. Costas was quoted insisting that 'There is a sense that we have to start thinking again'.[16]

By this stage in his career, Costas was immersed in the UK scene, with its internationalist focus. He had only occasionally intervened in Greek academia and politics. However, in 2005–6, he was invited to participate in the founding of the first Law School in Cyprus – at the national university. He welcomed the opportunity, seeing in it an echo of his experience setting up the Birkbeck Department decades earlier. He was one of a group of five legal scholars who acted as the new University of Cyprus Law School's directing committee, seeking (at least in Costas' case) to encourage the Birkbeck ethos.

Within a few years, his involvement in Greek political life was to intensify. In 2010, the Eurozone debt crisis erupted. The EU and the International Monetary Fund imposed a strict reform programme on Greece: the country's GDP was slashed by 28 per cent; salaries and incomes were halved. Costas found a voice in newspapers such as the *Guardian* and online forums where he could defend the Greek people and their resistance. After all, Greece was the most militant of the southern European countries that were subjected

16 Duncan Campbell, 'Move Over Jacko, Idea of Communism is Hottest Ticket in Town this Weekend' *The Guardian* (12 March 2009).

to the same neo-colonialist regime. Costas' articles were rapidly translated and republished in the Greek media. Old friendships were renewed. In May 2011, he was invited by the Greek *indignados* to address the occupation of Syntagma Square in Athens. Syriza, at that time a small radical left party, supported the resistance and was recognised as the organisation that could turn the popular indignation into a political force that could rule the country.

In 2015, Costas recalled Alan Hunt's words all those decades earlier: 'you're a lefty, you do legal theory, you have a strong accent: you won't go far in the English legal academy... try for a career in Greek politics'. Costas agreed to have his name listed on ballot papers for election in the Piraeus constituency for Syriza. His name went forward on the understanding that this would enable him to campaign but without an expectation (let alone the desire) to win the seat or leave Birkbeck. To his shock, even panic, a groundswell of support for Syriza resulted in his election as a Member of Parliament in his home city of Piraeus. On 20 September 2015, Costas became an 'accidental politician', a phase that became the subtitle of his book *Syriza in Power. Reflections of an Accidental Politician* (2017). After four decades in London, Costas returned to Greece, as Hunt had suggested all those years ago.

Although Costas continued to teach a Master's degree course at Birkbeck (enduring the gruelling circumstances of a weekly Athens–London commute), he was proud to be involved with the first ever radical government in Western Europe in the modern period. He no longer had to fret about his 'Greek accent' in Britain; instead, he was worried about his 'rusty Greek' in Greece.

Costas never stopped writing. During long and boring debates in Parliament, he could be seen writing academic books and newspaper columns in the debating chamber. During that time, he published three books in English and one in Greek: *Resistance and Philosophy in the Crisis*; *Syriza in Power: Reflections of an Accidental Politician*; *The Radical Philosophy of Rights*; and *Από την Έδρα στα Έδρανα: Εργα και Ημέρες μιας Αριστερής Κυβέρνησης* (English: *From the University Chair to Parliament's Benches: Life and Times of a Left Government*). It was a hectic and anxious time. Costas would spend hours preparing his interviews for TV or radio, worried that any mistakes when debating with opposition politicians could harm the precarious government. His legal training and oratory skills proved useful, as he was appointed the Chair of the House Standing Committee on Defence and Foreign Relations. This is the most senior committee in Parliament: it scrutinises Bills from the two ministries and acts as an oversight of the executive. Costas had to meet ambassadors, foreign secretaries, and other plenipotentiaries visiting Greece and had to travel all over Europe heading diplomatic missions. He insisted on giving university lectures in the various destinations wherever that was possible. It was a fast training period into international relations, its power plays, and hypocritical rituals. He was amused by the foreign office 'top secret' briefing papers which contained information freely available online. It was in his political role that Costas reflected that

> Lawyers live by the text. They learn to speak, write and interpret in particular ways. As a legal philosopher, I wrote and practised hermeneutics, rhetoric and semiotics. Deconstruction teaches that the meaning of the text continuously slides; hermeneutics, the importance of authorized communities of interpreters. I now moved to the other side as an occasional draughtsman of legal texts.[17]

Did the knowledge of critical legal theory help in his political work? By providing ways of understanding the circuits of political and economic power, it did. But it did not redesign institutions.

The Greek Parliament was perhaps not quite ready for Costas' style of debate and comportment. For the first time in its history, the names of Derrida, Habermas, and Legendre were spoken from the Chamber's lectern and entered the Greek Hansard. On one occasion, while chairing the parliamentary debates, Costas even managed to have the leader of the neo-Nazi Xrisi Avgi ('Golden Dawn') party marched ingloriously out of the chamber by Security. But Costas was also not quite ready for the long hours, smoke-filled committee rooms, and cloak-and-dagger negotiations between parliamentary representatives and their constituents. The strain was offset by the successes. The most important of these included: pushing through a parliamentary resolution recognising Palestine (which generated a fraught discussion about the difference between '*the* Palestinian state' or '*a* Palestinian state'); establishing the framework for introducing radical constitutional reform; negotiating and passing the Prespa Agreement between Greece and Northern Macedonia (which ended one of the longest running disputes in Greece's foreign policy); supporting a resolution introducing civil union granting rights to LGBTQ people and allowing changes to one's gender identity; and improving the position of refugees and immigrants.

Syriza lost power to the centre-right New Democracy party in 2019. Costas continued his party-political work as the President of the Nikos Poulantzas Institute (the left-wing think tank) and his regular columns in Greek as well as international newspapers and radio broadcasts. He continued (and continues!) to publish academic texts. In 2022, he published two collections, both in English and Greek. *Left Governmentality* reviewed

17 Costas Douzinas, *Syriza in Power* (Polity 2017) xi.

Syriza's period in government and included contributions by its main ministers. It was followed in 2023 by the edited volume *Life in Dark Times*, a reflection on the Left's response to the multiple disasters of neoliberalism. It was apt that the book opens with Jean-Luc Nancy's final published essay 'On Negativity', since Jean-Luc's combination of creative philosophical imagination, strong ethical stance, and political commitment has been an inspiration for Costas throughout his career. In 2025, Costas published *The Rule of Judges*, a short popular book on the reasons why the justice system has spectacularly failed in Greece, leading to widespread protests against judicial collusion with the government and big capital. His *Law's Desire*, a presentation of his wider work in Greek, was published in 2026. He continued writing on left and radical theory and was elected local councillor in his native Piraeus. His fortnightly page, *Current Political and Philosophical*, in the main progressive newspaper has made him one of the most prominent radical commentators in Greece.

By the second decade of the twenty-first century, he has supervised to completion over thirty PhD students. His books have been translated into many languages and he has engaged in extensive lecture tours of Latin America, South Africa, China, and Europe. His work continues to combine philosophical commitment, critical theory, and political engagement.

Costas' life is characterised by maverick critical thought and radical politics. He keeps saying that critical theory without politics is the reverse side of dogmatic formalism. But he also understands the importance of institutions. He recognises that they can become sclerotic and outdated, as well as being enemies of imagination and creativity. But, critical theory and radical thought need to create their own institutions, which is why he puts lots of energy into institution-building so that ideas acquire a home. Without the materiality of institutions, it is impossible to build traditions of critical theory and practice or to reproduce ideas and values across generations. But without principles, commitment, and passion, institutions eventually die. Theory and ideology need the support of bricks, mortar, and office although not necessarily of officeholders. Costas is proud of his contributions to the establishment of the Birkbeck Law School; he always strives to put his theories into practice. He did not always succeed; he sometimes failed, but he always tried again and failed better.

3

THE CRITICAL (LEGAL) PRAXIS OF COSTAS DOUZINAS

Illan rua Wall

There is an uncanny experience that sometimes happens when you read a close friend. As your eyes travel across the page, you begin to *hear* their singular voice in the words. This is possible, as Martin Heidegger says in a different context, because you have 'carried this voice with you'.[1] Memory makes syntax into cadence. In the act of reading a friend, the text takes on a different vibrancy. Roland Barthes cautions us about taking this to the level of method. He famously argued that we must not rely on the personality of the author to bind together their work: 'writing is the destruction of every voice, of every point of origin. Writing is that neutral, composite, oblique space where our subject slips away; the negative where all identity is lost, starting with the very identity of the body writing'.[2] The author cannot provide the category of identity for 'their *oeuvre*'. And up to a point that is right. The Douzinas which attaches to the 1987 essay, 'On the Deconstruction of Jurisprudence: Fin(n)is Philosophiae' is not the same as the Douzinas associated with 2023's *States of Exception*. Writing dissolves the writer *as far as the text is concerned*. But the voice, as Adriana Cavarero has shown, the corporeal, bodily nature of the voice persists, even only as an echo, despite the way that western metaphysics always tries to devocalise the Logos.[3] So we might reformulate Barthes' proposition. The *text* fragments the authorial voice. But to the friend who listens, the echo remains. This chapter seeks to

1 Martin Heidegger, *Being and Time* (State University of New York Press 2010) 153.
2 Roland Barthes, 'The Death of the Author' (1968) in David Graddoi and Oliver Boyd-Barrett (eds), *Media Texts, Authors and Readers* (Open University Press 1994) 166.
3 Adriana Cavarero, *For More Than One Voice: Towards a Philosophy of Vocal Expression* (Stanford University Press 2005).

DOI: 10.4324/9781032622224-3

read for these echoes, in order to bring together the critical legal praxis of Costas Douzinas.

Beyond Critical Legal Theory?

In his wide-ranging 2005 essay 'Oubliez Critique', Douzinas argues that critical legal theory must not get caught within extant structures and surfaces of society, that it must retain a radical edge by reaching out beyond a legal imaginary. In fact, the article argues that we should 'forget critique', which is a surprising position for someone who has spent their career defending expansive, philosophically inspired critical legal theories. I want to start precisely within this tension, because I will suggest that it helps to unlock both what comes before and after, if not quite uniting his oeuvre, then certainly drawing out a series of theoretical moves that are repeated again and again. 'Oubliez Critique' begins by pointing to a strong legal imaginary in critical theory. The legal archetypes of the legislator, the judge, the litigant/witness, the police and the clerk are deployed (explicitly or implicitly) across multiple different traditions. The forms of legal process itself seem to provide an apt metaphor for the Kantian critical project – the tribunal of reason calls which everything to account. Critique needs to establish and police the boundaries of knowledge. The 'critic is either the judge who makes distinctions, passes judgment and sets limits, or the policeman who guards those limits and ensures that the judicial fiat is translated into daily practice'.[4]

The more this imagination abounds, the more it begins to accord to the 'essence and form' of critique. That is, Douzinas argues, critique 'becomes law-like'.[5] And this is not limited to Kant:

> Hegel's end of history, Marx's communism, Bloch's spirit of utopia, Benjamin's angel of history, Derrida's messiah without the messianic are all judges in the court of final appeal, or more accurately the court of the last judgment; in other words they are legislators. Despite their differences, they set history's law, which is both inside history as its motivating power and outside as the all-seeing eye and looks back from the future. Law-giving acts as a judgment that judges the present from the perspective of a violence-free past or future.[6]

The critic-judge inscribes the limits of knowledge, the critic-police manage these limits, the critic-legislator establishes the frame against which society

4 Costas Douzinas, 'Oubliez Critique' (2005) 16 *Law and Critique* 50.
5 ibid 49.
6 ibid 52.

is judged, the critic-clerk inscribes and describes, turning away from law towards 'the real'. Douzinas argues that it is not that critique becomes legal, but that there is a more complex and sophisticated relation in critical-legal pairing. Critical legal studies cannot simply import the Frankfurt (or any other) School of critique into legal thinking. Rather, Douzinas hints that perhaps a thinking of law is much more important to the work of critical theory than anyone might like to admit.

The nub of the argument appears to arrive with Douzinas' final critical character. Reading Foucault's essay 'What is Enlightenment', he suggests a 'positive and transgressive' form of critique. This form of critique

> means developing *l'art de n'être pas tellement gouverné*, not being ruled so much or in this way. The business of critique is linked with resistance to governance or governmentality and with acts of desubjectification, attempts at detachment from the demands of bio-political power.[7]

The horizon of this 'other' critique, then, is ungovernability. But rather than a classical reading of ungovernability,[8] he connects it with the Schmittian warring subject.

> Without the universalising position of the philosopher or jurist/critic, the subject is a warring subject placed on the battlefield, surrounded by enemies, out to attain a particular victory and with a perspectival view of truth.... War as the model of the social bond facilitates a different type of critique, which would no longer be critique proper but acts of critical resistance, critical subversion or even an event of critical rebellion.[9]

This figure of the 'other critique' is not the legislator, judge, police or clerk. This is something more like a subversive. And so, in a simple sense, the essay argues that critique needs to maintain its subversive ends. 'It is by forgetting (the dominant types of) critique that we might be able to defy the law'.[10] In its most direct sense, the article reads as an argument for critical legal subversion rather than head-on assault. But there is also something more complex at play. I have, thus far, misquoted the title, which is in fact capitalised: 'OUBLIEZ CRITIQUE'. It is not shouted, there is no exclamation mark. But the capitalised French *oublier* (forget) is placed in the imperative tense. This is a law of memory, an injunction to 'FORGET CRITIQUE'. But

7 ibid 67.
8 Cf. Bal Sokhi Bulley, *Governing (Through) Rights* (Bloomsbury 2016); Ben Golder, *Foucault and the Politics of Rights* (Stanford University Press 2015).
9 Douzinas, 'Oubliez Critique' (n 4) 67–68.
10 ibid 69.

for an article which spends many pages in the depths of critique and which ultimately settles upon a position of ungovernability, framing itself as an injunction (or even a law) seems strange.

The key to this strange title lies in an article published three years previously. In 'Theses on Law, History and Time', Douzinas had asked 'can we forget by decree?'[11] The occasion for this slightly strange question was an account of a law of memory from Xenophon's Hellenica:

> In 403 BCE, when the Peloponnesian War had ended, the Athenian Democrats defeated the 30 tyrants who were ruling Athens subsequent to a coup. Cleocritos, the representative of the Democratic Party, could have acted as a vengeful conqueror and demanded the punishment of his enemies for the brutalities they had committed. Instead, his call to the Athenians was, 'let us forget the evils of the past'. The demos passed a decree banning the recollection of these traumatic events and the raising of lawsuits related to them, and the citizens took the oath: *me mnesikakein* – not to remember the evils but also not to use memory as a tool for evil. A clause in the decree exempted only the 30 tyrants and 31 of their henchmen. Instead, these 61 were executed. When one of the Democrats objected to the imposed forgetting, he was brought before the demos by the Democrat Archinos and sentenced to death. After that, the evils of the past were forgotten.[12]

Returning to this story at the end of the article, Douzinas explained, through Freud, that 'the unconscious is the guardian of memory; it selects what is to be remembered and hides the rest under a screen of fantasies and soothing memories'.[13] But this self-protective selection is never complete. The injunction to forget could never work *as a simple injunction* because the repressed would always return. In Xenophon's account, the injunction (law) is not alone. It is paired with the oath (the political):

> The promise the citizens give is performed in every moment when the traumas of the past return to haunt: 'I will not use the memory that returns precisely because it returns'. The oath neutralises memory without losing it, it disciplines memory by placing it in the midst of the polis, as a politics of forgetting acted out in the self-fashioning of citizens.[14]

11 Costas Douzinas, 'Theses on Law, History and Time' (2002) 7(1) *Melbourne Journal of International Law* 14.
12 ibid 1.
13 ibid 15.
14 ibid 15.

We might say that the citizen must *traverse* or *go through* the injuncted memory. The memory returns (how could it not) but it must be passed through. The injunction (law) and the oath (the political) operate together, entwined and inseparable. They generate a polis in which the memory exists as such, but it is struck through. At each moment, people may traverse the memory, but it is in abeyance.

We can read '*OUBLIEZ CRITIQUE*' through this sense of traversal. Douzinas injuncts us to *forget* critique. But even as he repeats this injunction to forget, critique (and its inseparable relation to law) *returns* over and again. Critique and critical legal theory must be overcome, but the act of overcoming seems to require the movement through the body of critique. This act of traversal sets the terms of what comes after. In this passage through critique, there is both a sense of its utility *and* of its exhaustion. In other words, the traversal is helpful but limiting; it is important to show both the ways in which the question of critique can help us understand law, capitalism, rights, politics, power and much else besides, but also to try to think beyond extant critical formations.

Traversing Human Rights

Douzinas' most important foray into the critical legal theory of human rights occurs in *The End of Human Rights*. Written as an extended reflection on the question of 'the subject', the book is at its strongest as it marshals an incredible breadth of political philosophy, bringing a panoply of voices and analyses out from within the human rights canon. It threads together different approaches and analyses to explore the ways in which rights shape (those who use them to change) the world. It would take another essay to explore these in any depth, but it is worthwhile to pull a number of key themes. The first, and perhaps most polyvalent, is the question of the subject – one which Douzinas argues is 'a defining characteristic of our modernity'. This begins with Marx and Burke, who identify the work of abstraction. The universal Man or Human is imagined at the core of the human rights project; the abstraction of humanity provides a grounding for dignity, autonomy, freedom and equality. But yet this abstraction itself is not neutral. Since Wollstonecraft, Louverture and Marx, the idealised universal Human is always already gendered (male), classed (bourgeois), racialised (white), able-bodied and sexualised (straight). Any deviation from the universal Man is treated as manifesting some peculiar particularity. The question of 'the subject', however, does not end with this critique of abstraction.[15] Rather,

15 See also, Jacques Rancière, 'Who Is the Subject of the Rights of Man?' (2004) 103 *South Atlantic Quarterly* 297–310; Danielle Celermajer and Alexandre Lefebvre, *The Subject of Human Rights* (Stanford University Press 2020).

through the centrality of Descartes and Kant in Western metaphysics, it helps to explain how the 'subject in all its various forms and guises, as self-identical, as ego or consciousness, as the *res cogitans*, the being behind thinking or thinking thing, is now the ultimate ground of all that exists'.[16] In this sense, human rights are not simply one form of (anti-political) politics; they are not simply a sentimental humanitarianism or a permissive morality of global empire as other critical accounts of the time suggested. Rather, they are an expression of something essential within Western metaphysics, the coming to fruition of a metaphysical formation.

This metaphysics also reveals another dimension, that is that the subject is both *subjectus* and *subjectum* – both the free autonomous, contentious subject and also subjected to law, dominated and controlled. 'In the composite terms of human rights, humanity represents the groundlessness of freedom, the potential of the future in the present, freedom not only as a will and choice but as the ability to wrench away from legal and historical determinations and open the unknown.... But the legal element of rights returns us to subjection, external determination and constraint'.[17] Bringing out this world historical significance of human rights was essential to the success of *The End of Human Rights,* it both elevated the significance of the matter under consideration (and by extension of the book itself) and, at the same time, underscored the importance of the supplementary, resistant reading of rights that it produced. This was not simply another critical account of human rights, the subtext of the book insisted, it saw rights in their world historical significance... warts and all.

The End of Human Rights pits itself against classical western accounts of the whole, enclosed subject, capable of effectuating itself.[18] There is no autonomous individual; she is already there in society, aculturing and incomplete. The book proposes a subject which is always already shattered. Drawing heavily on the post-structural tradition which had rearticulated structuralism's critique of the subject of western metaphysics as an axis of analysis, Douzinas' assault on the subject primarily comes through Lacan's split subject, the Levinasian ethics of alterity and Drucilla Cornell's imaginary domain. In these accounts of the incompleteness of the subject, a very different rights politics begins to emerge. Instead of the celebratory end of history accounts, we begin to grasp the dark side of anti-political activism which sidesteps ideology, leading to unstoppable proliferations of rights-claiming: 'rights legalise desire... they organise an economy of wants and

16 Costas Douzinas, *The End of Human Rights* (Hart 2000) 204.

17 ibid 226.

18 This is something of a favoured subject, being the subtext of a number of other books on rights – particularly Costas Douzinas, *The Radical Philosophy of Rights* (Routledge 2019).

fears and give public recognition to the subjects wishes'.[19] Later in *Human Rights and Empire*, the articulation of human rights and what Didier Fassin calls 'humanitarian reason',[20] comes into view, producing 'just' wars and 'moral' bombing campaigns, which intensify death and destruction on ever greater scales.

Ultimately then, poststructuralist theory does not provide ways to 'fix' the problems of liberal theory, but instead human rights become more carefully identified. As with 'Oubliez Critique', we traverse the rights canon with Douzinas, exhausting the conventional frameworks which undergird international human rights. The movement through the field is important, because it sets the conditions of emergence. In 2007, Douzinas gave an interesting gloss to his work on human rights. He pointed to Tom Campbell's 1983 book *Left and Rights: A Conceptual Analysis of the Idea of Socialist Rights* – a positivistic work of (largely) analytic legal theory – commenting that while he did not agree with many of the arguments, it had identified a key question that had troubled him for 20 years. The issue was the 'necessary and impossible attempt to marry socialism and rights'.[21] In a sense, Douzinas' analysis of human rights could be characterised as a thorough-going traversal of mainstream understandings of human rights, while insisting upon a certain supplementary form of rights which is excluded from their dominant deployment. This supplementary sense of rights carries a core liberatory kernel. In the age of revolutions, rights opened a fissure within the sovereign order: 'Human rights were the metaphysical principle which opened the distance between the ideal and the real and introduced the demands of justice into legal operations'.[22]

Here we might mark a crucial difference from Samuel Moyn's more recent account of human rights.[23] Moyn takes aim at the 'church histories' of human rights, which see human rights in all forms of rights or justice-claims across history. He insists that there is no necessary and inexorable progression from ancient or early modern notions of justice to the current doctrines of human rights. In fact, he argues that contemporary human rights essentially gain currency from the US presidency of Jimmy Carter. He claims that classical traditions of justice and rights are largely insignificant for the emergence of the contemporary rights and certainly don't explain their hegemony. On the

19 Douzinas, *The End of Human Rights* (n 16) 312.
20 Didier Fassin, *Humanitarian Reason: A Moral History of the Present* (University of California Press 2012).
21 Costas Douzinas, 'Left or Rights?' (2007) 34(4) *Journal of Law and Society* 618.
22 ibid 631.
23 See Samuel Moyn *The Last Utopia: Human Rights in History* (Harvard University Press 2010); Samuel Moyn, *Not Enough: Human Rights in an Unequal World* (Harvard University Press 2018).

face of it, there is a very obvious disagreement with Douzinas who insists upon the revolutionary and resistant scripts built within rights. But on closer inspection, the difference is much less marked. A major development of *The End of Human Rights* is the way Douzinas conceptualises that resistant kernel of rights. While the revolutionary tradition in the eighteenth century could open the gap between the ideal and the real, by the turn of the twenty-first century biopolitics had largely exhausted the potential of this modality of rights:

> Bio-power abolishes the line of separation between universal and particular, ought and is, human rights and rights. The two sides of the divide are collapsing into each other. They are merged through a zone of indifference, where passage from one to the other retains a certain rhetorical force but little axiological significance.... Dominant culture... has collapsed law, regulation and rights into a massive power of disciplining and normalization; democracy, the countervailing power, has turned into neoliberal management and moralistic exhortation and does not seem able to deal with the major conflicts of our time.[24]

Searching for a different grounds for this radical kernel, *The End of Human Rights* identifies the idea of 'right-ing' – a creative and antagonistic mode of claim making, wherein rights name a mode of dissensus. Douzinas roots right-ing in a 'non-metaphysical humanism' that 'would not treat people as synthetic entities for which the prosthetic operation of fragmentary rights satisfies disconnected wants'.[25] Right-ing would emerge in community, not rooted in 'obedience or tradition', but an emergent vibrance of resistant practices. In order to counter the tendency to church history, Moyn's account excludes that non-hegemonic element of right-ing, but he throws the baby out with the bathwater. As Douzinas writes in *States of Exception:* 'When the 70s is chosen as the beginning, all earlier moments of popular resistance that litter the traditions of natural law, natural rights, the rights of man, and recently human rights, are deleted'.[26] Over and again, clear-eyed contemporary critical analyses of rights identify new modalities of resistance and revolt gathered under the name of rights.[27] In other words, there are strong counter-hegemonic analyses of rights, and by focusing too much

24 Douzinas, 'Left or Rights' (n 21) 631–632.

25 Douzinas, *The End of Human Rights* (n 16) 215–216, my emphasis.

26 Costas Douzinas, *States of Exception: Human Rights, Biopolitics, Utopia* (Elgar 2024) 137.

27 See for instance: Lara Montesinos Coleman, *Struggles for the Human* (Duke University Press 2024); Golder, *Foucault and the Politics of Rights* (n 6); Sumi Madhok, *Vernacular Rights Culture* (Cambridge University Press 2021).

on hegemonic visions Moyn falls into a trap identified by Lara Montesinos Coleman. She writes that the failure to see the ways in which rights are given new meanings in social movement praxis, 'there is... a risk of being drawn into fantasy, fixing our coordinates in advance, and reading politics off a readymade theory or conceptual framework'.[28] Douzinas' account of rights maintains a suppleness. It provides a grounds to critique hegemonic forms of rights that pacify movements or provide cover for imperial violence. But it also insists that we are attendant to the spectacular ruptural forms of politics, and to the minor resistances of everyday life.

There is an interesting question here, which Ben Golder asks of fellow critics of human rights (Kennedy, Orford and Mutua).

> After having exposed its false claims to universality, its investment in and reproduction of a narrow liberal ontology, its propensity to circumscribe the field and possibility of politics, its inability to break with global capitalist ordering, its indebtedness to and repetition of colonial history, and a host of related criticisms... critical commentators on human rights nevertheless make a curious return to human rights. In this post-critical guise, human rights emerge in spite of their evident historical and political limitations as the site of reinvestment, reimagining and of futural possibilities.[29]

This poses an important question to my claim of traversal, because while Douzinas traverses rights, there is a question of whether the goal is to redeem or escape them. With human rights, certainly, it seems the aim is redemption.

The Thrashing Spirit and That Syntagma Feeling

In *States of Emergency,* Douzinas suggests that 'the motivation to critique... comes from two sources: the desire to *change* the way things are, the 'radical impulse', and the desire to *understand* the way things are, 'the truth impulse'.[30] This seems very reasonable, very palatable. 'Change' and 'understanding' could easily be the buzzwords of a contemporary neoliberal management handbook. While the change and truth drives are to be found throughout Douzinas' work, they are all too neat and rational to really

28 Peter Rush, 'Killing Me Softly with His Words: Hunting the Law Student' (1990) 1(1) *Law and Critique* 21.
29 Ben Golder, 'Beyond Redemption? Problematising the Critique of Human Rights in Contemporary International Legal Thought' (2014) 2(1) *London Review of International Law* 79.
30 Douzinas, *States of Exception* (n 26) 8.

accommodate his mode of critique. In this section, I want to suggest that rather than bifurcating his critical legal practice into this radical and truth impulses, Douzinas' work sits in tension. On one hand, there is the reasonable, well-mannered critic and on the other is a punk and utopian mode of critique. There is a constant movement between the proper (the hegemonic styles and habits of academic practice), and the *im*proper (the stylistically unruly and impossibly utopian). If the radical and truth impulse are proper to critique, as he suggests, then his work also captures the *im*proper doubles of these terms: what I will call a 'thrashing spirit' and 'that Syntagma feeling'. These others are disorderly; they refuse the calm, polite and well-ordered rationality that is supposed to mark lawyerly academic argument. In a sense, they are better captured by the Situationist cry of 'be reasonable, demand the impossible'.

If we look to two texts from the mid-1980s, we can see very clearly the truth/thrashing interplay. In Douzinas and Warrington's now canonical 'On the Deconstruction of Jurisprudence: Fin(n)is Philosophiae' (hereinafter 'Fin(n)is Philosophiae'), we see a thrashing spirit, aimed at traversing and exhausting the analytic legal tradition, with conservative natural lawyer John Finnis as the personification of the tradition. The article was published in 1987, in the bygone era of hegemonic analytical legal theory. Jurisprudence (or legal theory) modules began with natural law, worked through Austin and Hart, and ended with Dworkin, Finnis and Raz. In 'Fin(n)is Philosophiae' Douzinas and Warrington cut through the self-aggrandising rationality of the analytic jurisprudence. They argued that the analytic tradition (or linguistic philosophy more broadly) sought to create a fully transparent philosophical language, 'to free their discourse from the dangerous 'irrationality' of the always present rhetoric of language'.[31] They insisted that this narrative always produces itself using tools which it explicitly disavows. With Finnis, it is the rejection (and illicit redeployment) of rhetoric to ground his 'timeless logic' of natural law.[32] In particular, Douzinas and Warrington deconstruct his claims to self-evidence and obviousness, upon which his fundamental goods are grounded. They underscore Finnis' desire to 'exorcise the deviousness of figurality, to reclaim the clarity of the scientific language of Wittgenstein's *Tractatus*'.[33] Only to show the ways in which the text cajoles and threatens rhetorically. 'The text denies that it can be built on literary devices, but at the same time it has to use such conceits to establish its truth'.[34]

31 Costas Douzinas and Ronnie Warrington, 'On the Deconstruction of Jurisprudence: Fin(n)is Philosophiae' (1987) 14(1) *Journal of Law and Society* 33.

32 ibid 33.

33 ibid 39.

34 ibid 41.

In a certain light, 'Fin(n)is Philosophae' shares a number of similarities with Peter Fitzpatrick's later devastating deconstruction of Hart in the final chapter *The Mythology of the Modern Law*.[35] In it, Fitzpatrick shows the way that 'as a linguistic philosopher, Hart would not seek the essence of law... since... for Hart that was a misconceived quest. But [that was the]... quest on which Hart' embarked.[36] Despite the disavowal of myth, Hart found need of an origin story, where a 'primitive group' lived through primary rules, but gradually developed in sophistication to reach 'maturity' and 'civilisation'. 'Whatever else this antique story may be' Fitzpatrick commented wryly, 'it is not linguistic philosophy'.[37] As I say, there is a certain similarity, but at the level of style and strategy, 'Fin(n)is Philosophae' could not be more different. Where Fitzpatrick deployed a patient and calm mode of analysis, which tracked slippages and contradictions in a way that analytic philosophy could appreciate – even if the field had built up sufficient defence mechanisms to forestall that particular assault. Douzinas and Warrington thumb their noses at this 'polite' and 'respectful' academic mode. After five pages, they shift into 'literary refreshment', breaking the 'fourth wall' to address the reader: 'Let us pause here. We have a jurisprudential essay on the proper basis of natural law theorising. The next stage would then involve an assessment of the work's importance and quality in relation to that tradition. Usually that is'.[38] Instead they digress into an account of the romantics, and the manner in which they would deconstruct their own writing. This digression then helps them to playfully draw out the literariness of Finnis, which is too easily missed behind the more obvious bullying tone.[39]

There is no doubt, reading that article today, that it is a full-frontal attack on the analytic tradition, but it was a very particular attack on John Finnis – whose work signified the end of philosophy they argued. As Peter Goodrich explains in this book, 'Fin(n)is Philosophae' was 'an oedipal attack upon a domineering examiner' as well as a challenge to the 'theological hold [Oxbridge jurisprudence had] over the pedagogic reproduction of the legal academy and in significant part the profession'.[40] A seething rage, mixed with playful erudition. The article represents a thrashing spirit, in the vein of Zenon Bankowski and Geoff Mungham,[41] Angus MacDonald, Christopher

35 Peter Fitzpatrick, *The Mythology of the Modern Law* (Routledge 2002) 192.
36 ibid 192.
37 ibid 194.
38 Douzinas and Warrington, 'On the Deconstruction of Jurisprudence' (n 31) 36.
39 ibid 41.
40 Peter Goodrich, 'The Superfetation of Costas Douzinas' in Alexis Alvarez Nakagawa and Illan Rua Wall *Rights* (eds), *Resistance, Critique: The Critical Theory of Costas Douzinas* (Routledge 2026).
41 Zenon Bankowski and Geoff Mungham, *Images of Law* (Routledge Direct Editions 1976).

Stanley[42] and, of course, Peter Goodrich.[43] In a 1981 article, Alan Freeman had connected the truth-telling impulse of critique with delegitimation of existing legal apparatuses.[44] *Fin(n)is Philosophae* does not just get to a truth about Finnis, it delegitimates the entire framework that he embodied.

We can usefully read 'Fin(n)is Philosophae' alongside the more sober and prosaic 'Domination, Exploitation and Suffering' which was published a year earlier in 1986.[45] Gone is the playful, dynamic, post-structural style which would come to fruition in *Postmodern Jurisprudence*,[46] and which Douzinas along with Adam Gearey would later deploy with great effect in *Critical Jurisprudence*. There are no fireworks here – no auto-deconstruction, no '*nomopoieticon logopaignion*'.[47] Instead 'Domination, Exploitation and Suffering' is a worthy, careful and patient exposition of Marxist legal theory. It is not uncritical; indeed, the body of the piece points to places where Marxist analysis of the time was inadequate, and concludes by pointing to a sort of visceral affectivity that Marxism expresses – 'a 'feel' that something is wrong' and that extant explanations do not work.[48] This idea of the 'feel' comes late in the article; it is introduced briefly and with an apologetic tone. It feels surprisingly timid in the context of the discussion of structure, ideology, alienation and other meta-terms for Marxism, although it does contain an important early expression of what he will later describe as the paradox of *adikia* – to which I will return in a moment. Crucially, the contrast between 'Fin(n)is Philosophae' and 'Domination, Exploitation and Suffering' reveals the willingness for movement between the two modalities of this 'truth-drive' of his critical legal praxis, a movement between patient, calm criticism and a wild thrashing spirit.

The second impulse that Douzinas points to in *States of Emergency* – a drive to change – also needs to be seen through this same tension. One of the worries that has always harried critical legal studies has been the problem of 'positive alternatives' alongside the negation of critique. Despite the

42 Christopher Stanley, *Urban Excess and the Law: Capital, Culture and Desire* (Cavendish Publishing 1996).

43 Peter Goodrich, *Law in the Courts of Love* (Routledge 1996); Peter Goodrich, *Oedipus Lex* (University of California Press 1995).

44 Alan D Freeman, "Truth and Mystification in Legal Scholarship" (1981) 90(5) *Yale Law Journal* 1, 230. See James Stewart, *The Rise and Fall of Critical Legal Studies* (Edinburgh University Press, 2025) for further lucid discussion of thrashing.

45 Costas Douzinas and Ronnie Warrington's, 'Domination, Exploitation and Suffering' Marxism and the Opening of Closed Systems' (1986) 11(4) *American Bar Foundation Research Journal* 801.

46 Costas Douzinas, Ronnie Warrington and Shaun McVeigh, *Postmodern Jurisprudence: The Law of Text in the Texts of Law* (Routledge 1991).

47 Douzinas and Warrington, 'On the Deconstruction of Jurisprudence' (n 31) 44.

48 Douzinas and Warrington, 'Domination, Exploitation, Suffering' (n 45) 828.

tendency of some within that first wave in the USA to defend the virulent destructive critical legal methods against critiques of nihilism, many, like Roberto Unger, were clearly concerned that as a movement it did not do enough to produce different (more or less positive) approaches to law or society more broadly. While deconstructionist methods accelerated that thrashing impulse, amongst the BritCrits, there was also a much stronger sense that other political possibilities would be needed and were available. And in this context, a net was cast widely to seek to understand the predicament.[49] In a sense, we might pose this as the problem of the political. A great proportion of Douzinas' oeuvre can be understood as the question of how to think the political when its generative forces have been foreclosed by the 'end of history' and the weight of anti-political neoliberalism. Douzinas' response to the 'end of history' in the 1990s came in the form of a deconstructive ethics, drawing on Derrida and Levinas; alongside this was a psychoanalytical understanding of the drives and impulses, egos, superegos and ids. Later it would involve post-Heideggerian theories of being-together, and the heterodox natural laws of resistance. At each site of theoretical endeavour, he developed resources and frames which helped to reopen the question of the political. But at each moment, the political remained aporetic. This was not a simple platform for action. Each intervention was built around the paradox of *adikia*. One of the longest-standing themes of Douzinas' work has been that theories of justice *inevitably fail*. 'The dialectic between justice and injustice does not lead to a dialectic synthesis. Injustice is not the opposite of justice.... *Adikia* is both the gap between justice and injustice and the endless but impossible attempt to bridge it'.[50] This does not mean that we must give up on the work of *doing* justice. Nor that we should be melancholic about the work of justice. Quite the contrary, the question of *adikia* requires that we commit, with all our heart. Across the 1990s and 2000s, there was an ongoing attempt to find the terms to understand this aporetic sense of the political. But for Douzinas, the key moment occurs following the 2008 financial crash.

Building up until the end of 2010, a massive wave of popular unrest began to sweep Southern Europe and North Africa. In parts these movements were revolutionary, unsettling long-standing regimes in Tunisia and Egypt. Elsewhere they expressed a distinct anti-capitalism, challenging ideologies of economic crisis and austerity in Spain, Greece and the USA. Douzinas attended protests against EU enforced austerity in Syntagma Square in Athens. While his texts were always open to insights from social movements,

49 Nicholas Blomley, *Law, Space and the Geographies of Power* (The Guilford Press 1994); Bob Fine and Robert Millar (eds), *Policing the Miners' Strike* (Lawrence & Wishart 1985).
50 Costas Douzinas, *Philosophy and Resistance in the Crisis* (Polity Press 2013) 80.

in the wake of Syntagma the texts drip with a new set of affects and draw on a new wellspring of material. While still tarrying with the same history of philosophy, they increasingly draw on a different register. One scene in particular seemed to crystallise this Syntagma feeling:

> I had just finished my invited address to the Syntagma Square occupation in Athens and members of the multitude were lining up to speak. A man in the queue was showing signs of stage fright. But he proceeded to give a beautiful speech. When I inquired, he nonchalantly told me that when he started speaking he was just mouthing words. A stranger inside him was dictating what to say.[51]

In Syntagma, the crowded affects and atmospheres of resistance collected those involved and gave them a new sense of the political. He comments in *Philosophy and Resistance in Crisis* that they reminded him of 'the scary thrilling days of 1973' and the overthrow of the Colonel's regime in Greece.[52] In the foment of unrest, the paradox of *adikia*, which he had traced conceptually across his thinking, gets restated afresh. 'The Tahrir and Syntagma Square occupiers are the contemporary children of *adikia's* return.... In modernity, the reaction to *adikia* takes the form of (the right to) resistance'.[53] Where theories of justice sought to resolve the dialectic in the abstract, *adikia's* return to the Squares of North Africa, Europe and North America in 2011 named something different. It was a concrete manifestation of an emergent resistant subjectivity, a form of commitment to overcoming the injustice of contemporary neoliberal management societies.[54] The radical drive here was not just for change. But that change would be driven from the streets, from these new subjectivities that were being born in disobedience and resistance: 'Disobedience is transformed from a personal moral act to collective emancipatory practice. The biopolitical project to control individual bodies and minds, and turn the people into a pliant body politic, fails. This is what power fears most'.[55] What was a 'feel' that Marxism manifested in 1986, in *Philosophy and Resistance in Crisis* is a fully developed philosophical theory of the closure of the political, and the site from which creative forms emerge. That Syntagma feeling then is the moment of commitment, a faith in the ruptural quality of collective dissent and resistance. It was a drive to change, but driven from below. What Douzinas' Syntagma feeling diagnoses, I want to suggest is that visceral refusal of the foreclosure

51 Douzinas, *Syriza in Power* (Polity Press 2017) 19.
52 Douzinas, *Philosophy and Resistance in the Crisis* (n 50) 6.
53 ibid 80.
54 Costas Douznas, 'Athens Rising' (2013) 20(1) *European Urban and Regional Studies* 136.
55 ibid 138.

of politics in the 1990s and 2000s. Holding firm against the narrow reformism of hegemonic human rights, against the neoliberal settlement which crowned lawyers and bureaucrats. Douzinas was a philosopher in need of a people. A theorist of ruptural subjects, in a time where rupture was managed and policed. When the rupture called, after Syntagma, how could he not respond.

A Praxis of Critique

I want to finish by suggesting that what connects these sites of critique is a threefold praxis of traversal, exhaustion and overcoming. Because there is no stable grounding 'outside' from which to critique, we must always start within the field. Douzinas starts *within* jurisprudence, human rights or analyses of global capitalist forms. He situates the field in question within the broad sweep of the history of ideas, and pairs it with the most dynamic of contemporary radical philosophy. At times, this leads to a rigorous scholarly analysis which tracks the emergence of contemporary forms; at other times, it is playful, poetic or downright confrontational. At the heart of this is a fundamental orientation that things are not as they seem, that the stories that law (or human rights, jurisprudence, etc) tells of itself are not all-powerful. Douzinas seems to insist at each moment that we must go *through* these forms, exhausting the affective pull of their imperial hegemonies. And in this traversal, we begin to find the resources to overcome their gravitational pull.

Douzinas' work is made up of shards of critique that lacerate structures of power, legal orders, political regimes and economic apparatuses. Piecing these shards together does not give us a complete theory. From his early work on deconstructive techniques, there was a distinct suspicion of completeness. There can be no simple complete expression of his theory, because in Douzinas' work, critique *does not resile in identity*. There is no 'law is...' or 'human rights are...'. Or if there is, then they are momentary identities (dynamic, emergent and changing). Law's identity is not given, once and for all, but it moves with a dialectical or processual unfolding. Reading across an oeuvre we find no singular theory, but instead a plenitude of theories. It is in the theory of *adkia* that he comes closest to a meta-theory, but the aporetic nature of the gap between the substance of injustice and the impossibility of justice can never unite. What is left then, is an extraordinary praxis of critique. A praxis of traversal, exhaustion and overcoming.

4

THE SUPERFETATION OF COSTAS D

Peter Goodrich

The narrative upon which I draw is political, comedic, amicable, and biographical. Others are better equipped than I to calibrate, colligate, and catabolise the celivagous arc and titanic trajectory of our subject's career. From lecturer in law to member of the Greek Parliament, and back again, the chart of his progress is that of postmodernism colliding with the real, of theory collapsing into the quotidian, and of jurisprudence fending off the paraffle and bamblustering of political palabra and pabulum. Latterly an advocate of radical rights, I knew Costas D in his youth, the early and iconoclastic Douzinas, the inaugural comedy as traceable through inebriate evenings, now lost to liquification, and diurnal gems such as 'Fin(n)is Philosophiae', and the immortal 'Suspended Sentences', with its nyctograph, the '*whiskoletterosmotron*' or recumbent reverie and temulent tobacco trance as writing machines. These formed part of *Postmodern Jurisprudence*, a co-authored collection of essays, collective cerebrations that appeared, heaven forfend and turn back the clocks, revise the calendar, to great excitement and plaudits in 1991.[1] It is this inaugural work, a trio of authors aiming at a triptych of volumes, that will be my focus and specifically their driving force, the rebirth of Douzinas as we knew him.

The scene was set in the late 1980s and the admixture of the post-ignition of the 1960s with the first substantive intimations of the *finisecular*, or fin-de-siècle, racial reckonings and climate change. To give a sense of jurisprudence circa 1990, an anecdote can guide the way. In conversation with an Oxford law colleague, the dialogue turned to the narrowing of the jurisprudence

1 Costas Douzinas, Ronnie Warrington and Shaun McVeigh, *Postmodern Jurisprudence: The Law of Text in the Texts of Law* (Routledge 1991).

DOI: 10.4324/9781032622224-4

curriculum. The view she expressed was that when H.L.A. Hart governed the law faculty it was open to difference and covered 'all the schools of jurisprudence'. There was a richness to the theory in the Oxford school, because Hart, unlike his successor, was not threatened by other views, and so the curriculum included both positivism and natural law. Hart was happy to appoint a critic of his work, Ronald Dworkin, but that, they mused, would not happen today. Now, she continued, that would be deemed too threatening and only positivist jurisprudence, black letter law, commercial consultancy, remain. What is most striking in the conversational observation, in the affect of disappointment, is the extraordinary supposition that the duet of positivism and natural law covers the full scope and ambit of jurisprudence, that this little enclave and alcove of analytic legal philosophy is all that there is to glean and garner of the global discipline. No critical legal studies, no critical race theory, feminism ignored, postmodern jurisprudence unborn, the grand traditions of the global south, Scandinavian legal realism, uBuntu theories of justice, Indian legal philosophy, the plethora of Renaissance traditions of astrojurisprudence, jurisliterature, *lex amatoria*, let alone Karl Marx,Frederick Engels, or Eugeny Pashukanis, to name but a few, did not exist. As Costas D put it orally, one must recognize oration as his most formidable talent, 'the grand narratives of the Enlightenment are crashing down on our heads', and black letter law with its wholly white connotations formed the asphyxiating walls of the epistemic prison house of the law faculty. That is where things stood when, armed with a recent PhD in the legal philosophy of freedom of expression, examined not without trauma at the London School of Economics School of Law, with Professor John Finnis as the external, the young man from Piraeus, with a larger than usual intelligence bump on his dodypate, emerged vociferously on the legal academic scene.

For a long time, not far off a decade, Costas in the main talked, fired up with a passion for the alliterative theory of Douzinas on deconstruction, on the project of taking both text and law apart. The one paper he did publish, and which was later to become a pivotal chapter in *Postmodern Jurisprudence*, was 'On the Deconstruction of Jurisprudence: Fin(n)is Philosophiae'. Co-authored with Ronnie Warrington, in the stifling atmosphere of what was in essence the jurisprudence of the 1950s, in which the most radical debate in jurisprudence was the abstract deliberation on whether morality was a part of law, the walls had to come down. In retrospect, the incandescent yet endemically convivial rage of the not so youthful critical legal scholar seems almost too tame in its academicism, its indirection, in the certainty of its doubt. All critique, however, is relative to context and circumstance, to the negation of what is, so as to engender the not yet.[2]

2 Pierre Legrand, *Negative Comparative Law: A Strong Programme for Weak Thought* (Cambridge University Press 2022).

Marxist in purpose, postmodern in method, 'Fin(n)is philosophiae' was in part an oedipal attack upon a domineering examiner but is more broadly to be understood as impugning the Oxbridge establishment, its status, its jurisprudence, its theological hold over the pedagogic reproduction of the legal academy and in significant part the profession.[3] The outsider, the Greek, had been slighted, rebuffed, not recognized by the gatekeepers of the discipline and the response is the elegant punning deconstruction aimed at 'finnising' them off.

Haunted by the erudition of Ronnie Warrington, driven by the political verve and parricidal energy of Douzinas, a regnant text is torn to shreds. Lucid, playful, and approachable, 'our text fully anticipates its own deconstruction, and becomes the most accessible text of modern jurisprudence';[4] the authors dissect the authorial hubris and the logical fault lines in the Oxford philosopher's account of the theory of a Christian natural law. Like Caesar's Gaul, or the Nicene creed, the argument has three parts. The first is the critique of the apodictic character of Finnis' argument, the second is the rhetorical deconstruction of its textual progression, and then finally there is its emanation, the joker in the pack, the sense of play and possibility. The literary character of all ratiocination undermines the self-evidence or certainty of grand narratives and absolutist assertions of truth, while poetics, and specifically the flowers of diction, undo the law.

The essay starts with the paternal figure, 'a reading of an important text of modern natural law'.[5] One might inquire as to why a text that transpires, in this analysis, upon deconstruction, to be so misguided and self-undermining is 'important', but this conferral of status is a recognition of its place in the established order of legal academic reproduction and, published by the Clarendon Press, it carries the imprimatur of status and, as the author himself modestly puts it: 'The book was conceived, begun, and finished in the University of Oxford, whose motto could be placed at the end of Part Three'.[6] It is self-confessedly a work of analytic jurisprudence and the preface also names the friends who form the author's milieu, Plato, Aristotle, the Church Fathers, and Thomas Aquinas, and then amongst contemporaries, H.L.A. Hart, Michael Detmold, Joseph Raz, J.L. Mackie, and Neil MacCormick.

3 This was published first as Costas Douzinas and Ronnie Warrington, 'On the Deconstruction of Jurisprudence: Fin(n)is Philosophiae' (1987) 14 *JLS* 33. It is worthy of note that the editors of the special issue remark in the introduction that Douzinas and Warrington 'reject critique and... epitomize post-modernist themes'. (Peter Fitzpatrick and Alan Hunt, 'Critical Legal Studies: Introduction' (1987) 14(1) *Journal of Law and Society* 2).

4 Douzinas, Warrington and McVeigh (n 1) 90.

5 ibid 75.

6 John Finnis, *Natural Law and Natural Rights* (OUP and Clarendon Press 1980) preface, and the motto is *Dominus illuminatio mea*, the Lord is my light, or God speaks through me.

Finnis also mentions, in a short aside, that the book was 'mainly written in Africa... at the University of Malawi' but, just to make the obvious point, there is no hint that any African joined the circle of friends or merited any specific thanks or intellectual debts, let alone membership of the community of 'ongoing dialogue', of *civitas* and *polis*. The culture of erudition, back then, the preface is signed March 1979, is colonial and the epistemic is imperial and patristic. The philosophical canon and the law of text were obvious, and it is this self-evidence that begins the deconstructive argument.[7]

In Finnis' argument, the Principle of Practical Reasonableness assures certain values, such as knowledge, truth, preservation of life, and the common good. These values underlie the concept of justice as the vehicle of human flourishing. Such is simply the case and presumably especially so if one's self-professed bibliographic motto is *Dominus illuminatio mea* and one is writing *in partibus infidelium*, in Malawi, which sounds dangerously like malaria. Assertion, in classical terms dogma, is the word of the Lord that needs to be reverenced rather than inquired into or challenged. Thus, for Finnis, the principles 'are obvious – obviously valid – to anyone who has experience of inquiry into matters of fact or of theoretical judgment...'[8] The founding principles are self-evident, obvious of course, indubitable, and not to be questioned as they form the basis, the vehicle, for the philosopher's necessary progression towards the truth. Reason and text depend upon these presuppositions or in jurisprudential argot little *grundnorms*. The problem is that their assertion is their only defence; they are truths 'willy-nilly', and correlatively any challenge to them is to be excluded *ab initio*, as groundless, absurd, impotent, and nihilistic. The text of this philosophical sovereign, Finnis' telos, 'commands (cajoles, bullies or rewards) the subject (reader) who is forced to submit to the threat of sanctions (putting to silence)'.[9] Finnis speaks the law by means of threats, bullying, intimations of execution, on the one side seducing with the knowledge and light of the sovereign pedagogue and on the other destroying the absurdities, the folly of the sceptic, or in this instance, the deconstructive theorist. Certainty pummels scepticism, and truth must overwhelm doubt.

The bad father or mendacious parent is then exposed by means of undermining the claim to an unmediated truth. An apodictic or self-evident verity requires reasoning free of all but the crystalline precepts of logical analysis, the text of truth, of verdict and law, being supposedly without literary intervention or rhetorical ornamentation. Deconstruction, however, supposes the opposite. Language is dialogic, the bearer of social histories, of

7 Douzinas, Warrington and McVeigh (n 1) 77.
8 Finnis (n 5) 69.
9 Douzinas, Warrington and McVeigh (n 1) 90.

previous uses, of the figures, tropes, and flowers of speech.[10] The argument is that philosophy cannot escape its own literariness and using a passage from Keats' 'Endymion', the argument is made that the words, the text, the law, are nothing but rhetoric, the literary expression and 'fleuristic imagery' that carries argument as linguistic expression and verbal play. The tour de force of the analysis lies in the deconstruction of the figures of Finnisian advocacy of natural law and the seven reigning values of life. Rhetorical analysis evinces a humanistic search for origins, an aesthetic of longing for the classical polis, an absent origin upon which to legitimate contemporary institutions. The text then takes aim against the sceptic in a series of attacks upon a straw figure who is variously impotent, irrational, possibly mad, a blind and powerless fool. The sceptic, another name for literature, must be expelled from the text and Christian principles must reign or, in one glorious epigram: 'our Fin(nis) becomes our aim', a deathbound subjectivity, a theology of the last days. Against such Christian nihilism, the arguments of the natural lawyer are inverted to show an analysis 'going to pieces', reason riddled with metaphor, literature undoing philosophy, rational argument depending upon fiat, dogma, imposition, and bullying.

In the idiom of the time, in a context of debates between materialism and idealism, Marx versus Hegel, 'Fin(n)is philosophiae' and its deconstructive method, its irreverent tone and playful reversals, were deemed marginal, lacking jurisprudential gravity, more punning than political. It is more accurate, however, to view this early exercise in textual deconstruction as an expression of a minor jurisprudence, a subaltern, Southern, and loosely Hellenic, language acting out in the academic sphere a challenge to the hegemony of analytic legal philosophy, the dominant hierarchy of jurisprudential status, and the imperialism of legal method. A Greek and an East European Jew at a provincial university were demanding the right to expression, to a language of their own, and simultaneously making a claim to a jurisprudential territory for those excluded chorologically, affectively, and intellectually from the dominant language and the then current discursive formation. As Minkkinen ably argues, a minor jurisprudence aims to introduce a different, deterritorialized, language and is political in the sense of broaching a programme outside of extant or major jurisprudential traditions. What is at play is precisely the end of a specific regime of legal philosophy and an opening to the lure of the novel, the desire for difference, the affect and excitement of change.[11]

10 For a legal version of this argument, see the use of Bakhtin in Julen Extabe, 'The Dialogical Language of Law' (2022) 59 *Osgoode Hall Law Journal* 429.

11 See Panu Minkkinen, 'The Radiance of Justice: On the Minor Jurisprudence of Franz Katfka' (1994) 3 *Social and Legal Studies* 357.

The critique of natural law theory, not being an analysis of class, history, and the economic foundations of legal consciousness, was deemed by leftist lawyers to fall within the idealist camp and to be irrelevant, excessively Francophile, a continental obscurity, in the eyes of the analytic brigade. Finnis certainly did not deem the critique to merit a reply, though such could be either that it was too threatening, or, more likely, that it lacked the seriousness necessary to the inscription of the sacred words of jurisprudential knowledge, the *ius divinarum* of which Finnis was mouthpiece and amanuensis. A divide subsisted but mainly because of the novelty of the deconstructive method in the hands of lawyers. The greater question, however, is proleptic: what did *Postmodern Jurisprudence* portend? The clearing of the ground, the decapitation of the parental figures, and the confrontation with comrades embedded in vulgar materialism spoke to possibility rather than actuality, to texts rather than institutions or doctrines. The critique, if we move to the final chapter of *Postmodern Jurisprudence*, 'Suspended Sentences: A Novel Approach to Certain Original Problems of Copyright Law', is gauged to that most unsettling of critical positions, attention to becoming, to what Ernst Bloch termed the *novum*, the introduction of the new, meaning precisely that which and those who have no place and no language in the extant legal order.

Being gauged to texts and literary criticism of the jurisprudential regimien, *Postmodern Jurisprudence* is correctly viewed as aesthetic. It is the metaphoricity of Finnis' text that is playfully taken apart to reveal an acerbic and ominous affective core. To dismiss such an explosive and irreverent exercise as merely aesthetic is to miss the point entirely. This is in part, as Derrida so notably evidenced, because the war in the libraries, the smoke in the stacks, the clash of arms in journals, and the battle of books *in toto* are exercises in 'scribble – writing power'.[12] Armies conquer, grammar governs. It is also because the aesthetic prefigures and circumscribes the political or, as Jacques Rancière puts it, the artistic distribution of the sensible generates the perception, the spectacle, of the common and, in our instance, the common law.[13] Political and legal change have to be prefigured, imagined, argued, and inserted into extant practices and *Fin(n)is Philosophiae*, like any end, is also an opening or new beginning, superfetation in a narrative and, perhaps better put, a comedy of as yet to be inscribed positions. The not yet, or, to borrow a phrase, the democracy to come, may be haunted by the ghosts, the revenants, of the past but it is also a fissure in the present, a diffraction

12 See Jacques Derrida, 'Scribble (Writing-power)' (1979) 58 *Yale French Studies* 116. For further elaboration of the concept of politics involved, see also Derrida, *Positions* (Athlone 1981).

13 Jacques Rancière, *The Politics of Aesthetics: The Distribution of the Sensible* (Continuum 2004) 12.

of existing discourses, a space of possibility. It is in this sense of novelistic projects, of being post in the full connotations of sending a message as well as laying down novel parameters for the discipline that the final chapter of *Postmodern Jurisprudence* thinks collectively and dramatically about issues of doctrine intersecting with theory, dogma confronting critique.

Entry for content, exit for style, the last chapter begins by stating that it is a chain novel. It is part of a collective enterprise and a contribution to a community of thought. This is particularly true in that the chapter started its public life as a live theatrical performance during the critical legal conference at Newcastle University in 1987. Parts were assigned and a lively dialogue ensued to what it must be admitted were mixed reviews: why this novel form and how would it reach the working class? What could it mend? On the other side, it was viewed in a comradely spirit as something fresh, an exciting venture, a movement in a new direction towards a plurality of thought and diversification of thinking. The chain novel was not a new concept, originating as it does in the work of Ronald Dworkin, but the theatrical performance gave it a terpsichorean twist and a disruptive radicalism. It was no longer merely suggesting a further chapter in an ongoing text, but rather a version of poor theatre, an interaction with a present community, a jurisprudential intervention that was both histrionic and, in its context, provocative.[14] What was it then that was said at the end of the book, what parting message, envoi or call to action? The last words, a pun, 'the name of the Judge has always been (voir)-vere'. The reference is jurisliterary, to the trial of Moby Dick and the pun is see the truth as opposed to only speaking it.

First, it is playful, by which I mean both that it took the initial form of a theatrical performance and that as printed theatre it is consistently dialogic, a form associated with foundational texts and mobile conversation. In a stronger, architectural sense, the theatrical roots of law and the history of the spectacular modes of its performance were suggestive of a historical reaching back, not just to jurisliterary sources such as Shakespeare, Keats, Cervantes, and Borges, but also a theoretical insistence upon the long recognized though seldom utilized *auctoritates philosophorum et poetarum*, cited by Lord Coke but returning of course to the *mos italicus* and Roman law. The theatrical staging is an epistolary play addressing copyright and infringement, podium and Bar, practice and theory, as well as postulating questions about academic norms, publishing, and plagiarism. Three lecturers, by implication our three authors, D.W.M., publish a paper, 'Suspended Sentences', itself the title of the chapter addressing the eponymous article, which it is claimed draws substantially from an unpublished thesis by a student supervised by two of the defendants. The case, of

14 Ronald Dworkin, *Law's Empire* (Belknap Press 1986) 228–238.

course, raises manifold hermeneutic questions of similarity and difference in the expression of both legal and literary compositions. What ensues is a correspondence between the journal editor and the authors, between lawyers and clients, expert witnesses and academics, student and teachers, as well as court and litigants. A wild dialogism between disparate stakeholders but with a common manifestation in literary expression and epistolary exchange. And as we know, the letter always arrives at its destination. Here that terminus is initially a lengthy reading of Melville's Billy Budd to evidence the degree to which law is literature and literature is law leading to the conclusion, on the one hand that the verdict in Billy's case repeats the crime it condemns, and more directly stipulates 'If the law has always been used, somewhat quixotically, to patrol the borders of copyright, *Billy Budd, Sailor* in its reversals and suspensions shows the need and opens the space for a legal poetics'.[15] It is that bold goal, that noble and time-honoured enterprise that fills the final pages.

To suspend the sentence is to give it time, to allow an *interstitium* or transitional space between law in the books and law in action. It is one definition of justice, the allowance of listening, attending, hearing, sensing both subject and cause prior to determination. The suspension is essential, and references not only the pre-law of judgment but the anticipatory distribution of the sensible through art and imagination. Before rules, prior to writing, there is the poetics of invention, the imaginal world that forms the criterion of decision, the affects and sensibilities that attend to conception and then inscribe determination. In *Postmodern Jurisprudence*, the process is both graphic and detailed. Writing is a physical activity, a sensorium inside the scriptorium, and here a sense of being ill at ease: 'I know what it is. This vague feeling of discomfort. The law, yea the law. They want to confiscate my whiskoletterosmotron'. There is the novelistic crux, law crushing inspiration, the elucubrations of the 'long, sleepless, tormented night'.[16] The oneiric or hypnopompic suspension of frontal exegesis gives way to the physical description of corporeal endeavour, lying on a bed trying to write upside down. More than that, the creative act requires the use of the *whiskoletterosmotron*, an '[a]pparatus for the osmosis of graphic characters representing sounds used in speech with spirits distilled from grains (CED)'. No law without repression, and no repression without passion, and the *whiskoletterosmotron* is the figure of searching for and finding access to that repressed affect, that well of feeling which will impel invention and decision.

Such brief description – my powers are limited – does but scrimption of accuracy, scantling justice to the range and play of genres, disciplines,

15 Douzinas, Warrington and McVeigh (n 1) 243.
16 ibid 267.

positions, persons, and texts that the novelistic chapter on suspensions enacts. It magnificently exemplifies the link, both etymological and heuristic, between theatre and theory. Theory is the play of thought, the theatrical assemblage and performance of concepts which in 'Suspended Sentences' takes the hypnopompic form of recumbency, horizontal positioning to allow the body to think. A materialist enterprise: the mode of production determines thought and so the inference to resupine reverie, and now to moving interviews, mobile thinking was in anticipation of much to come. It was also a manner of introducing the unconscious into the elaboration of the process of thinking. Life and thought are twins, however separate the legalist will endeavour to make them. Not even worth trying because the effort is much better expended in the play of integration and of understanding the interrelations, both the irrelation and the imbrication, estrangement – that uneasy feeling – and epiphany – the excitations. And the *whiskoletterosmotron* presents a moment of revelation, of cutting loose, inhabiting youthful or at least mid-30ish desire. At the level of the word, the machine, the allegory of the temulent verbal wrecking ball, is a reference to another play of deconstruction, the atomization of words. For the *whiskoletterosmotron*, the word is merely and exorbitantly a sign. It is composed of protons and phonemes, neutrons and nouns, sub-atomic particles and adjectives, and I could go on, but the point is that the lexical items are simply representations of things absent and can be dissected in their very materiality as well as being thrown into the realm of their symbolic proliferations. In the latter aspect, breaking down the words is a mode of materialist analysis which addresses the composition of the syntactic items in the here much contested terms of who and with what authority, in what context and in relation to whom, has this statement been made. Jurisprudence, the second order of doctrine, should not go unchallenged:

> the molecules of the words and the sentences get through the breeder and they get into all sorts of funny shapes and colours, and smells and lengths... they burst their cage. Do you get me, you ejected injunction of injected ejaculations? You bale bailee, bowler-hatted bailiff, liffyan leave of appeal for money... you garnishee of the Master of Rock and Rolls.[17]

A healthy irreverence marks the final chapter and exemplifies both the chains of the legal tradition and the novel that the inventive can inscribe:

> We need evidence that you haven't copied. Evidence my ass. I'll give you the video sweetheart, the video. I wrote this bloody piece lying on my

17 ibid 269.

> back staring at the roof, see it? There. I destroyed 144 biros, no less; the bloody things won't work for more than two minutes if you write lying on your back. Lying on my back. That's the only way the osmotron works.[18]

It is a scene that could be torn from the pages of Borges' story of Pierre Menard, or possibly Pierre Bayard's work on plagiarism of the future.[19] To lie down to write, recumbent to rectify, the *whiskoletterosmotron* allows the play of words as images, as materialities, as corporeal phantasmata, the body becoming the crucible of affect and the trigger of expression. And so, to the greatest freedom of conclusions, that the unconscious is interminable, the dream continues, and if allowed, the reverie persists. The book ends without marching orders, instructions, rules, but in and with aporia and, in precision, '© suspended', or, if one allows the index as terminus of the interior syntagm, then *mot finale* as *mot juste*, is simply and appositely 'self 48'.[20]

The hedonism, the degree zero and pleasure in writing, and, exit for style, the encounter with the self are all features of an implicit injunction to self-awareness in the deliberative exteriorization of the unconscious as it writes, the objective unconscious as Coccia loosely frames it.[21] To borrow again from Coccia, 'it is delicious to write, to be no longer yourself but to move in an entire universe of your own making'.[22] The hedonic ground of scholarly activity, the ability to choose a community of thought, the freedom of calculated indiscipline amongst the disciplinators and particularly the juridifiers, the lawyers, the filing clerks, is a first step, if not to anarchy, at least to a libertarian politics. The *whiskoletterosmotron* is most directly a method of libertine erudition, a left hedonism, radical humanism of mutual recognition and egalitarian prospects.[23] In the case of the book, this community of three, there is a mingling of student and teacher, disparate colleagues, and most pertinent for present purposes of distinct jurisprudential traditions. In contrast to the anecdote of Oxford closures of thought, *Postmodern Jurisprudence* admits the Greeks and the Romans, natural law and positivism, Marxism, deconstruction, narratology, poetics, pragmatism, and in sum, a plurality of semionauts. Aesthetics, feminism, critical race theory,

18 ibid 268.
19 Jorge Luis Borges, 'Pierre Menard: Author of Don Quixote', in Anthony Kerrigan (ed.), *Fictions* (Grove Press 1962); Pierre Bayard, *Plagiat par anticipation* (Minuit 2009).
20 ibid 303 and the 'self' is the last entry for 'writing'.
21 Emanuele Coccia, *Sensible Life: A Micro-ontology of the Image* (Fordham University Press 2014) 52: 'Every sort of image is the Being of knowledge that acts outside of the subject, a sort of objective unconscious'.
22 ibid 62.
23 I take libertine erudition from the expansive work of René Pintard, *Le Libertinage érudit dans la première moitié du XVIIe siècle* (Slatkine 1983).

and intersectionality *avant la lettre*, were yet to come. The doors, however, were open for others to walk through.

Finally, the superfetation, the second birth of Costas D. I do not by this mean resurrection or anything remotely Christian, Orthodox, or otherwise, but rather the living on of the book, or *vivitur ingenio* to use the proper emblematic motto. 30-odd years – increasingly odd – since its publication, what insight can the decades add, what perspective, what scholium upon the deeds of *Postmodern Jurisprudence* can be offered in summation? First, a point already adverted to, the creation of an intellectual cause in legal theory, the building of a non-school and the occasions of impact. Postmodernism served its critical purpose and then fled the scene. That is only because we are all postmodern now, that is our context and the political reality of our torrefacted times: 'postmodernity is not an epoch... it is always with(in) us'.[24] The driving force and propulsive desire of the book was to bring the legal academic establishment to account, to challenge the hegemony of legal positivism from a non-structural position. The inherited and dominant theory of law was imperialistic, patristic, legalistic, agelastic, and white. That hegemony was challenged by the critique operated via the *whiskoletterosmotron*. Even Goodrich on the mailbox rule was subjected to reversal by dialing in the phoneme: 'the post comes before the prior, the letter before the phone, endless circulation before... fixity of meaning and the order of law'.[25] Here then, in endless circulation, in prospect rather than retrospect, in the post, which is to say in epistolary form, a boundary was shifted, a style subverted, and the opening of a school inaugurated. Call it the Birkbeck non-School, to which this volume is in many senses a tribute connected centripetally, peterly perhaps, to passage through Gower Street, visits to Malet Street, and critical hammers honed to keep knocking away at the bricks in the wall. Costas D was presciently concerned to galvanize a new generation of legal scholars, to set the post afoot abroad the polity and the common law world. Unusual for law, a host of doctoral students were recruited to Birkbeck and then entered the legal academy. The most successful in this respect was the third author, Shaun McVeigh, tierce, whose career at Melbourne Law School, Victoria, Australia has been devoted to training postgraduates who then went into the antipodean legal academy and changed its face. From the London schola to Australia is a pronounced expanse, no small feat, big feet, and a similar range of influence or theoretical acumen, of libertine erudition, spread out also into the UK law schools, to Keele, Kent, Warwick to name but a trio of institutions where

24 Douzinas, Warrington and McVeigh (n 1) 134.
25 ibid 129.

the occult of critical legal ideas have been kept aflame, in Handbooks and Pocketbooks, New Developments, Dangerous Supplements, curricular orientations, and research agendas.

Second, the concept of a non-School is that of resistance to conclusion and concludency. As Thomas Mathiesen, the Norwegian abolitionist, so persuasively argued some years before the coining of the postmodern, novelty has to be unfinished. By this, he meant that attempting to topple and replace, to substitute one programme for another, was bound simply to repeat existing structures with new facades.[26] In conclusion, schemes and other completed programmes are predicated upon the extant forms, upon the current institutional conditions of possibility, which are precisely what the abolitionist, or in our case the toppler of grand narratives, seeks to overcome. To be postmodern is to be indisciplined in the positive heuristic sense of being both in the plurality of disciplines and resistant to the strictures and impositions of the disciplinary with its rods and followers.[27] The resistance to finality is predicated upon an insistent openness of thought and an aesthetic attention to appearances, to the material manifestations of the real. The Birkbeck non-School, the postmodern jurisprudential academy is one without programmes, dictates, disciplinary flowcharts, or status aspirations. In their place is a critical stance, apperceptive aspiration, and a hedonic freedom of thought. Far from being the demise of politics into aesthetics, the hedonic materialism of the *whiskoletterosmotron* addressed a politics to come in the globalized form of networks, connectivities, and the *perpetuum mobile* or constant mobility of the community of thought.

It is the role of theory to anticipate, to stage the political in advance of actuality, to think the possible. It is in this radical and optimistic sense of the practice of theory that the hedonic and aesthetic character of the non-programme gains its proper purchase. In an important sense, both facets of thinking novelty, felicific and artistic ethics, human betterment and improved living conditions, are aspects of theory in its etymological root sense of theatre, of seeing, performing, inventing models of what is to come, enacting prospects, opening the community of thought to the diversity constitutive of dialogue. It is here that Douzinas took his place and played his role, adding a powerful voice to the plurality of intellection and the parliament of speech. As to method, and the *whiskoletterosmotron*, it provides a vital reminder, a cautionary curatorial and community building note of hedonism and of *homo ludens* to the civilizing endeavour.

26 Thomas Mathiesen, *The Politics of Abolition Revisited* [1974] (Routledge 2015) 47: 'the alternative lies in the unfinished, in the sketch, in what is not yet fully existing. The "finished alternative" is "finished" in a double sense of the word'.

27 For a fulsome discussion of indiscipline as freedom of method, see Legrand (n 2) ch. VII.

Play and pleasure, enthusiasm for thought, the fun of dialogue and the contestation of ideas, passion and performance are triggers of intellectual action and of theoretical amity. As the superfetation of Costas D admirably indicates, these forms of ideational motion emerge also in dreams, or the recumbency of hypnopompic conception, in trance and reverie, in play and laughter.

5

JUST LISTENING

Gilbert Leung

There is a difference between thinking and theorising. Theory constructs discourses that operate within a matrix of time, place, and power, pointing towards 'truths' whose radiance wanes once attention has turned elsewhere or when paradigms or academic fashions have changed. Theory encloses, limits, hypostasises. It answers questions within these discursive limits but cannot grasp what comes before the question. Before the question there is nothing to grasp. There is only a listening to the archaic and silent promise of what is to come into question.[1] Thinking comes before theory and is first and foremost the heightened sensitivity to listening.

When it comes to law, there is a lot to hear. A cacophony of rules, declarations, prohibitions, and injunctions. Behind these, one can hear differing interpretations, intentions, sources, founding 'fathers'. One can hear without comprehending. This is law as background noise, occasionally piercing through and grabbing attention, or law as the silent hum of an operating system, the imperceptible maintenance of force and violence. But to hear and

1 Cf. Jacques Derrida, *Of Spirt* (University of Chicago Press 1989) 129 footnote 5. Here, Derrida addresses the 'question of the question'. Given that a question is given in language, the question of the question ultimately asks what comes before language. Much of this is inspired by Heidegger and the way he thought the prior commitment of language to language itself, what he called '*Zusage*': 'promise, agreement or consent, originary abandonment to what is given in the promise itself' (130). I suspect another way to consider this is through the question of the question in law. Given that a mode of questioning—interrogation, examination—is already part of law and legal language, the question of the question might ask, who or what authorises the question and what comes before law?

DOI: 10.4324/9781032622224-5

to comprehend requires listening,[2] and to listen to law implies obedience. If obedience is not to be the only thing one hears, the critical ear cannot listen only to law; it must also pay attention to what is of the law and beyond it—law's divine companion, justice.

Greek Dike is the goddess of justice.[3] Depicted on an amphora, dating back to the sixth century BCE, there is a representation of Dike beating *Adikia* (injustice) with a long hammer.[4] While this may be interpreted as symbolically sexual,[5] a more direct interpretation is that of the superiority of justice prevailing over injustice, a familiar trope throughout the ages. Whereas *Adikia* is shown as an 'ugly, barbarian woman with tattooed skin',[6] her vanquisher—in beautiful female form—is an early indication that justice is identifiable, knowable, desirable. This is what justice looks like from a certain point of view, and theories of justice continue to bear witness, each theory claiming to know her better than the last.

But, 'the theory of justice is the oldest failure of human thought', writes Douzinas.[7] Whether 'Homer, the Bible, and Plato' or Mill, Rawls, and Dworkin, it has been a case of intrinsic futility, rather than failed implementation. In the archaic justice (*dike*) of the Anaximander fragment, we can hear the spectral cry of injustice (*adikia*). This is not merely the absence of justice, but a primordial dislocation and disjointure that renders the application of justice impossible, imbuing tragedy with meaning.[8] Failure is intrinsic to justice because it is mired in injustice. We should therefore turn our attention away from theories of justice and focus instead, Douzinas argues, on the 'sense of injustice':

> We are surrounded by injustice but we don't know where justice lies. This is the paradox of justice: while the principal has been clouded in uncertainty and controversy, injustice has always been felt with clarity, conviction and a sense of urgency. We know injustice when we come across it; its truth is felt. However, every time a theory of justice is put into practice, it soon degenerates into another instance of injustice.[9]

2 Cf. Jacques Derrida, 'Heidegger's ear: Philopolemology' in John Wallis (ed), *Reading Heidegger: Commemorations* (Indiana University Press 1993) 188.
3 Jacques de Ville, 'Mythology and the Images of Justice' (2011) 23(3) *Law & Literature* 349.
4 ibid 348.
5 ibid
6 See 'Adikia' (Theoi) <https://www.theoi.com/Daimon/Adikia.html > accessed 20 June 2025.
7 Douzinas, *Philosophy and Resistance in the Crisis* (Polity 2013) 80.
8 ibid 78 ff.
9 ibid 80.

Adikia is no longer she who *dike* vanquishes, the overcoming of injustice by justice. Instead, *adikia* becomes the unending struggle between law and justice. In this thinking, justice is deific only insofar as its transcendence cannot be contained within the edifices of theory—'we don't know where justice lies'. Injustice, on the other hand, acts directly on the body and feels pain when the hammer strikes. This does not mean *adikia* is vanquished. On the contrary, she fights back: 'The sense of injustice, which prepares militants, is history's judgment and reparation for the original and enduring *adikia*'.[10]

The word 'sense' is not about 'making sense' of injustice. Nothing is made or constructed, especially not a theory of injustice. On the contrary, 'sense' here is materiality and corporeality; it is sense as physical sensing. Resistance, fighting back, 'is the bodily reaction to hurt, hunger, despair, to an overwhelming sense of injustice'.[11] This is the resistance of 'dissidents and revolutionaries… the Tahrir and Syntagma square occupiers'.[12] The myriad examples of such resistance have in common the irrepressible desire to change the current order, a 'righting' born from the sense of injustice.

Even though there is no making sense of injustice, this does not mean injustice cannot be 'known'. Direct knowledge—or in a more strictly Kantian idiom, 'apprehension'—of injustice, through the senses, is the point at which one knows what one feels, whether it be hurt or hunger. Such knowledge is not theoretically determined, but intuitively apprehended. We not only sense injustice; by directly sensing it, we also know that the cause of the sensation is unjust. How then can we know a situation is unjust when it is not directly experienced and without having to resort to an abstract theory of in/justice? Perhaps the only way is through the use of empathy and imagination. We must imagine ourselves as other and elsewhere and let the pathos of the situation unfold through the senses.

As an example, let us imagine, with Derrida, what is at stake when faced with the stranger. For Derrida, amongst others, the ethical relation to the stranger is one of hospitality. Without the possibility of hospitality, the relation to the other is reduced to an ontology of rejection, the immiseration if not impossibility of coexistence. To think in terms of pure or unconditional hospitality is to think in terms of the absolute welcoming of the other, the imperative to say

> yes to who or what turns up, before any anticipation, before any identification, whether or not it has to do with a foreigner, an immigrant, an invited guest, or an unexpected visitor, whether or not the new arrival is

10 ibid 79.

11 Douzinas, *States of Exception* (Elgar 2023) 96.

12 Douzinas (n 7) 80.

a citizen of another country, a human, animal, or divine creature, a living or dead thing, male or female.[13]

Pure hospitality is, however, impossible. One clue as to why is in its etymology: 'The word "hospitality" derives from the Latin *hospes*, which is formed from *hostis*, which originally meant a 'stranger' and came to take on the meaning of the enemy or 'hostile' stranger (*hostilis*), + *pets* (*potis, potes, potentia*), to have power'.[14] Any act of hospitality contains within it a trace of hostility. To welcome the stranger, the host must first have the capacity to do so. There must be a demarcation between inside and outside, a primal *nomos* that the stranger crosses, enabling them to arrive, turning estrangement into familiarity. But if hospitality is to be maintained, the host must remain a host in *a priori* relation to a guest. Indeed the host must make a sovereign decision to welcome the other into the home, a power relation that is also a potential source of hostility. For within the concept of 'host' lies the idea of 'hostage'. In retaining the sovereign power to lay down the conditions of hospitality, the host keeps their guest hostage to their preconditions, a prisoner of their encounter.

Even within an apparently pure hospitality lies the trace of the hostage. If one relinquishes sovereignty over the home and bids the other to '"come inside", "come with me", not only toward me, but within me: occupy me, take place in me, which means, by the same token, also take my place, don't content yourself with coming to meet me or "into my home"'; what happens is a paradoxical substitution of host and hostage.[15] With pure hospitality, an infinite cycle takes place wherein the positions of both host and hostage are simultaneously assumed. Derrida concludes, 'these substitutions make everyone into everyone else's hostage'.[16] Because of this, hospitality can only always be impure, that is to say, conditional; and in the tension between host and hostage, hospitality and hostility, lies the impossibility of justice and the immanent pain of injustice.

Politically, the stranger could be said to be the figure of the foreigner and the migrant. If one of the hallmarks of the political left is a tendency towards a welcoming of the other, an ever greater hospitality and opening of borders, then at stake are precisely the deconstructive aporias inherent in hospitality. The host empathises with the suffering of the stranger and beckons them in from the cold. But once inside, the guest continues suffering as hostage

13 Jacques Derrida, *Of Hospitality* (Rachel Bowlby trans., Stanford University Press 2000) 77.

14 John Caputo, *Deconstruction in a Nutshell: A Conversation with Jacques Derrida* (Fordham University Press 1997) 110.

15 Derrida (n 13) 123.

16 ibid 124.

to the host's dominion and rule. Empathising further, the host attempts to relieve the hostage's suffering by sacrificing themselves to the point of substitution—the host becomes the hostage.

For those on the political right, it is perhaps this pain of self-sacrifice and substitution that is most acutely felt as injustice. At the same time, the political categories of left and right are not simple binaries. When we consider them in any way other than in their most ideal forms, they become relativised, where one can be more or less hospitable, more or less open, more or less welcoming of the other. Injustice is felt regardless of political orientation, whether one is revolutionary or reactionary, dissident or conservative.

For Derrida, the negotiation of the aporias inherent in hospitality involves 'knowing how to transform and improve the law' without which unconditional 'hospitality would be in danger of remaining a pious and irresponsible desire, without form and without potency, and of even being perverted at any moment'.[17] But how does one know 'how to transform and improve the law'? Legal theorists may fail simply by invoking a theory of justice to answer this question. Conversely, while a sense of injustice can provoke the desire to change the situation, to move away from injustice, any thinking of where to go risks becoming trapped in and by theory.

Justice and injustice, *dike* and *adikia*, while not opposites are nonetheless relational. Justice is the (divine) will to heal an ontological wound that cannot be healed because injustice exists. Neither justice nor injustice can be fully captured in theory, which is why a material sense of injustice, felt on the body, is a useful way to think beyond the abstractions of theory. But what if a similar approach were applied to justice? What could an atheoretical sense of justice be—one that is also materially grounded and felt on and/or by the body?

Refrain

Theory encloses, limits, hypostasises. It answers questions within these discursive limits but cannot grasp what comes before the question. Before the question there is nothing to grasp. There is only a listening to the archaic and silent promise of what is to come into question. Thinking comes before theory and is first and foremost the heightened sensitivity to listening.

In his meditation on 'Heidegger's Ear', Derrida notes Heidegger's insistence that hearing must be thought starting from listening and not the other way round.[18] Though hearing is a physical sense, the organs of hearing are not

17 Jacques Derrida, *Cosmopolitanism and Forgiveness* (Mark Dooley and Michael Hughes trans., Routledge 2001) 22–23.

18 Derrida (n 2) 188.

necessary to be disposed towards hearing. Derrida recalls Heidegger's view that 'we do not hear because we have ears, but we have ears because we hear'.[19] Moreover, '*Wir Hören, wenn wir ganz Ohr sind*'—'We hear when we are all ears', though '*ganz Ohr*' might metaphorically represent being entirely reduced to a single ear. An alternative rhetorical formulation might ask: who needs ears when we *are* all ears? Being-all-ears, listening to what disposes itself to being heard, is a unique form of receptivity. If thinking comes before theory and the heightened sensitivity to listening is the material precondition of thinking, then one may be able to speak of the sense of justice as a thinking of justice (not a theory of justice), which is, in effect, a listening out for justice.

What might justice sound like? Given its elusiveness, perhaps the best way to answer is through speculative metaphors. For example, borrowing from the experience of music, it might sound as if it were a 'cadence': the movement, flow, transformation, and resolution of (harmonic) tension that links and drives one progression to another. Even with no musical training, we know cadences when we hear them, even if we cannot name them as such. They are central to the aesthetic experience of most music, particularly in the Western tradition. They contribute to the subjective experience of a piece sounding 'right' and can generate endless states of mind: (dis)satisfaction, (in)completeness, anticipation, suspension, sublimity, divinity, surprise, complexity, intrigue, elegance, mystery, intensity, etc.

But what if justice, in all its ineffability, gestures only through silence? Silence is constitutive not only of language but also of music. There are the silences (technically speaking 'rests') in melodic lines as well as the silences that pace the rhythm and provide colour through syncopation. Rhythm and syncopation, like a 'rhythm stick', act on the body, causing it to sway in the ecstasy of dance. And even if we take silence as something more than this, or rather, strictly speaking, as something infinitely less, namely a form of radical nihilism that marks the existential limit of all sense, then at the very least one could say that being 'all ears' in the face of this limit, a demand of justice will have already touched the senses. This demand is one of *just listening*, without end, to the endless end, precisely because there is no end.

Theories of justice are, at best, the rigid crystallisations of a thinking of justice. Yet all writing, perhaps with the exception of poetry, crystallises thinking, including this essay set in type. Theories of justice fail because they can only ever be incomplete and provisional. At the same time, the restless thinking of justice—h/earing it—demands both its articulation and deconstruction.

19 ibid

6

WILD MERCURY TEXT

Douzinas... Bentham... De-Ontology

Adam D. Gearey

This essay, a lost chapter from *Postmodern Jurisprudence*, imagines a reading of Bentham's *Deontology*. We will interrupt Bentham's title and read it as De-ontology in order to invite it to a wandering away from itself: an errancy of its own; as if Lucie Austin – snakes in her hair – leads old man Jeremy from the circumgyration of his garden into the wilderness: a last turn... steps beyond...following whispers from elsewhere. So, we will read with an eye and an ear to the voices in *Deontology*; voices that speak of many strange things, but most importantly of a superfluity that allows itself to be ventriloquized by magistrates and moralists, lends itself to description, calculus and "springs of action" – and makes possible an economy of its own exploitation.

Proposing a reading of a text that never took place would present insuperable problems to any approach other than that inaugurated by Douzinas, Warrington and McVeigh. Already a tripling, a dozening of voices. Douzinas et al. Douzinas and others. Elsewards. *Postmodern Jurisprudence,* echoing *Finnegans Wake*, is a play of voices. Like Joyce's unreadable novel, *Postmodern Jurisprudence* introduced a poetic method, a way of reading/writing, which, if honestly performed, articulates texts as generators of endless meanings. However, the ludic deconstruction practised by *Postmodern Jurisprudence* has unforeseen effects. A reading that did not take place generates meanings to come. What sense can we make of this process?

The reading consciousness moves backwards and forwards cutting its own paths and loops as it sounds out the text that holds its attention. The point is that *Postmodern Jurisprudence* misses some of the stranger elements of Bentham's economy of happiness. At the same time, *Deontology* remains blind to some of the consequences of its own argument. Certain

DOI: 10.4324/9781032622224-6

themes in the margins of *Postmodern Jurisprudence*, energized by feminist critique, will be mobilized to amplify submerged voices in *Deontology* that tell of a surplus central to both moral and political economy. What are the terms in which surplus can be thought? Answering this question takes us beyond both positivism and postmodern legal theory; indeed, one of the legacies of Douzinas et al is a re-engagement with themes that have been present in both conventional and critical canons. Perhaps it is time to listen to voices that have seemed to speak past each other.

This chapter will develop in the following way. The first section of this essay will outline Douzinas, Warrington and McVeigh's method. *Postmodern Jurisprudence* had a somewhat reductive approach to positivism, but in keeping with the creative methods of the text, we will read the voices of *Deontology* to get at their productive instabilities. As we need to begin with everything in its right place, the second section focuses on the principles of deontology. These are put forward by a philosopher/teacher who speaks for Bentham. Bentham saw deontology as a way of revising utilitarianism in order to bring together morality, jurisprudence and political economy.[1] This is why the deontologist gives advice to the magistrate who has much to learn about the art of governance. We will then listen to the political economist who applies the principles of deontology to the production and distribution of wealth. Underlying this entire project is the axiom that everyone desires their own happiness. The prudent use of self-interest is fundamental to individual and communal well-being.

This presents a huge set of themes, not least the redefinition of utilitarianism. We will touch on this concern, but our focus will be somewhat different. The third and fourth sections of the essay will elaborate these arguments. Bentham's subject is not the cliched "social moron" of certain forms of liberal legal theory. Deontology takes seriously the embodied subject: "[m]y happiness and my unhappiness are as much a part of me as [my] organs."[2] This is the moral subject as a man of mucus, snot, toothache and indigestion; a fun-seeking farting insomniac anti-colonialist vegetarian (so concerned about the poor diets of others as to propose laws against not eating well) prone to remorse and wild dreams; embedded in relationships with human and more than human others.[3] Hart, Posner and others who have looked back to Bentham have arguably failed to engage with this expansive, fleshy figure.[4] At least one line of analysis spinning out from the torsion

1 Jeremy Bentham, *The Works of Jeremy Bentham*, ed. John Bowring, *Chrestomathia* Vol 8 (William Tait 1843) 213–214.
2 Jeremy Bentham, *Deontology* Vol 1 (Longman 1834) 161.
3 .Jeremy Bentham, *The Collected Works of Jeremy Bentham: Writings on Political Economy* Vol 1 (Michael Quin ed, OUP 2016) 26, 29.
4 See Richard A. Posner, 'Blackstone and Bentham' (1976) 19(3) *The Journal of Law and Economics* 569–606; Richard A. Posner, 'Bentham's Influence on the Law and Economics Movement' (1998) 51 *Current Legal Problems* 425–For general overview, see Alain Strowel,

of *Deontology* and *Postmodern Jurisprudence* is a re-engagement with the claims of both positivism and law and economics. However, this essay will concentrate on a slightly different issue that takes us back to the Benthamite subject of morals and economy. The real problem is that Bentham is unable to realize the play of his own text. So, we will listen to a strange voice speaking in *Deontology;* this is a voice that addresses Felicity and venerates her as the personification of deontology, the goddess Felicitas. Is this the voice of a poet? Maybe. But Felicity's history passes through many strange junctions. After all, she lent her name to utilitarian calculus. Appearing with cornucopia and staff, a caduceus entwined with serpents (a symbol that means she has at least some relationship with Hermes/Mercury), Felicitas presides over the fecundity of life and economy as the realization of the maximum of happiness. However, there is something else at work. We will address it in the fourth and fifth sections.

To realize the disruptive energies that pass through Felicity we will need to distort Bentham's title. He knew that something was afoot. Trapped within the word deontology is another word; a word that may mislead us: ontology. What is at stake in deontology's ontology of bodies? It requires more than an acknowledgement that the moral body is physical and socially orientated. To focus this argument we will need to read the figures and metaphors of *Deontology* as they point towards a deontological re-framing of Bentham's themes. Deontology, a term explained in detail presently, suggests that we should think differently about Bentham's phantasy of economy: a cornucopia of permanent increase without real sacrifice or loss. We will invite Felicitas to attend to our de-ontological endeavours and to help us grasp a "real" that is concealed within Bentham's vision of the endless production of wealth; a real "slippery as an eel" (Bentham 1834 I 241). As the chapter condenses its conclusion, we will turn to feminist critiques of *Postmodern Jurisprudence* and to the de-ontological alembic that will allow the future distillation of arguments about the surplus that underlies law and economy.

Read Again Read Better

Whilst Bentham's name does not appear in *Postmodern Jurisprudence,* the text does make a reference to the Benthamites; a lost tribe who committed themselves to a crude utilitarian philosophy.[5] This portrayal owes something to Hart's assessment of his master. Indeed, it would be fair to say that

'Utilitarisme et approche économique dans la théorie du droit. Autour de Bentham et de Posner' (1992) 37 *Archives de Philosophie du Droit* 143–171.

5 Costas Douzinas, Ronnie Warrington and Sean McVeigh, *Postmodern Jurisprudence* (Routledge 1991) 13.

Hart, rather than Bentham (or even Austin), is the target of the critique of positivism that *Postmodern Jurisprudence* puts forward. Hart is the focus of a reading that moves through hermeneutics to a celebration of a ludic form of deconstruction. It would be possible to re-habilitate Hart, and to deepen and strengthen this reading, but this is not the project put forward by this essay. Rather, we must take a few steps back, and return to one of Bentham's last texts and one that re-framed earlier concerns. Bentham is not corrected by Hart. If anything, Hart subjects Bentham's madness to the spirit of gravity. Opening *Deontology*, we come across a terrain more peculiar than that imagined by *Postmodern Jurisprudence*.

We will read this positivist text (if that is what it is) as already polyvocal. The tangled etymologies of "positivism" provide essential clues. Reconstruction of root meanings suggests that the word relates to that which was settled or is somehow completed and set aside as finished. The sense is of an active construction of something, and the turning away or letting be of that which has been created. These etymological roots give us the sense of settling, but a settling that allows slippage and movement. Once we examine the foundations of a structure, we find the play that holds up a building may also bring the whole edifice crashing down or going up in flames like Borley Rectory.

As a consequence of this method, it is necessary to abandon, or at least suspend, an interpretative practice that positions one text as somehow superior to another. How does this approach make something provocative of the two texts? There are a number of elements to the argument. The poetic method of *Postmodern Jurisprudence* urges us to read with an eye and an ear to textual figures and metaphors as they are the seams around which an argument may be turned. As part of this poetic method, we will also listen to textual voices that are also vectors of argument not under the control of their author. Elaborating the method for reading *Deontology* requires further adaptation of concerns from *Postmodern Jurisprudence*. In particular, the presence in the text of deities. Hermes was very much the presiding spirit of the book, but he had very few messages about positivism. We will therefore have to reckon with the presence of Felicitas as the anima of deontology. The goddess, like Hermes, works between worlds and is well suited to be a mediator of morality and economics.

The method of reading can be further nuanced by taking into account certain feminist critiques of *Postmodern Jurisprudence*. One of the most significant criticisms accused the book of falling into a trap posed by the very binaries it was attempting to deconstruct.[6] This is similar to the re-reading of the book outlined above. But whilst our reading is based on the claim

6 Sara Ahmed, *Differences that Matter* (Cambridge University Press 2009).

that *Postmodern Jurisprudence* does not quite grasp the disruptive energies present within positivism, the feminist critique stressed a slightly different point. The text failed to honour its own claim to read voices excluded by conventional jurisprudence. Douzinas et al were blind and deaf to the ways in which different bodies are spoken for, or silenced, and effectively re-asserted this tradition of silencing and blindness. We will review the terms of this argument more thoroughly in the last section of the essay. To what extent can we engage with this provocative criticism through the method that we have been outlining?

Our method will be soldered together in the following way. *Deontology* requires us to ignore distracting significations present in the title of the book: the "ontology" of *Deontology*. So, we will read ontology back into the word because Bentham's text effectively initiates this way of reading its own disruption. Ontology can then be connected to the feminist concern with bodies. The "de" speaks of a contradictory distancing and intensification, and resonates with the etymological tensions inherent in positivism suggested above. As a prefix, "de" signifies the undoing of a verb's action. Presently we will link this with a deflation of Bentham's claim to an economy of perpetual increase. Also, usefully (in a non-utilitarian sense) "de" echoes both the "de" of deconstruction and the "D" of Douzinas. Once we read deontology de-ontologically we come across working, desiring bodies, the energies that flow through them and the sacrifices that they have to make to sustain flows of happiness.

The Body With Organs

> In a word. Deontology, or Private Ethics, may be considered the science by which happiness is created out of motives extra-legislatorial – while Jurisprudence is the science by which law is applied to the production of felicity.[7]

Bentham's "word" might be a sentence, but it would seem that the sovereign masters of pleasure and pain have been dethroned. We need to examine these terms in a little more detail, as the moral science of deontology is not such a sharp break with its predecessor. Bentham has realized that jurisprudence must be revised and make room in its province for a more nuanced way of reasoning. Deontology cannot rely on coercion, and can only persuade by the logic of its arguments. The norms of happiness are not based on conventional philosophy, nor on the ruminations of Oxford moralists. The wisdom of the ancients must also be viewed somewhat sceptically.

7 Bentham, *Deontology* I (n 2) 28.

Deontology provides an *index expurgatorius*, an expurgation of misleading rubbish from the body and the mind. Deontological reason is an irritant, a caustic, a way of encouraging the body to cleanse itself.[8] To "do" deontology is to read one's own body, to summon one's own health. *Deontology* is as much a book about organs as morality: "[t]he organ may be subservient to the pleasure, but the pleasure is subservient to the body."[9] Pain and pleasure leave their traces on the skin and in the memory. "Recollection" is a matter of the mind and the body: the tingle, the burn. *Deontology* addresses the body with organs.

Deontological thinking begins with the grasp of a fundamental point: you desire your own happiness. There is no need to look deeply into the self. Provided one is disciplined enough to create the correct sentiments and practices, one's faculty of judgment becomes more sophisticated. Enjoyment is essential to well-being, but the "offspring of wealth" is an unruly child.[10] As enjoyment consumes resources, the prudent man must learn management and balance so that any expenditure produces more happiness. judgment is its own organ. If looked after, it auto-generates. This is right and proper for the moral science. The healthy body is the seat of a healthy soul. As deontologists train to understand and manage their own pleasures, they become their own "tribunal" – the best possible judge of what counts as happiness.[11] There is no substitute for a lifetime. The master of deontology cultivates a moral prudence that expresses itself socially as "effective benevolence." Effective benevolence is ultimately well-being: a "sensibility" of being "alive to pleasure and pain" and which, as will be demonstrated, links the happiness of the individual to the happiness of others.[12]

This is precisely why debauchery, intoxication and its physical expression through vomiting are the opposite and the strange cousin of prudence. Debauchery is the mark of a pleasure that has taken over the self. Ill-being comes from the failure to balance pleasure and pain. Pleasure has become a source of physical and mental destruction. Bentham, like Brecht's Baal, knew nothing was harder than the quest for fun. However, debauchery requires the same cultivation of habits as prudence. Drunks work hard to refine their drunkenness. However, the difference between drunken vomiting and the expurgations of deontology is that whilst the former is a repetition of a failure of self-control, the latter is the expression of an ongoing self-discipline. Expurgation of the toxic allows the culturing of good habits. Deontology's gentle ministries work with this logic. They remind the sufferer that the

8 ibid 48.
9 ibid 48.
10 ibid 40.
11 ibid 136–137.
12 ibid 16.

pleasure sought through intoxication is a form of self-regard. There is nothing wrong in seeking pleasure, but the happiness that comes from prudence is far superior to that of dissolution.

So, deontology's only "axiom" is that one desires happiness.[13] Return to deontology's ambition to bring together jurisprudence, morality and political economy. Bentham conceives of an "economy of happiness"[14] that is fundamentally linked to "the production of the maximum of wealth and the maximum of population."[15] Malthus, the arch miserabilist, should have marked this last point well. The growth of population will not, for Bentham, outstrip supplies of food. As we will see, an expanding population is an essential element in the economy of happiness. We will return to this point, as we have arrived at an important theme for the redefinition of utilitarianism. Bentham confesses that his jurisprudence did overprivilege the idea of penal law and legislation. Legislation might be necessary to order a community, but the methods of the legislator and the magistrate are different from those of a deontologist. Morality has very little to do with coercion and legal obligation. Indeed, the only "ought" in deontology is that "ought [should be] be banished from the vocabulary of morals." Bentham fulminates against doctrines of duty and the "sumum bonum" determined by those philosophers who deny the truths that any sensible person can discover.[16] It might suit the lawgiver to link obligations to duties but this is obscurantism.[17] Emphasizing duties means that the subtleties of moral reasoning have been abandoned.

Bentham's thinking is a variation on the concern with self-interest that one might find, for example, in Adam Smith.[18] Bentham acknowledges his debt to Smith in matters of political economy whilst also nuancing his thinking. Bentham also refers to Mandeville, and whilst he does not agree with the claim that private vices are public virtues, there is a sense in which he is building on these earlier arguments. As my happiness is irretrievably linked to yours, then in morality, as in political economy, I must act in my self-interest to generate general happiness. Or, more precisely, I must use my share of communal wealth, my capital, in such a way as to increase my own wealth and the wealth of the community. For Bentham, nature's "first law" is that you must find your own happiness in that of others.[19] It is important to note that this law is not really a law. By Bentham's own argument it cannot be an

13 ibid 278.
14 Jeremy Bentham, *Deontology* Vol. 2 (Longman 1834) 105.
15 Bentham, *Writings on Political Economy* (n 3) 33.
16 Bentham, *Deontology* I (n 2) 38.
17 ibid 10.
18 ibid 50.
19 ibid 17.

"ought" statement. It is inscribed in our own nature: in our "near-ness" to ourselves.[20] Bentham means that we understand that self-interest and happiness coincide; but other meanings emerge from this nearness. Is this the law of near-ness to self as mediated by capital? We will return to this point. For the moment, let us stick with the voice of the teacher of deontology.

The lessons put forward by the teacher of deontology are connected with other features of the text. Bentham names at least two allegorical figures. Timothy Thoughtless squanders his talents in drunkenness and debauchery – preferring instant pleasures to careful living and the nurture of his talent.[21] The story of Walter Wise shows that one must train one's energies: invest in order to recover more.[22] To stress a point made above, we should not confuse Walter with the stereotypical liberal subject. Whilst Mr. Wise certainly carries with him the cast of the bourgeois figure of political economics, he is a vegetarian and animal lover. He is, moreover, a man of sentiment and benevolence who knows that his happiness depends on that of others: "the mutual dependence of every human being upon… others of the human race."[23] But Mr. Wise is prone to doubts, nightmares and troubling self-examination. We will come back to Mr. Wise's fears, as we are still assembling the lessons of deontology.

Refined by deontology, utilitarianism is a dedication to the transformation of the body and its sentiments. The subject of happiness is deeply embedded in the social relationships that radiate out from the family to include all those others affected by the prudent man's behaviour. The happiness principle is one of social connection and other regarding prudence.[24] No wonder, then, that sections of Volume 2 read like *How to Make Friends and Influence People*.[25] As happiness is a social relationship, moral science requires subjects to be in control of themselves. For instance, 'natural' relationships of inferiority and superiority must be conducted in such a way as to not give offence. The moral subject must work to discipline his passions and emotions, and order his mind so as not to be distracted by wasteful thoughts. Bentham suggests that one should make use of blank moments between social interactions. One strategy recommended is to imagine discourses between the great figures of the past from which edification might be gained. For instance, what might one learn from listening to Milton and Smith talk to each other? There is always "work to be done."[26] There are

20 ibid 18.
21 ibid 118–121.
22 ibid 156.
23 Bentham, *Deontology* II (n 14) 40.
24 ibid 173–174.
25 Dale Carnegie, *How to Make Friends and Influence People* (Simon and Schuster 1936)
26 Bentham, *Deontology* II (n 14) 295.

practical matters to which one should attend. Most importantly, eructation and "the emission of that species [of gas] from the lower part of [the alimentary canal]" must be subjected to rules so as not to upset others.[27] The trick with the latter is to position one's self so that "the direction... [of] the blast will not reach any person." As far as belching is concerned, one must let the air escape "from the smallest possible aperture at the corner [of the mouth]."[28] If you are seated at table with others, it is better to cover your mouth than "puff... out effluvia." The "laws of amity," of which deontology is the inheritor, take the Aristotelean practice of friendship as a social virtue.[29] Whether or not there is such a thing as a friend, it would be fair to say that one would not want to cover one's neighbour with effluvia.

The moral subject is not limited to relationships with human others. Happiness extends beyond the human race to animals, who, in comparison with human babies, are more sentient and convivial. Although animals cannot reason, they can suffer, and as suffering is an index of pain, animal suffering counts against general happiness and is morally reprehensible. The extended field of morality is articulated in a re-shaping of the famous metaphor from *An Introduction to the Principles of Morals and Legislation.*[30] "[T]he chain of virtue" that "girdle[s] the whole of the sensitive creation" means that meat is murder: "happiness" must be "communicate[d]" through our actions "to lower natures" as animals are "intimately associated with that of the human race."[31] The animal becomes index and talisman of our relationships with others. If we do not understand that it is in our self-interest to treat animals well, we will never understand that the same applies to human others.

These lessons are carried forward when the teacher addresses the magistrate. The magistrate would do well to keep the principles of deontology in mind as he calculates with the "instruments" that govern the public sphere. He must draw up a balance sheet of pleasure and pain. There are precise instructions for this *personarum privilegiatarum*. Pleasure and pain have to be broken down into measures of intensity and duration. The catalogue then works through differentiations and oppositions. To understand the different dispositions of human beings, one must take into account certain variables: health, strength, hardiness, education, resoluteness of body and mind, moral and religious constitution, gender, climate, age, culture, government

27 ibid 237.
28 ibid 239.
29 ibid 239.
30 Jeremy Bentham, *The Works of Jeremy Bentham* Vol 11 (John Bowring ed, William Tait 1843).
31 Bentham, *Deontology* I (n 2) 213.

and rank in life.[32] These distinctions produce positive and negative terms that can then be mapped onto further distinctions which are meant to bring the formal operation of the code as close as possible to the human reality it is trying to measure.

Yes, the magistrate can use his discretion; and yes, the catalogue is only an approximation of reality. The springs of action give the grid of analysis, but Bentham is aware that they are somewhat dead on the page.[33] The drive for precision and exactness renders the catalogue unusable, and it risks collapse under its own divisions, subdivisions and clarifications of detail. Bentham anticipates Fuentes the Memorius. Utilitarianism is not really fit for purpose if "[it] offers too vague and undefined an impression to the mind."[34] As a deontologist, the magistrate cannot be a legislator. He must reason differently, reject "dogmatism" and the urge to hold forth from an "elbow chair."[35] The correct starting point for the "principles of utility" is not self-abnegation, sacrifice and asceticism of duty, but personal interest. Personal interest, directed towards the realization of "the greatest possible portion of felicity" can be coordinated with "the maximum of obtainable happiness" and the "end of morality... eternal happiness" achieved.[36] How? Utilitarian calculus should be replaced with "felicity."[37]

Bentham Invokes the Goddess

Whilst this might seem quite strange, Felicitas is the appropriate deity. After all, she graced the coins of the Roman Empire, and her beneficence was a symbol of the Emperor's wise stewardship.[38] She was also venerated as the deity of successful military commanders, and even though she has now taken up a different office and a new name, there is still something of the "spur and bridle" to her.[39] She had, of course, served Bentham at a somewhat earlier point, lending her name to felicific calculus: *plurimorum maxima felicitas*. But now, Felicity's "maternal" disposition guides the prudent man. She watches over those things that can increase, but also trickle away. She is the deity of flows:

32 ibid 32.
33 Bentham, *Deontology* II (n 14) 324.
34 Bentham, *Deontology* I (n 2) 34.
35 ibid 34.
36 ibid 12.
37 ibid 35.
38 See Hendrik Wagenvoort, 'Felicitas Imperatoria' (1980) 1 *Studies in Greek and Roman Religion* 59–83.
39 Bentham, *Deontology* II (n 14) 8.

> In her eyes happiness is a treasure of such value, and interest, and importance, that she would not willingly lose the smallest portion of it. She watches it in all its wanderings, and would fain bring it back to every bosom from whence it has escaped.[40]

Felicitas presides over deontology. She first appears in the text as a mother standing with her daughters.[41] She provides an allegorical realization of moral education. The practices of well-being, the "gymnastics" of the "body" and the "mind" are guided by her gentle hand. Felicity instructs through her "maternal kindness."[42] Her frowns serve to check misconduct through the desire of the prudent one to see her happy again and to witness a "recompense" of "smiles" (the kind of psychic dilemma that Laing might refer to as a knot: "I am unhappy that you are unhappy"). As Felicity presides over deontological reasoning, we know that she encourages the training of one's judgment. judgment becomes richer the more one considers the "seemingly unimportant events of life."[43] But then a peculiar simile. The patterns of judgment so formed are like "flakes of snow" succeeding one another. As the snow "gathers," so "our habits are formed."

This metaphor cuts against the sense of Bentham's argument, as it appears to describe something that just happens: an impersonal and anonymous process outside of individual control. This is most inappropriate as a figure of prudence and provokes a re-reading of one of the statements from *An Introduction to the Principles of Morals and Legislation* that grounds utilitarianism:

> The simple pleasure of the ear, excited by the perceptions of the chirping of birds, the murmuring of waters, the rustling of the wind among the trees. The pleasures of the smell, excited by the perceptions of the fragrance of flowers, of new mown hay, or other vegetable substances, in the first stages of fermentation. The agreeable inward sensation, produced by a brisk circulation of the blood, and the ventilation of it in the lungs by a pure air, such as that in the country frequently is in comparison of that which is breathed in towns.[44]

The sensorium is alive: the world is a play of light and sound, and the body is vigorous in the world: it glories in simply being there; flesh connected with

40 ibid 9.
41 Bentham, *Deontology* I (n 2) 138.
42 Bentham, *Deontology* II (n 14) 266.
43 Bentham, *Deontology* I (n 2) 169.
44 Jeremy Bentham, *The Works of Jeremy Bentham* Vol 1, 21 (John Bowring ed, William Tait 1843).

all that flows. You are in a world where labour has taken place. Things are kept up well. You are in a fecund place. The "first stage of fermentation" is part of this cycle of the seasons of which you are part. Through inward sensations this social, natural and animal world becomes knowable to you. You are far from the town. The air is pure. You are in touch with the body of the goddess which is all around you. Whose voice is speaking? How does this passage fit into the sober text of *Deontology*?

The voice from *An Introduction to the Principles of Morals and Legislation* is celebrating superfluity. Felicitas is present with her cornucopia of plenty. But there is still more. The roots of the words "felicity" and "surplus" connect with those of the words "to suck" and "to suckle." Whilst the metaphorical sense is clear, this also seems quite inappropriate for Bentham's argument. The image of the child at the breast could be connected with errant senses that we have been tracing above. At the same time, the drift of meaning could be limited by interpreting the metaphor as one of nurture: Felicity works to bring up her child, just as deontological reason works to educate the sensibility. Even so, the gendered nature of the metaphor seems off key. Furthermore, simply assuming parental "joy" risks making invisible the hard work of childcare. If we allow that there are other themes at work, themes not yet quite visible, we may be on the right track. The missing concerns are ones of work and sacrifice. Let's just note, for the moment that sacrifice is "mischievous."[45] If we can read these into the text, then we may be able to understand the strange dynamics of Bentham's moral economy. In order to do this, though, we must listen to one more voice. The voice of the political economist. We must see what he makes of Felicity, before we can finally hear what mutters, screams, curses, works, sweats and wriggles in Bentham's text.

The Commerce of Happiness

Happiness is not a quantitative phenomenon. An increase in happiness is a psychic increase. The arithmetic of happiness is a measure of social connections. In this sense, it has "geometrical" properties. This takes us to the link between happiness and wealth, and the fundamental connection between moral and political economy. Wealth is the material form taken by happiness: it is an aggregate of things that can be enumerated, put to use and enjoyed (indeed, the idea of poverty, of less-ness, stands as anti-wealth; the stubborn existence of what "falls to the poor" and can only diminish to nothing).[46] Labour might be the source of wealth, but in Bentham's Smithian

45 Bentham, *Deontology* I (n 2) 34.
46 Bentham, *Writings on Political Economy* (n 3) 2.

understanding, labour must be put to work by capital to produce wealth. That portion of wealth given over to increase is called capital. Those who make use of their stock of capital to work with land and labour have control of a quite miraculous substance: something that expands, and, if well managed, keeps expanding. Moreover, working to increase our "stock" (or enjoying it) is what makes us human. Bentham's moral man works hard all day and enjoys himself moderately in the evening. In this life of industry and repose, we are "most near" to ourselves.[47] The "atoms" out of which national wealth is composed come from the growth of capital, which "adds to the stock of an individual" and are not taken from anyone else.[48]

But, wealth is something used, and in being used, or consumed, it diminishes. So, the man of prudence must ensure that increase comes from productive consumption. Provided that wealth is subject to increase, any "sacrifice" is re-incorporated into a much grander increase. There is a necessary sacrifice of wealth in providing the means of security that protect the economy from internal and external enemies; likewise, the requirements of subsistence must also be sensibly managed. As we know, wealth is sacrificed in personal enjoyment, but the wise man knows that his pleasures must be kept in check. Once the enjoyment of enjoyment or the "commerce of happiness" is realized, it links distribution and production in a virtuous cycle of increase.[49] Productive capital puts more capital into circulation. Capital in circulation can be exchanged for other forms of capital. If this capital is invested in production, one can assume that it would go on to produce more capital which can in turn be exchanged and re-invested in production. As capital increases, wealth increases. As wealth increases, happiness increases.

The irrefutable logic of deontology means that there is no such thing as expenditure with real loss. Such losses as do take place are occasioned by poor actions of government (interventions into the spontaneous actions of the market) or unwise individuals' decisions. This is also perhaps why Bentham entertains a certain suspicion towards money. Money must be used by productive industry to enable increase, and the problem with taxation and government bounties is that they frequently put money into the wrong hands. When the spontaneous interactions of the economy are properly operational, "canals, docks and ports" appear through individual initiatives, metals and resources are extracted from land, towns develop and spread, machinery appears as labour divides and subdivides itself.[50]

47 ibid 13.
48 ibid 40.
49 Bentham, *Deontology* I (n 2) 164.
50 ibid 67.

Who best to preside over this economy of abundance? It cannot be the magistrate. Happiness cannot be legislated. Return to first principles. As we are the best judge of our own happiness, those who have shown themselves to be most skilled in the nurture of self-interest have the "power, knowledge and inclination"[51] to "direct national industry."[52] Hence the importance of private morals. Law may be used to urge men of property to achieve certain ends, and this is one of the correct aims of government. But the role of government and law is minimal: support private power, defend title to property and the security of money. This leads onto a much wider politics of "liberty": the use of privately owned things towards ends deemed proper by their owners.[53]

Felicity is the anima of this economy of happiness:

> Show me the man who throws away more of the elements of felicity than he creates, and I will show you a fool and a prodigal. Show me the man who deprives himself of more good than he communicates to another, and I will show you a man ignorant of the elementary arithmetic of morality.[54]

As the political economist ventriloquizes the teacher of deontology, Bentham nods in approval and the magistrate applauds. Here are the norms that articulate the polity; norms that link together personal and public governance. "Show me the man" booms the political economist. Timothy Thoughtless comes to mind. We know the "fool and the prodigal" has failed the test. He is unable to do the moral arithmetic and can manage neither himself nor his things. Poor Tim is lost to personal and social happiness, exiled from the interlocking circuits over which Felicity presides. This is exactly why Thoughtless and his kind must be subject to the "oughts" of law. Walter Wise receives deontology's "imprimatur."[55] He is marked by the goddess and knows himself as her offspring.

So far so good. Happiness names the increase of wealth. The increase of wealth will take place provided it is left to those with an enlightened sense of self-interest. However, doubts begin to disturb this bullish argument. Walter Wise may have developed habits of prudence and management, his busy days might distract him from dark thoughts, but he is still assailed by forebodings. Unable to sleep at night, insomnia heralds the infirmities of the body that break into his ordered life.[56] In his "ripe years" he must face the

51 Bentham, *Writings on Political Economy* (n 3) 167.
52 Bentham, *Deontology* I (n 2) 34.
53 ibid 36.
54 ibid 165.
55 ibid 9.
56 Bentham, *Deontology* II (n 14) 105.

approach of death. Wheezing and coughing, the moral man's expulsion of mucus is a cruel parody of political economy. Something plentiful is automatically given away. Expectoration without return. There is no escape from the truth. The organs that are as much part of you as your own happiness will fail. Your energies will run down like a cheap pocket watch. Your "nearness" to yourself will be replaced by infinite distance. Too much already. Political and moral economy come together to provide some comfort. The "consolation[s] of old age" are when "we may say, I shall not entirely die"[57] as you will be remembered through your property.[58] Deontology assures the anxious man a form of material afterlife.

There is something wedged in the smooth circuit of economy. We can return to Felicity to try to figure this unworking. As a figure of infinite fertility, it would appear that she has been recruited to serve the economy of moral empire; a role in which she is somewhat compromised. Certain peculiarities appear to take on significance. Felicity appears to have daughters but no partner. The teacher of deontology is certainly never represented as anyone other than one who passes her messages along. Moral men are merely her supplicants and pupils. It would seem that Felicity simply brings forth. She is her own cornucopia, an auto-generating fecundity. She must guarantee the increase of population that is one of the pillars of Benthamite political economy. This increase is most un-natural. It has no real body. Felicity has no organs. She presides over a system of production and distribution without cost, waste or compromise. Surely, this is a fantasy that avoids confrontation with the labour of the female body. But it is not just the labour of the female body that has disappeared. The commerce of happiness effaces all labouring bodies. After all, labour unlinked to capital is entirely unproductive and irrelevant to the generation of wealth.[59] Those who labour are invisible: crushed to dust in the cogs that grind out someone else's happiness.

De-Ontology

We can now return to the question asked in the first section of the essay.

The feminist criticisms of *Postmodern Jurisprudence* saw parallels between the criticism of positivism launched by the text and its own failure to understand what it had effaced. This criticism focused on the question "who speaks?" Who authorizes the voices that are heard in legal theory? The voice of the master speaks: Austin, Bentham, Hart. This argument is then effectively turned on "the postmodernists." Their text authorizes

57 ibid 73.
58 ibid 105.
59 Bentham, *Writings on Political Economy* (n 3) 43.

them to speak, and – moreover – despite the author's protestations, others remain silent. They announce that they will be sensitive to voices that are excluded from jurisprudence. But just how sensitive are they? Does the name "Douzinas et al." simply serve as the paradoxical stabilizer of its own mastery of unstable meaning? If so, ludic deconstruction would turn out to be a most dishonest game.

This essay has tried to develop a method of reading that takes these criticisms seriously. We have proceeded on the assumption that the text to be read was already reading the text reading it. Like the feminist strategy, this method of reading *Deontology* does not seek a pre-existing position from which to speak. Rather, and again like the feminist strategy, it tried to locate an "intertextual space" or "gap" where meanings circulate and "renewal" and "transformation" might be possible.[60] But, to what extent does this deal with the real point at stake? Does "postmodern theory" operate as "a gendered modality of enunciation"?[61] This cannot be confused with the banal claim that postmodernism is somehow "male."[62] The feminist approach aims to read in what *Postmodern Jurisprudence* left out, failed to see or hear. To talk back, in this feminist sense, is to speak of bodies.

Law does indeed appear as a body in *Postmodern Jurisprudence.* The corpus of law "must either digest or transform the non-legal into legality, or it must reject it, keep it out as excess and contamination."[63] The problem is that this body of law is undifferentiated. It is organized around its purgation of excess and contamination. Perhaps this corpus is closely related to that of Bentham's moral man. The controlling metaphor presupposes a universal body. Whilst its gender is not specified, it would seem that this universal body is male. It is not a body constituted by difference. There is no indication that law's body is "gendered" or "racially marked;" "healthy or unhealthy," "able-bodied or disabled."[64] These criticisms are clinched by turning to the engagement with *Antigone* in *Justice Miscarried.* Douzinas and Warrington are accused of further obscuring sexual difference by mapping it onto a prior difference between the "divine [and the] human."[65] This division is made the origin point for a corpus of law that effaces the materiality of human difference.

Have we repeated the same errors? The same blindness? If we talk of gods and goddesses are we effacing human differences? Felicitas' commerce

60 Ahmed (n 6) 8.
61 ibid 15.
62 ibid 15.
63 Costas Douzinas and Ronnie Warrington, *Justice Miscarried* (Harvester Wheatsheaf 1995) 25.
64 Ahmed (n 6) 25.
65 Douzinas and Warrington (n 63) 26.

between *Deontology* and *Postmodern Jurisprudence* would at least suggest that it was not necessary to move to *Justice Miscarried* in order to complete a critical reading of the earlier text. We have also tried to read bodies back into the problematic centre of political and moral economy, and to trace the various meanings that gather and disperse around the goddess. Admittedly, it is a heterosexual body, and Felicitas also "worked" for the Emperor. There is nothing inherently subversive about her. It is unlikely a feminist reading would make such an essentialist claim. The issue is perhaps the most un-natural nature of this divine body. But in reply to the criticisms of *Postmodern Jurisprudence*, it is not the case that the appearance of the goddess effaces other bodies. The goddess' staff links her with Tiresias – and a body that slides between differentiations.

Under this sign of errancy, bodies become unfixed in de-ontology. Consider the following problem that opens up at the centre of the springs of action – the key text for the magistrate. Resoluteness of mind is displayed through bodily signs; in particular the way in which a person's face expresses how they are feeling. A footnote acknowledges that there are many exceptions to this rule. Cromwell, for instance, had a hard heart but was also frequently disposed to voluminous tears. An anecdote from Tacitus that is meant to offer further evidence of how dispositions express themselves tails off in disruptive details. A man who claims to have had a brother "never had a brother." Did he have a sister? What is worse, as soon as Bentham turns his attention to the distinctions between sexes, the marks of difference have become disruptive: tears unsex Cromwell.

But the body is not just unfixed in de-ontology. We have discovered an invisible structure that holds bodies in place and erases their labour. The voices of *Deontology* circulate around this strange erasure – something like Beckett's Unnamable; but only something like: for at the core of de-ontology is something given, and, for the moment at least unlike Beckett, nameable: surplus value. De-ontology has revealed the ontology within de-ontology as the work of desiring bodies and exploited energies:

> The generosity of the poor is generally visible in personal services, in the dedication of their time, in the exposure of their persons, in the risks they run.[66]

The ragged trousers philanthropists appear in Bentham's text; or rather, their entrance is in the terms of de-ontology: the economy of happiness runs on their gift of time and energy. De-ontology does not see the precarity of labour in the economy. What appears is the generosity of a class whose work

66 Bentham, *Deontology* II (n 14) 235–236.

seems to be freely given. As we have seen, the only sacrifices that Bentham countenances are those offset by an increase in capital, or necessary investments in productive infrastructure. Like Smith, Bentham sees labour as the generator of wealth, but without capital, labour has no input into the economy. At least Smith had a slightly more developed sense of class than Bentham; for the latter, the social elements of the economy are primarily those roles linked to production and distribution. The sacrifice of lives in production does not figure in Bentham's political economy, or is presumably offset in the felicific calculus as the pains of the few. To the extent that labour appears at all, it is either in the form of a growing population, eager to take up work, or those condemned to poverty; thrown out of work in times of economic downturn. The poor are a problem for the magistrate; an unfortunate output of the economy of happiness that might have to be picked up at public expense; a theme where something like class war flickers at the edge of Bentham's text: *maxima felicitas*.

We have suggested that there is a sense in which de-ontology might be more alive to these problems than in the arguments that the teacher of morality, the political economist or the magistrate put forward. If there is a de-ontological imaginary unworking of Bentham's arguments from within, then perhaps we have found a place where what has been made invisible might reappear; where the ill health that founds that economy of happiness might slowly begin to reveal itself. The hyphen of de-ontology is this placeholder – a dash, a pause, an anticipation of something to come – the re-inscription of labour and surplus value into moral economy.

This blind spot might be where the de-ontological unworking of de-ontology leaves us. The phantasy of an ever-replenishing cornucopia of capital has hit against the real. It is not as if this structure of the real ignores bodies, as it puts all to work. The differences of race, gender and ability are not invisible. They structure the real. The real difficulty is to think about how they are active in the production of surplus value, and how this problematic can be deployed in jurisprudence. *Postmodern Jurisprudence* shares a fundamental message with feminist critique. We need to put at the centre the question of "distributive justice" and work at understanding the forces that "inscribe certain subjects" as worthy of note, and others as invisible.[67] To get at the real requires more than a theory of distributive justice. De-ontology offers a way of getting at the fundamental injustice of capitalism as a mode of production.

67 Ahmed (n 6) 66.

Differences That Mutter: Trumpets and Eructations

Can we now bring down the curtain on our reading with a final scene? As the prince is borne away, minor characters step forward to the flourish of trumpets and announce the new order. Such a neat resolution would seem inappropriate. It would be wrong to fold all the voices of this essay into a single authoritative statement. To remain authentic to *Postmodern Jurisprudence* (if that is not itself a trap) is to understand how it continues to be provocative; how it remains relevant to ongoing critical writing and thinking. Already, though, its legacy is somewhat tangled. Following the book's lead, "'the crits" might have abandoned Bentham too soon, and in so doing neglected a radical tradition that runs through the Owenites and the Chartists to John Watt who engaged in earnest discussion with Engels in the Manchester Hall of Science.[68] A similar question might be asked of those writers in the traditions of positivism and law and economics. In claiming Bentham for a certain liberalism, has a more radical legacy of his work been forgotten? Might *Postmodern Jurisprudence* suffer a similar fate? Who talks about postmodernism anymore? The general re-working of titles that has been a theme in this essay reaches a terminal point. Perhaps we should not be so hung up. The title, the name of the master, the imprimatur of the text obligates. Might this obligation be a species of the ought that de-ontology should try to understand? If so, it would be an unworked obligation; a continuing bastard inheritance from Bentham's most strange book: *Krapp's Last Tape* re-written as moral philosophy. What would a de-ontological obligation resemble? As this essay unspools, we cannot deal with this point, but it may be that de-ontological obligation is bound up with *Postmodern Jurisprudence.* Hart was wrong: the metaphor for obligation in Bentham is not the weight of something pressing down, but how the effaced can be made to count.[69]

The "post" of *Postmodern Jurisprudence* is yet to arrive. Or it may be lost in the mail. Perhaps it even arrived a long time ago and got trapped under the mat like Hardy's famous letter. The possibilities that the book opened spread backwards and forwards in time. In travelling back to Bentham, we entered the ruins of Ur and wandered amongst the shadows cast by the concepts of happiness, wealth and happiness. Our expedition did not set itself the task of reconstruction. We have tried to work with a de-ontological method and open the flux between Bentham and Douzinas et al. This movement eddies and swirls into other texts written by Douzinas,

68 See John Seed 'Unitarianism, Political Economy and the Antinomies of Liberal Culture in Manchester 1830–1850' (1982) 7(1) *Social History* 1–25.

69 HLA Hart, *Essays on Bentham, Jurisprudence and Political Philosophy* (Clarendon Press, 1982) 130–131.

Warrington and McVeigh. We have very briefly reviewed a theme from *Justice Miscarried*, and the currents from this text would carry us further towards other works where themes relevant for a moral economy of surplus value wait like slack water before rapids. The clue, taken from *Postmodern Jurisprudence*, is the requirement for an engagement with "the real." There has not been space enough in this essay to properly engage with this Lacanian term, and, indeed, a psychoanalytic framing is largely absent from *Postmodern Jurisprudence*. Nevertheless, we have certain orientating points that send the compass needle spinning. Despite the arguments put forward by Douzinas et *al. in Postmodern Jurisprudence*, the work that needs to be done is not storytelling. Following the feminist strategy, it might be that the legacy of our authors is to appreciate the labour of bodies whose work is the source of wealth: a sacrifice that makes ill-being the hidden foundation of Bentham's commerce of happiness.

The legacy of *Postmodern Jurisprudence*?

The gift to. Given.

Read again. Read better.

7

REFLECTIONS ON POSTMODERN TRUTH AND POST-TRUTH

Elena Loizidou

I was an undergraduate studying Law and Politics at the University of Keele between the years 1988–91. In my last year of studies, I elected the option of Jurisprudence taught by Shaun McVeigh. The group of legal theory enthusiasts was small, but the seminars were filled with ideas and vibrant discussions. Shaun McVeigh, a ferocious reader and a dedicated scholar, made sure that he introduced us to both classical and contemporary theoretical perspectives on law, sparking our imagination and our desire to read more. It certainly inspired me to do so and pursue, after my graduation, a Master's of Laws in Legal Discourse and later on a PhD at the University of Lancaster, where Costas Douzinas and Peter Goodrich, amongst other critical legal theorists, had set up camp. It was not, though, at Lancaster that I first encountered Costas Douzinas. I met Costas Douzinas for the first time in the first draft of *Postmodern Jurisprudence: The Law of text in the texts of law.*[1] Chapter 2, 'From the Book to the Text: Hermeneutics, Critique Deconstruction'[2] of the book was circulated in our Jurisprudence class by Shaun McVeigh, who was one of the authors of the book along with Costas Douzinas and Ronnie Warrington. The chapter both dazzled and enthused me. I was seeing in writing for the first time what I intuitively sensed about the law; the law was a language that could be interpreted, but depending on how we interpret the law, it could open us to expansive and exciting social, political, and material possibilities or close the world to us. I will engage

1 Costas Douzinas, Ronnie Warrington and Shaun McVeigh, *Postmodern Jurisprudence: The Law of Text in the Texts of Law* (Routledge 1991).
2 ibid 29–51.

DOI: 10.4324/9781032622224-7

with the chapter's understanding of the relationship between truth, interpretation, and postmodernity below, but before I proceed, I wanted to explain why I chose this book to celebrate the work and contributions to the Critical Legal and Human Rights Scholarship of Costas Douzinas. The first reason is obvious: it is the first book that I encountered by Costas, it is engraved in my mind, and it is one that I return to over and over again when I am writing and thinking about critical legal theory. The second reason, perhaps, is less obvious. It is not because I am interested, of course I am, in understanding the connection or disconnection between postmodern truth and post-truth and its implications on law, but rather because I want to pay homage to Douzinas' ability to write with others, and perhaps unintentionally to align the critical legal project with the idea of collaboration. Costas Douzinas, as a writer, thinker, and scholar, is able to produce impressive scholarship in collaboration with others. It is not easy; I would say, it is a challenge to align one's thinking with others and more difficult to write with others. Whilst for most of us, writing is a solidarity activity, for Douzinas, it is not the only way of writing books. Douzinas has, of course, written over five books on his own, but he also wrote with others. *Postmodern Jurisprudence* is the first of three books that he co-authored with friends. Others include *Justice Miscarried: Ethics and Aesthetics in Law* with Ronnie Warrington[3] and *Critical Jurisprudence: The Political Philosophy of Justice* with Adam Gearey.[4] As one of the founding members of the Critical Legal Studies movement in the UK, Douzinas must have been aware that radically transforming legal scholarship and establishing a new movement requires writing that challenges orthodox jurisprudential positions—something that cannot be accomplished by one person alone. The creation of movements requires collaboration at all levels, including with writing. This is a lesson that he transmitted to a new generation of critical legal scholars. This edited collection, edited by two, Alexis Alvarez-Nakagawa and Illan Rua Wall, former doctorate students of Douzinas and, of course, accomplished critical legal scholars, is a testament to this. Along with the scholarship of Douzinas in this chapter, I would like to punctuate and celebrate the collaborative spirit that he contributed to the critical legal studies movement in the UK.

Let us turn now to our reflections on the concept of postmodern truth as articulated in *Postmodern Jurisprudence* and the phenomenon of post-truth. A preliminary introduction to *Postmodern Jurisprudence* is necessary here. *Postmodern Jurisprudence* sets us on an adventure that takes us from

3 Costas Douzinas and Ronnie Warrington *Justice Miscarried: Ethics and Aesthetics in Law* (Edinburgh University Press 1995).
4 Costas Douzinas and Adam Gearey, *Critical Jurisprudence: The Political Philosophy of Justice* (Hart 2005).

modernity to postmodernity. We know from its preface that it has an ambitious objective, to undo the jurisprudence of modernity, which 'constructs theories that portray law as a coherent body of rules and principles, or of intentions and expressions of a sovereign will.[5] It goes on to explain rather colourfully that the jurisprudence of modernity 'is obsessed' with one particular desire 'to dress the exercise of political power in legitimacy'[6] and that its strategy is to unify all legal texts into a single veil, that is reproducible, circulatable and repeatable.[7] *Postmodern Jurisprudence*, on the other hand, is suspicious of 'attempts to create large-scale, totalizing theories in order to explain social phenomena'[8] and instead, it attends to subjugated knowledge, stories, that are present in texts but have somehow either been forgotten or excluded. Each book chapter meticulously offers a critique of the jurisprudence of modernity as well as theories that situate themselves at a distance from theories of modernity.

I turn now to Chapter 2, 'From the Book to the Text: Hermeneutics, Critique Deconstruction'[9] as it is the chapter that we find an engagement with the question of truth or how we arrive at truth. As we all know, law is invested in delivering the truth as well as justice. Legal theory is invested in explaining how law arrives at the truth or justice. Legal theory is interested in the process of delivering truth and justice. Whilst the jurisprudence of modernity understood the process of delivering truth to arrive from the application of the legal text, bereft of prejudices that will be produced objectively by a conscious and rational subject, theories of interpretation, on the other hand, reject this proposition. The truth about the meaning of a text cannot be universal or mechanically produced. It is, instead, the product of history and language. The subject itself is also a product of its historical context and language. The chapter sets out to first present the turn to hermeneutics popular in social sciences, anthropology, and law in the 1990s but also to critique one of the most established theorists at the time of hermeneutics, Hans-George Gadamer, and then point to the limits of Gadamer's understanding of the production of truth.

For Gadamer, the meaning and truth of texts are inextricably linked to the prejudices and prejudgments that we bring to it as readers.[10] I would read, for example, a newspaper article on gender from where I am situated, a cis queer woman who acquired knowledge about gender theory in the 1990s. I will evaluate legal decisions on queer subjects from this position. Gadamer,

5 Douzinas, Warrington and McVeigh (n 1) ix.
6 ibid.
7 ibid ix–x.
8 ibid x.
9 ibid 29–55.
10 ibid 34.

of course, by recognizing that we may bring to a legal text our own prejudices, does not suggest that we should carry on with these prejudices. By recognizing our prejudices and those of the culture we find ourselves in, that we are not neutral recipients of knowledge, information, culture, and so forth, we can assess or keep in check our prejudices and pre-judgments and amend them accordingly. Truthful meaning arises from the process of recognition of prejudices, assessment of them, and amendment of these prejudices.[11] As Douzinas, Warrington, and McVeigh observe, 'Th[is] operation assumes that the text forms a unity, a consistent whole, that allows the continuous readjustment between part and whole and shows certain interpretations to be better than others'.[12] While Gadamer's theory of interpretation may strike a blow to the jurisprudence of modernity, and positivist thinkers, a welcoming contribution for the authors of *Postmodern Jurisprudence*, it still reveals certain limits. Firstly, apart from holding on to the unity of a text, it assumes that a text in itself is true.[13] The second criticism that Gadamer's theory of interpretation faced is that of lack of objectivity, of being subjective and therefore retaining the prejudices that he proposes his theory of interpretation set out to not exactly ameliorate, but rather situate. Gadamer's response to this criticism has been one that acknowledges the creating attributes of interpretation but at the same time argues that the new meaning or truth that emerges through this process—acknowledgement, evaluation, and amendment of prejudices—produces truth that does not belong to the subject but rather to the interlocutors of different positions. As Douzinas, Warrington, and MacVeigh explain through this process 'the text is a harmony of voices', a fusion of previous opinions and interpretations that have been handed down to us'.[14] This allows the authors of *Postmodern Jurisprudence* to conclude that 'Gadamer seems to have replaced the allegiance to personal prejudice or meanings given in the text with an allegiance to the past'.[15] My aim here is not to provide a summary of Gadamer's theory of interpretation and production of truth but rather to use it as a springboard to show how *Postmodern Jurisprudence*'s critique of Gadamer gives way to talk about the more desirable postmodern theory of truth.

As you have noticed, Gadamer's robust critique of the universality of truth is haunted by an enduring attachment to the past. The past is presented as a collaborator in the production of truth and meaning. This position, nevertheless, carries certain risks. While considering past meanings can illuminate the present, unreflective appeals to the past—such as the rhetoric

11 ibid 34–35.
12 ibid 35.
13 ibid 35.
14 ibid 37.
15 ibid.

invoked by the 'Unite the Kingdom' movement, which frames migration as a threat and longs to return to an imaginary 'pure' UK—reproduces the same exclusionary universality that Gadamer sought to avoid. The authors of *Postmodern Jurisprudence*, through their engagement with deconstruction, offer a way out of this trap.

Drawing on Derrida's deconstructive theory, Douzinas, Warrington, and McVeigh invite us to see the text, the legal text specifically, not as something that is steeped in tradition, but rather as a play of signs. To that respect, the meaning of text is never fixed, nor fully present, but rather 'a trace of presence and absence', 'temporarily deferred', 'repeatable'.[16] The repeatability is an important characteristic of the sign. When a sign is repeated, it is not repeated in the same way, producing inevitably difference. To this effect, as they explain, '[i]n repeating, the sign defies all distinguishing lines between original and copy, authentic and derivative, essence and expression, context and form'.[17] Whilst this may suggest that we will never reach the intention of its author, as even the author themselves are not fully present to their writing, or that there is no universal truth to a text, it does not mean, as what some often suggest, that 'we do not need truths'.[18] It simply means, the authors of *Postmodern Jurisprudence* write, that we must be vigilant to the operation of claims to truths. We should, for example, not allow claims to the obvious natural truth to go unexamined. Such truths, they explain, are steeped in violence, precisely because they hold close to their heart the idea of the universality and unity of texts. For example, recently gender-critical feminists suggest that only biological and not re-assigned women are women. Deconstruction, the philosophical position that *Postmodern Jurisprudence* adopts, will not take such claims to truth and knowledge about subjects as truth. On the contrary, it will point to the different categories of 'woman' and include trans women within this category. No word, or sign, or subject for that matter is ever static, but rather is constantly in the process of becoming other. In this respect, if we stick to the example of who occupies the category of woman, deconstruction will suggest that there is no original woman but rather a constant resignification of who a woman is. Any attempt to claim as true a certain category of woman and not another is both violent and exclusive.

The idea of constant resignification and instability of meaning has often been critiqued as both introducing the idea of truth of a text and, in our legal context, relativism. Though, if we notice Douzinas, Warrington, and McVeigh's analysis of interpretation, truth, and meaning points not to

16 ibid 47.
17 ibid.
18 ibid 51.

relativism, but rather to be mindful that when universal claims to truth are made, we should note the exclusions that they bring along and the violence that they may impose on those who may be affected by them.

While the *Oxford Dictionary* traces the use of the post-truth back to 1985, the term entered the dictionary in 2016. The dictionary tells us that the term post-truth 'originated in the US. It is defined as '[r]elating to or denoting circumstances in which objective facts are less influential in shaping political debate or public opinion than appeals to emotion and personal belief'. Lee McIntyre identifies numerous examples of post-truth that include the lies that brought about the Brexit referendum voting results, as well as the US presidential election results in 2016, and the denial of the climate crises.[19] We can add to this list the lies told by public officials that the Covid public inquiry has recently uncovered, including those of former Prime Minister Boris Johnson, former Health Secretary Matt Hancock, and also former Prime Minister Rishi Sunak, in relation to various decisions they made—such as the procurement of personal protective equipment (PPE) and the 'Eat Out to Help Out' scheme. The evidence increasingly suggests that delays in decision-making, the awarding of PPE contracts, and the implementation of the scheme were driven less by scientific advice and more by political interests.

My aim here is not to delve into post-truth examples, but rather to consider to what extent postmodern ideas of truth align with those of post-truth. This link has been made and prompted McIntyre to consider that post-truth may be 'a fusion, whereby largely left-wing relativism and postmodern attacks on the idea of truth from decades ago have now simply been co-opted by right-wing political operatives'.[20] If there is an alignment between post-truth and postmodern truth, then the ideas of postmodern truth, meaning, and subjectivity proposed by the authors of *Postmodern Jurisprudence* risk corrupting the expansive and inclusive idea of truth and its making that they proposed in 1991. Is the check on universal truth, by pointing to the non-existence of original meaning, to the play of signs and repetition with difference, leading to the proliferation of opinions verified by emotions, such as sadness, anger, etc.? And if this is the case, if we can point to such alignment, what will be the effects on not just legal theory but moreover on judge-made law?

As we have seen earlier, *Postmodern Jurisprudence* was, of course, written as a response to modern jurisprudence, which was steeped in the rational project of Enlightenment. At the same time, whilst it may not be an object of emotions being part of our interpreting meaning, as Foucault

19 Lee McIntyre Lee, *Post-Truth* (MIT Press 2018).
20 ibid 6.

did in 'Nietzsche, Genealogy, History',[21] by putting the body and emotions at the centre of undoing traditional interpretations of histories that focused mainly on great figures and events, it still never suggests that truth should be foregone. Nor does *Postmodern Jurisprudence* suggest that we should only be succumbing to 'confirmation bias'—a characteristic of post-truth proponents—following only those opinions, texts, and social media that confirm our own bias. Confirmation bias turns itself into a new universal where it does not allow anything that contradicts one's opinions formed in silo to be challenged. On the contrary, as we have already seen, their intervention into the philosophies of meaning and truth of legal texts, and texts in general, stems from the dangers of universalizing and naturalizing our opinions. Additionally, post-truth, unlike *Postmodern Jurisprudence*, rejects the existence of truth altogether, whilst *Postmodern Jurisprudence* asks us to be vigilant to all claims that are all-encompassing, exclusionary, and promote an all-knowing attitude.

I could write more about how *Postmodern Jurisprudence*'s understanding of truth and our relation to it and post-modern truth. My aim here, though, was to offer a brief chapter that situates *Postmodern Jurisprudence*—a classic in the critical legal studies oeuvre—within contemporary discussions about post-truth. This chapter leans towards a need to think of this relationship more and embrace the lessons of this book, to be vigilant and ready to dismantle any claims to truth as well as any claims that challenge the existence of truth. Instead, like Douzinas and his collaborators in *Postmodern Jurisprudence* suggest, we should be always ready to challenge whilst thinking with any claims that aim at naturalizing the world we find ourselves in as well as creating violent exclusions. The aim here was not just to celebrate the thinking and huge transformation in legal studies that this book offered but also to celebrate Douzinas' collaborative spirit and his strong belief in collective and open thinking of how we do things. To all this, I raise a glass.

21 Michel Foucault, 'Nietzsche, Genealogy, History' in Michel Foucault (ed), *Language, Counter Memory, Practice* (Basil Blackwell 1997) 139–164.

8

THE VERY SHORT STORY OF DOUZINAS' LAW AND IMAGES (THAT AWAITS ITS REBUTTAL)

Ozan Kamiloglu

Costas Douzinas gave his inaugural lecture as a professor in 1999, not on critique of human rights, for which he is probably most widely recognized, but on images and law. Since 1996, starting with the article *Whistler vs. Ruskin: Law's Fear of Images*, Douzinas has written many articles on the relationship between law and images until 2012. A close reading of these works reveals a recurring core argument, articulated across different texts with varying degrees of nuance and expansion.[1] In this brief chapter, I will examine how this central argument evolves throughout Douzinas' engagement with law and images, and consider how his perspective fits within the broader framework of his intellectual trajectory.

In his first single-authored article on law and images,[2] Douzinas examines the 1877 libel case of *Whistler v Ruskin*, in which art critic John Ruskin publicly condemned eight of Whistler's paintings. Ruskin's argument rested on two claims: first, he argues for the truth of his claims, and second, he argues that they are 'fair and bona fide criticisms'. This argument obliges the court to 'pass judgment upon aesthetic principles and judgments of taste; the law was called upon to judge art, the normative realm to regulate aesthetics'.[3] It is this uneasy intersection that becomes a foundational tension in Douzinas' work, prompting a sustained inquiry into the normative dimensions of visual judgment within legal frameworks over the years. Douzinas

1 For example, several pages of these two articles are exactly the same: Costas Douzinas, 'Law and the Image' (1999) 7 *Gramma: Journal of Theory and Criticism* 15; Costas Douzinas, 'The Aesthetics of the Common Law' (1997) 17 *Studies in Law, Politics and Society* 3.
2 Costas Douzinas, 'Whistler v. Ruskin: Law's Fear of Images' (1996) 3(19) *Art History* 353.
3 Ibid.

DOI: 10.4324/9781032622224-8

revisits this theme in two subsequent articles: 1986 'The Alta(e)rs of Law: The judgment of Legal Aesthetics'[4] and 2008 'Sublime Law: On Legal and Aesthetic Judgments'[5] In both, he draws on the case of *Re St Stephen Walbrook* [1986], where judges were similarly tasked with making an aesthetic judgment—this time concerning the design of an altar in a church.

The intersection of law and aesthetic judgment provides Douzinas with a compelling framework to reintroduce a central philosophical figure in his work on law and images—as well as in his writings on human rights—Immanuel Kant. Douzinas frequently turns to Kant's *Critique of judgment* mainly to highlight how, contrary to law, modern aesthetic judgment is disinterested in use, end, purpose or motive of the act/work.[6] The aesthetics is a judgment of pure form,[7] and separate from knowledge and justice, all of which are 'separate institutions operated by a distinct group of experts'.[8] This Kantian tripartite division enables him to construct associations that mark the nature of this distinction. 'Law is the combination of reason and necessity; for law, art is the combination of sensuality and luxury' Douzinas argues.[9] 'Images are sensual and fleshy; they address the labile elements of the self, they speak to emotions and they organize the unconscious. They have power to short circuit reason and enter the soul without the interpolation or intervention or language or interpretation' suggests Douzinas at the Introduction of, *Law and the Image*, edited with Lynda Nead. Douzinas consistently contrasts the domains of art and law, arguing that: 'Art is assigned to imagination, creativity and playfulness while law to control, discipline and sobriety. There can be no bigger contrast than that between the open texts and abstract paintings of the modernist tradition and the text of statutes'.[10] A decade later, he reiterates this opposition: 'Art and the subjective responses it evokes are diametrically opposed to the reasoned and objective resolution to questions of doctrine and law'.[11] This modernist separation—between justice and aesthetics, image and law—creates a conceptual gap that Douzinas continues to explore and theorize throughout his work.

4 Costas Douzinas, Shaun McVeigh and Ronnie Warrington, 'The Alta(e)rs of Law: The judgment of Legal Aesthetics' (1994) 9(4) *Theory, Culture & Society* 93.
5 Costas Douzinas, 'Sublime Law: On Legal and Aesthetic judgments' (2008) 4 *Parallax* 18.
6 Sometimes Kelsen, Burke and Hegel also help Douzinas to explain the modern condition.
7 Douzinas, 'Whistler v. Ruskin' (n 2) 353.
8 Douzinas, 'Law and the Image' (n 1) 15; Douzinas, 'The Aesthetics of the Common Law' (n 1) 3.
9 Douzinas, 'Law and the Image' (n 1); Douzinas, 'The Aesthetics of the Common Law' (n 1) 3.
10 Douzinas, 'Law and the Image' (n 1); Douzinas, 'The Aesthetics of the Common Law' (n 1) 3.
11 Douzinas, 'Sublime Law: On Legal and Aesthetic judgments' (n 5) 18.

After constructing this 'modern' demarcation of closed systems of judgment, the majority of the articles focus on the reasons (continuities) and consequences (complexities) of this presumption of demarcation of the form of law and that of taste or image. He argues for 'Law's fear of images', repeatedly, to highlight centuries-long continuities that have been carried to the modern law.[12] Since images are 'too worldly, too sensual and potentially corrupt, too contingent and transient, and so was replaced with the word', or policed by the law.[13] The law, Douzinas claims, 'loves and fears images, it both prohibits them and organizes its own operation in a highly spectacular and visual manner'.[14] This interplay between love and fear and the idea of the policing of images allows Douzinas to delve into the theological history of Byzantium in several articles, introducing iconophilia and iconoclasm of religion and arguing for a continuity between pre-modern religion and modern law. In different articles, he discusses the iconomachia or 'complex legal administration of aesthetics' and claims that 'In the same way that icons were excluded from churches, figures and imagery [...] banned from the law'.[15] Law demonstrates its fear of images through banning images, in a continuity with iconoclasts of Byzantium, and 'In modernity, unrepresentable Deus whose imago reached all corners of the empire has been replaced by sublime law, which, although invisible, can be known through its proliferating images'.[16] The sublime thus becomes a conceptual bridge between theology and modern jurisprudence. Douzinas writes 'the prohibition on images becomes the transcendental condition of representation, of imagery and of the law. This is the crucial moment at which the idea of invisibility passes from the divine to law and from theology to jurisprudence. The law becomes the absolute or transcendent force of modernity, expressed in the theory of the sublime'.[17]

In his later works, partly inspired by Rancière[18] and others, he rethinks the relationship between the image and the law, moving beyond the earlier

12 Douzinas, 'Whistler v. Ruskin' (n 2); Douzinas, 'Law and the Image' (n 1); Douzinas, 'The Aesthetics of the Common Law' (n 1); Douzinas, 'Sublime Law: On Legal and Aesthetic judgments' (n 5).

13 Costas Douzinas and Lynda Nead, 'Introduction' in Costas Douzinas and Nead, Lynda (eds), *Law and the Image: The Authority of Art and the Aesthetics of Law* (Chicago University Press 1999) 8. See also: Douzinas, 'Law and the Image' (n 1); Douzinas; 'The Aesthetics of the Common Law' (n 1) 3; Douzinas, 'Sublime Law: On Legal and Aesthetic judgments' (n 5).

14 Douzinas, 'Law and the Image' (n 1); Douzinas, 'The Aesthetics of the Common Law' (n 1) 3.

15 Douzinas and Nead, 'Introduction' (n 13) 8. See also: Douzinas, 'Law and the Image' (n 1); Douzinas; 'The Aesthetics of the Common Law' (n 1) 3.

16 Douzinas and Nead, 'Introduction' (n 13) 12.

17 Douzinas, 'Sublime Law: On Legal and Aesthetic judgments' (n 5).

18 Jacques Rancière, *The Politics of Aesthetics* (Gabriel Rockhill tr, Continuum, 2004) 7–46.

dichotomies that had shaped his initial arguments. The new theoretical tools he adopts and develops consider the image as a 'complex administration of an era's available ways of seeing'.[19] This definition enables him to return to the iconomachia of images, where love and fear of images become a regime of images that 'determine our ways of seeing, of attaching symbolic constructs to missing, lost or dead objects and making them appear natural, inescapable or truthful in their absence'.[20] This theoretical turn deepens Douzinas' engagement with law and images, bringing figures such as Pierre Legendre, Jacques Lacan and Jean-Paul Sartre into the conversation on the iconomachia of images and their relationship to law.[21] Looking at this turn in his thinking, Douzinas' trajectory in law and image theory mirrors his evolving approach to human rights: initial oppositions and boundaries give way to a more intricate interplay of forces—gaze, subjectification and aesthetic-political regimes. His work increasingly emphasizes the fluidity and complexity of these relationships, rather than their separation.

At the end of his last article on law and images, Douzinas issues a call to 'responsibility' for lawyers and scholars: 'To revive an aesthetic of justice, in the name of a justice whose judgments lie outside or beyond the law, expressions of a higher tribunal to which the law is called to account, when its eye turns into an ossifying gaze'.[22] With this, he gestures toward the realm of natural law and human rights, where judgment transcends the positivist boundaries of legal justification. An invitation to rethink Kant's *sensus communis* which is the source of both legal and aesthetic judgment, 'higher or right reason organizes those judgments of sense and compares universal forms'.[23] This moment of convergence reveals a key intersection in Douzinas' thought: the relationship between law and images is not merely aesthetic, but deeply ethical and political. His invocation of *sensus communis* signals a broader concern with the conditions under which justice can be imagined and enacted beyond the strictures of legal formalism.

Douzinas' work on law and images can also be situated within the broader history of critical legal theory in the UK, particularly through his involvement with the Critical Legal Conference and the founding of *Law and Critique* during the 1980s and 1990s. In those years, Douzinas and others challenged the mainstream legal academy by drawing on French post-structuralists, deconstruction, psychoanalysis and semiotics. Their interventions exposed law as a contingent fiction, shaped by specific historical and

19 Costas Douzinas, 'A Legal Phenomenology of Images' in Oren Ben-Dor (ed), *Law and Art* (Routledge-Cavendish 2011) 249.
20 Ibid 250.
21 Ibid.
22 Ibid 258.
23 Douzinas, 'Sublime Law: On Legal and Aesthetic judgments' (n 5).

ideological conjunctures. Therefore, by exposing the fear of law from unstable, sensual and fleshy images, they simultaneously expose the mainstream legal academy's fear of critical theory. In his most recent work, *States of Exception*, Douzinas looks back to the history of legal theory in the UK, associating aesthetics and anti-formalism with the 1980s, ethics with the 1990s and early 2000s and politics and resistance with the late 2000s. These phases are clearly traceable in his writings on law and images. In his early work, aesthetics is treated as a distinct and threatening domain that unsettles legal rationality. By the 2000s, Douzinas begins to develop more nuanced conceptual tools—phenomenology of the image, the scopic field, the mirror image, the regime of visibility, the gaze. While these tools enrich our understanding of law's symbolic and visual dimensions, they stop short of establishing a fully political or resistant relationship between law and image. Although Douzinas' more recent work on human rights and political theory moves beyond the frameworks of Levinas, Derrida and Lacan, his theory of the image still awaits a final turn—one that would fully integrate politics and resistance into the aesthetic-legal nexus.

If each of these epochs contains, in a dialectical way, a critique of the one preceding it, the complex tools of deconstruction and psychoanalysis that Douzinas and others have used in their analysis of law and image, still await their rebuttal. Law with a capital 'L' may be sublime as Douzinas claims, but that of law with lower case 'l' remains terribly purposeful and precise in ordering bodies, communities, voices, capital and property. This tension underscores the need for a conceptual framework that situates law and images within the politically resistant phase of critical legal theory, and this is where Douzinas' law and image awaits its negation. The challenge is to move toward a mode of theorization that confronts law's material effects and symbolic power through resistance, struggle and transformation. Only then can the image become not just a site of critique, but a force within the politics of law.

To continue along the path opened by Douzinas, Goodrich and other critical legal theorists, we must ask: what are the questions of a politicized debate on the law and images that will negate its predecessor? I propose three starting points: first, we need to understand the neoliberal aesthetics of justice, the ordering of bodies for maximum efficiency, control and surveillance. The cynical and spectacular aesthetics of justice in the neoliberal era operate on the principle of managed transparency, screens and data where the mechanical gaze of justice eats itself like an ouroboros. The law, with a small 'l', in its daily activities, is an archiving machine that lives increasingly in the digital, behind the screen, above the data. It is embedded into the global regime of surveillance and borders. Even if there is nothing behind the veil that hides the law, and we live on the earth that is only crust without an interior, that crust is what we build our lives out of, and what we are buried into. Peter Goodrich points to a shift in the medium from text to screen in 2013, the year the Supreme Court uploaded its first video to its own YouTube channel;

> The classical trinity of ordo, lex, medium holds true for the contemporary world. Each new medium underpins a new world and a changed form of law. Thus, the current move from text to screen because the new mode of humanist letter is in the form of the scroll page; the new emblems of legality are Court TV, Judge Judy, Boston Legal, CSI, the screens that range from real-time news, cameras in court, to Planet Hollywood and IMAX.[24]

If the medium has changed dramatically, we need new tools of analysis that can understand the law and its relationship with images. This could also allow us to go beyond anthropocentric consideration of the law.

Secondly, if the past decade of social movements—Black Lives Matter, Me Too and decolonial struggles—has taught us anything, it is the imperative to historicize law in relation to its complicity in producing layered systems of oppression, alienation and interpellation, and to look at 'the lives of others'. Every single life matters, demands attention and holds a truth that is frequently invisible to the methods of western philosophy, phenomenology or psychoanalysis of 'othering'. These movements proposed to be seen, not as the absolute victim, but as resistant subjects demanding justice. A politicized analysis of law and images in this context must respond to the multiplicity of relationships between legal structures and visual regimes. It must move beyond sweeping generalizations that span millennia or universalize the human condition. Instead, it requires attention to micro-histories—specific, situated narratives that reveal how law and image intersect in lived experience.

Finally, the idealized aesthetics of judgment should not be revived in the hope of unity or moral clarity. Instead of teleological desires for order, care and solidarity should be prescribed, and instead of a 'higher tribunal', we should look for the lowest possible one. Douzinas sets the task of legal iconology as 'to develop a critique of regimes of visuality that will complement the critique of ideology'. Perhaps, however, legal iconology should move beyond toward an investigation of the everyday life of icons and the people who live among them—how icons rise, how they fall and how they shape the textures of lived experience

24 Peter Goodrich, 'Screening Law' (2013) 21(1) *Law & Literature* 1.

9

TOWARDS A LEGAL PHENOMENOLOGY OF SOUNDS

Douzinas' Legal Aesthetics Beyond the Image

Julia Chryssostalis[1]

Douzinas' Legal Aesthetics

For Costas Douzinas, aesthetics, and its significance and relation to law, has been an important and constant preoccupation. We can trace this strand of his work throughout his extensive writings on critical legal theory by distinguishing between three main periods in his rich intellectual trajectory over the last forty-five years or so. In the first period, signposted by *Postmodern Jurisprudence*,[2] the first book he co-authored with Ronnie Warrington, aesthetics was central to the task of undoing the closure of the legal text and the 'noble lie' of its internal coherence and consistency. Exploring specifically the form of law, of legal writing and the literary aspects of law, the book examined the aesthetic forms that the legal text deploys and, while 'norming' the legal text *qua* legal, remain excluded, hidden, and repressed, at the margins of legality as its secret underside. The second period of Douzinas' work, which focuses on ethics, the normativity of law and justice, can be similarly signposted by *Justice Miscarried*, the second book that Douzinas and Warrington wrote together.[3] Here, aesthetics, the literary field in particular, is the privileged domain in which the questions of justice and of the relationship between ethics and law are articulated. Aesthetics, in this juncture, is the site at the

1 Westminster Law and Theory Lab, Westminster Law School, University of Westminster. I would like to thank Illan Rua Wall, Brandon LaBelle, and Patrick Hanafin, without whom this piece would never have been written.

2 Costas Douzinas, Ronnie Warrington and Shaun McVeigh, *Postmodern Jurisprudence: The Law of Text in the Texts of Law* (Routledge 1991).

3 Costas Douzinas and Ronnie Warrington, *Justice Miscarried. Ethics, Aesthetics and the Law* (Harvester and Wheatsheaf 1994).

DOI: 10.4324/9781032622224-9

other side of the law, an outside that is always already within, from where to begin a reawakening of law's ethical sensibility and sense of justice. Literature here does not simply bring ethics to law. Literature, as the writing of the impossible, is a writing that follows law in its breach and its failure and allows us to imagine and hope for another justice. Finally, the third period of Douzinas' work on law and aesthetics is marked by a shift from the text to the image. It covers a relatively long period of time and begins with the publication of *Law and the Image*, a collection of essays that were written by legal theorists, art historians, and art theorists in the late 1990s, and that Douzinas co-edited with art historian Lynda Nead.[4] This was the first book of its kind in that it put legal theory, art theory, and art history in conversation with one another. Douzinas' own contribution[5] explored law's order of images and introduced the idea of regimes of visuality, a year before Jacques Rancière published his discussion of aesthetic regimes.[6] In the following years, Douzinas continued to work on law and aesthetics in several texts that were published as journal articles and book chapters.[7] These investigated, on the one hand, the legality of the image and the aesthetics of law; the order of images and the normative regimes of visuality and visibility that determine, frame, and control what and how we see as well as how we are given to the world to be seen; the nature of legal and aesthetic judgment; and the legal phenomenology of images; and, on the other hand, proposed the critique of iconology as a new field 'perhaps more important than the well known critique of ideology.'[8]

4 Costas Douzinas and Lynda Nead *Law and the Image. The Authority of Art and the Aesthetics of Law* (University of Chicago Press 1999).

5 Costas Douzinas, '*Prosopon* and *Antiprosopon*: Prolegomena for a Legal Iconology' in Douzinas and Nead (eds) (n 4) 36–67.

6 Rancière first introduces the concept of 'aesthetic regime' in *The Politics of Aesthetics: The Distribution of the Sensible* (Continuum 2004), which was originally published in French, in 2000, as *Le partage du sensible; esthétique et politique* (La fabrique éditions). It should be noted that Douzinas' and Rancière's concepts do not coincide despite their similarities. Douzinas briefly explains the difference between his concept of 'regimes of visuality' and Rancière's concept of 'artistic/aesthetic regimes' in a footnote in his contribution to a collection of essays on law and art. There, he notes that, although both are epochal concepts, Rancière's 'aesthetic regimes' is a concept that 'is limited to art and aesthetic considerations' whereas his 'regimes of visuality' is a concept that 'covers all aspects of imagery and vision' Costas Douzinas, 'A Legal Phenomenology of Images' in Oren Ben-Dor (ed), *Law and Art: Justice, Ethics and Aesthetics* (Taylor and Francis 2011) 258, fn 4.

7 'Law and the Image' (1999) 7 *Gramma* 15; 'The Legality of the Image' (2000) 63 *Modern Law Review* 813; *Νόμος και Αισθητική. Λογοτεχνία, Τέχνη, Δίκαιο [Law and Aesthetics. Literature, Art, Law]* (Papazisis 2004, in Greek); 'The Aesthetics of Law' in Daniel McClean (ed), *The Trials of Art* (Ridinghouse 2007); 'Sublime Law: On Legal and Aesthetic judgments' (2008) 14(4) *Parallax* 18; 'Foreword. The Blindness of Law and the Insight of Justice' in Michael Stolleis (ed), *The Eye of the Law. Two Essays in Legal History* (Birkbeck Law Press 2009); 'A Legal Phenomenology of Images' in Ben-Dor (ed) (n 6) 247–258.

8 Douzinas (n 6) 253.

What started therefore in the 1980s and 1990s as a literary jurisprudence, one whose engagement with aesthetics focused on the text, from the late 1990s and 2000s onwards, through the turn to the image, gradually became an aesthetic jurisprudence, or *ars juris*, a body of work that studies different aspects of the aesthetic dimensions of law, legality, and normativity, and, concentrating on vision, how our senses, or *aesthēses*, generally are captured and governed by the law. Moreover, the texts that Douzinas published during this period, with their analyses of the order of images, and the regimes of visuality, visibility and representation, indicate a further shift in his engagement with aesthetics, one that is framed by the broader turn to politics in his work during this time.[9] Further, although his attention in these writings remains on law's field of representation, it now moves from the unrepresented and unrepresentable other of the law, that concerned him in the 1980s and 1990s, to the very ordering of the domain of representation and the encoding of our sense of seeing: how we see and are being seen, and how we judge what we see as beautiful, truthful, and normal. Finally, his theorisation of legal and aesthetic judgment enables him to re-work some earlier pieces on aesthetics[10] and integrate them now into what emerges as a complex aesthetics of law.

To be sure, Douzinas' legal aesthetics is developed around the text, the image, the eye, and vision. References to the other senses are sparse, limited to hearing, often indirect, and found elsewhere in his writings. For instance, in the 'Introduction' to *Postmodern Jurisprudence*, he and Warrington write that the task of postmodern critiques is to 'give voice to,' that is render audible and make heard, 'the echoes of what has been silenced in the corridors of the law.'[11] While in *Justice Miscarried*, drawing on Levinas, they refer to hearing and to the ear as intrinsic to ethics and justice, and as such as having priority over vision and the eye, and the principle of *audi alteram partem* as 'the first principle of natural justice.'[12] Moreover, in fact

9 During this same time, Douzinas was also working on his first solely authored book, *The End of Human Rights: Critical Thought at the Turn of the Century* (Hart 2000), that signalled a turn to a more pronounced concern with politics, and subsequently resistance, in his work. Translated into several languages, *The End of Human Rights* was followed by a series of books – *Human Rights and Empire: The Political Philosophy of Cosmopolitanism* (Routledge 2007), *The Radical Philosophy of Rights* (Routledge 2019) and *States of Exception* (Elgar 2024) – as well as numerous journal articles, essays and edited collections on the philosophy, history, and practice of human rights.

10 These were: 'Signifying 'Alta(e)rs. The Aesthetic of Legal judgment,' that originally appeared as chapter 10 of *Postmodern Jurisprudence* and was co-written with Ronnie Warrington and Shaun McVeigh; and 'The most perfect beauty in its most perfect state.' Sir Joshua Reynolds and an Aesthetic of the Spirit of the Laws,' that was co-written with Ronnie Warrington as chapter 8 of *Justice Miscarried*.

11 Douzinas, Warrington and McVeigh (n 2) xii.

12 Douzinas and Warrington (n 3) 175.

in the same text, Douzinas and Warrington connect the act of stating, or saying, the law, *juris-diction*, with that of hearing the law.[13] A thought, that much later Douzinas picks up and develops in 'The Metaphysics of Jurisdiction,' where he examines precisely, what he calls, the 'acoustic economy' of jurisdiction.[14]

In what follows, I am not so concerned with identifying the significant but somewhat overlooked thread of law and aesthetics in Douzinas' work and tracing it through his writings. Instead, I want to bring into relief and build on these 'minor' writings on sound and hearing in order to connect them to his work on legal aesthetics to take it beyond vision and the image. For this purpose, I use one of Douzinas' own texts, the chapter he contributed to Oren Ben Dor's edited collection of essays on *Law and Art*,[15] where he develops a legal phenomenology of images. 'Hacking' the piece's textual/material arrangement,[16] I set out to 're-write' it, from inside out, into a new piece on sound, hearing, and the distribution of the heard and the audible. It should be clear that the idea here is not to ventriloquise Douzinas on law and sound. Rather, by shifting from image to sound in his legal phenomenology, this contribution experiments with iteration, as a partial re-writing of his text that writes *with* his text, following it like a thread, an Ariadne's thread if you want, or indeed using it as a weft, in order to weave a new text, that seeks to explore an aspect of the sensible, namely the heard and the audible, that Douzinas has written little about and has not dealt with in his work on legal aesthetics.[17]

The Phenomenology of Sound

The law has taken a strong interest in the organisation and regulation of sound, and of what is heard in the public domain more generally, *since* the Third *Commandment*, the trial of Socrates for impiety and for corrupting the youth, and *Plato's attack* on new trends in music as a threat to orderly

13 ibid 174–175.

14 Douzinas, 'The Metaphysics of Jurisdiction' in Shaun McVeigh (ed), *The Jurisprudence of Jurisdiction* (Routledge Cavendish 2006) 29. A brief mention of the hearing can also be found in the 'Foreword' Douzinas wrote to Michael Stolleis' book, *The Eye of the Law*. Stolleis (n 7).

15 Douzinas 'A Legal Phenomenology of Images' in Ben-Dor (ed.) (n 6) 247–258.

16 Douzinas' piece is divided into four sections: 'the phenomenology of the image,' 'the scopic field,' 'regimes of visibility,' and 'legal aesthetics.' I have maintained this arrangement, but due to space constraints, I have brought together Sections 2 and 3 into a single section on the acoustic field and its regimes.

17 To indicate this operation in the text of this chapter, Douzinas' text from 'A Legal Phenomenology of Images' is in blue italics.

society and the good functioning of the *polis*.[18] Indeed, history, poet Anne Carson reminds us, 'is full of unacceptable noises: high pitch, gossip, talkativeness, hysteria, wailing and ritual sounds.'[19] For its part, the law has sought to control and police sound, to censor and ban 'dangerous' and 'offensive' music, and to silence 'illicit' or 'deviant' speech in secular and church courts alike, through such torts as defamation and slander, and such crimes as treason, blasphemy, heresy, and scolding. Moreover, by gendering, racialising, or infantilising the voices of those that are deemed socially inferior or are outright excluded, the law has habitually sought to preserve the King's, (or indeed, as the case might be, the Father's, the Settler's, and the Corporation's) 'peace' by turning voice into noise and rendering the unheard inaudible.[20] So, while music regulation and censoring have a long and rich history across political regimes, religious contexts, geographical locations, and temporal spaces, equally sound more generally, whether this concerns particular sounds (e.g. drumming), noise, voice, speech, or silence, also has a rich and long history of regulation and control. Yet, *why* this is the case? *What makes* sound *threatening?*

After all, 'sound is a fact of life'[21] – even if it does not quite 'fit the familiar world of physical things.'[22] Being intangible, immaterial, and weightless, it is instead a physical phenomenon, where a vibration is conveyed through the

18 Plato, *Laws* 700a–701b, Loeb Classical Library 187 (Robert Gregg Bury tr, Harvard University Press 1926).

19 In the publisher's synopsis of Anne Carson, *The Gender of Sound* (Silver Press 2025).

20 Several examples spring to mind here: first, the widespread popular disturbances in fourteenth-century England, known as the 'Great Rumour,' that preceded the Peasant Rebellion of 1381, and involved villagers in England asserting their freedom by refusing to work for their lords and requesting exemplifications based on the Domesday Book; second, scolding, as a specifically female crime from the thirteenth century onwards, that penalised women for being outspoken in public, i.e. having a 'vicious tongue,' being quarrelsome with neighbours or authorities, and speaking publicly (as it was considered immodest for women to do so); third, the colonial authorities' ban on drumming first in Jamaica, in the 1696 'Act for the better Order and Government of Slaves,' then in South Carolina, in the 1740 Slave Code (an 'Act for the Better Ordering and Governing of Negroes and Other Slaves in this Province') that was passed following the Stono rebellion of 1739, as well as in nineteenth-century colonial legislation in Barbados, and Trinidad and Tobago; fourth, the recent rejection in a referendum in 2023 in Australia of the proposal to amend the constitution to establish a First Nations (Aboriginal and Torres Strait Islander Nations) Voice to Parliament; and finally, a new set of rules that were introduced in the UK by the Police, Crime, Sentencing and Courts Act 2022 amending s.12.1 of the Public Order Act 1986, giving new powers to the police to impose conditions on protests if they reasonably believe that the noise generated by the protest 'may result in serious disruption to the activities of an organisation which are carried on in the vicinity' of the protest (s.12.1 (aa) Public Order Act 1986)– an organisation such as, say, for instance, the British Parliament.

21 James Parker, 'The Soundscape of Justice' (2011) 20 *Griffith Law Review* 963.

22 Jonathan Rèe, *I See a Voice. A Philosophical History of Language Deafness and the Senses* (Harper Collins 1999) 19.

air as a wave. In fact, as early as in Aristotle's *De anima*, sound is understood as '...a kind of motion of the air,'[23] that is produced by 'something striking against something else,'[24] (by a 'vehement percussion or separation,'[25] comments later Algazel). In Boethius' *De Institutione Musica*, sound is thought to move in a wave-like fashion. 'When air that is struck creates sound,' Boethius writes, 'it affects other air nearby and in this way sets in motion a circular wave of air.'[26] This movement takes place in polycentric circles, very much like when a pebble thrown from above falls into quiet water: 'first it causes a wave in a very small circle; then it disperses clusters of waves into larger circles, and so on until the motion, exhausted by the spreading out of waves, dies away.'[27] Building on this Aristotelian account – in which sound was conceived as the effect of the vibratory movement of bodies 'break[ing]'[28] or 'disturbing the surrounding air,'[29] that was generated by some form of collision, striking, hitting, breaking, or shaking – the medieval acoustic imagination considered sound as a phenomenon, whose key ingredients being air and violence, was a kind of '*passio*, or suffering, of the air'[30] (as one of the commentators of (pseudo-)Aristotle's *Problemata* put it). Finally, for the early moderns, sound was thought of as 'air in motion itself,'[31] more specifically 'repercussed air' that is sensed by the soul;[32] in other words, a 'verberation,'[33] or in Descartes' formulation, a 'certain vibration of the air

23 Aristotle, *De Anima* II. 8, 420b11-12 (Robert Drew Hicks tr, Cambridge University Press 1907).

24 ibid II. 8, 419b4ff.

25 Algazel, *Physica*, *Tractatus Quartus. De anima vegetabili et animali et humana* 3.3 in Eva St. Clair, 'Algazel on the Soul: A Critical Edition' (2005) 60 *Traditio* 47, 64.

26 Boethius, *Fundamentals of Music*. [*De Institutione Musica*] Book 1, S.14 (Calvin Bower tr, Claude V. Palisca ed, Yale University Press 1989) 21.

27 ibid.

28 Simon de Faversham (c.1260–1306), Quaestiones CXIV in Aristotelis libros de anima [Vatican City, Biblioteca Apostolica Vaticana, MS Vat. Lat. 10 135 fols. 87r-118r, second half fourteenth century] cited in Alison Cornish '*Sonus qui non est vox*. Sound and Voice in the Body Politic' (2019) 2(1) *Biblioteca Dantesca: Journal of Dante Studies* 1, 4.

29 Daniel Heider, 'Suárez on Sound and Hearing', (2017) 50(2) *Anuario Filosófico* 323, 326.

30 Pietro d' Albano, *Expositio Problematum* 11.1, cited in Charles Burnett, 'Sound and its Perception in the Middle Ages' in Charles Burnett, Michael Fend and Penelope Gouk (eds), *Second Sense: Studies in Hearing and Musical judgment from Antiquity to the Seventeenth Century* (Warburg Institute 1991) 60.

31 Martin Schoock, 'De Natura Soni et Echus' in Veit Erlmann (ed), *Reason and Resonance: A History of Modern Aurality* (Zone Books 2014) 33.

32 ibid.

33 According to the Oxford English Dictionary, the word *verberation* appears at precisely this point in time in English (the first recorded use is in 1609) and is now rare. According to Michel Chion, the term ought to be 'revived' to refer to the specific vibration that sound is. Michel Chion, *Sound: An Acoulogical Treatise* (James A. Steintrager tr, Duke University Press 2016) 16 ff.

striking our ears.'[34] Ubiquitous, fleeting, incorporeal, and invisible, sound is a physical phenomenon that has an inexplicable ability to touch our psyche. It can delight us, surprise us, and overwhelm us, intrigue us, seduce us, soothe us, as well as haunt us.

Let us now *summarise the central functions of* sound. *In the most general sense,* sound is the *object of* hearing, and to hear is to *perceive* the sounds *the world* produces. In this way, sound makes what is going on around us perceptible. It is a 'potent and necessary means for accessing and understanding the world'[35] and for orientating ourselves in it. Hence, its first function is indexical. The world is soundful, audible, 'for hearing,'[36] Jacques Attali writes. By tracing a sound to its source, whether the latter is immediately present or absent, visible or invisible, proximate or distant, tells us something about ourselves, our bodies, our fellow creatures, and the world around us. The sound of footsteps, for instance, suggests someone is approaching or moving away, voices indicate presence, a heartbeat life, and the sound of breathing good health or ill. Equally, birdsong can reveal the time of day, as well as my location; tapping on the window, that it is raining; drilling next door, that my neighbour is having work done to their house; an engine revving high, that a car is accelerating; and a siren that somewhere there is some sort of emergency. We are both surrounded by and immersed in sound. In fact, it is one of our earliest sensations. We perceive sound in the womb from the fourth month of our foetal life.[37] In our homes, radios, televisions, domestic appliances, and ringtones are part of the soundscapes of our everyday lives. Sirens, horns, engines, and noises of all kinds form part of the urban soundscape. Sound is everywhere. And today, more than ever before, with what James Parker calls the 'planetization of machine listening,'[38] no places and no sounds are off-limits throughout the biosphere: seas, forests, rivers, mountains, ice-caps, and coral reefs[39] have become audible, perceptible – not only by scientists but by anyone with access to the internet.[40]

34 René Descartes, *The World and Other Writings* (Stephen Gaukroger tr and ed, Cambridge University Press 2004) 5.

35 Douglas Khan in Jonathan Sterne, 'Sonic Imaginations' in Jonathan Sterne (ed), *The Sound Studies Reader* (Routledge 2012) 7.

36 Jacques Attali, *Noise. The Political Economy of Music* (Brian Massumi tr, University of Minnesota Press 1985) 3.

37 On this point, see further Chion (n 33) 12 ff, discussing Dolto and hearing in the womb at four months.

38 James Parker, 'The Planetization pf Machine Listening' (2025) 52 *Critical Inquiry* 21–47.

39 ABCiview, 20 November 2020, 'Scientists use sound to monitor Great Barrier Reef's health' <https://www.youtube.com/watch?v=B5WS2dleh88>.

40 Interestingly, not only scientists but everyone is invited to take part in Google's 'bioacoustic mission' and become part of Google's listening collective monitoring the sounds of coral reefs. For more information on Google's platform 'Calling in our corals,' see <https://blog.google/outreach-initiatives/arts-culture/how-to-protect-coral-reefs/>.

Secondly, sound provides a form of connection: it is 'a means of us 'touching' at a distance,'[41] it has a 'haptic' quality, one could say. There is a relationality and sociality in sound. When I purposefully make a sound that I direct to others, I reach out to them to communicate information, thought, and emotion, even when we are beyond the reach of each other, even before language or music,[42] even if this is between human and nonhuman.[43] A dog barking, a baby crying, members of an orchestra tuning their instruments before playing music together, are all examples of such sonic reaching out and connecting. In this sense, the function of sound is relational, significational, and although sound is an integral part of language, it is not limited to it. Michel Leiris, for instance, in his genealogy of language in *Á cor et á cri*, lists a variety of cries, of pain, joy, pleasure, fear, thrill, which, even if inarticulate, he locates 'on this side of speech.'[44] In doing so, what Leiris emphasises in his close and detailed study of the cry is how sonority and sound are essential parts of signification, how sound as such, in other words, is meaningful.[45] Moreover, in language, sound and meaning are connected but this connection is an arbitrary one. As *structural linguistics argues, the signifier*, or sound image, has an *arbitrary link with the signified, through which we* can understand *the sign/concept*. This in turn then means that to know a language means precisely to know its sounds, the way its sonorities are organised into a system of oppositions and differences and linked to meaning; its phonology and phonetics; be able to differentiate between its verbal and non-verbal sounds; and to pick up differences in pitch, rhythm, and expressive variation. As Chaucer's Eagle puts it in *House of Fame*, 'speche is soun/ Or elles no man mighte hit here,'[46] while a few centuries later, the eminent French linguist and historian of the French language, Ferdinand Brunot, inaugurating the *Archives de la Parole* [*Archives of the Spoken Word*] in 1911 at the Sorbonne, adds that the spoken word, 'in its essence

41 David Hendy, *Noise. A Human History of Sound and Listening* (Profile Books 2013) 14. *Cf* here Schafer, who says the same about hearing. R. Murray Schafer, *The Soundscape: Our Sonic Environment and the Tuning of the World* (Destiny Books 1993) 11.

42 Consider here the case of baby talk (see Hendy, *Noise* 14). And of the 'musilanguage' of 'singing Neanderthals' (see further, Steven Mithen, *The Singing Neanderthals* (Weidenfeld and Nicholson 2006)).

43 Here, the classic example is that of a dog barking. For the scholastic discussion, see briefly Susan Boynton, Sarah Kay, Alison Cornish and Andrew Albin, 'Sound Matters' (2016) 91 *Speculum* 998, 1006.

44 '…en deça de la parole'. Michel Leiris, *Á cor et á cri* (Gallimard 1988) 34.

45 On this point, also Don Ihde, *Listening and Voice. Phenomenologies of Sound* (2nd edn, SUNY Press 2007) 4.

46 Geoffrey Chaucer, *The Hous of Fame* 762–763 <https://www.gutenberg.org/cache/epub/45027/pg45027-images.html#hfIII>

and nature, is an assemblage of sound and noise.'[47] It is not by accident that we can only emit vocally what we hear,[48] yet we often forget how soundful the word is;[49] or to put it differently, how the very materiality of the word consists in sound. It is as if, once we acquire language, sound becomes 'language's remainder,' Michel Chion observes – a remainder 'shared by music and the so-called shapeless zone that we call noise.'[50] Simply consider here the hubbub of indistinct chatter. Or remember the experience of hearing a language you do not know. 'The foreign tongue is first a kind of music before it becomes language,'[51] Don Ihde notes; a kind of melodic, 'organised noise'[52] we could say, using Jacques Attali's well-known definition of music.

Finally, in the more restricted sense of the work of art, sound *is given to us in the form of* music; the art, according to Jean Jacques Rousseau, 'of combining sounds in a manner pleasing to the ear,'[53] 'pleasing' precisely

47 Ferdinand Brunot, 'Discours d'inauguration des Archives de la Parole', Sorbonne, 3 June 1911. Recording <https://gallica.bnf.fr/ark:/12148/bpt6k1279113> Disque 1, at 00:00:40–43.

48 Chion (n 33) 15

49 Ihde (n 45) 4.

50 Chion (n 33) 15

51 Ihde (n 45) 157. Jean Jacques Rousseau puts this point even more emphatically when he notes in his 'Dictionary of Music' that 'if speech did not begin by Song, it is at least sure that there is singing everywhere there is speaking.' *Essay on the Origin of Languages and Writings related to Music* (John T. Scott tr and ed, Dartmouth College Press 1998) 438. On this point, similarly also Friedrich Nietzsche, for whom, as Kathleen Higgins notes, 'the human capacity to experience music… is something like a transcendental precondition for the possibility of language.' Kathleen Higgins, 'Nietzsche on Music' (1986) 47 *Journal of the History of Ideas* 662. Interestingly, in linguistic analysis this aspect of speech is referred to as *prosodic* and is distinguished from the *syntactic* aspect. Its features, pitch, volume, stress, emphasis, convey emotional significance and variation rather than grammatical structure and signification.

52 Attali (n 36) 4, where he defines music as 'the organisation of noise' that 'reflects the manufacture of society; [and] constitutes the audible waveband and vibrations and signs that make up society.' *ibid.*

53 Rousseau, 'Dictionary of Music', 437. Strikingly, Rousseau's *über*-mechanistic definition of music, more apt perhaps to muzak than music, could not be further away from a long tradition that understands music as divine and emphasises its formidable and miraculous character, particularly its transformative and (psych)agogic powers – a theme which is famously played out in the myth of Orpheus. We also find it in lesser-known contexts, as in Sophocles' satyr play, *Trackers,* for example, in which we witness the birth of music, in the form of a tune coming out of a cave, in which baby Hermes uses something dead (the shell of a dead tortoise) to turn it into something that 'sings' (a lyre). In philosophy, the nature of music, and its role in cosmic order as well as civic and contemplative life, have been significant themes at least since Pythagoras and Plato, while throughout the life of the Church, the use of music in the liturgy has been an important subject of heated discussion and controversy. I have in mind here particularly the Patristic theology of music with its emphasis on psalmody and voice and the suppression of instrumental music in worship in the early Church; Boethius' deeply influential *De institutione musica* in the early middles ages, with its understanding of music as central in a theologically grounded cosmic order; the fierce

because they are arranged into forms according to a certain way, or system, of ordering.[54] Made of sound, a tune, a song, or a symphony *becomes available to us* when it is performed, when it is sounded. When it does, it comes and passes, it appears and fades, it comes and expands. Music is after all 'sonorous air,'[55] mobile, immaterial, 'transparent,' and 'incorporeal,' as Italian pianist and composer Ferrucio Busoni has famously described it. *It is through its* sonic *presentation* that the musical work *offers itself to the world.* What characterises it, particularly in its instrumental form, is that it does not refer to things, or to the world. Rather, being non-linguistic and non-representational, music is powerfully expressive of emotions, moods, and feelings. Indeed, according to one definition, music is 'the art of expressing sentiments and passions through the medium of sound;'[56] or, in Arthur Schopenhauer's words, music is 'the language of feeling and of passion.'[57] Meaning in music, then, writes Don Ihde, 'does not lurk elsewhere, but it is *in* the sounding of the music.'[58] As such, especially when compared to language, music 'is "opaque"... a dense embodied presence,'[59] in which, moreover, our bodily sense is engaged in a listening that 'participates' in the movement of the music.[60] We 'feel' the music in our body, and listen to it, not just with our ears, but with our whole body:[61] straining towards it, for instance, attending to it, or 'keeping time,' moving our head rhythmically, and tapping our feet,

controversies in the Western Church around polyphony in the Middle Ages, and instrumental music during the Renaissance, as well as the role of humanism on the Reformation theology of music; and the 'codification' of the liturgy in the Council of Trent, especially the part that regulated the relation between the music and the text. On the Reformation theology of music and the role that humanism played in it, see especially (Hyun-Ah Kim, *Humanism and the Reform of Sacred Music in Early Modern England John Merbecke the Orator and* The Booke of Common Praier Noted (1550) (Routledge 2018).

54 This is a classical point that can be traced to Plato's *Laws* and Boethius' opening pages of *The Fundamentals of Music.* The sense of hearing, Boethius writes, 'very often actually finds pleasure if the modes are pleasing and ordered, whereas it is vexed if they are disordered and incoherent.' Boethius (n 26) 2.

55 Ferrucio Busoni, 'Sketch of a New Aesthetic of Music' in *Three Classics in the Aesthetics of Music* (Dover Publications 1962) 77

56 Fermo Bellini, *Manuale della musica: Ovvero introduzione alla scienza ragionata di questa arte* (Milano 1850) 9.

57 Arthur Schopenauer, *The World as Will and Idea* Vol 1 (3rd edn, RB Haldane and J Kemp tr, Kegan Paul 1891) 336.

58 Ihde (n 45) 155.

59 ibid.

60 I draw this point from Ihde (n 45) 155–156.

61 Oliver Sachs in *Musicophilia* attributes this point to Nietzsche, quoting him as saying that 'we listen to music with our muscles' but without providing a reference (Oliver Sachs, *Musicophilia, Tales of Music and the Brain* (Picador 2014) xi) . The only point I found close to this in Nietzsche is in *Twilight of the Idols*, par. 10, where he says that '*rhythm... speaks* to our muscles' – which is not quite the same, especially if viewed in the context of Nietzsche's own argument.

hands, or fingers, sometimes voluntarily and sometimes not. At the same time, music being one form of, what Jean-Luc Nancy calls, the 'sonorous present, [it] is the result of space-time: it spreads through space, or rather it opens a space that is its own, the very spreading out of its resonance, its expansion and its reverberation.'[62] In so doing, music fills space, its auditory space (what is after all an *auditorium* if not precisely an auditory space, a space for/of listening?), in a way that is 'omnidimensional and transversate' says Nancy,[63] its sounding expanding through obstacles, encompassing, engulfing, and penetrating listening.[64] This is why, although the sonorous for Nancy more generally is 'tendentially methexic (that is, having to do with participation, sharing or contagion),'[65] music in particular, has the power of bringing and binding people together. Sharing a tune often also involves sharing the emotion that this evokes, while singing together, or making music together, is a plural act. It involves a performative articulation of plurality and is not simply many people singing. As such, music, Nancy notes,

> harbors a force of communication and participation that all forms of secular, religious, or aesthetic power that have succeeded each other through our history have not failed to recognise since at least the time when the term *mousikē* designated the ensemble of forms and exercises of expression of a wider sense than the single sense signified by words.[66]

Perceived sounds – i.e. sounds that I hear – and sound imagery – i.e. sounds that I recall in memory (that I remember hearing) and sounds that I 'presentify'[67] in fantasy (that I imagine hearing) – *form a continuum: they bring to*

62 Jean-Luc Nancy, *Listening* (Charlotte Mandell tr, Fordham University Press 2007) 11.
63 ibid.
64 I owe this point to Ihde (n 45) 156.
65 Nancy (n 62) 10
66 ibid 52. On the institutional function of music, the classic study of some of the early sources on regal acclamation as part of the Medieval liturgy (and its significance) is Ernst Kantorowicz, *Laudes Regiae. A Study in Liturgical Acclamations and Medieval Ruler Worship* (University of California Press 1946). On the significance of glory in the liturgies of power more generally, see Giorgio Agamben, *The Kingdom and the Glory. For a Theological Genealogy of Economy and Government*, (Lorenzo Chiesa with Matteo Mandarini trs, Stanford University Press 2011 [2007]), especially his analysis of liturgical acclamations and angelical hymns in relation to the structures and operations of power. Peter Goodrich picks up this thread in Agamben and explores the choral and acclamatory qualities of the common law in 'Spectres of Law: Why the History of the Legal Spectacle Has Not Been Written' (2011) 1 *UC Irvine Law Review* 773, 793 ff. On the liturgical roots of anthems, see Emanuele Conte, 'Il popolo é una multitudine che canta. Osservazioni storiche sulla funzione istituzionale della musica' in Giorgio Resta (ed), *L' armonia nel diritto. Contributi a una riflessione su diritto e musica* (Roma Tre Press 2020).
67 This is Ihde's term for 'rendering present' in fantasy, on whom I mainly rely for this analysis (Ihde (n 45) 131).

consciousness what is not present. Sounds *give* acoustic *form to the invisible and make present what is absent.* Hearing the wind howling during a storm while in my office on the sixth floor of the Little Titchfield Street building, remembering the wind roaring from a barren hilltop on a Greek island, and listening to one of Mozart's wind concertos or to the humming sounds that the wind makes as it goes through the aeolian harp strings of Luke Jerram's acoustic wind pavilion, *Aeolus*,[68] in Canary Wharf, in London, *are experientially different activities.* And yet, despite that, perceptual and imaginative modes of sonic experience can happen at the same time. For instance, I can be surrounded by background music or 'white noise' (say, the sound of the wind blowing through trees on an app on my phone), and find that I can continue to read, think, or indeed 'hear' myself thinking. The co-presence of these modalities of sonic experience depends on a certain balance between them. If there is an increase in the intensity and volume of the 'external' sound, or a change in its constancy, its presence penetrates my awareness, becomes distracting and I find that I can no longer read, or think, and that my train of thought has been interrupted. The 'external' sound has now become intrusive, invasive. What's more, I am defenseless against it, since the ear 'cannot be shut,'[69] for 'we have no ear-lids to close sound off,'[70] as Michel Chion has famously said. At the same time, this invading, intrusive character of sound is not only felt in auditory perception but also in sound imagery and memory.[71] We have all had, for example, a 'catchy' tune, or 'earworm' as it is often called, for a day or two 'stuck' in our heads, meaninglessly playing again and again until it eventually fades away.[72]

68 https://www.lukejerram.com/aeolus/ and https://www.youtube.com/watch?v=AynhY5A-iVQ

69 Jacques Lacan, *The Sinthome - The Seminar of Jacques Lacan, Book XXIII*, ed. , transl. (Jacques Alain Miller, ed, A.R. Price tr, Polity Press 2016) (Sem.1/ 18.11.1975) pp??

70 Michel Chion, *Audio-Vision: Sound on Screen* (Claudia Gorbman trans, Columbia University Press 1994) 33.

71 Both Franz Kafka and Edgar Allan Poe engaged with this intrusive, disruptive and overwhelming character of sound. I am thinking here of Kafka's early text, 'The Great Noise' in relation to auditory perception and Poe's short story 'The Tell-Tale Heart' in relation to sound imagery. On Kafka and sound more generally, see Kata Gellen, *Kafka and Noise: The Discovery of Cinematic Sound in Literary Modernism* (Northwestern University Press 2019).

72 More rare and much more disquieting than 'earworms' is the case of musical hallucinations – which apparently are the most common form of non-psychotic hallucination. These come on suddenly and full-blown, without obvious cause, in most cases replaying music heard in childhood. They are highly repetitive, loud, cannot be stopped by effort or will and, as Oliver Sacks observes, 'interfere with perception or conversation in a manner that never occurs with normal musical imagery.' Oliver Sacks, 'Commentary: The Power of Music' (2006) 129 *Brain* 2528, 2531. On musical hallucinations, see also Sacks (n 61) 49.

The most familiar type of auditory imaginative activity, however, is inner speech, the voice in the mind or internal voice, the hidden or internal monologue, that often accompanies everyday human activities, commenting, counselling, reminding, criticising, or chastising. At its most basic, inner speech describes the experience of hearing myself think; the voice that I hear in my mind when I think or read; a voice that is most singularly and uniquely mine *and* simultaneously the voice of the Other, of language and the Law, Socrates' *daemon*, the voice that the philosopher has to silence in order to philosophise.[73] What distinguishes it from other forms of auditory imagination is first, that, this is '*thinking as and in a language*;'[74] second, that, despite evading objectification,[75] it is mine – it is 'the ongoing presence of a dimension of my own thinking,'[76] says Ihde – and hence, it is very different from the well-known disembodied 'voices' heard in psychosis that may be in my head but I do not consider 'mine;' and finally, that it is an 'almost continuous aspect of self-presence:'[77] indeed, by being a background or an accompaniment to the rest of my experience, it forms precisely *my* thinking self-presence, the intimate interiority which, by co-implicating the Other of language, '"lets be" [for me] a World as a significant phenomenon.'[78]

A phenomenology of sound thus *examines how* sound *discloses things, bringing them into presence. The primary meaning of the expression 'this is the* sound *of something' is not that the* sound *comes after the thing in a sequence where the thing leads to* sound. *On the contrary, it is the* sound *that* anticipates the thing, that announces and brings forth the thing for us: for example, the bell is brought forth by its ringing, the bird by its song, the clock by its ticking. It is the sound that reveals the unseen and the invisible: the siren, the wind, the heart, the distant star. It is through sound that we can identify the thing: X calling Y, an ambulance rather than a fire truck passing by, an argument rather than a conversation taking place next door, an analogue radio tuning rather than a digital one. Sound indicates, identifies and *poses*, i.e. renders perceptible and present, *the thing for a subject.* Being soundful, the world 'is given' into what is present, is 'presentified,' and listening, in Ihde's words, '"lets be," lets come into presence the unbidden giving of sound.'[79] At the same time, this presence, as Jean-Luc Nancy explains,

73 On this point see Nancy, (n 62) 1–2. Also, Ihde (n 45) 140.
74 Ihde (n 45) 118.
75 ibid 139.
76 ibid 121.On the 'mineness' of inner speech, also 139.
77 ibid 134.
78 ibid 144.
79 ibid 109.

> is not the position of being present... It is presence in the sense of an 'in the presence of'... a *present* that is not a being (at least not in the intransitive, stable, consistent sense of the word), but rather a *coming* and a *passing*, an *extending* and a *penetrating*. Sound essentially comes and expands or is deferred and transferred... It is a present in waves on a swell, not in a point on a line; it is a time that opens up, that is hollowed out, that is enlarged or ramified, that envelopes or separates, that becomes or is turned into a loop, that stretches out or contracts, and so on.[80]

As such, Nancy continues,

> [t]he sonorous present is the result of space-time: it spreads through space, or rather it opens a space that is its own, the very spreading out of its resonance, its expansion and its reverberation. This space is immediately omni-dimensional and transversate through all spaces: the expansion of sound through obstacles, it's property of penetration and ubiquity, has always been noted.[81]

Thee Acoustic Field and Its Acoustic Regimes[82]

Religion, ethics, and law have a long history of policing sounds, and of what is heard in the public domain more generally. Religious, ethical, and legal norms code, define, and delimit the heard and the audible: what is heard, what is being made heard, what can be heard, and what cannot be heard, or indeed should remain unheard. *The normative control of the* acoustic domain *takes the form of an economy of permitted* and protected sounds, on the one hand, *and a criminology of... dangerous, threatening, and fallen*

80 Nancy (n 62) 13.
81 ibid.
82 The concept of 'acoustic regime' I am putting forward here is based on Douzinas' concept of 'regime of visuality,' which he develops in two essays, 'The Legality of the Image' (Douzinas (n 7)) and 'Prosopon and Antiprosopon' (Douzinas (n 5)). It is in the latter that Douzinas first speaks of the 'order of vision' (p. 51), of 'iconic regimes' (p. 48), 'imagistic regimes,' and 'regimes of imagistic representation' (p. 59; also 64). Niall Atkinson also uses the concept of 'acoustic regime' in 'Sonic Armatures: Constructing an Acoustic Regime in Renaissance Florence' (2012) 7 *Senses and Society* 39, and in *The Noisy Renaissance. Sound, Architecture and Florentine Urban Life* (Penn State University Press 2016). He uses the concept differently than the way that I do here. For Atkinson, 'acoustic regime' refers to the sonic signalling of civic and religious activity and action in the context of pre-modern Florence where, as he argues, civic and church bell ringing marked and orchestrated the daily rhythms of civic and religious life. As such, for Atkinson, 'acoustic regime' has a more narrow and administrative/disciplinary sense than the broad, normative sense which I develop and use here.

sounds, noises, voices, music, and speech, on the other. To put it differently: even if sound dwells in the air, the unseen, and the invisible, its field, i.e. *the* acoustic *field, has always been divided.* This division involves what Brandon LaBelle, drawing from Jacques Rancière,[83] calls a certain 'distribution of the heard:'[84] a set of norms that define and delimit the heard and the audible by stipulating what can (and ought to) be heard, when, where, by whom, and at what volume and pitch, and what should be unheard. In this sense, a *nomos*, or distribution, of the heard consists of the regimes of audibility that precisely form and norm the acoustics and sonic experience of social and civic space and the economies of attention that determine our capacities for listening. Indeed, *[e]ach epoch develops its own peculiar and historically changing* 'acoustic *regime*' that precisely shapes and regulates the soundscape and acoustic domains of our daily lives, sociality, morality, and politics. *Such regimes form a combination of* permitted and prohibited sounds *and amount to a complex administration of an era's available ways of* hearing. *These epochal regimes exist in all cultures even though their naturalisation inhibits their identification. Such regimes become de-naturalised and can be examined when* what is heard *becomes the target of political and ideological confrontation.* For, in regulating the acoustic domain, acoustic regimes are not always bound to the audible or to sound only but also, and importantly, concern the orientation of attention, care, and attunement, and as such are bound both to the audible and the inaudible, the said and the unsaid, the silence and the silenced. In this respect, it is important to recall LaBelle's point that how one is heard, '[h]ow one's voice, for example, is registered, given value, or positioned within the distribution of the heard comes to reflect the complex and highly charged acoustic dimensions always already at play.'[85] As these dimensions involve inequalities and imbalances of power, they in turn link to questions of community, belonging, and solidarity, of shared understandings of responsiveness and responsibility to others, and to struggles over equality, freedom, recognition, and justice.

Consider, for instance, Solon's extensive and profound legal reforms in the sixth century BC, that reshaped the public and private life of pre-classical Athens. As part of these reforms, Solon enacted laws forbidding speaking ill of the dead, as well as speaking ill of the living in certain public spaces, such as temples, public offices, courts of law, and festivals,[86] in which the

83 Rancière (n 6).
84 Brandon LaBelle, *Acoustic Justice. Listening, Performativity, and the Work of Reorientation* (Bloomsbury 2021) 14.
85 ibid 23.
86 Plutarch, *Plutarch's Lives. Solon* 21.1 (Bernadette Perrin tr and ed, Harvard University Press 1914) https://www.perseus.tufts.edu/hopper/text?doc=Perseus%3Atext%3A2008.01.0063%3Achapter%3D21%3Asection%3D

context made it impossible for someone to respond to and account for what was being said about them. Read in the register of the acoustic, these laws are important *not* because they seek to control the circulation of potentially defamatory speech and thus foster civility and harmonious co-existence (by limiting the 'nasty' things said, that could 'poison' the ears of the Athenians). Rather, their significance lies in their re-coding of the acoustics of the civic domain of the *polis*, and the relations within it. By reconfiguring what should and should not be heard around a basic principle of fairness and justice, namely the injunction to hear the other side, the law sought to reshape basic norms of sociality, which in turn 'inform[ed] a greater collective imaginary for how speaking out and hearing each other are fundamental to forging a just society.'[87] At the same time, it should be clear, however, that this egalitarian imaginary, being limited to male citizens, was deeply gendered. Women were positioned completely differently within the aural architecture of the *polis*. In fact, Solon's reforms also comprised sumptuary laws that regulated in detail women's behaviour in civic space, including their participation in festivals, processions, and funeral rites. According to Plutarch, these laws 'did away with disorder and licence'[88] in these public contexts, and especially, with what Anne Carson calls, 'the uncontrolled outflows of female sounds'[89] – wailing, sobbing, shrill laments, shrieking, screaming, and the *ololyga*, 'a high-pitched piercing cry uttered at certain climactic moments in ritual practice... or at climactic moments in real life... and also a common feature of women's festivals.'[90] By restricting to a minimum female noise, and sonic expression and outpouring, these laws (along with those of Charondas regulating funeral lament in Catania a few decades later) in effect proscribed and silenced these specifically female sounds in civic spaces as excessive, offensive, unacceptable and ultimately intolerable. By reducing the volume and the pitch of the particularity and positionality of female sounding, these laws ensured that what was determined as specifically female sounding remained underheard in the *kosmos* of the pre-classical and classical *polis*. For the law narrowed down both the boundaries of female audibility and the 'reverberant geometries'[91] framing female subjectivity.

The normative control of the acoustic domain in antiquity did not concern only what should be heard and how, and whose voice was noise and whose *phōnē semantikē*; in other words, it did not only concern acoustic norms that organised sociality and norms that either authorised or denied

87 LaBelle (n 84) 22.
88 Plutarch (n 86) 21.4.
89 Carson (n 19) 14.
90 ibid 12.
91 I owe this term to LaBelle (n 84) 38.

recognition and participation. It also concerned norms that delimited the acoustic horizon of community, inclusion, exclusion, and the base of commonality. Boethius, in *De institutione musica*, reports the story of Timotheus of Miletus,[92] the most infamous and controversial musician of ancient Greece, who was forced out of the city of Sparta for adding a string to his *kithara*. According to the expulsion decree, which Boethius reproduces in its entirety,[93] Timotheus' musical innovation seems to have breached all sorts of norms, at once civic, ethical, *and* musical. His case allows a rare glimpse in the interface between the normative and the acoustic. For one, adding an extra string had made his music more capricious, signalling a shift to complexity and virtuosity, but also (and crucially) a rejection of the grandeur and simplicity of the (traditional) ancient style. Second, it had introduced polyphony, which had 'polluted the hearing of the young'[94] and had steered them away from the virtue of moderation, which Timotheus had been entrusted to teach in his music lessons. And, finally, it had changed the structure of the pitches in the octave, which in turn had altered the mode of the music being played (from enharmonic to chromatic). At issue here was not the musical novelty and merit of such a shift. Rather, given the significance of music in ancient Greek civic life,[95] which meant that particular musical genres and musico-poetic types (paians, hymns, *nomoi*, etc) had a civic character, and were sanctioned for particular private and public festivities, sacred feasts, and solemn occasions,[96] playing the 'right' type of music (say, a *nomos*) at a given festivity in the 'wrong' mode (say chromatic) would have been considered not just a shocking and outrageous breach of the city's musical laws but also an affront to the city's laws and ways of life *tout court*. From this perspective, the *polis* emerges as a 'sensitive' sonorous and aural construction, where the tensions between identity and its disruption are played out.[97] Timotheus' challenge to the 'old Muse,' as he put it

92 Timotheus of Miletus was a lyrical poet and musician who lived in the late fifth and early fourth century BC (446–357 BC). He was famously an exponent of 'new music.'

93 Boethius (n 26) 4–5; although the authenticity of this decree has been contested. On this point see, Thomas Mathiesen, *Apollo's Lyre: Greek music and music theory in antiquity and the Middle Ages* (University of Nebraska Press 1999) 68, fn 84.

94 'Πολυφωνίαν εἰσάγων λυμαίνεται τάς ἀκοάς τῶν νέων.' Greek in the original, as cited in Boethius (n 26) 4.

95 On this point see instead of others, Zartaloudis, *The Birth of Nomos* (Edinburgh University Press 2018) 339 ff.

96 According to Aristides Quintilianus, for instance, *nomoi* were so called because they were melodies established by law to be used in certain private and public festivities. Aristides Quintilianus, *De Musica* II.6 (Reginald Pepys Winnington-Ingram ed, Teubner 1963) 59.1–8.

97 I draw this point from Brandon LaBelle, *Acoustic Territories. Sound Culture and Everyday Life* (Bloomsbury 2019) 36.

himself,[98] was therefore for Sparta, not 'simply' a matter of aesthetics but one of public order. The new sonority that his innovation produced breached the bounds of audibility of the *polis*, of what the *polis* could hear. Allowing and including Timotheus' 'new music' in its acoustic horizon would require for the polis to shift the boundaries of the audible making possible the coming of a future community. By expelling Timotheus and silencing the 'new music' instead, the *polis* sought to seal off its commonality from disruption and disturbance. Yet in drawing a hard line between sonorous identity and difference, between established, dominant, and deviating sonority, the *polis* also eliminated the possibility of transformation.

The question of polyphony, and the threat that it posed to an acoustic order regulated through civic ideals of harmony, *concordia* (the agreement of musical chords, and of hearts), and the authority of a dominant tradition, never disappears after this point. In the Middle Ages, it is central in the controversy concerning the Church's singing practices, which in turn involved a contestation of the Church's established distribution (or *nomos*) of the heard (and the audible), the logics that determined sonorities as protected and proscribed sounds, and ultimately the normative control of the acoustic domain. In the ninth century AD, Abbot Honoratus, who was the abbot of an important monastery just outside Rome,[99] became the addressee of a bull issued by Pope Leo IV after the 'most unbelievable report reached [the latter's] ears,'[100] namely that Honoratus found 'distasteful the beauty of Gregorian chant,' was not following the rite of the Church 'in all its details in the sung parts and readings,' and was singing what must not be sung, using chant practices outside the Gregorian canon. The purpose of the decree, the first papal document to focus exclusively on sacred music, was not only to chastise Honoratus for his 'presumptuous audacity' not to sing in the tradition that was given to him, i.e. the Gregorian tradition, and sing otherwise, but also to issue a general command to all abbots, 'under sentence of excommunication that, in the singing and readings in your churches, you carry them out in no other way than that which Pope St. Gregory handed down,' and 'if anyone should try, now or in the future, in any way whatever, to lead you back or turn you aside to any tradition besides the one which We gave you, We not only command that he be excommunicated… [but] that he shall remain in perpetual anathema.' The papal bull thus distinguished between, on the one hand, permitted, established, and 'beautiful' monophonic psalmody, and,

98 Cited in Mathiesen (n c93) 68.

99 Robert Hayburn mentions that this was the monastery of Farfa, which in the ninth century was, according to the *Chronikon Farfense*, one of the two most important monasteries in Italy. Robert Hayburn, *Papal Legislation on Sacred Music. 95 AD to 1977 AD* (Liturgical Press 1979) 8.

100 Cited in Hayburn (n 99) 8–9. All subsequent quotations in the text are drawn from here.

on the other, prohibited, novel, and inappropriate polyphonic singing, set up the standard of what could and could not be heard in the acoustic domain of the Church and of course the dire consequences for transgressing it. In this way, the bull established a regime that proscribed polyphonic singing and endorsed Gregorian chant. This acoustic regime remained in place for at least three centuries and continued to influence the Church's 'distribution of the audible' for many centuries beyond that. For even when much later polyphony had gained acceptance in the singing practices of the Church, it continued to be criticised and often ridiculed.

This controversy concerning sacred music, moreover, was not the only one in the Church, where, crucially, hearing and the acoustic domain more generally hold particular significance. After all, the Church is first and foremost a community of hearers. As Paul says in *Romans* (10:17), *fides ex auditu*, 'faith cometh by hearing.' It is through the ear that the Word reaches the heart and gets hold of the soul, delivering it to wisdom and divine illumination. Normative questions, therefore, about hearing and ways of hearing the divine message were 'a recurring theme of doctrinal debate both within and between denominations and jurisdictions.'[101] The issue was to ensure that music, as Pope John XXII put in his *Extravagantes Communes*, did not 'intoxicate the ear without satisfying it... [and] instead of promoting devotion, prevent it by creating a sensuous and indecent atmosphere.'[102] To achieve this, it was imperative to 'prohibit, cast out and banish from the Church of God'[103] all music that stirred the passions and 'derailed' the soul from the road to salvation. During the Renaissance, a new set of musical practices challenged the Church's acoustic regimes. This time the issue was not polyphony as such[104] but a whole host of new questions: the intelligibility of the text when music was used, the use of instrumental music in worship, the creeping secularism of some musical practices, and the intrusion of the 'profane, lascivious, and impure' in churchly expression. It should be noted that these matters emerged in the context of the Western Latin Church. In the Eastern Orthodox Church, the hold of the Patristic opposition to musical instruments was such that the question of using instruments in the liturgy never arose and any overtone of profanity or lasciviousness in the church

101 James Parker, *Acoustic Jurisprudence: Listening to the Trial of Simon Bikindi* (OUP 2016) 17.

102 Cited in Hayburn (n 99) 21.

103 ibid.

104 Interestingly, polyphony continued to be an issue in some quarters in relation to convents. Monson recounts the fascinating story of the attempts made to reform convent musical practices during the twenty-fifth session of the Council of Trent by banishing polyphony and excluding professional musicians from nuns' churches and how in the end convent polyphony was saved. Monson, 'The Council of Trent Revisited' (2002) 55 *Journal of the American Musicological Society* 1, 19–22.

musical practices was fiercely and uniformly policed.[105] Music was, and had been historically, performed vocally in its entirety. Praise was sung, as continues to be sung to this day, *a capella* – or 'in the manner of the chapel' – without instrumental accompaniment. In the Western Latin Church, on the other hand, instrumental music began to be used in the late medieval period. As both the conceptions of music and liturgy started to change during this time, by the fifteenth and early sixteenth century, a range of musical practices seemed to put at risk the sense of 'utmost reverence' that all those present at the mass should feel, so much so in fact that a number of synodal and conciliar decrees before, during, and after the Council of Trent[106] (that was convened to deal with the Reformation) marked them out 'as particular abuses of the proper churchly attitude.'[107] These practices included church music without liturgical character, the curtailment of liturgical texts, the inclusion in the mass of non-churchly songs in the vernacular, worldly and lengthy organ compositions, and the text becoming unintelligible in the delivery of the psalmody.[108] A clear indication of the concerns, the stakes, and the reasons it was felt necessary to regulate 'everything' in the liturgy, that is to say the mass in all its aspects, can be found in a well-known passage on mass reforms from the proceedings of the Council of Trent:

> Canon 8. Since the sacred mysteries should be celebrated with utmost reverence, with both deepest feelings toward God alone, and with external worship that is truly suitable and becoming, so that others may be filled with devotion and called to religion:... Everything should indeed be regulated so that the Masses, whether they be celebrated with the plain voice or in song, with everything clearly and quickly executed, may reach the ears of the hearers and quietly penetrate their hearts. In those Masses where measured music and organ are customary, nothing profane should be intermingled, but only hymns and divine praises. If something from the divine service is sung with the organ while the service proceeds, let it first

105 James McKinnon, 'The Meaning of the Patristic Polemic Against Musical Instruments' (1965) 1 *Current Musicology* 69. According to McKinnon, in the Patristic tradition the opposition to musical instruments, which was fierce and uniform, was mainly due to their association 'with prostitution, luxurious banquets, and the obscenities of the theatre' and to a lesser extent with pagan rites (69). This overall condemnation of musical instruments was further reinforced by ecclesiastical legislation that refused baptism to players of aulos and kithara unless they renounced their trade (*ibid.*), while in fourth-century Alexandria, a law threatened with excommunication a cantor who learned and persisted in playing the *kithara* (ibid.)

106 On this point, see Karl Gustav Fellerer, 'Church Music and the Council of Trent' (1953) 39 *The Musical Quarterly* 576, 578 and 580.

107 ibid 577.

108 ibid 577.

> be recited in a simple, clear voice, lest the reading of the sacred words be imperceptible. But the entire manner of singing in musical modes should be calculated, not to afford vain delight to the ear, but so that the words may be comprehensible to all: and thus may the hearts of the listeners be caught up into the desire for celestial harmonies and contemplation of the joys of the blessed.[109]

In other words, the purpose of the reforms that the legates to the Council of Trent proposed for discussion in the general congregation in September 1562 was to ensure that the entire content of the liturgy 'reach[es] the ears of the hearers and quietly penetrate[s] their hearts.' How could this be made possible? By making sure that nothing profane or ostentatious in the song and music disrupts the atmosphere of 'utmost reverence' and devotion during the mass; that the singing is measured and does not distract the ear with 'vain delight;' and that the text comes through clearly and is understood by all. By excluding everything that could distract, disrupt, or delight the ear, and therefore also the heart, of the listener away from the piety, solemnity, and devotion that the mass required, the reformed acoustic regime of church music that the legates proposed would restore the 'feeling [indeed the *aesthēsis*] for the sanctity of place' that these new church practices had destroyed. At stake in these proposals was thus not just what the Christian subjects heard: 'good' monophonic psalmodies as opposed to 'bad' polyphonic singing; or 'good' *a cappella* singing as opposed to 'bad' instrumental music; but *how* they heard. At stake, in other words, in the normativity and governance of the acoustic domain of the Church was how the hearts of the listeners would be 'penetrated' and captured ('caught up') into a particular form of desire, in this case that 'for celestial harmonies and contemplation of the joys of the blessed,' that would in turn lead to forms of action that would deliver the listener to salvation. What this passage from the proceedings of the Council of Trent reveals then is the clarity with which the legates understood what was at stake in the governance of the acoustic domain. Namely, that, if it is through song that the law, the Word, reaches our heart, it is through the ear that our heart is led. And it is the ear that is precisely the aperture through which the law gets under our skin, seizes our hearts as well as our minds, takes hold of our words and our actions, commands our obedience.[110] At the same time, even more importantly, in my view, the passage also reveals how deeply they understood that the aesthetic, indeed the sensorial, and the normative combine in the operation of the legal insti-

109 Cited in Monson (n 104) 9. The translation in Hayburn (n 99) 27 is slightly different.
110 On this point, see further Julia Chryssostalis, 'Nomos is an Air. Hearing as a Juridical Faculty' in Danilo Mandic et al (eds), *Hear* (University of Westminster Press 2023).

tution; and that the character of institutional attachment is fundamentally an aesthetic-sensorial one.[111] Which effectively means that the ways through which a normative order embeds itself into its subjects and is lived out in their bodies, in their desires and in their affects, are aesthetic, go through the senses.

By Way of Conclusion: Douzinas' Legal Aesthetics Beyond the Image?

At this point, I would like to offer some brief reflections on what I have been trying to do in this piece and on whether Douzinas' legal aesthetics can be taken beyond the image. What I have provided so far is a first attempt to sketch a legal phenomenology of sound by following the steps that Douzinas makes in his text, 'A Legal Phenomenology of Images,' which he wrote in 2011. As such, my piece is an experiment, very much inspired by the early work of Douzinas and the sort of irreverent, playful, and joyous deconstructive corps-à-corps with the canon that *Postmodern Jurisprudence* inaugurated. In undertaking this experiment, I pursue two questions: first, can Douzinas' piece on the phenomenology of the image be re-written for sound? What new additions and new arrangements would such a text require? Second, can Douzinas' oculocentric legal aesthetics be reworked beyond the eye and vision? What would a legal aesthetics attending to sound and acoustics add to our sense of law and justice?

Writing this piece revealed to me that at the heart of the first set of questions lies a certain isomorphism that underlies our understanding of the senses more generally. In practice, we think that if we substituted one sense for another, sight with hearing for instance, we would be simply shifting the object of our attention from image to sound, from the visible to the audible, from one phenomenality to another. However, this isomorphism is both problematic and misleading. For sure, there are affinities and constants in the ways in which, to paraphrase Jean-Luc Nancy, our senses sense and sense is sensed, or perceived, through the senses. Yet this isomorphism, particularly of seeing and hearing, is premised on a privileging of visual presence as the conceptual referent of knowledge and understanding. What we miss consequently is the dissymmetry and difference between the senses, the specific ways in which the audible is not commensurable with the visual, and the sonorous remains untranslatable to a philosophical grammar and lexicon developed for the visual plane; in other words, for that which presents itself to view. For the sonorous, Nancy observes,

111 Peter Goodrich, 'Introduction: Psychoanalysis and Law' in Peter Goodrich (ed), *Law and the Unconscious: A Legendre Reader* (Macmillan 1997) 17.

> outweighs form. It does not dissolve it, but rather enlarges it; it gives it an amplitude, a density, and a vibration or an undulation whose outline never does anything but approach. The visual persists until its disappearance; the sonorous appears and fades away into its permanence.[112]

With this in mind, the question becomes: can we think and know philosophically without the grammar of 'what presents itself to view – form, idea, painting, representation, aspect, phenomenon, composition – but arises instead in accent, tone, timbre, resonance, and sound[?]'[113] Further, how does this matter in the specific context of law?

This brings me to the second set of questions concerning the role and significance of visuality in Douzinas' aesthetics. That is to say: how much Douzinas' legal aesthetics is tied to the eye, the image, vision, visuality, and visibility? How it attaches to the visual aesthetic object, the text, the icon, the painting, the sculpture? And importantly: what of the organising concepts of his aesthetics remain relevant to a sense of legal aesthetics that is broadly focused on *aesthēsis*, *qua* 'sensible cognition,'[114] and thus seeks on the one hand to understand the legal *sensorium*, and on the other attend to the hierarchies and regimes of the sensible, in other words its distributions and *nomoi*.[115] The key point for me here is that Douzinas in his legal aesthetics (very much like Jacques Attali in relation to the political economy of music), does not theorise about the image; he theorises *through* the image. What he theorises about is the distribution of the sensible, the aesthetic regimes through which a given order embeds itself into its subjects and the way in which the subject's institutional attachment is part of an aesthetic economy of normativity. Which is how, despite the 'oculocentrism' of his aesthetics he can also exhort us 'to open our ears, prick up our ears, develop an active hearing, when listening to the law... [indeed] confront the community of the sovereign of the One and All with the plurality of many ears.'[116]

112 Nancy (n 62) 2.

113 ibid 3.

114 Alexander Baumgarten, *Aesthetica* (Georg Karl Aschenbrenner and William B. Holther, Olms Verlag 1970 [1750–58]); §1.

115 Dan Matthews and Illan Rua Wall raise an objection along similar lines in their introduction to a series of essays on legal aesthetics in the *Journal of Law, Culture and the Humanities*. See Dan Matthews and Illan Rua Wall, 'Legal *Aesthēsis*: Affect, Space and Encounter' (2023) 19(2) *Journal of Law, Culture and the Humanities* 186, 187–188.

116 Douzinas (n 14) 31.

10

THE MATERIAL DOUZINAS

Andreas Philippopoulos-Mihalopoulos

And Yet

At first instance, Douzinas' work on aesthetics and the law does not engage with materiality. There are few references to Deleuze, or post-Deleuzian, feminist or queer literature at least of the type usually connected to new materialism and the recent emergence of materiality. There is not a great deal of engagement with what it means to link law with space, bodies, the nonhuman, the planetary and the elemental. References to how the law is generated are confined to ethics, psychoanalysis and indeed aesthetics and the judgments that spill over to law. Even in his work on art and aesthetics, there is little in terms of how art is generated, the tangibility of the form, the handling of the material. At first instance, for those of us interested in dealing with the law on a material level, Douzinas seems unwilling or unable to contribute.

And yet. On a personal level, Costas loves and appreciates art. He also appreciates objects, bodies, elements (his long-distance swimming is a material immersion in a Greek element – a love we share). He appreciates spaces and the opportunities that these spaces allow – often connected to the flowing materiality of good quality wine. He loves the night and the talks that take place when lights dim and faces lean towards one another to confess or lie beautifully. For these reasons, I have always suspected otherwise. And for one added, personal reason: he discerned in me a nascent preoccupation with materiality and art production much earlier than I did, as early as when I was doing my PhD at Birkbeck, when my theoretical interests were a tad too abstract (oh yes) even for Costas. He told me, 'you think and act more like an artist than a lawyer.' He meant it as a compliment, I think. And

DOI: 10.4324/9781032622224-10

then he carried on with some Lacanian references about the Real, of which I remember almost nothing. For these reasons, I want to bring out the material Douzinas.

The Locus of the Material

My intervention focuses specifically on Douzinas' work on law and aesthetics. It is my intention to flesh out the materialist in his writings in the same way that he sniffed out the artist in me. It is a gesture of complicity but also of friendship. Complicity because I feel I know more than I read of Costas the scholar/pedagogue/polymath/father figure/mother hen figure/politician: you know how it is, when you look up to someone and as a result cherish the sparkles of intimate conversation as gateways to their more concealed and vulnerable sides.

And friendship in the second form of friendship as described by Douzinas in his work on Syriza: friendship as *filotimo*, 'the aesthetic aspect of ethics. It is to try your best and get pleasure from the effort and perfection of the work and its fruit: a tasty meal, a beautifully painted wall, a well composed sonnet.'[1] Douzinas' writing is brimming with *filotimo*: it has the material quality of perfectly formed pieces of conversation made to persuade and entice but also show that there are things well beyond what you think you have understood.

And this is the clue to materiality he offers: Douzinas' aesthetic work (the rest too but I am only making a case for this here) dwells in a chiaroscuro of barely grasped absence. There is always something withdrawn, concealed, beyond phenomenological reach. Counterintuitively, this is the locus of materiality, the material Douzinas who is folded in Douzinas' material. Materiality is revealed in absence: the material becomes relevant when it unveils its immaterial. This interplay is a direct consequence of a heady mixture familiar to and indeed embodied by many of us critical legal thinkers: a law that never fully reveals itself, a justice that delivers in concealing her gaze, the image of law beyond the text of law, the aporia as the defining moment of the delivery of the law. Derridean thought coupled with legal metaphysics and personal longing for this something more, this beyond, not quite here but promised here. The future of a promise. This is deeply personal too: it's the thinking process of a person who has embodied the left thought and strived to practise it, however imperfectly, in his life and career. It is a deferral of justice through the promise of actual, material ethics of respect for alterity.

1 Costas Douzinas, *Syriza in Power: Reflections of an Accidental Politician* (Polity 2017) 256.

Matter/Materiality

In quoting Pseudo-Dionysius on how the light enlightens us only by concealing itself,[2] Douzinas points to the folding between the visibly concealed and the invisibly revealed. This folding (and I insist on calling it so rather than dialectic, a Deleuzian folding that never prioritises and never synthesises but keeps on folding and unfolding in baroque twirls like a line of flight that pushes the possible from within) finds its perfect expression in his work on the *Antiprosopon*,[3] the other side of the Byzantine icon that is revealed to the awe and devastation of the enemy. It is always the other side that is revealed, never the thing itself, just like the face of power is shown in its concealment: a female Venice by Veronese, her face always shaded in the serene nebulae of the ceiling, folded in the almost promiscuous visibility of such concealment. 'The sublime is obscure, it overawes.'[4] But in the core of its concealment lies the absolute apophantic materialisation of its apophatic matter: the icon is fully present yet *Acheropoitos*, namely a nonpainted image, or rather an image not painted by human hand (*a-chera*, 'no hand'). The artist's hand has been directed by god, the material identity of the image is visibly hidden in order to allow for the absolute invisibility of matter to be fleshed forth.

The distinction between matter and materiality can be thought of in similar terms: matter as what would be left if materiality were to be removed.[5] Matter as the object *qua* object, the inaccessible material assemblage that can never become a concept or an a priori but is always co-emerging folded in with materiality. In Douzinas, when the image is phenomenologically present, the matter of the image (its material, its production, its thingness) withdraws.[6] In similar ways in both my academic and artistic practices, when materiality is ontologically present, matter withdraws. This withdrawal enables materiality to flow into agentic entanglements and material considerations. But since matter is co-emergent with materiality, matter dwells in that constant paradoxical penumbra of being both always present (with materiality) and always withdrawn (in order for materiality to emerge). In the same way, for Douzinas images are atmospheric emergences that circumvent logos and address the senses directly. In his earlier work with Ronnie Warrington on Reynolds, they write that his 'Discourses are their own perfect double:

2 Costas Douzinas, 'Prosopon and Antiprosopon: Prolegomena for a Legal Iconography', in Costas Douzinas and Lynda Nead (eds), *Law and the Image: The Authority of Art and the Aesthetics of Law* (University of Chicago Press 1999) 44.

3 ibid.

4 ibid 55.

5 I have written on this in 'Performing Metaphors' (2021) 24(1) *Theory and Event*.

6 Costas Douzinas, 'A Legal Phenomenology of Images', in Oren Ben-Dor (ed), *Law and Art: Justice, Ethics and Aesthetics* (Routledge 2011).

they indicate not the truth in painting, but that this truth, if it exists, is not available in non-plastic forms.'[7]

Desire for the Stage

Desire runs through Douzinas' texts in waves and lances. It is not a material desire a la Deleuze but a Lacanian desire, always chasing the impossible even in visual terms: 'Visuality is anchored on the desire to perceive the invisible and ineffable.'[8] Yet desire is already part of the economy of power, taking pride of place on stage. In the ambit of the divine, the fetishisation of icons by both inconophiles and iconoclasts during the Byzantine iconoclastic conflicts points to the ineffable that could not be represented. Christ depicted is the materialisation of desire to be (in the image of god) and to control the divine by converting it into flesh. And although this attempt at representation, this desire to possess, can never be fully materialised ('the icon *tends* towards him'[9]), it still claims centre stage in the economy of incarnation that introduces the matter of transcendence into history through the material image of a god in human flesh. Idem for law, and indeed the law of law: 'But even the categorical imperative law, that law that pre-exists me, must be staged, in the same way that the absent presence of God was staged before modernity.'[10]

And here is the Christian ethical moment of materiality fully fleshed out: 'Through the recognition of the absolute otherness of the divine image, narcissistic desire – the desire of the self in its image – is transposed into an acceptance of radical otherness (of the image, the other) and into desire for the other.'[11] This acceptance of the other is the ultimate ethical project for Douzinas. Art and law are the last bastions of such a transposition: 'by reconciling us to radical alterity and by introducing us to difference, the law helps the imagistic staging of the world for the subject.'[12]

And yet. By staging the world, the law does not only reconcile us to radical alterity and difference. Douzinas is aware of the limits of this theologisation of the law when he writes: 'We increasingly see our relations with others and the world through a contractual imagery. A fictional frame of promises, agreements and contracts filters the way we see a large part of relations with others. This contractual framework is replacing other ways of seeing human

7 Costas Douzinas and Ronnie Warrington, *Justice Miscarried: Ethics and Aesthetics in Law* (Edinburgh University Press 1994) 301.
8 Douzinas (n 2) 45.
9 ibid 43.
10 ibid 57.
11 Douzinas (n 6) 251.
12 ibid 256–257.

relations, such as sympathy, care and love. It operates both as a mise-en-scene, a staging of human relations, and as a screen which approaches relations, encounters and emotions according to a model of offer, acceptance and consideration. While such an economic model is staged and artificial, it relies on the naturalising ability of the legal institution.'[13]

But the Stage Is Taken

This is all good. But we the non-anthropocentric thinkers, we the anthropocenic emergences, we the crits, now have the responsibility to go further than phenomenology and criticise the instances when new material manifestations affect us negatively. Law is not only staging the world as contractual. Law stages *itself*, twitter-based, media-obsessed and fully narcissistic, feeding the desire for public expression of that most illusionary of liberties, the contractual freedom. Law no longer mediates between us and whatever else, but itself becomes this whatever-else, ontologically becoming a body beyond direct human control.[14] By staging itself, law meddles not just with the phenomenological mediation between subjects and world, but with the very ontology of the world and the taken-for-granted category of subjects. Law staging itself means that the world becomes absorbed in law's representation of the world: the only possible world is the one offered by the staged law. This is not simply a question of phenomenological perspective but an intervention on the level of ontology: by staging itself, law alters not just the representation of the world but the world itself.

This is the new order of things: it has become impossible to defend the faith in the ineffable because the signifier is all there is. There is no outside. There is no longer anything that can afford the luxury of the chiaroscuro. The fully lit stage is the only thing we have, a totalising atmosphere of a glossy flatness. We are witnessing a collapse of the distinction between representation and object. We see that the face of the other, Douzinas' major point of ethical responsibility, is succumbing to a totalising ontology of signs, an affective maelstrom of planetary impact. As problematic as it was, we are no longer even able to say 'I see myself because somebody sees me.'[15]

13 ibid 257.

14 Yet always part of an assemblage in which human and nonhuman bodies converge. See my work on 'Lively Agency: Life and Law in the Anthropocene' in Irus Braverman (ed), *Animals, Biopolitics, Law: Lively Legalities* (Routledge 2016). In that sense, law needs to be rethought in the manner of Niklas Luhmann's [e.g., *Law as a Social System* (K Ziegert trans, F Kastner, R Nobles, D Schiff and R Ziegert ed, OUP 2004)] post-humanism as an autopoietic body whose connection to human conscience is only a matter of contingency.

15 Douzinas (n 6) 253.

The gaze of the other replaces any possibility of awareness of self. The flatness disallows any search for even a disgruntled, marginalised identity.

And yet, for these reasons, one must try and salvage the face of the other from being absorbed by this flatness. One must pluralise it, make it more-than-human, make it planetary. One must use any means one has left. Douzinas' aesthetic project is to show how law and image, and art more broadly, are not only compatible and continuous (historically and currently) but also the final social spaces of radical otherness. In this, the new materialism project can learn from Douzinas' oeuvre. For what is the ultimate purpose of a material turn in law if not to move beyond identity politics and into a planetary materiality where flows of ethical positioning enable bodies to be seen?

11

THE PARADOX OF NON-HUMAN RIGHTS

Alexis Alvarez-Nakagawa

> The continuously changing conceptions of humanity are the best manifestation of the metaphysics of an age.
>
> *Costas Douzinas*[1]

Deeply intertwined forces are propelling us toward a foreseeable yet not entirely certain end. The relentless expansion of extractivist technologies under neoliberalism is rendering the planet increasingly inhospitable for both human and non-human life. We stand at a critical juncture, shaped by a technological crisis of unprecedented scale.[2] Much as human rights were introduced as a response to the social and political turmoil of an epoch defined by the Second World War, non-human rights are being proposed today as a solution to our ongoing techno-environmental malaise. Animals, rivers, mountains, rainforests, ecosystems, machines, AIs, and robots are increasingly recognized as subjects of rights in various jurisdictions,[3] and legal systems now seem driven by a push to 'decentre the human'. From

1 Costas Douzinas, 'The Paradoxes of Human Rights' (2013) 20(1) *Constellations* 55.

2 Our technological framework, or what Martin Heidegger has called *Ge-stell*, is in crisis not only because our technological choices have surpassed the threshold where they destabilize the conditions that make the planet habitable for humans (the 'parametric conditions of human existence'), but also because this destabilization will necessarily bring about the 'end of human technology', either as such (if humans are wiped off the face of the Earth) or as it has been understood (if humans change the basic techno-onto-epistemic choices that have defined human technology so far). For Heidegger's remarks on *Ge-stell*, see *The Question Concerning Technology and Other Essays* (William Lovitt tr, Harper and Row 1977) 20.

3 In jurisdictions as varied as the US, India, Brazil, Saudi Arabia, Ecuador, Spain, and New Zealand, among others.

DOI: 10.4324/9781032622224-11

climate change to the treatment of sentient and non-sentient beings to the regulation of artificial intelligence, non-human rights are advanced as a new form of governmentality in a world dominated by a sense of an impending end—not just of history but of the world itself.[4]

If human rights once seemed to herald an era of perpetual peace—an illusion shattered by the 9/11 attacks and the ensuing 'war on terror'—advocates of non-human rights now speak in a more modest and pessimistic tone, aiming to offer a legal and ethical framework to avert (or administer) a looming ecological and technological catastrophe. It could be said that the 'postmodern condition', described by Jean-Francois Lyotard as the end of the 'grand narratives',[5] has given way to different 'narratives of the end'. As news about devastating wildfires and floods, global plagues, a third world war, and the dangers posed by new technologies pop up on the flat screens of our various devices every day, we seem to be suspended in an agonizing movement towards an extinction that is yet to fully materialize. From the dream of perpetual peace to the spectre of perpetual end, in which the eschatological extends indefinitely, non-human rights have emerged as a paradigmatic, or perhaps symptomatic, legal idiom of our times.

While those who advocate for non-human rights aim to transcend the limitations of human rights, they adopt much of the latter's theoretical foundations and modes of practical implementation. Therefore, if, as Joan Scott provocatively put it, human rights have offered 'nothing but paradoxes',[6] why should non-human rights be any different? If paradox has been the 'organising principle of human rights'[7] from beginning to end, how can we be reassured that paradox is not also formatting the new emerging discourse of non-human rights? In other words, are we fated to continue 'suffering the paradoxes of rights'[8] as they move beyond the human? Are non-human rights the 'revolution' that will save us, the 'paradigm shift' our legal systems need,[9] or merely a new iteration of the rights obsession of an exhausted

4 For a nuanced overview of various contemporary formulations of these 'endings', see Déborah Danowski and Eduardo Viveiros de Castro, *The Ends of the World* (Rodrigo Guimarães Nunes tr, Polity Press 2016).

5 Jean-François Lyotard defined the postmodern condition as an exhaustion with and incredulity towards grand narratives. See Jean-François Lyotard, *The Postmodern Condition: An Essay on Knowledge* (Manchester University Press 1984).

6 Joan Wallach Scott, *Only Paradoxes to Offer: French Feminists and the Rights of Man* (Harvard University Press 1996).

7 Costas Douzinas, *Human Rights and Empire* (Routledge 2007) 8.

8 Wendy Brown, 'Suffering the Paradoxes of Rights' in Wendy Brown and Janet Halley (eds), *Left Legalism/Left Critique* (Duke University Press 2002) 420–434.

9 See David R. Boyd, *The Rights of Nature: A Legal Revolution that Could Save the World* (ECW Press 2017), and, more recently, Saskia Stucki, who suggests that we might be 'at the onset of the next, and perhaps most profound, human rights revolution—a non-human

late-liberal political imaginary confronting environmental catastrophe? Dipesh Chakrabarty, among others, has written that the mansion of modern freedoms and rights rests on an ever-expanding foundation of fossil-fuel consumption and energy-intensive institutions.[10] If that is the case, then the current expansion of rights to include non-humans is a development that warrants closer scrutiny.

This chapter attempts to address some of these questions and in doing so it takes inspiration from Costas Douzinas' examination of the 'paradoxes of human rights'.[11] While some of the paradoxes he describes also apply to non-human rights, this chapter focuses on a paradox unique to the latter: non-human rights are intended to redefine humanity's relationship with non-humans in non-anthropocentric ways, yet they operate within and reinforce human-centric legal frameworks. As non-human beings are recognized as subjects of rights based on their similarity (or identity) to humans, the extension of subjectivity to non-humans becomes a projection of humanity. Rather than making humans more attentive to the world beyond the human, non-human rights render us blind to its inherent properties. They thus produce a 'decentring' that paradoxically favours a new 'recentring' of the human.

The chapter proceeds as follows. It begins with a reflection on the idea of the end of human rights in Douzinas' work and then moves on to the question of non-human rights as a 'discourse of the end'. After all, the so-called 'end of human rights' can be seen both as a cause and a consequence of the current rise of non-human rights. The chapter then enquires into the ontological and anthropological foundations for granting rights to both humans and non-humans. This examination serves as a basis for exploring the paradoxical nature of extending rights to non-human beings. It also highlights the relationship between non-human rights and a broader movement that now spans philosophical, economic, scientific, and technical discourses and practices—one that reveals the metaphysics of an age obsessed with erasing non-human alterity and projecting a disembodied humanity as the universal form and measure of all existence.

---

rights revolution'. See Saskia Stucki, *One Rights: Human and Animal Rights in the Anthropocene* (Max Planck/Springer 2023) 7.

10 Dipesh Chakrabarty, 'The Climate of History: Four Theses' (2009) 35(2) *Critical Inquiry* 208. For a related discussion on how fossil fuels have both enabled and constrained democracy in the 20th century, see Timothy Mitchell, *Carbon Democracy: Political Power in the Age of Oil* (Verso 2011).

11 See, specifically, Douzinas, 'The Paradoxes of Human Rights' (n 1) 51–67. Notably, however, Douzinas' entire body of work on human rights is characterized by his effort to unveil the paradoxical nature of human rights.

The End of Human Rights?

The question of—and for—the 'end' has been a part of human rights discourse from the very beginning. The discourse gained momentum at the proclaimed 'end of history' and in a strange way its heyday coincided with the proclamation of the 'death of man'. It could be said that much of Douzinas' 'trilogy of rights'[12] deals with reconciling the 'death of man', as announced somewhat stridently by Foucault in the 1970s, with the rise of human rights after the collapse of the Berlin Wall in 1989. Douzinas seeks to understand how, amid a crisis of the modern subject and its human embodiment, human rights 'triumphed on the world stage', uniting 'left and right, the pulpit and the state, the minister and the rebel, the developing world and the liberals of Hampstead and Manhattan'.[13] Douzinas wonders how it can be that on the eve of the death of man (in the face of clear signs of his dissolution as a metaphysical foundation), human rights emerged as the lingua franca of ethics and politics. If the victory of human rights represents a fulfilment of the Enlightenment's emancipatory promise, the death of man is the clearest evidence of its failure. How is it possible for both events to coexist? What does the simultaneity of these opposing, 'non-simultaneous' drives tell us? Is it that man has not quite died? Is it that human rights have not truly triumphed?

As Douzinas indicated, 'the announcement of the "death of man" [was] accompanied by the most protracted campaign to reclaim the individual, as the triumphant centre of our postmodern world and to declare freedom, in the form of autonomy or self-determination, as the organizing ideal of our legal and political systems'.[14] Perhaps this contradiction is reconciled by the fact that the apparent triumph of human rights discourse coincides with its persistent empirical neglect; an irony that has gradually discredited human rights and led to their current 'existential crisis'. 'It is an undeniable fact', states Gabriel Marcel 'that human life has never been as universally treated as a vile and perishable commodity as during our own era'.[15] Indeed, the human rights age has been also the era of genocide, ethnic cleansing, of the Holocaust. While Man (with a capital 'M') ascended to the transcendental realm previously occupied by God, man (in lowercase) was murdered in all sorts of unimaginable ways. The gap between normative humanity and empirical humanity highlights the distance between human rights and their realization. The disparity between the formal recognition of human dignity

12 See Costas Douzinas, *The End of Human Rights* (Hart 2000); *Human Rights and Empire* (n 7); *The Radical Philosophy of Rights* (Routledge 2019).

13 Douzinas, *The End of Human Rights* (n 12) ibid. 1.

14 ibid 17.

15 Gabriel Marcel, *Creative Fidelity* (Robert Rosthal tr. Fordham University Press 2002) 94.

and the abandonment of humans as 'mere life' in everyday existence arguably signals the predictable end of human rights.

This glaring contradiction has taken its toll on the idea of human rights, and over the past 25 years, many have pointed to the 'end of the human rights era',[16] the 'endtimes of human rights',[17] its 'twilight',[18] or the 'collapse of the global human rights regime'.[19] David Kennedy has argued that the moment of human rights has passed and that they are 'no longer the way forward'.[20] From a different perspective but with similar despair, Douzinas predicted the 'end of human rights' if they were to continue straying from their radical origins and utopian ends.[21] The ubiquity of this diagnosis is evident in recent calls to start looking forward, to 'end with the endism' that has pervaded the field.[22] If anything, this 'endism' suggests a critical juncture for human rights. In a time of multiple interlocked crises—or 'polycrises', as it is commonly referred to today[23]—when most social and institutional arrangements of modernity seem to be crumbling under their own weight, it is no surprise that 'the ideology at the end of history' would follow suit.

Though the crisis of human rights can be traced back to its very inception, it became fully visible only at the turn of the century. The humanitarian rationale, first invoked in Bosnia and Kosovo and later in the US-led interventions in Afghanistan and Iraq, demonstrated how easily human rights could be co-opted to justify war efforts and imperial agendas. Among progressive campaigners, leftist intellectuals, activists from the Global South, and even some liberal scholars, human rights increasingly came to be seen

16 Michael Ignatieff, 'Is the Human Rights Era Ending?' *The New York Times* (New York, 5 February 2002) <https://www.nytimes.com/2002/02/05/opinion/is-the-human-rights-era-ending.html> accessed 15 December 2024.

17 Stephen Hopgood, *The Endtimes of Human Rights* (Cornell University Press 2013).

18 Eric Posner, *The Twilight of Human Rights Law* (OUP 2014)

19 Haythem Guesmi, 'The Global Human Rights Regime Has Collapsed' (*Aljazeera*, 1 September 2023) <https://www.aljazeera.com/opinions/2023/9/1/the-global-human-rights-regime-has-collapsed> accessed 15 December 2024.

20 David Kennedy, 'The International Human Rights Regime: Still Part of the Problem?' in Rob Dickinson, Elena Katselli, Colin Murray and Ole W Pedersen (eds), *Examining Critical Perspectives on Human Rights* (Cambridge University Press 2012) 34.

21 Douzinas, *The End of Human Rights* (n 12) 371–380.

22 César Rodríguez-Garavito-, 'Human Rights at 75: The End of Endism' (*Open Global Rights*, 1 December 2023) <https://www.openglobalrights.org/human-rights-75-end-of-endism/> accessed 15 December 2024. On the trend of human rights 'endism', see Ruti G. Teitel, 'From Human Rights to Humanity's Law' in András Sajó and Renáta Uitz (eds), *Critical Essays on Human Rights Criticism* (Eleven International Publishing 2020) 111-132.

23 Adam Tooze, 'Welcome to the World of the Polycrisis' *Financial Times* (London, 28 October 2022) <https://www.ft.com/content/498398e7-11b1-494b-9cd3-6d669dc3de33> accessed 15 December 2024.

not as instruments of liberation but as tools of oppression. The absence of human rights rhetoric within the Madrid, Athens, and Occupy Wall Street protests after the 2008 economic crisis, as well as during the 'Arab Spring' protests starting in 2010, highlighted its limited relevance to some of the most pivotal political and social movements of the time. All this was reaffirmed in states' responses to the global Covid-19 pandemic, where human rights principles and standards, overshadowed by economic, medical, or political considerations, seemed to play no significant role in guiding the actions of governments. In parallel, for better or worse, warring states no longer seem to invoke universal human rights as the main justification for their belligerent actions. In both Ukraine and Palestine, the discourse of human rights has not functioned as the primary organizer of the rhetoric of war, as other narratives centred on geopolitics, territory, or security take precedence. While human rights have played a part in the criticism of both wars and still retain some relevance in specific local contexts, their hegemony as a universal lexicon of politics and law appears to be in decline on a global scale.

It could thus make sense to see the emergence of non-human rights as yet another consequence of the twilight of human rights. Is this the realization of the long-predicted 'death of man'? Does the decline of the human rights discourse finally coincide with the fulfilment of Foucault's prediction that Man would disappear 'like a face drawn in sand washed by the sea'?[24] If the question of the subject was already controversial in human rights discourse, as the scholarship abundantly shows,[25] it takes on new nuances with the emergence of non-human rights. With these new rights, the *monosubject* of human rights fragments into a multitude of non-human subjects granted with human-like entitlements. If the human is no longer the sole subject of rights and now shares this status with animals, rivers, and machines, does this mean that humans have lost their privileged place in the law? If the enduring crisis of human rights has not marked its 'end' but rather their growing political irrelevance, will non-human rights deliver the final blow? Is this, at last, the end of human rights?

The Metaphysics of Our Age

We cannot answer these questions without first considering how the concept of human rights came into being and how this development was tied to the

24 Michel Foucault, *The Order of Things: An Archaeology of the Human Sciences* (anon. tr, Vintage 1994) 387.

25 Douzinas has addressed this issue extensively in his trilogy of rights. Jacques Rancière has presented one of the best-known philosophical accounts on the question of the 'subject' of human rights. See 'Who is the Subject of the Rights of Man?' (2004) 103 *The South Atlantic Quarterly* 297–310.

formation of a modern anthropology and ontology. The subject of human rights emerged through the gradual assimilation of three once distinct notions—the person, the subject, and the human being. It was only through the long historical process by which these categories came to be folded into one another—a process that unfolded over centuries—that human rights could be conceived at all, let alone rise to prominence as a powerful political and legal discourse in the twentieth century. A full account of how these notions became historically entangled, and of the far-reaching consequences this entanglement had for Western culture, lies beyond the scope of this chapter. It is nevertheless important to emphasize that this identification profoundly shaped modern understandings of what it means to be human—and, by implication, what it means to be non-human.[26]

The new anthropology that emanated from the crystallization of the three interlocking categories gradually converged with an emerging ontological framework that, among other things, established a particular separation between human and non-human beings, whereby the former are placed in the privileged position of moral subjects and the latter relegated to morally irrelevant objects. Bruno Latour argued that modernity has often been defined in terms of humanism—saluting the birth of Man or, more recently, announcing his demise—while neglecting the simultaneous birth of 'non-humanity' (the world of things, objects, animals, and nature).[27] This asymmetrical understanding is evident in the prominence human rights have gained in the modern political imaginary.[28] Whereas in antiquity the notions of person and subject were applied to a vast range of non-humans, modernity restricted these categories to humans beings.[29] The assimilation between person, subject, and human enabled the emergence of 'humanity', while rendering invisible the 'non-humanity' that served as its contrast.

The Onto-Anthropological Convergence

Western modern ontology, which Philippe Descola has termed 'naturalism', posits a continuity in the physicality of entities (humans and non-humans

26 For a genealogical account of the assimilation between the notions of person and subject, see my 'Who is the Subject of (Non) Human Rights' in Alexis Alvarez-Nakagawa and Costas Douzinas (eds), *Non-Human Rights. Critical Perspectives* (Elgar 2024).

27 Bruno Latour, *We Have Never Been Modern* (Catherine Porter tr, Harvard University Press 1993) 13.

28 Douzinas is correct in saying that the French Declaration of the Rights of Man and Citizen could be considered the 'manifesto of modernity'. See Douzinas (n 1) 55.

29 See on this Yan Thomas, 'The Subject of Right, the Person, Nature: Remarks on the Current Criticism of the Legal Subject' in Yan Thomas (ed), *Legal Artifices: Ten Essays on Roman Law in the Present Tense* (Chantal Schu̇tz and Anton Schu̇tz tr, Edinburgh University Press 2021).

alike are made of matter) and a discontinuity in their respective interiorities (only humans are conceived as intentional agents).[30] This dualist ontology set the parameters for a correlative anthropological dualism: humans are divided between the internal, immaterial qualities—rationality, sentience, consciousness, autonomy, agency, and will—that are considered unique to them, and the external, physical attributes shared with non-humans.[31] This continuity/discontinuity explains why animals have been treated as figures of both sameness and otherness in Western culture: from a physical point of view humanity is a form of animality, the species *Homo sapiens*, but from a psychological point of view it is a unique state of being, possessing spiritual attributes that animals do not have.[32] The modern idea of the human subject is thus a product of onto-epistemic inflections that contrast inner (spiritual/psychological) and outer (material/physical) attributes.

As Foucault pointedly remarked, modern anthropology places humans in a unique metaphysical, epistemological, and moral position.[33] It attributes to the human being not only a material but a transcendental existence. The fact that humans' faculties are 'internal' does not make them less transcendental—just as our *inner* rational soul relates to God and transcends the material plane in theological thinking, the modern Kantian transcendental subject is prior to empirical experience. Modern transcendentalism establishes a hierarchical relationship between the inner and outer aspects of the human being: due to its transcendental nature, the spirit (or reason) is meant to govern and subdue the body. Through the reflective privilege granted by its transcendental interiority, the human being can objectify its external self. Consequently, the subject is not identified as a body but as the possessor of one—the subject is the proprietor of its empirical self.

This thinking positioned humans between two opposing magnitudes: as bodies, they are objects (no different from animals or inanimate things); as subjects, they are transcendental creatures. That internal-transcendental disposition distinguishes humans from non-humans, marking them as

30 Philippe Descola, *Beyond Nature and Culture* (Janet Lloyd tr, The University of Chicago Press 2013).

31 Historian R.G. Collingwood memorably asserted that 'nature' has no 'inside' and thus no history: 'in the case of nature, this distinction between the outside and the inside of an event does not arise. The events of nature are mere events, not the acts of agents whose thought the scientist endeavours to trace [... consequently] all history properly so called is the history of human affairs'. See RG Collingwood, *The Idea of History* (New York 1976) 212.

32 As Tim Ingold explains, human beings can be defined either as a species of animal or as a condition distinct from the animal. See Tim Ingold, 'Humanity as Animality' in Tim Ingold (ed) *Companion Encyclopedia of Anthropology: Humanity, Culture and Social Life* (Routledge 1994) 15.

33 Foucault is referring to Kant in particular. See Foucault (n 22).

exceptional. The ontological privilege granted by their reflective consciousness, intentionality, and transcendental subjectivity makes humans the point of reference of being—in the modern age 'man becomes the relational centre of that which is as such'.[34] Dispossessed of interiority, in contrast, nonhumans are excluded from knowledge and action; as such, they cannot stand as the paradigmatic form of existence. Because of its interior-transcendental attributes, the human subject stands as the metaphysical foundation and epistemic principle of intelligibility of the world: humans become the measure of all things.[35]

From this perspective, 'naturalism' can also be considered a form of 'monism'. Or, more precisely, as a dualistic way of apprehending the world that relentlessly strives for unification. Its monistic drive to reconcile the opposing ends of its inherently impossible binary structure leads humans to constantly work through the contradictions therein, searching for a unifying principle between two irreconcilable and incompatible fields of phenomena. This occurs in two alternative ways, each privileging one extreme of the opposition. The first gives rise to different forms of empiricism, realism, and materialism, while the second gives shape to various kinds of spiritualism, idealism, and constructivism. On the one hand, to counter the dizzying effect of a plurality of interiorities, naturalism projects a unified physical world (a 'mononaturalism') of reassuring regularities, immanent laws of universal character, a kind of irreducible 'reality' or 'materiality'—that is, a natural world that exists independently of human beings. Despite our individual and cultural differences, naturalism affirms that we all inhabit one natural world governed by the same laws. On the other hand, the naturalist framework also seeks unification by pushing in the opposite direction, proposing the existence of a transcendental unifying principle beyond the empirical world of nature. This ultimate totalizing source can take various forms: God, Man, the Spirit, Culture, or any other empty signifier powerful enough to act as a foundational source or teleological principle.[36] Transcendence inevitably affirms the superiority of the signifier and establishes a hierarchical relationship between the two opposing sets: the material world is subordinated to the transcendental principle of unification. In this latter case, naturalism

34 Martin Heidegger, 'The Age of the World Picture' in Heidegger (n 2) 133.
35 ibid.
36 I am partially departing from Descola's description, which posits that the dualist problem of naturalism is addressed either through natural monism or cultural relativism (pluralism). See Descola (n 25) 290. However, I think that what Descola refers to as cultural relativism can also be understood as a form of spiritual monism, as it necessarily relies on the idea that all human beings possess a 'culture' (even if this culture manifests in multiple different ways). In other words, the concept of culture (an empty signifier) serves as the ultimate unifying principle.

looks for unification by transcending and therefore negating the primacy of what it sees as the 'natural' element within the dualistic opposition.

A naturalist world presents its inhabitants with an intractable problem: how to establish relations between phenomena and entities separated by an ontological original fracture (the 'great divide'). Since the naturalist framework starts with detachment and differentiation (spirit/matter, culture/nature, humans/non-humans), relationships and connections emerge as something to be actively constructed.[37] To describe naturalism as a 'dualist ontology', thus excluding the production of such laborious entanglements, is to tell just half of the story.[38] Modernity has oscillated between two ways of seeking unification in the face of naturalism's dualist dilemma: in the physical plane by positing a common material background or in the transcendental by affirming a totalizing unifying principle.

The Natural Contract

The modern onto-anthropological convergence produced a privileged form of transcendental existence—humanity—as the necessary counterpart to a reified and dispirited nature. In Classical thought, nature was seen as a standard, a telos to which all things tended or aspired, serving as a critical principle above human institutions and customs. In replacing nature with God as the supreme authority, Medieval theology devalued nature, stripping it of its ancient transcendent power. This shift in perspective paved the way for a new conception of nature in modernity—one in which nature became inanimate: a mathematizable, measurable, homogeneous, and divisible substance, famously characterized by René Descartes as 'extension'.[39] Nature

37 See generally Marilyn Strathern, *Relations. An Anthropological Account* (Duke University Press 2020), and more specifically her 'Epilogue' in Alexis Alvarez-Nakagawa (ed), *The Non-Human Turn in the Law* (British Academy/OUP forthcoming).

38 It is in this spirit that Latour says that moderns 'have never been modern'. Despite their claim to respect the split between nature and culture, moderns constantly produce 'attachments' or 'entanglements' (proliferating 'hybrids'). See *We Have Never Been Modern* (Catherine Porter tr, Harvard University Press 1993). There is a 'fabulous dissonance' inherent in the modern project between what moderns say about the detachment of phenomena and what they do—creating ever more attachments. As Latour notes, 'modernism was always about attachments'. See 'Love Your Monsters. Why We Must Care for Our Technologies as We do Our Children' (2011) 2 *Breakthrough Journal* 22.

39 See René Descartes, *Meditations on First Philosophy* (John Cottingham ed tr, Cambridge University Press 2013) Meditations 2 and 4. This way of conceptualizing space as extension contrasts with the ancient and Medieval view of the world as a network of qualitatively distinct places, interconnected by routes of travel rather than by abstract geometric points. See Jordan Branch, *The Cartographic State: Maps, Territory and the Origins of Sovereignty* (Cambridge University Press 2014).

became the non-human physical backdrop against which human history unfolds.

Reduced to inert matter devoid of intrinsic value, nature also became the object of conquest for the human subject, who sought its mastery by uncovering its regularities, patterns, and laws. The creation of 'subject' and 'object' came out of this process, which transformed humanity into a universal subject and nature into an absolute object. The dispirited nature of modernity, as an all-encompassing totality, could then only relate to the totality of spirited humanity. Relations of collaboration, conflict, belonging, possession, freedom, and constriction were defined between these universal all-encompassing magnitudes. If humanity (rather than individual human beings) was the counterpart of nature, as total agent it must stand and act—dwell, use, know, work, and produce—in opposition to an objectified nature. The flipside of ontological naturalism was thus humanism, not only as an expression of human exceptionality but as the universalization of an essentialized human form distinct from empirical humans.

While the onto-anthropological convergence confined moral and epistemic subjecthood to a single species, it simultaneously introduced a hierarchical divide within that species. As Descola notes, within the naturalist framework, humans' uniqueness arises from their ability to distinguish themselves from non-humans but also from one another.[40] The interior traits regarded as markers of humanity were not evenly distributed among all humans. Some humans were seen as lacking the logocentric qualities associated with humanity, effectively rendering them no better than animals or mere objects.

This discontinuity within the human species was constructed by associating certain physical attributes with the properties of the non-human world. While masculinity and whiteness were linked to distinctly human traits such as reason, spirituality, and culture, women, racialized peoples in colonial territories, and the poor in metropolitan areas were associated with corporeality, materiality, and nature.[41] These oppositions reflected a hierarchical ordering: reason was placed over the body, spirit over matter, and culture over nature. This resulting hierarchy helped justify the subjugation of those deemed inferior due to their insufficient detachment from nature and bodily instincts. This peculiar onto-anthropology of the moderns permeated our political and legal arrangements, establishing a 'natural' order—one that

40 Descola (n 30) 191.

41 Carolyn Merchant, *The Death of Nature: Women, Ecology, and the Scientific Revolution* (Harper & Row 1990) 1ff; Val Plumwood, *Feminism and the Mastery of Nature* (Routledge 1993) 19–21, 41ff; Sylvia Wynter, 'Unsettling the Coloniality of Being/Power/Truth/Freedom: Towards the Human, After Man, its Overrepresentation. An Argument' (2003) 3(3) *New Centennial Review* 266.

justifies itself through the supposed naturalness of certain forms of social stratification—effectively constituting a kind of *natural contract*.[42]

It thus follows that the idea of rights historically extending outward from a narrow conception of 'the human' has become a common trope in legal and political discussions. This form of moral evolutionism, particularly championed in progressive contemporary liberal thought, portrays the gradual inclusion of hitherto excluded human (and now non-human) beings as rights-holders. The circle of humanity has certainly expanded in recent years—at least in formal terms—through the legal recognition of rights previously denied to women, Black and Indigenous peoples, and various so-called 'minorities'. However, the subjects newly admitted to the circle are still judged against the dominant idea of the human being that justified their exclusion in the first place. In other words, while one no longer needs to be a white male to be considered a subject of rights, one must still meet the logocentric traits once exclusively attributed to them. Thus, inclusion has involved different forms of exclusion: new subjects were admitted only if they conformed to the dominant idea of the human, excluding and rendering invisible other characteristics. And just as women and people of colour have been admitted to the circle of humanity for their likeness to white males, non-humans are now being granted entry by being judged according to the logocentric traits that define abstract humanity. Since humans set the standard, bringing non-humans into the realm of the subject requires demonstrating how non-humans resemble humans.

Widening the Circle: Inclusion as Exclusion?[43]

The extension of rights to non-humans is typically mediated by the interplay of 'similarity' and 'difference',[44] nurtured by the ontological determinations of naturalism. If moderns seek to suture the ontological wound presupposed

42 Of course, this natural contract is quite different from the one Michel Serres has in mind in *The Natural Contract* (Elizabeth MacArthur and William Paulson tr, The University of Michigan Press 1995).

43 This section builds and expands upon Alexis Alvarez-Nakagawa (n 23) 109–113.

44 Catherine MacKinnon refers to the 'like-us model'. See her 'Of Mice and Men: A Feminist Fragment on Animal Rights' in Cass R Sunstein and Martha C Nussbaum (eds), *Animal Rights: Current Debates and New Directions* (OUP 2004) 263. Other scholars refer to the 'similarity argument'. See Taimie L Bryant, 'Similarity or Difference as a Basis for Justice: Must Animals be Like Humans to be Legally Protected from Humans?' (2007) 70 *Law and Contemporary Problems* 208. In my opinion, both ideas place too much emphasis on the 'like-us/similarity' aspect of the process, while in fact the 'difference argument' (the 'not-like-us model') also plays a significant role. As we will see, in this comparative process, things are considered similar to X but also different from Y. For this reason, I prefer to frame it as an 'interplay between similarity and difference'; it could alternatively be understood as the interplay between 'identity' and 'difference', as similarity here

by naturalism by finding ways to relate entities deemed fundamentally apart, then in the case of non-human rights this dynamic unfolds through metonymic comparisons that extend qualities long regarded as uniquely human to non-human entities—qualities that are often not strictly analogous to non-human traits, but only loosely connected to them.[45]

Animal rights perhaps provide the clearest example of how the circle of humanity widens through the interplay of similarity and difference. A paradigmatic case of this reasoning has been presented by philosopher and animal rights advocate Peter Singer, who considers extending rights to conscious or sentient animals as an 'expansion of the circle of concern of morality'.[46] For Singer, sentience justifies granting rights to animals—he has also supported granting rights to animals with certain cognitive abilities, while also defending the corresponding idea of stripping rights from humans who fail to meet certain cognitive-based thresholds.[47] According to Singer, granting rights only to sentient humans constitutes 'speciesism', a form of discrimination akin to racism. This theoretical position is more or less standard in current literature on animal rights. For example, Tom Regan, a prominent animal rights scholar, asserts that non-human beings should be recognized as moral agents and 'subjects-of-a-life' provided they possess abilities that indicate internal traits such as consciousness, autonomy, and intentionality.[48] Many other animal rights advocates likewise prioritize cognition, sentience, or a combination of the two.[49]

This paradigmatic reasoning, common in scholarship, has also been adopted by litigants and courts in judicial processes recognizing personality and rights for non-human animals. Intelligence, sentience, and, in some

---

represents a way of speaking about identity (a 'weak identity', since, for obvious reasons, the resemblance between humans and non-humans cannot be considered complete).

45 Douzinas is therefore correct in referring to them as 'metonymical rights'. See *The End of Human Rights* (n 12) 258.

46 Singer initially advocated for taking animals' interests seriously on the grounds that they are capable of experiencing pleasure and pain, similar to human beings. See *Practical Ethics* (Cambridge University Press 1979). This does not alter my argument here, as such feelings are highly dependent on cognitive capacities. Even when connected to bodily sensations, pain and pleasure are subjective ('interior') experiences, so animals would still be considered objects of ethical consideration due to possessing interior attributes akin to those of human beings.

47 Peter Singer, *Animal Liberation* (Penguin 2015). Singer argues that humans who lack or lose such cognitive faculties due to malformation or lesions may not fully qualify as persons or subjects of rights. This claim is striking but not novel, as this internal differentiation among humans is an integral aspect of naturalism. See also, Singer's *Writings on an Ethical Life* (Harper Collins 2000) 88.

48 Tom Regan, *The Case for Animal Rights* (University of California Press 1983).

49 See, for example, Steven Wise, *Rattling the Cage: Toward Legal Rights for Animals* (Perseus 2000), which prioritizes cognitive capacities, or Gary Francione, 'Animals and Us: Our Hypocrisy' (2005) 2502 *New Scientist* 51–52, which prioritizes sentience.

cases, biological and DNA similarities have been the most frequent criteria used by the Nonhuman Rights Project and other NGOs litigating animal rights cases.[50] These traits have also been utilized by courts in granting rights to animals in Argentina, Colombia, Brazil, Ecuador, India, and Pakistan, among other countries.[51] Interestingly, the same characteristics have been used to emphasize the intrinsic difference between humans and animals in order to deny animal rights. Various courts in the US, for instance, have concluded that animals 'cannot bear any legal duties, submit to societal responsibilities, or be held accountable for their actions' due to their fundamental difference from humans.[52] In these cases, litigants argued that non-human beings should not be treated as mere objects because of their intelligence and biological similarities to humans. Their argument centred on the 'proximity' of non-humans to humans with respect to their interior properties. Following this line of reasoning, if proximity allows inclusion within the circle of moral concern, 'distance' permits exclusion.

The interplay of similarity and difference also plays a significant role in the 'rights of nature' discourse. Here, nature and natural entities—such as rivers, mountains, and rainforests—are anthropomorphized in order to be granted rights and recognized as legal persons. Legal scholar Christopher Stone, often regarded as the initiator of the rights of nature, saw these rights 'as an additional stage in the protracted process of extending legal recognition' to previously excluded human beings. For him, by granting rights to nature, 'we are cultivating the personal capacities *within us* to recognize more and more the ways in which nature—like the woman, the Black man, the Indian and the Alien—is like us'.[53] In line with this thinking, rights of

50 It should be noted that biological similarity is typically considered alongside the alleged intelligence and sentience of the animal in question, rather than in isolation (physical similarity *reinforces* the extension of rights to non-humans). Furthermore, biological similarity does not contradict the core principles of ontological naturalism, which upholds the *continuity* between human and non-human bodies.

51 See Tercer Juzgado de Garantías de Mendoza, 'Presentación efectuada por. A.F.A.D.A. respecto del chimpancé Cecilia Sujeto no humano', 3 November 2016, Expt. No. P 72.254-15 (Argentina); Corte Suprema de Justicia 26 July 2017, AHC4806-2017 (Colombia) – this ruling was later reversed; Superior Tribunal de Justiçia, Recurso especial N°1.797.175 – SP (2018/0031230-0), 21 March 2019 (Brazil); Supreme Court of India, Animal Welfare Board of India v. A Nagaraja and Ors., 2014 7 SCC 547; High Court of Islamabad, Islamabad Wildlife Mmgt. Bd. v. Metropolitan Corp. Islamabad, W.P., No. 1155/2019, 21 May 21 2020 (Pakistan).

52 People ex rel. Nonhuman Rights Project, Inc. v. Lavery, 124 A.D.3d 148, 152 (N.Y. App. Div. 2014).

53 Christopher Stone, 'Should Trees Have Standing? – Toward Legal Rights for Natural Objects' in *Should Trees Have Standing? Law, Morality and the Environment* (OUP 2010) 29 (emphasis in the original). As he did not clarify, we can assume that 'like us' refers to people like Stone, a white, educated, US-American male. He ends the sentence with a parenthetical remark, adding that 'we will also become more able realistically to

nature advocates regard nature and natural features as *living agents*, autonomous individuals or singularities with intentionality, identity, and, in some cases, sentience. This way of conceiving natural features as indivisible and living wholes, that is, as bounded, discrete, and atomistic entities, reflects a distinctly human (individualist) scaffold.[54]

In various cases, advocates invoke Indigenous understandings of these entities as living, agential, conscious, sentient, spiritual, and intentional beings. In doing so, they present rights as emerging from or as translations of Indigenous philosophies and cosmologies.[55] In other cases, they draw from scientific and pseudo-scientific theories that revive various forms of organicism and conceive of the Earth as a system or living whole. Attributing human traits to nature and natural entities renders the latter morally deserving of legal protection and justifies extending them fundamental rights, such as the right to life and the right not to be harmed. From Ecuador and Bolivia to New Zealand and India, governments and courts have embraced this perspective as well as activists.[56] In some recent cases, advocates have even sought the recognition of intellectual rights for nature and natural entities,

define, confront, live with, and admire the ways in which we are all different'. Note that the ability to deal (confront, admire, live) with difference is subordinated to a prior act of assimilating that difference.

54 Moreover, there seems to be a 'bios bias' in the rights of nature discourse, with this organic bias recently being characterized as anthropocentric. See Christine J. Winter and David Schlosberg, 'What Matter Matters as a Matter of Justice?' (2024) 33(7) *Environmental Politics* 1205–1224.

55 As Descola argues, however, the ethics underlying the rights of nature seem to align more closely with puritanism and Western *Naturphilosophie*. See (n 25) 199. Much of the time, the rights of nature discourse distorts Indigenous philosophies, as the concept of 'nature' embedded in these rights often bears little resemblance to Indigenous understandings. See Mihnea Tănăsescu, *Understanding the Rights of Nature: A Critical Introduction* (Transcript 2022) 43–44. The tendency to associate the rights of nature with Indigenous philosophies mirrors a broader political and cultural trend that promotes 'becoming Indigenous' in the Anthropocene. For a critique of this trend, see David Chandler and Julian Reid, *Becoming Indigenous: Governing Imaginaries in the Anthropocene* (Rowman & Littlefield 2019). It is therefore unsurprising that significant parts of Indigenous movements in countries where the rights of nature have been recognized remain indifferent or even critical of these rights. See Craig M Kauffman and Pamela L Martin, *The Politics of the Rights of Nature* (MIT 2021) 125.

56 See Constitución de la República de Ecuador, 20 October 2008; Bolivia's Act 71 in 2010 – Ley de derechos de la Madre Tierra and Act 300 in 2012 – Ley marco de la Madre Tierra y desarrollo integral para vivir bien. Te Awa Tupua (Whanganui Claims Settlement) Act 2017; Record of Understanding for Mount Taranaki, Pouakai and the Kaitake Ranges, 20 December 2017. See High Court of Uttarakhand, Mohd. Salim v. State of Uttarakhand and Others, Writ Petition (PIL) No. 126 of 2014, 20 March 2017; Uttarakhand High Court, Lalit Miglani v. State of Uttarakhand & Others, Writ Petition (PIL) No. 140 of 2015, 30 March 2017, 64.

acknowledging them as 'co-creators' of artistic works.[57] Since the arts have been historically seen as manifestations of human singularity, this strategy highlights nature's proximity to humanity's inherent 'spiritual' qualities.[58]

Attempts to extend personhood and rights to machines, robots, AI, and digital creations underscore the fact that the human remains the benchmark by which the worthiness of new candidates is assessed for entry into the circle of moral concern. Unlike with animal rights and the rights of nature, no significant piece of legislation or case law has recognized rights to these artificial entities. Certain anecdotal cases have garnered public attention, however, such as the 2017 granting of honorary citizenship to a humanoid robot named Sophia in Saudi Arabia,[59] and the recognition of residency for an online system mimicking a seven-year-old boy in Tokyo.[60] While these instances are of largely symbolic significance, they reveal a growing willingness to engage with the 'machine question',[61] as also reflected in a surge of legislative initiatives on AI regulation in recent years and a growing scholarly discussion on 'robot rights'. Notably, a 2017 European Parliament resolution advised the European Commission to consider granting 'electronic personhood' to the most advanced autonomous robots.[62] In other instances such considerations have focused on practical challenges arising from the integration of AI and robots into various social and economic spheres. Some US cities, for example, now regard robots operating on sidewalks as pedestrians.[63]

57 Patrick Barkham, 'Legal Bid for Ecuador Forest to be Recognised as Song Co-creator' *The Guardian* (London, 25 October 2024) <https://www.theguardian.com/world/2024/oct/25/legal-bid-for-ecuador-forest-to-be-recognised-as-song-co-creator?CMP=share_btn_url> accessed 15 December 2024.

58 Humans have been regarded as the 'artistic animal'. In the words of the anthropologist Alexander Alland, 'the creation and appreciation of art in its many forms are uniquely human activities' and 'true artistic behaviour is seen in no species other than *Homo sapiens*. Not even a hint of it occurs in the natural behaviour of other species'. See *The Artistic Animal: An Inquiry into the Biological Roots of Art* (Anchor Books 1977) 21, 24.

59 Andrew Griffin, 'Saudi Arabia Grants Citizenship to a Robot for the First Time Ever' *The Independent* (London, 26 October 2017) <https://www.independent.co.uk/tech/saudi-arabia-robot-sophia-citizenship-android-riyadh-citizen-passport-future-a8021601.html> accessed 15 December 2024.

60 Anthony Cuthbertson, 'Artificial Intelligence "Boy" Shibuya Mirai Becomes World's First AI Bot to Be Granted Residency' *Newsweek* (New York, 6 November 2017) <https://www.newsweek.com/tokyo-residency-artificial-intelligence-boy-shibuya-mirai-702382> accessed 15 December 2024.

61 David J. Gunkel, *Robot Rights* (MIT Press 2018).

62 European Parliament Resolution with Recommendations to the Commission on Civil Law Rules on Robotics (2015/2103(INL)) (European Parliament, 16 February 2017), para 59(f).

63 Matthew Stern, 'Sidewalk Robots Are on The Way' *Forbes* (New Jersey, 6 April 2021) <https://www.forbes.com/sites/retailwire/2021/04/06/sidewalk-robots-are-on-the-way-but-probably-later/?sh=3c6124127ee0> accessed 15 December 2024.

As with animal rights and the rights of nature, much of the debate on AI rights revolves around whether certain machines have attained a level of intelligence, self-awareness, and autonomy comparable to that of humans. The Turing test, which deems a machine intelligent only if it can convince a human that it too is human (by imitating human behaviour to the point of being indistinguishable), has deeply shaped the contours of these debates. In this context, similarity or proximity to human behaviour is equated with intelligence. The very term 'artificial *intelligence*' implies machines intended to resemble this human attribute and, as is generally acknowledged, most AI is programmed to approximate human behaviour. Other discussions have focused on whether AI could develop consciousness or sentience, which would make it deserving of legal subjectivity, while yet others have placed emphasis on the agency of electronic, digital, or automated systems, such as programmes that buy and sell shares or self-driving cars. These developments have sparked debates around the criminal and civil liability of such entities. It is worth noting that those who oppose granting entitlements to robots often do so based on a 'similarity/difference' framework, arguing that machines cannot be rights bearers because they are biologically and/or ontologically different from human beings.[64]

Like any discourse shaped by a plurality of actors and practices, non-human rights encompass diverse and sometimes conflicting formulations. The examples above are necessarily condensed and selective, but they arguably reflect the underlying assumptions and ideas driving much of the non-human rights advocacy, particularly its most visible and representative parts. These cases suggest that non-humans enter the circle of moral concern not for their distinct characteristics, but for their purportedly human attributes. Non-human rights advocates typically portray non-humans as unitary, free, and willing agents, and, like human individuals, as autonomous and formally equal to others.[65] The assumption underlying non-human rights is that entities of equal standing should be treated alike—if non-humans are similar to humans, they should be afforded the same treatment that is, in this case, rights or legal subjecthood.[66]

Non-human rights expand the circle of moral concern by erasing non-humans' inherent alterity. Non-humans are included in the circle at the cost of excluding what defines them as non-human. This necessarily involves

64 Lantz Fleming Miller, 'Granting Automata Human Rights: Challenge to a Basis of Full-Rights Privilege' (2015) 16 (4) *Human Rights Review* 369.

65 It should be noted that the very notions of 'subject of rights' and 'legal personhood'—now being extended to non-humans—implicitly suggest the existence of such attributes. An entire ontological worldview is implicit within the rights discourse. See on this Wendy Brown (n 8) 429.

66 Bryant (n 34) 207.

failing to recognize non-humans on their own terms, thereby obscuring their characteristic or defining attributes.[67] If non-humans are considered morally worthy and deserving of legal protection only because of the properties they are perceived to share with humans, their distinctiveness is discounted; we are blinded to their distinguishing faculties. In this way, they are both *included through exclusion* and *excluded through inclusion*—brought inside and kept outside the supposedly enlarged circle of humanity.[68]

Humanity on Steroids

The paradox of non-human rights does not stem from the view that non-humans possess faculties once thought to be exclusive to humans. Rather, it lies in the related but distinct assumption that these attributes must necessarily mirror human capacities. We easily assume that non-human traits can be explained by reference to human characteristics.[69] But acknowledging that non-humans can represent and act upon the world—that they may be intelligent, willing agents—does not necessarily mean assuming they do so in human ways.

By relying on human traits as the benchmark for moral and legal worthiness, non-human rights frameworks not only project an anthropomorphic image onto the world but also impose an anthropocentric measure of non-human existence. As a result, even if non-human rights blur the distinction between humans and non-humans by attributing similar properties, they also surreptitiously re-establish a hierarchical relation between them. Establishing a moral scale based on traits such as rationality, agency, and will (originally conceived as inherently human) creates an association between humans and non-humans that inevitably places humanity at the top.

The very acts of 'recognizing' and 'measuring' the proximity of non-humans to humans expose an absolute asymmetry between the two.[70]

67 As MacKinnon aptly noted in relation to animal rights: 'seeking animal rights on a like-us model [...] misses animals on their own terms, just as the same tradition has missed women on theirs'. See (n 35) 263–264.

68 For an illuminating description of the dynamics of inclusion and exclusion in our legal orders, see Hans Lindahl, 'Inside and Outside Global Law' (2019) 41(1) *Sydney Law Review* 1–34 and, more generally, *Fault Lines of Globalization: Legal Order and the Politics of A-Legality* (OUP 2013).

69 Robert Garner, *Animals, Politics and Morality* (Manchester University Press 1993) 35.

70 Recognition always entails a form of asymmetry between the one who recognizes and the one who is recognized—between the valuer and the evaluated. For an understanding of valuing as a form of reification, and thus a form of 'devaluing', see Martin Heidegger, 'Letter on Humanism' in Martin Heidegger, *Basic Writings* (David F Krell ed, Frank A Capuzzi and J. Glenn Gray tr, Routledge 1977) 141.

Moreover, such acts of measurement render non-human difference irrelevant—or even harmful. Difference, in fact, can become an obstacle to recognising the moral worth of non-humans.[71] Similarity/identity ultimately necessitates the foreclosure of difference. The more human-like an entity is perceived to be, the more it is regarded as entitled to rights; the more it differs, the fewer protections it is believed to deserve. This reinforces a natural order grounded in a universalized conception of humanity. Rather than eliminating anthropocentrism from the law, expanding the circle of moral concern to include non-human beings might thus be its ultimate realization.

Erasing non-human 'otherness' typically involves assimilating non-humans into a continuum of variations of the same, implying that they are fundamentally like us (albeit less developed or evolved).[72] Despite non-human rights appearing to shift the focus away from humans in favour of non-humans, they ultimately recentre humans as the benchmark of non-human worth. Rather than contravening the fundamental ontological commitments upon which the anthropocentrism of naturalism is based, the extension of rights to non-humans on the basis of proximity to human beings reinforces the naturalist framework, whether expansion is grounded in a shared spiritual interiority or in shared physical traits (e.g., similar biological attributes, genes, DNA).[73]

Non-human rights do not herald a new era in which humans relinquish their central place in existence. On the contrary, they contribute to the creation of a hyper-human, 'all too human' world. They function as a homogenizing force that absorbs all of existence under a universal human umbrella—an illusory attempt to erase alterity. Non-human rights privilege unity over multiplicity, sameness over difference, resulting in an effective 'flattening' of the world—a 'flat ontology' in all its splendour—that seeks to render all beings formally equivalent, stripping away exteriority.[74] They embody a totalizing impulse to transcend human biological and physical limitations by projecting an inflated humanity. They do not diminish humanity; they amplify it. These rights are humanity on steroids.

71 For this see Bryant (n 44) 210.

72 See Eduardo Kohn criticizing 'reductionist solutions that flatten important distinctions between humans and other kinds of beings'. See *How Forests Think. Toward an Anthropology beyond the Human* (University of California Press 2013) 7.

73 Descola (n 30) 194.

74 Of course, this flat ontology differs in significant ways from the one advocated by Manuel DeLanda—who coined the term 'flat ontology' in contrast to vertical or hierarchical ontologies—where no object holds ontological priority. Yet it shares with it a significant aspect: an obsession with equalizing—or flattening—individuals, even if this entails sacrificing ontological difference. See *Intensive Science and Virtual Philosophy* (Continuum 2002) 58.

Non-human rights are not the only new development marking this scenario of self-human affirmation but part of a broader shift in our political and technical imaginaries—perhaps a desperate reaction as our fantasies of absolute control unravel in the face of climate catastrophe. After the 'end of narratives', a new 'grand narrative' is in the making, permeating various philosophical, economic, scientific, and technical discourses. Unsurprisingly, this is also a narrative about endings—the end of biological man, a geological epoch, of the 'natural' world.

The idea of the Anthropocene, which has rapidly gained traction among natural and social scientists, is a prominent expression of this new techno-political imaginary. First proposed by Nobel-winning chemist Paul J. Crutzen and his collaborator, marine science specialist Eugene F. Stoermer, the term Anthropocene was to mark the beginning of a new geological era, defined by humanity's capacity to determine the global environment and reshape the planet.[75] For advocates of the Anthropocene, humans became a major geological force as their industrial activities changed the most basic physical processes of the earth[76] and altered the planet's geological strata.[77] Through technology, humans produced climatological and geological effects that were once solely the domain of nature. This fusion of humans with the objects they create—machines and technical instruments—mirrors the rapid human appropriation of the non-human world. In the Anthropocene, nature has become 'human nature'; wild, pristine, or untouched environments no longer exist.

The Anthropocene also marks the end of humans as distinct entities, as they become interwoven with their technologies and the no-longer natural world they shape around them.[78] Natural and human history converge as humanity merges with the planet.[79] Geological time and human chronological histories collapse. As Chakrabarty puts it, to see human beings as

75 Paul J Crutzen and Eugene F Stoermer, 'The Anthropocene' (2000) 41 *IGBP [International Geosphere-Biosphere Programme] Newsletter* 17.

76 As Oreskes put it: 'There are so many of us cutting down so many trees and burning so many billions of tons of fossil fuels that we have indeed become geological agents. We have changed the chemistry of our atmosphere, causing sea level to rise, ice to melt, and climate to change'. See Naomi Oreskes, 'The Scientific Consensus on Climate Change: How Do We Know We're Not Wrong?' in Joseph FC Dimento and Pamela Doughman (eds), *Climate Change What It Means for Us, Our Children, and Our Grandchildren* (Harvard University Press 2007) 93.

77 'What geologists can now see in rocks—from the subtle (think changes in the ratios of carbon and oxygen isotopes) to the gross (think plastic residues in marine sediments) points to large-scale, far-ranging and utterly pervasive human impacts'. See Naomi Oreskes, 'Does the Anthropocene Matter?' (2024) 330(1) *Scientific American* 89.

78 Following Ingold's distinction, we could say that this marks the end of the human as a species but not 'as a condition'. See (n 32) 15, 21.

79 Chakrabarty (n 10) 201, 207.

geological agents 'scale[s] up our imagination of the human [...] to call ourselves geological agents is to attribute to us a force on the same scale as that released at other times when there has been a mass extinction of species'.[80] Therefore the Anthropocene carries a bitter irony: if humans are narcissistically conceived as a force capable of reshaping the Earth, they are also seen as victims of an age that heralds extinction. Humanity is both super powerful agent—a geological and climatological force—and helpless victim. The fantasy of human mastery unleashed by the Anthropocene is countered by ubiquitous images of human disenfranchisement.

As the Anthropocene has emerged from the unintended consequences of human choices, its advocates argue that humans must confront their anthropogenic powers and learn to manage them for the greater good. The solution to the environmental damage we have caused thus lies in further deepening our technical mastery of the planet—shaping the climate and geophysical phenomena to our will through various forms of environmental 'management'.[81] The dream of a planet-machine designed, engineered, and constructed by humans should be pursued to its conclusion. Thus advocates believe that the negative effects of the Anthropocene can be countered by intensifying the forces causing it.[82] Crutzen, for example, has been a vocal supporter of large-scale geoengineering projects aimed at artificially optimizing the environment to prevent climate change.[83] Rather than representing a self-reflective moment in which humanity acknowledges its limitations and finitude in the face of environmental catastrophe, then, the Anthropocene—as the term itself suggests—announces the 'Age of Man', the era of a 'planetized Humanity', in which humans aspire to become a 'God Species',[84] transforming the planet in their image.

It should be noted that the Anthropocene coincides with a historical moment that the young Karl Marx prefigured in his early writings—a moment in which humanity, aided by science, industry, and technology, has the capacity to produce nature in such a way that it 'appears as his work and his reality'.[85] At this stage, man would 'contemplate himself in a world he himself has created'.[86] It should be no surprise that this solipsistic 'empire of the same' is emerging with unprecedented intensity in late capital-

80 ibid 206–207

81 Crutzen and Stoermer (n 75) 18.

82 ibid.

83 Paul Crutzen, 'Geology of Mankind' (2002) 415 *Nature* 23; 'Albedo Enhancement by Stratospheric Sulfur Injections: A Contribution to Solve a Policy Dilemma?' (2006) 77 *Climate Change* 216.

84 Mark Lynas, *The God Species: How Humans Can Really Save the Planet* (Fourth State 2012).

85 Karl Marx, *Early Writings* (Rodney Livingstone and Gregor Benton tr, Penguin 1974) 329.

86 ibid.

ism. The identity-driven thinking of the Anthropocene aligns closely with a world economy structured around the exchange principle, which necessarily demands the 'equivalence of non-equivalents'. Capitalism renders dissimilar things comparable, making everything universally commensurable and fungible—turning inherently different things into exchangeable commodities.[87] If the rise to prominence of human rights coincided with that of neoliberalism,[88] then the emergence of non-human rights might signal a new phase in capitalist exploitation. After all, imagining humanity as extending over nature provides the ontological foundation for the spiralling emergence of new forms of extractivism. From genetically modified organisms and biotech enhancements to the datafication of life and geoengineering,[89] the technological ethos of late capitalism is to reshape organic and inorganic life on Earth. If so, there is a timely convergence between the political economy of late capitalism and the political ontology of the Anthropocene. The flattening of distinctions between forms of existence accelerates the capitalist drive toward reification: if earlier forms of capitalism subjected fetishes to the law of equivalence, in the age of the capitalist Anthropocene 'equivalence itself becomes the fetish'.[90]

It becomes clear then that this anthropogenic grand narrative aligned with contemporary capitalist modes of extractivism, a narrative of which both non-human rights and the Anthropocene are momentous expressions, attempts to bridge the separation between humans and non-humans by erasing the existence of one of these poles. The non-human world dissolves into a universal inflated and flattened humanity. As Frédéric Neyrat observes, this is a form of denialism—maybe not that different from climate change

87 Max Horkheimer and Theodor W Adorno, *Dialectic of Enlightenment. Philosophical Fragments* (Gunzelin Schmid Noerr ed, Edmund Jephcott tr, Stanford University Press 2002) 4.

88 For the coupling between human rights and global neoliberal capital, see Douzinas (n 1) 65. On the joint ascendancy of human rights and neoliberalism, and how human rights functioned as the 'moral framework' for the market society, see Jessica Whyte, *The Morals of the Market: Human Rights and the Rise of Neoliberalism* (Verso 2019).

89 Arguably, the increasingly popular idea of 'ecological reparations' could also be included here as efforts to 'reconstruct' the Earth. These are forms of what Frédéric Neyrat calls 'eco-constructivism'. See *The Unconstructable Earth. An Ecology of Separation* (Drew S Burk tr, Fordham University Press 2019). According to Neyrat, modern humanity is trapped in a Sisyphean cycle of destruction and reconstruction.

90 Horkheimer and Adorno (n 73) 12. It could be said that the production of the 'non-place' in late capitalism—the erasure of spatial and cultural difference, of the local and particular—can be seen as yet another manifestation of this drive toward homogenization. As Marc Augé argues in *Non-Places: Introduction to an Anthropology of Supermodernity* (John Howe tr, Verso 1997) these spaces of transience and anonymity—airports, highways, shopping malls—reflect a form of social and cultural levelling (again, a 'flattening'), where the distinctiveness of place is subordinated to global circulation and standardized experience.

denialism—marked by 'a refusal to recognize the existence of one of these terms for the benefit of the lone identity of the other term'.[91] The goal is not to embrace the multiplicity and plurality of entities, but to create the One: a unified world, or to borrow the term John Law uses in a slightly different context, a 'One-World-World'.[92] Whether this represents yet another iteration of the transcendental attempt to reconcile the dualism of naturalist ontology or signals the rise of a different, *anaturalist* ontology, as Neyrat suggests, remains unclear.[93] In any case, he is correct in asserting that this grand narrative is not postmodern but hypermodern. It is a recycling of the modern project of domination over nature through instrumental reason, technification and artificialization, reinforcing its original aims without addressing the problematic dynamics it unleashed or its anthropocentric drive toward conquest.[94] In other words, these trends burn with the Enlightenment's flame while also casting its long and enduring totalitarian shadows.[95]

Without denying the planetary impact of human action or humans' vast power in shaping their environment, and without neglecting the multiple entanglements and relationalities between human and non-human worlds, critically scrutinizing the anthropogenic grand narrative involves recognizing that non-human rights, the Anthropocene, geoengineering, and other related discursive expressions offer an intoxicating cocktail that reaffirms human supremacy.[96] These developments are part of shared political, economic, and technical imaginaries of human aggrandizement that envision a disembodied, spiritual humanity subsuming the world—a positivist 'religion of humanity', as Comte once envisioned.[97] As in Christian eschatology, which tells us that the son of God died and shed his human flesh to be reborn as a god, humanity 2.0 aspires to leave its bodily constraints to become one with a fully humanized planet. A definitive triumph of the spirit over obsolete animal physicality.

The ancient desire to transcend biological finitude is emerging today with unprecedented force amid catastrophe. Its intensification and increased

91 Neyrat (n 89) 4.
92 John Law, 'What's Wrong with a One-World-World' (2015) 16(1) *Distinktion: Journal of Social Theory* 126–139.
93 Neyrat (n 89) 4.
94 ibid 3.
95 On the totalitarian nature of Enlightenment and its relation to humanity's desire for domination over nature, see Horkheimer and Adorno (73) 4.
96 It goes without saying that transhumanism, accelerationism, and certain strands of posthuman thought are embedded within this broader discourse. The drive for connectivity and the 'network fever' that characterize much of contemporary social theory are likewise part of this trend. On this latter point, see Alain Pottage, 'Why Nature Has No Rights' in Alvarez-Nakagawa and Douzinas (n 26) 39–65.
97 On this see Boris Groys, 'Genealogy of Humanity' (2018) 88 *e-flux Journal* 1.

visibility occur during a new cycle of capitalist exploitation as humans find themselves in a state of heightened fragility.[98] Confronted with the real prospect of extinction, humanity's existential anxiety is sublimated through the projection of an unbounded, all-encompassing version of itself. As Heidegger observed, 'man, precisely as the one so threatened, exalts himself to the posture of the lord of the earth. In this way the impression comes to prevail that everything man encounters exists only insofar as it is his construct. This illusion gives rise in turn to one final delusion: It seems as though man everywhere and always only encounters himself'.[99]

Is this yet another indication that (against the odds and predictions) the human has not yet died? Is this a new kind of humanism—a 'non-human humanism'? Man is erased from the sands of our shores, only to reappear on another in a different guise.

Conclusion

Twenty-five years ago, midway through *The End of Human Rights*, Douzinas took a provocative stance on the subject of rights. The question of who should be regarded as subject of human rights appeared obvious to him: 'rights exist for the sake of humanity, they are the acme of humanism'. And yet, he acknowledged, 'if we question the self-evidence of common sense, the intellectual reasons for creating human rights instead of rights for all living beings are not clear'.[100]

Interestingly, the rise of non-human rights signals both the end of human rights and its unchecked expansion—it is both an *end* and a *new beginning*. Admittedly, non-human rights are already part of the broader discursive trajectory of human rights. Thus, it comes as no surprise that some scholarship has started to question whether human rights are exclusively human, considering non-human rights as 'a necessary dialectical derivation',[101] 'the logical extension of human rights', or simply 'part of the same normative enterprise'.[102] Non-human rights supporters have recently started to see non-human rights as the 'fourth generation of human rights'[103] or as 'new human

98 ibid 4.
99 Heidegger (n 2) 27.
100 Douzinas, *The End of Human Rights* (n 12) 184. In light of his more recent work on the 'rights of robots', one might add that Douzinas would now say 'for all living and *non-living beings*'. See Costas Douzinas, 'Do Androids Dream of Having Rights' in Alexis Alvarez-Nakagawa and Costas Douzinas (eds), *Non-Human Rights. Critical Perspectives* (Elgar 2024).
101 Paola Cavalieri 'Are Human Rights Human?' (2005) 4(2) *Logos* 2.
102 Alasdair Cochrane (2013), 'From Human Rights to Sentient Rights' (2012) 16(5) *Critical Review of International Social and Political Philosophy* 655–675.
103 Andrew Vincent, *The Politics of Human Rights* (OUP 2010) 147.

rights',[104] recalling Stone's characterization of them as an 'additional stage' in the long process of extending rights to the entire human genus.[105] In this context, it is revealing of this tendency that some animal rights scholars, who have typically been at the forefront of these discussions, are calling for a 'One Rights' approach—a unifying normative umbrella for both humans and non-humans,[106] 'a new (post-)human rights paradigm for the Anthropocene'.[107] Approaches that make human rights the paradigmatic model for the rights of non-humans are clearly in tune with the discursive efforts of a monistic world. The reason that non-human rights are commonly seen as a desirable normative framework for the Anthropocene is clear: as we have seen, both ideas belong to shared political, economic, and technical imaginaries that aim to expand humanity beyond the confines of the human, realizing aspirations for a 'One-World-World'.

It thus makes sense to ask whether the end of human rights marks the dawn of the non-human, or whether the seemingly opposite trajectories of human and non-human rights are actually in furtive alliance. Have the utopian ends of the former not turned into the New Atlantis of the latter, where, to use Francis Bacon's words, 'the enlarging of the bounds of human empire, to the effecting of all things possible' becomes a reality?[108] The transcendental narcissism that characterizes human rights appears to be expanding through the non-human-rights project's imperialist desire

104 See Tomasz Pietrzykowsky, 'Animal Right' in Andreas von Arnauld, Kerstin von der Decken, Mart Susi (eds), *Cambridge Handbook of New Human Rights: Recognition, Novelty, Rhetoric* (Cambridge University Press 2020) 243–252; and William F Schulz and Sushma Raman, *The Coming Good Society: Why New Realities Demand New Rights* (Harvard University Press 2020).

105 Stone (n 53). This discussion has primarily unfolded within the fields of animal rights and the rights of nature. However, it is important to note that most scholars and advocates of machine rights also view these rights as either human rights or a variation of them. For an overview, see John-Stewart Gordon, 'Human Rights for Robots? A Literature Review' (2021) 1 *AI and Ethics* 579–591. Some scholars, such as David Gunkel (n 61), prefer to speak of 'robot rights'.

106 See Saskia Stucki and Tom Sparks, 'The Elephant in the (Court)room: Interdependence of Human and Animal Rights in the Anthropocene' (*EJIL: Talk!*, June 2020) <https://www.ejiltalk.org/the-elephant-in-the-courtroom-interdependence-of-human-and-animal-rights-in-the-anthropocene/> accessed 15 December 2024. See also Stucki (n 9) 9. This normative approach relies on the 'One Health' (or 'One Welfare') perspective in the natural sciences, which argues that the interconnectedness of human, animal, and ecosystem health should lead to an integrative, unifying framework. See Jakob Zinsstag, Esther Schelling, Lisa Crump, Maxine Whittaker, Marcel Tanner, Craig Stephen (eds), *One Health: The Theory and Practice of Integrated Health Approaches* (CABI 2021).

107 Stucki (n 9) 12.

108 *The New Atlantis* (Watchmaker Publishing 2010) 42.

to extend humanity beyond its bodily limits.[109] This is a self-aggrandizing project that erases difference and eliminates alterity. Non-human rights acknowledge the multiple relationships between humans and non-humans, yet redirect this relationality to serve the interests of an exceptional humanity that encompasses all of existence. This humanization is problematic not only because of the narcissistic and impoverished image of the world it projects, but also because of the solutions it brings forth: from geoengineering to the datafication of life, humanity's *Ge-stell* is invested in the creation of the *more-than-human*—not as a reduction of the human in favour of the 'other-than-human', but as an amplified humanity accompanied by a consequent flattening of the world.

Rights are indeed the 'ideology of the end', as Douzinas pointed out.[110] Not so much because they mark 'the end of ideologies', as Fukuyama had it,[111] but because they signal the progressive assimilation of all that exists into humanity. Notably, Hegel thought that the 'end of history' would be the complete identification between the Spirit and the world rather than the mere overcoming of political conflict and antagonism.[112] In the journey of the Spirit, human consciousness recognizes its identity with the rational structure of reality, thereby transcending historical oppositions. The journey leads the Spirit back to itself in a process of self-appearance and self-manifestation: 'All activities of the Spirit are nothing but various ways of reducing what is external to the inwardness which the Spirit itself is, and it is only by this reduction, by this idealization or assimilation of the external that the Spirit becomes and is the Spirit'.[113] The interior world of humankind becomes the world as such. In this Hegelian theodicy, the human spirit and the world merge into one, fulfilling a long-standing desire for reconciliation and unification. At this last stage, humanity is finally free because 'it does not will anything alien, extrinsic, foreign to itself'.[114] In the solipsistic and monistic world of the end of history, the Spirit becomes absolute (universal and infinite), and humanity is at last free to desire itself and nothing else.

Both human and non-human rights can be seen as a promise of the fulfilment and a haunting reminder of this ravaging dialectic, which reveals a human yearning to achieve unity, not merely to regard oneself as a part of

109 As imperialism begins with the assertion of the singularity of the self, the desire for a humankind that encompasses the planet is simply the natural conclusion of a humanity conceived as extraordinary.

110 Douzinas, *The End of Human Rights* (n 12) 246.

111 Francis Fukuyama, *The End of History and the Last Man* (Penguin 2012).

112 Georg Wilhelm Hegel, *The Philosophy of History* (J. Sibree tr, Dover 2004) 488ff.

113 Georg Wilhelm Hegel, *Philosophy of Mind, Part Three of the Encyclopaedia of the Philosophical Sciences* (W. Wallace and A. V. Miller tr, OUP 2007) § 381 Zusatz. Translation slightly modified.

114 ibid 489.

the world, but to perceive the world as a reflection of the self. This is a violent form of reconciliation through self-assertion which seeks only mastery. It is yet another variation of the master-slave dialectic. We must therefore not push this evolving dynamic to its ultimate conclusion—the complete erasure of alterity—but to find a way out of it. In other words, we should break free from the 'end' of which we have been in relentless pursuit.

12

THE ERRANCY OF RIGHTS AND THE REFUSAL OF THE LAW

Patrick Hanafin

> We should not stop arguing that no-one should be without rights.[1]
>
> The demand for rights can be used also for a politics of rupture and radical change.[2]
>
> Politics is something that is declared in the face of policing, defined as the law that prescribes what emerges and what is heard, what can be counted and what cannot be counted.[3]

The work of Costas Douzinas on the theory of human rights provides us with an example of how the errant letter of rights arrives in the hands of those who are without them.[4] This errancy of rights provides us with a way of reimagining rights themselves and points towards an emancipatory politics to come. Using Jacques Ranciere's work on the orphan letter and Maurice Blanchot's work on refusal I argue that Douzinas' work puts rights in the hands of those who should never have had them and points to a certain refusal to be ordered by the biopolitical order. In the original analysis of orphan letters, Plato notes how literature is an orphan letter in the *Phaedrus*.[5] Rancière uses

1 Costas Douzinas, *States of Exception: Human Rights, Biopolitics, Utopia* (Elgar 2023) 177.
2 ibid 171.
3 Jacques Rancière, 'The Cause of the Other' (1998) 4(2) *Parallax* 28–29.
4 See Costas Douzinas, *The End of Human Rights* (Hart 2000); *Human Rights and Empire: The Political Philosophy of Cosmopolitanism* (Routledge 2007); *The Radical Philosophy of Rights* (Routledge 2019); Douzinas (n 1).
5 See Jacques Rancière, *The Flesh of Words: The Politics of Writing*, (Stanford University Press 2004) 102.

DOI: 10.4324/9781032622224-12

this allusion to the orphan letter to develop a thinking of democratic literature. As he puts it: 'Writing is... the orphan utterance, deprived of the voice that gives it meaning and legitimacy, diverted from the trajectory by which the *logos* is a principle of life'.[6] It subverts the dominant discourse. Similarly, rights in the hands of the oppressed, or 'rights of the street'[7] as Douzinas calls them, are, to paraphrase Hector Kollias: 'paradigmatic of the errant letter, reach[ing] every and any addressee, can be read by anyone, including *particularly* those who *should not* read them'.[8]

Rights as Orphan Letters

The inscription of rights in legal texts represses their original revolutionary force and instead orders them, in the process, divorcing them from the individual material beings who are deemed to possess them as subjects of law. Such a policing of rights hides their insurrectionary origins and political force, just as liberal political discourse more generally represses the representation of conflict. In *Disagreement*, Jacques Rancière paints a resolutely bleak picture of the conflict-free biocratic-juridical state where 'the law... divests the state of the politics of which it once divested the people'.[9] However, such a diagnosis does not leave us without hope of resistance and political action. The order of the police can be interrupted by the becoming political of the people (the uncounted) via political action or political subjectivation. As Sam Chambers reminds us, such a becoming political of the people occurs:

> But seldom, and only by way of a never predictable, and always insurrectionary, moment. This is a moment when a given order of domination and a given regime of hierarchy are radically called into question by the emergence of a political subject, a demos. Importantly, the demos that undoes a given order does not and cannot exist prior to its surprising and unpredictable appearance on the stage of politics.[10]

Such a conflictual model may allow us to think about the possibility of the reappropriation of rights as the 'action of subjects who, by working the

6 ibid 103.
7 Douzinas (n 1) 172.
8 Hector Kollias, 'Taking Sides: Jacques Rancière and Agonistic Literature' (2007) 30(2) *Paragraph* 90.
9 Jacques Rancière, *Disagreement: Politics and Philosophy* (University of Minnesota Press 1995) 112.
10 Samuel A. Chambers, *The Lessons of Rancière* (OUP 2012) 8–9.

interval between identities, reconfigure the distributions of the public and the private, the universal and the particular'.[11]

As Etienne Balibar has observed: 'Democratic citizenship is conflictual or it does not exist'.[12] In speaking of what he terms the 'conflict-shy forms of government' in the developed world which deny the 'insurrectionary element'[13] of politics, he proposes the model of a 'counter-counter revolution' as a mode of resisting this tendency.[14] Such moments of counter-counter revolution irrupt within the ordered realms of the political to reveal the impossibility of a democratic citizenship without conflict, disobedience and insubordination, provoking us to question accepted modes of thinking liberal democracy, sovereignty and citizenship in order to bring to the surface in Patchen Markell's rich phrase: 'the spirit of insubordination that animates [democracy]'.[15] This writing of insubordination animates Douzinas' writing. It is a writing in the narrative voice in Blanchot[16] and Derrida's[17] sense which contests the narrating voice of biopolitics and hegemonic neoliberal laws. As Douzinas states: 'Political conflict and resistance always return and defy claims of social inertia. Politics operates and rights work fully only when an excluded group or a radical ideology challenges the social hierarchy. In such cases, rights become a battle cry and a weapon for those who fight for radical change'.[18]

Such incidences of interruption irrupt within the realm of the police order to reveal the impossibility of a democratic citizenship without conflict, disobedience and insubordination, provoking us to question accepted modes of thinking sovereignty and rights.[19] Such an exercise allows us to interrogate the limit point of the police order in an impolitical fashion. This is a thinking which calls for continuous intervention in the police order with the aim of expanding the space of what *Rancière* terms politics, 'the ongoing creation of equality'.[20] Such acts of resistance can be seen as a means of appropriating rights in the service of equality. In such a moment rights become errant,

11 Jacques Rancière, *Hatred of Democracy* (Verso 2006) 61–62.
12 Etienne Balibar, 'Resistance, Insurrection, Insoumission' in *La Proposition de l'Egaliberte: Essais Politiques, 1989–2009* (Presses Universitaires Francaises 2010) 347.
13 Etienne Balibar, *We the People of Europe: Reflections on Transnational Citizenship* (Princeton University Press 2004) 119.
14 ibid 125.
15 Patchen Markell, 'The Rule of the People: Arendt, Arche and Democracy' (2006) 100(1) *The American Political Science Review* (February) 2.
16 Maurice Blanchot, 'The Narrative Voice' in Maurice Blanchot (ed), *The Infinite Conversation* (University of Minnesota Press 1993) 379–387.
17 Jacques Derrida, *Parages* (Stanford University Press 2011) 130–131.
18 Douzinas (n 1) 176.
19 Markell (n 15) 2.
20 Jacques Rancière, *On the Shores of Politics* (Verso 2007) 84.

wandering from their proper place as dead letters in biocratic constitutional documents into modes of political subjectivation in the mouths and hands of the oppressed. This errancy of rights leads to them becoming something other than what the police order intended them to be. Rights re-emerge in the mouths of those who should not have them, in 'the movement by which these available words take hold of and divert from their intended path people who had not been concerned with dealing with logos or the community'.[21] The errancy of the letter of rights creates a space for their unexpected and improper use not as means of binding through repetition in the biocratic order but as an opening to a thinking of a radical politics of law and rights.

Rights are then not just *dispositifs* which exclude and order but can be appropriated by those who should not have them in order to provoke an always provisional redistribution of the sensible. In other words, what is possible is, to use Bonnie Honig's phrase, a staging of 'dissensus by working with materials provided by the city of consensus'.[22] In viewing rights as orphan letters available to all to adapt and use in the staging of dissent, we have an insight into the agonistic nature of law. This reading of rights is an attempt to provide an agonistic counterpart to the appropriation of rights by power.[23] Through such contestation it is possible, as Honig reminds us, to shift: 'the terms of the current partition and gain some adjustment in its partition of the sensible'.[24] Such a challenge could be put in Rancièrean terms as the instantiation of what he calls: 'the community of sharing... membership in a single world which can only be expressed in adversarial terms, and a coming together which can only occur in conflict'.[25] As Todd May puts it:

> Politics is not to be confused with the success or failure of change, even if change is its goal. Politics is a process. It is the emergence of collective subject acting under the presupposition of its equality, an acting that disrupts a particular police order. This does not mean that the question of political effects or political change is unimportant. It is of the highest importance. Political movements often fail. However, we must distinguish the existence of politics from its effectiveness. Otherwise, we risk

21 Jacques Rancière, 'Balzac and the Island of the Book' in *The Flesh of Words: The Politics of Writing* (Stanford University Press 2004) 94–112.
22 Bonnie Honig, *Antigone Interrupted* (Cambridge University Press 2013) 146.
23 See Bonnie Honig, 'Antigone's Two Laws: Greek Tragedy and the Politics of Humanism' (2010) 41(1) *New Literary History* 4.
24 Honig (n 22) 145.
25 Rancière (n 20) 49.

> missing it in the moment of its happening, and on the other hand, ascribing it where it does not exist.[26]

In Douzinas' claiming of rights, something other than rights is formed: a new mode of resistance to the hegemony of institutionalized neoliberal rights discourse. As Douzinas notes: 'Human rights have become an integral part of power relations, preceding, accompanying and legitimizing the penetration of all parts of the world by the new order'.[27]

Policing Rights

As Tim Campbell reminds us, conflict lies at the heart of politics as 'the radical possibility of its own negation'.[28] For Campbell, the valorization of order in political discourse 'immobilizes and negates conflict'.[29] This approach coincides with Roberto Esposito's diagnosis of the repression of conflict in liberal political discourses in his 'Ten Thoughts on the Political'. As Esposito observes:

> if antinomy lies outside of the language of philosophy and politics it is because it constitutes its unrepresentable foundation, untranslatable into its universal law and in any case always emerging from the margins and the gaps in the philosophical narrative.[30]

Esposito, in a different manner to Rancière, has examined such a praxis for the purposes of rethinking the political in terms of conflict rather than consensus.[31] In comparing both thinkers, Etienne Balibar demonstrates their potential similarity as impolitical thinkers:

> this critique asks us to pass beyond the position of values (and especially legal values, or forms of legitimation of law or the state, but also of civil

26 Todd May, 'Rancière in South Carolina' in Gabriel Rockhill and Phillip Watts (eds), *Jacques Rancière: History, Politics, Aesthetics* (Duke University Press 2009) 116.

27 Douzinas (n 1) 191–192.

28 Tim Campbell, 'Thinking the Law with Roberto Esposito' (2011) paper presented at the Annual Meeting of the Association for the Study of Law, Culture and the Humanities, University of Nevada, Las Vegas, 12 March 2011.

29 ibid.

30 Roberto Esposito, *Dieci Pensieri Sulla Politica* (Il Mulino 2011) 30–31.

31 See Roberto Esposito, *Terza Persona: Politica della Vita e Filosofia dell'Impersonale* (Einaudi 2007); *Immunitas: The Protection and Negation of Life* (Polity 2011); *Dall'Impolitico all'Impersonale: Conversazioni Filosofiche* (Mimesis 2012); 'The *dispositif* of the Person' (2012) 8(1) *Law Culture and the Humanities* 17–30.

society or revolutionary action) and to turn toward the genesis or creation of those values and the antinomies involved in that event or process.[32]

As Balibar notes in trying to draw out similarities between impolitics and disagreement:

> policing, in general, is a matter of demands; it seeks to give everyone a fair share in the distribution of the common good, by authoritarian or contractual procedures. Democratic politics, in contrast, has as its unique criterion the 'share of the shareless': that is, the requirement of equality set off against social identity or personal merit.[33]

He observes that: 'politics is constituted by the incessant encounter between its own egalitarian logic and the logic of policing, "which is never set up in advance"'.[34]

He goes on to argue: 'There is indeed something impolitical in the way Rancière develops his radical critique of consensus and the common good (commonwealth) or in the way he shatters unitary, identity-based representations of communities'.[35]

Esposito is concerned with the deactivation of *dispositifs* such as that of the juridical person in favor of the expansion of the space of the common. For him, the notion of the person inherited from Roman Law constitutes a mode of disembodying the individual, of devaluing the material in favor of the abstract. This valorization of an abstract rational subject over the mere life of actually existing individuals leads to the denigration of the flesh in favor of abstract reason. Individual lives are devalued in favor of a politics which rules over these lives. As Esposito observes: 'The person doesn't coincide with the body in which it inheres, just as the mask is never one with the actor's face'.[36] As such it can be seen as a *dispositif* which allows the material lives of individuals to be subjected to power, to be constructed as objects of power. For Esposito this notion of material singularities coming together to act in common provides an example of the power of a collective being in common of material lives. This is a politics *of* life not a politics *over* life.[37] This critique of the dominant narration of the political as order highlights what erstwhile colleague of Rancière, Etienne Balibar has called the

32 Etienne Balibar, 'What Is Political Philosophy?' in Gabriel Rockhill and Phillip Watts (eds), *Jacques Rancière: History, Politics, Aesthetics* (Duke University Press 2009) 95–104.
33 ibid 102.
34 ibid 102.
35 ibid 103.
36 Esposito, *Dall'Impolitico all'Impersonale* (n 31) 25.
37 Esposito, *Terza Persona* (n 31).

repressed 'insurrectionary element'.[38] of politics. Balibar calls for a 'counter-counter revolution' as a mode of resisting this tendency.[39] Such moments of counter-counter revolution irrupt within the ordered realms of the police order to reveal the impossibility of democracy without conflict, disobedience and insubordination, provoking us to question accepted modes of thinking liberal democracy, sovereignty and citizenship. Such a thinking of Rancière allows us to create 'zones of hegemonic struggle that work against the consensual idyll of the state'.[40]

One way of doing this would be to take a concept like Balibar's 'right to politics' which implies that no one can be emancipated from above but only through one's own acts[41] and discover how it might provide a means of how such an interruption occurs at the heart of the police order and in so doing makes us rethink rights in a more emancipatory key. In this mode we see rights as being appropriated by those who were not supposed to have them, mimicking their use quite successfully but not being deluded into thinking that rights can be the end point of the struggle. Starting from the principle of equality one is always required to intervene in the police order to readjust the distribution of the sensible, a constant throwing oneself at the system without any guarantee of success and eventual incorporation into the police order. In this mode of the 'right to politics' the self declares itself speaks/appropriates the errant word/orphan letter of rights, as an active participant in political affairs. This can be seen as a working of the interval between order and conflict, a staging of dissensus which manifests the repressed conflict which is at the heart of politics. It is an instance of the stubborn refusal of mere life to be categorized and ruled. Indeed, to borrow Judith Butler's phrase such refusals can be seen as: 'critical acts of resistance... incendiary acts that somehow, incredibly, live through the violence they oppose, even if we do not yet know in what ways such lives will survive'.[42] Douzinas' work is a means of bringing to the surface the repressed 'insurrectionary element' at the heart of rights thinking.

(W)ri(gh)ting Rights

For contemporary regimes of biopower, what is essential is that the life of individual citizens is formed by law and power.[43] This forming of life has, as one of its aims, the need to make all acts predictable. The unforeseen act

38 Balibar (n 13) 119.
39 ibid 125.
40 Simon Critchley, *Infinitely Demanding* (Verso 2007) 130.
41 Etienne Balibar, *Politics and the Other Scene* (Verso 2002) 167.
42 Judith Butler, *Frames of War: When is Life Grievable?* (Verso 2009) 62.
43 See further Costas Douzinas (n 1) Chapter 1.

or the disorderly word, the word not sought or extracted by the agents of power, shocks the complacency of the biocratic state. Such disorderly words testify to a short-circuiting of the order of the state, in which the fiction of politics as order is exposed. As J.M. Coetzee has put it, such words 'may have a meaning quite different from what the lexicon says, where the metaphoric spark is always one jump ahead of the decoding function, where another, unforeseen reading is always possible'.[44] Such unforeseen readings and detournements of accepted understandings are not tolerated and order must be seen to be restored after they have been uttered.[45] Every word must remain in its place. The surprising word which issues from nowhere, authorized by no one and with no end other than as an appeal, constitutes what Maurice Blanchot has termed 'the right to unexpected speech'.[46]

The writing of Douzinas could be seen to enact Roberto Esposito's description of writing as 'moving from the first to the third person'.[47] As Esposito notes, such a writing is:

> not reducible to a defined category, to the point that instead of speaking from the neutral, one speaks as the neutral, by which is meant a one hundred and eighty degree turn in our entire logical and semantic apparatus leading to the passage from the first or second person to the third person.[48]

This is a writing which does not seek to appropriate identity and form selves, but is, rather, what Blanchot calls a 'communism of writing' which constitutes 'plural speech'.[49] Such plural speech for Blanchot: 'short-circuits all speech. [It is] an urgent and violent appeal, a decision for rupture... it is only the urgency it announces, bound to an impatient and always excessive demand, since excess is its only erasure'.[50] It is a writing of selves which exceeds fixing. As such, it does not impose a form, but can be seen in Deleuze's terms as writing as becoming:

> To write is... not to impose a form... Writing is a question of becoming, always incomplete, always in the midst of being formed... it is a process... Writing is inseparable from becoming... always has a component of flight that escapes its own formalization... To become is not to attain

44 JM Coetzee, *Diary of a Bad Year* (Vintage 2008) 23.
45 See Douzinas' discussion of the fear of Douzinism in Greece in Douzinas (n 1).
46 Maurice Blanchot, *Les Intellectuels en Question* (Farrago 2000) 36.
47 Esposito, *Terza Persona* (n 31) 159.
48 ibid 157–158.
49 Maurice Blanchot, *Political Writings 1953–1993* (Fordham University Press 2010) 85.
50 Maurice Blanchot, *L'Amitie* (Gallimard 1971) 116.

> a form… but to find the zone of proximity, indiscernibility, or undifferentiation where one can no longer be distinguished from a woman, an animal, or a molecule – neither imprecise nor general, but unforeseen and non-preexistent, singularized out of a population rather than determined in a form.[51]

As such, it is emblematic of Blanchot's attempt to seek 'liberation from [the] exclusionary powers of concepts themselves'.[52]

Douzinas' counter-model of rights does not constitute a rejection of rights as such, but forces us to rethink the way in which we imagine rights as tools of emancipation in so-called liberal democratic societies. As Hannah Arendt has reminded us: 'the Rights of man… had never been philosophically established but merely formulated… had never been politically secured but merely proclaimed'.[53] This declaring or indeed dictating of rights in the ordered State represses their original revolutionary force and instead orders them, in the process divorcing them from the individual material beings who are deemed to possess them as subjects of law. Such ordered forms of right hide their insurrectionary origins. In order to address this paradox, Arendt formulates the notion of 'the right to have rights' as a mode of thinking the limitations of institutionalized rights discourse.[54] A call such as Arendt's 'right to have rights' forces us out of the complacency of thinking that the mere declaration of rights is the end of the struggle for rights and freedoms.

In his book *The Radical Philosophy of Rights*, Douzinas uses the example of Maurice Blanchot's right to insubordination as an example of what he terms 'righting rights'.[55] This is an apt example and helps shed light on Douzinas' critique. Blanchot's right to insubordination was contained in a document called *The Declaration of the Right to Insubordination in the Algerian War* in 1960. This Declaration, more commonly known as the Manifesto of the 121, issues a call to refuse to take arms against the Algerian people. It called for a questioning of the actions which the state perpetrated in the name of the people. It was part of the strategy of insubordination in response to the persecution of those who supported the anti-colonial cause in Algeria and coincided with the trial of Francis Jeanson and the other so-called '*porteurs des valises*' in September 1960. In this trial, the authorities used treason laws against those who carried money out of the country for the FLN, the Algerian anti-colonial movement. The Jeanson trial was

51 Gilles Deleuze, 'Literature and Life' (1997) 23(2) *Critical Inquiry* 225–226.

52 Zakir Paul, 'Introduction: Affirming the Rupture' in Maurice Blanchot (ed), *Political Writings 1953–1993* (Fordham University Press 2010).

53 Hannah Arendt, *The Origins of Totalitarianism* (Harcourt, Brace, Janovitch 1951) 446.

54 ibid 296. See also Costas Douzinas (n 1) chapter 1.

55 Douzinas, *The Radical Philosophy of Rights* (n 4) 190.

an example of the state's attempt to re-impose order on the insurrectionary elements who threatened national unity by supporting the cause of the anti-colonial movement in Algeria. Indeed, the state went so far as to order speech in the trial to such an extent that the presiding judicial authorities forbade the utterance of the words 'Algerian war' during the case and imposed the official state description of the war as a 'police action'. Such a 'capture of speech' is what the strategy of refusal and insubordination of Blanchot and his companions contest. Such a strategy of insubordination is all that remains when citizens' voices go unheard and they are forced to corroborate in a false narrative of national unity. It is a refusal to accept that citizens and their words can be formed by the state. As the Manifesto states:

> The undersigned – considering that everyone must come to an opinion about acts that it is henceforth impossible to present as trivial episodes of an individual adventure... considering that they themselves, in their place, and according to their means, have the duty to intervene, not to give advice to men who have to decide personally when faced with such grave problems, but to ask those who judge them not to be taken in by the equivocal aspect of words and values – declare
>
> - We respect the refusal to take arms against the Algerian people, and we judge this to be justified
> - We respect the conduct of the French citizens who consider it their duty to bring help and protection to the oppressed Algerians in the name of the French people, and we judge this to be justified
> - The cause of the Algerian people, which contributes to ruining the colonial system in a decisive way, is the cause of all free men.[56]

The Declaration makes the move from dictation to contestation, from the mere declaration of rights to an active performance of rights. It is a response to state violence which is both an act of witnessing and an active witnessing. Instead of imposing a community of citizens bound together by force of law and state power, the Declaration called for an effacement of the sense of community built on identity. In De Gaulle's France, the dominant politics saw the nation as having a homogeneous identity that needed to be put to work in maintaining order and stability. As Blanchot had written in his 1958 essay 'The Essential Perversion', De Gaulle had posited an imaginary void in the political that required to be filled.[57] For De Gaulle, this void would be filled with the illusory French nation, made up of one homogenous people with an identity. Two years later the Manifesto of the 121 would

56 *Manifesto of the 121*, 1960.
57 Blanchot (n 49) 8–14.

respond to this 'essential perversion' of law and politics by refusing all identity. The perverse commonality offered by De Gaulle was exposed by the event of the Declaration, which pointed instead to the possibility of community beyond the formed lives of the biocratic state.

The Declaration, in effect, acted as a 'counter-law' which challenged De Gaulle's perversion of true politics. In a short essay entitled 'Refusal' written in 1959, in opposition to De Gaulle's capture of power and the denigration of democratic citizenship, Blanchot had noted that refusal was a means of exposing the perversion of democracy that was being carried out. He noted that: 'Those who refuse and who are bound by the force of refusal know that they are not yet together. The time of common affirmation is precisely what has been taken away from them'.[58] Similarly, Douzinas' call for a politics of rights to come[59] is a refusal of the accepted neoliberal politics of human rights.

Etienne Balibar has attempted to make a link between Blanchot's right to insubordination and Arendt's right to have rights and its implications for a more radical thinking of rights. For Balibar, Blanchot's right to insubordination is an example of:

> 'right without the law', which is founded on nothing other than its own claim and its exercise… right without the law is a suspension or interruption which takes us to the limit where the juridical order turns against itself… There is a very great affinity between right without the law and the right to have rights, which are like the inversion of each other, [a] negative side… possessed of an affirmative power – and [a] positive side… filled with dispossession.[60]

It is in this sense that Blanchot's insubordinate performance can be seen in terms of what Balibar has termed a 'right to politics'. Such a 'right to politics' implies that no one can be emancipated from above, but only through one's own acts.[61] In this mode of the right to politics, the self declares itself not as the subject matter of rights, but as an active participant in political affairs.[62] As Balibar observes, an intervention such as the Declaration and the thinking behind it annul the condition of subjectivity:

58 ibid 7.
59 See Douzinas (n 1) Chapter 10.
60 Etienne Balibar, 'Blanchot l'insoumi' in M Antelme et al (eds), *Blanchot dans son siècle* (Sens Public 2009) 303.
61 Balibar (n 41) 167.
62 Indeed, Douzinas took part, as a minister, in the Syriza government. See Costas Douzinas, *Syriza in Power: Diary of an Accidental Politician* (Polity 2017).

> The insubordinate one is... s/he who refuses and... annuls the condition of the subject (subject of law, subject of power, subject of sovereignty)... The gesture of insubordination is the return to that primary moment which conditions the very possibility of obedience... There is a fundamental disobedience which precedes and makes possible at once submission to authority, to the law, to institutional power to the extent that it is the condition of free men... and insubordination when it is provoked by the degeneration or the disqualification of political authority, the perversion of law... when torture is used, or when they declare a war which doesn't have as its objective the defense of the nation... it is a question of evoking under the name of insubordination a "non-negative" mode of refusal'.[63]

For Balibar, disobedience then becomes the only possible positive condition of law: 'to disobey the law is not equivalent to obeying the law, but without a possibility of disobedience there is no legitimate institution of obedience – a thesis that does not have its foundation in the idea of human nature, but is rooted in the pragmatic understanding of how democratic regimes, 'constitutions of liberty', emerge and collapse in history'.[64] Disobedience does not lead to an overcoming of law which would lead to either anarchy or totalitarianism, but rather creates the possibility for action and for the cultivation of freedom. As Balibar observes:

> there is no political community without the inclusion of a principle of disobedience or dissidence within the legal frame of obedience itself, which radically challenges the purely legal understanding of the law, and refutes the sovereign tautology, 'law is law'... What is strange, indeed remarkable, is that the 'negative' argument provides the institution with its only possible positive condition, and the positive argument entirely concerns a 'dialectical' inclusion of the negative within the positivity of the law, albeit not in order to overcome it, rather in order to give it life.[65]

This detournement of the term 'right' gives it the sense which Michel Foucault gave it when he spoke of moving: 'in the direction of a new right, one which must indeed be anti-disciplinary, but at the same time liberated from the principle of sovereignty'.[66] Douzinas' work is such an instance of a new right, and reminds us that the demand to engage in insurrectionary politics of rights remains an unending one. The disavowal of conflictual

63 Balibar (n 60) 297.
64 Etienne Balibar, '(De)constructing the Human as Human Institution: A Reflection on the Coherence of Hannah Arendt's Practical Philosophy' (2007) 74 *Social Research* 735.
65 ibid 737.
66 Michel Foucault, *The History of Sexuality* Vol 1 (Vintage 1990) 90.

engagement at the heart of democratic politics in favor of a managed consensus in which individuals are formed as citizen subjects calls for a rethinking of accepted modes of sovereignty and subjectivity. Douzinas' thinking points us in such a direction.

Acts of writing such as Douzinas' are critical acts of resistance and can be seen as a means of appropriating rights in the service of equality.[67] In such a moment rights become errant, wandering from their proper place as dead letters in biocratic constitutional documents into modes of political subjectivation in the mouths of the oppressed. This literariness of rights is an interesting one to pursue, making them something other than what the police order intended them to be. This reading of rights is an attempt to provide an agonistic counterpart to the appropriation of rights by power in the name of humanity to engage in imperial wars and suppression of citizens 'in quest of a politics that is not reducible to an ethics nor founded on finitude'.[68] Through such contestation it is possible, as Honig reminds us, to shift: 'the terms of the current partition and gain some adjustment in its partition of the sensible'.[69] However, success in a political sense is not always possible yet even if

> 'The action of dissensus may fail in instrumental terms while nonetheless succeeding for, in such action, equality is enacted and experienced'. Butler points this out: 'in the asking, in the petition, we have already become something new'.[70]

Conclusion

Douzinas' work constitutes a stubborn refusal to submit to the biocratic order, to the order of the proper name. The action of refusing this biopolitical order points to the beginning of a resistance to biopolitical modes of production. In their discussion of refusal as a mode of political resistance, Michael Hardt and Antonio Negri refer to Etienne de la Boetie's politics of refusal in which resistance can be performed as much in a deliberate refusal to support tyranny as in the violent toppling of the tyrant. As de la Boetie exhorted: 'Resolve to serve no more, and you are at once freed'.[71] It is in such a refusal that Hardt and Negri see the beginning of a liberatory politics.

67 See Douzinas (n 1) Chapter 10.
68 Honig (n 23) 4.
69 Honig (n 22) 145.
70 ibid 143.
71 Etienne de la Boetie and P Bonnefon, *The Politics of Obedience: The Discourse of Voluntary Servitude* (Black Rose Books 1975) 52–53.

However, for them, it is only the beginning. The larger project requires for them the creation of:

> A new social body, which is a project that goes well beyond refusal. Our lines of flight, our exodus must be constituent and create a real alternative. Beyond the simple refusal, we need also to construct a new mode of life and above all a new community.[72]

The beginning of the outline of such a coming community can be seen in Douzinas' work on rights. He, in effect, performs what Michel Foucault has termed '[the] right to bear witness, to oppose truth to power... That right to set a powerless truth against a truthless power'.[73]

72 Michael Hardt and Antonio Negri, *Empire* (Harvard University Press 2000) 204.
73 Michel Foucault, *Michel Foucault: Essential Works 1954–84, Volume 3: Power* (J Faubion ed, R Hurley trans, Penguin 2002) 330.

13

THE ELECTRICAL DIALECTIC

Cormac Deane

In the final paragraphs of his 2010 essay '*Adikia*: On Communism and Rights', Costas Douzinas writes about politics as a kind of entanglement:

> The individualism of universal principles forgets that every person is a world and comes into existence in common with others, that we are all in community. Being in common is an integral part of being oneself: a self is exposed to the other, it is posed in exteriority, the other is part of the intimacy of a self.[1]

For Douzinas, the need to make these statements arises because of the liberatory energy that fires talk of human rights. This energy has proven so powerful in modern liberal democracies that the status of the person as an individual with rights threatens to decouple that person entirely from the community. To conceptualise 'every person' as entangled in this way is an attempt to draw a political path along the many lines of connectedness that Douzinas reminds us we are not only subjects of but also subject to. In this short essay, I would like to broaden the field of types of connectedness that Douzinas has in mind in the '*Adikia*' essay, in particular by considering the modes of connectedness that are enacted by the *techne* of modern infrastructure, and by the electricity grid in particular.

The fact that we are all connected through infrastructure is both obvious and obscure. Obvious because indispensable systems of transport, energy,

1 Costas Douzinas, '*Adikia*: On Communism and Rights' in Costas Douzinas and Slavoj Žižek (eds), *The Idea of Communism* (Verso 2010) 99.

DOI: 10.4324/9781032622224-13

information, goods and services are viable only if interchange is possible among their nodes. We all know that 'to be modern is to live within and by means of infrastructures',[2] as Paul N. Edwards puts it. But, 'historically, infrastructures dominate through invisibility'[3] for two main reasons: because they are kept out of plain sight (underground, under the oceans, in outer space, in inaccessible facilities, far from population centres); and, for a closely related reason, because the materiality of infrastructure is understated in all the ways that bodies, technologies and the earth itself are routinely de-emphasised at the expense of values that are supposedly transcendental, neutral, conceptual and weightless. For example, the term 'cloud computing' is more ideologically palatable than the transcontinental, energy-intensive, physical network of data centres and cables that makes it possible. The ties that bind are, then, inescapable and also, as Douzinas suggests, desirable. The dialectic that is 'being in common' is also obvious and obscure. For these reasons, I propose here to adapt Douzinas's dialectic of exteriority/intimacy for a political theory of infrastructure.

The expansion of the political outwards, upwards, downwards and sideways from the human is a project that is already ongoing. Generally speaking, new materialist, posthumanist approaches to other life and other objects redescribe the field of politics in ways that emphasise entanglement and interconnectedness as actually existing material realities. In so doing, they re-position the status of 'others' and 'things' and they alter understanding of the material and immaterial connections between them; some are critical of the enmeshment of capitalism in the human sensorium, while others find liberatory potential. A partial list of these approaches includes: Jane Bennett's 'thing-power',[4] Haraway's 'species-being',[5] Braidotti's 'enfleshed materialism'[6] and 'symbiotic interdependence',[7] Hird's 'sociable life',[8] Morton's interspecies and ecological ethics,[9] Esposito's 'common immunity',[10] Latour's

2 Paul N Edwards, 'Infrastructure and Modernity: Force, Time, and Social Organization in the History of Sociotechnical Systems' in Thomas J Misa, Philip Brey and Andrew Feenberg (eds), *Modernity and Technology* (MIT Press 2003) 186.

3 Vicki Mayer, 'The Second Coming: Google and Internet Infrastructure' (2019) 18 *Culture Machine* 9.

4 Jane Bennett, 'The Force of Things: Steps toward an Ecology of Matter' (2004) 32 *Political Theory* 347.

5 Donna J Haraway, *When Species Meet* (University of Minnesota Press 2008).

6 Rosi Braidotti, *Metamorphoses: Towards a Materialist Theory of Becoming* (Polity 2002).

7 Rosi Braidotti, 'Affirming the Affirmative: On Nomadic Affectivity' (2006) 11/12 Rhizomes https://www.rhizomes.net/issue11/index.html>.

8 MJ Hird, *The Origins of Sociable Life* (Palgrave Macmillan 2009).

9 Timothy Morton, *The Ecological Thought* (Harvard University Press 2012); Timothy Morton, *Hyperobjects: Ecology and Philosophy After the End of the World* (University of Minnesota Press 2013).

10 Roberto Esposito, *Immunitas: The Protection and Negation of Life* (Polity 2011).

'interactionism',[11] Stiegler's treatment of 'transindividuation',[12] Galloway and Thacker's elemental dynamics of networks,[13] Wark's 'vectoral' power,[14] Bratton's 'interfacial relays *between* addressable objects',[15] and Zundel and Holt's 'organizational in-between'.[16]

Contemporary with these has been the development of two closely related fields – infrastructure studies and media archaeology. These developments ought to be considered *en masse* because they all attempt to consider not simply this thing and that person, or these machines and those nations, this medium and that message, or this animal and that diet; instead, they are interested in what might be called the 'operative functioning'[17] of any of these combinations. Instead of an ontology that seeks to understand being, what must be kept in view are processes of becoming, sequences of doings and concatenations of affordances. Both of these fields retain a strong interest in the sedimentary layerings of *techne* that have unforeseeable, complex and even nonlinear effects on social and political life (see Parikka on sedimentation).[18] They also have in common a powerful focus on the modern period as a time when transformations have taken place that, while they have roots in earlier periods, represent a significant rupture with what went before. Graham and Marvin put this technological entanglement at the centre of modernity: 'As a "bundle" of materially networked, mediating infrastructures, transport, street, communications, energy and water systems constitute the largest and most sophisticated technological artefacts ever devised by humans'.[19]

In other words, infrastructure studies and media archaeology may be seen as ways of parsing entanglements in such a way that the interconnectedness of the technological and the political becomes hard to ignore. To return to Douzinas's vocabulary, they produce the dialectic of exteriority and intimacy that he asserts as unavoidable and as vital for political action. In particular, this essay discusses a pervasive infrastructure – the electricity

11 Bruno Latour, 'On Interobjectivity' (1996) 3(4) *Mind, Culture, and Activity*, 228-245.
12 Bernard Stiegler, 'Anamnesis and Hypomnesis: The Memories of Desire' in Arthur Bradley and Louis Armand (eds), *Technicity* (Litteraria Pragensia 2006) 14–26.
13 Alexander R Galloway and Eugene Thacker, 'Sovereignty and the State of Emergency' (2005) 2 *Kritikos n.p.*; Alexander R Galloway and Eugene Thacker, *The Exploit: A Theory of Networks* (University of Minnesota Press 2007).
14 McKenzie Wark, *The Vectoralist Class* (2015) 65 *e-flux* n.p..
15 Benjamin Bratton, *The Stack: On Software and Sovereignty* (MIT Press 2016) 575.
16 Robin Holt and Mike Zundel, *The Poverty of Strategy: Organization in the Shadows of Technology* (University of Cambridge Press 2023) 348.
17 Aud Sissel Hoel and Iris van der Tuin, 'The Ontological Force of Technicity: Reading Cassirer and Simondon Diffractively' (2013) 26 *Philosophy & Technology* 187.
18 Jussi Parikka, *A Geology of Media* (University of Minnesota Press 2015).
19 Steve Graham and Simon Marvin, *Splintering Urbanism: Networked Infrastructures, Technological Mobilities and the Urban Condition* (Routledge 2001) 10.

system – in these terms and explores a small sample of historical attempts to understand it in political terms. As will become clear, the various valences of electrical connectedness suggest that dialectical thinking is a possible, even an inevitable, response to infrastructure per se. In what follows, I would like to compare the responses of three very different modern thinkers who struggled with the political implications of modern infrastructure, and for each of whom electricity abounded in dialectical potential: Edmund Burke, Vladimir Lenin and Carl Schmitt.

The Greek Grid

A slightly later piece of writing by Douzinas provides a second starting point: *Philosophy and Resistance in the Crisis: Greece and the Future of Europe* (2013). As trenchant economic reforms emanating from Brussels were implemented in Greece following the global financial collapse that started in 2007, it became clear that the burden of repaying debts to banks that had made bad loans was falling on the shoulders of the Greek people.

> Under the bailout agreements, however, taxation has hit the poorest especially hard. VAT at the top rate has been imposed on food and even *souvlaki*, the Greek fish and chips. The *souvlaki* tax has been followed by increases in direct taxation and an especially objectionable property tax collected through electricity bills and leading to power disconnection if not paid.[20]

Attempting to collect electricity charges through a property tax, while obnoxious, was at least politically clarifying. The citizen's relation to the state has long been articulated in terms of land rights and the payment of tributes or taxes; the subdivision and parcelling of land is at the basis of the law as *nomos*. So when electricity was charged through the same system, the relation of the citizen to the state was explicitly mediated as infrastructural. Electricity is not something that one may use or not use, buy or not buy, but it is as fundamental to modern living as having a place to live. The threat of disconnection is far more than the withdrawal of a service.

As things developed, a 'can't pay won't pay' response swept across communities in Greece to this and to other measures: 'Members of the electricians' union refused to disconnect the non-payers or reconnected them after private contractors had cut them off'.[21] The point to make here about the

20 Costas Douzinas, *Philosophy and Resistance in the Crisis: Greece and the Future of Europe* (Polity 2013) 47.

21 ibid 99.

electrical infrastructure is that it was not only symbolically but actually the thing that bound people in a collective. The Greek example makes clear that the private citizen's connection to the grid is also their connection to society and community. In that context, when people refuse to pay or when electricians refuse to enforce the penalties, '[d]isobedience is transformed from a personal moral act to collective political resistance',[22] as Douzinas puts it.

The connection that comprises any electrical circuit or system is the core of its dialectical challenge. Electricity must flow from one thing or place to another in order to be. This fundamental characteristic means that, the moment when electrical current is first harnessed and rudimentary attempts are made to engineer it (from roughly 1750 onwards), it is immediately deployed in political contexts. The capacity of electricity to relay energy at a distance and in an instant contains all of the paradoxes of political belonging that animate political debate in the modern era, where the great questions concern the problems of governance at scale (e.g. mass populations, standing armies, central banks) and at a distance (e.g. centralised states, global empires). It was precisely these challenges that occupied the rising bourgeois political class of 18th-century Britain, among them Edmund Burke.

'Electrick communication every where'

Burke died in 1797, so he did not live to see electricity being deployed in any infrastructural way. It took another century for nascent electricity grids to take shape (the Edison Electric Light Station in London and the Pearl Street Station in New York both date from 1882). But as early as 1775 he deploys electricity metaphorically in a speech to the House of Commons on the restive American colonies (*Speech on Conciliation with America).* For Britain's 'extensive and detached Empire',[23] he identifies the key challenge of political representation at a distance, holding up for (rather facetious) comparison the dissatisfaction of being governed from London as it has been experienced even within Great Britain:

> But America is virtually represented. What! does the electric force of virtual representation more easily pass over the Atlantic, than pervade Wales, which lies in your neighbourhood; or than Chester and Durham, surrounded by abundance of representation that is actual and palpable? But, Sir, your ancestors thought this sort of virtual representation, however ample, to be totally insufficient for the freedom of the inhabitants

22 ibid 99.
23 Edmund Burke, *The Writings and Speeches of Edmund Burke*, vol III (Warren M Elofson and John A Woods eds, OUP 1996) 125.

of territories that are so near, and comparatively so inconsiderable. How then can I think it sufficient for those which are infinitely greater, and infinitely more remote?[24]

In order to describe a theoretical (and so, for him, impractical) connection between polities, Burke here reaches for 'electric force' to express his scorn. Electricity is held in suspicion and becomes associated, throughout Burke's career, with all that opposes the key principles of what is natural, traditional and virtuous. Electricity both actualises and symbolises the wave of technological transformation that ushers into power the wrong kind of people, i.e. the bourgeoisie. That rise is in many ways describable as a technological transformation, as it is connected to the networks of capitalist expansion, financialisation, transport, speed, population growth and, most prominently for Burke in the French context, mass communication.

Burke's biographical context is worth remembering here, as he had spent the four years running up to the *Speech on American Conciliation* as the London agent for the General Assembly of the Province of New York.[25] This, along with his other political roles, meant that Burke was at the centre of a global imperial network of power. Although the greater part of his political career was spent in opposition, he was nevertheless continually concerned with the power of the parliament and of the sovereign and of the extreme difficulty of spreading Britishideas and principles across the world. So he is one of the first modern philosopher-politicians that we have who is at the interface of empire, receiving and sending correspondence, acting remotely at a distance, debating budgets for a global navy, attempting to influence the governance of America, India, Ireland and elsewhere, but with an infrastructure that is clearly not up to the task. He sees and senses the disconnect that threatens to erupt between traditional modes of sovereign power and the modern methods of logistical expansion, and it is the struggle to preserve the former by using the latter that proves insurmountable in his lifetime.

More than 20 years after his *Speech on American Conciliation*, Burke conducted an exhaustive post-mortem of the French *ancien régime*. In his *Second Letter on a Regicide Peace* of 1796, he tries to trace back to the class upheavals that had led to the disaster of the Revolution:

The chain of subordination ... was broken. Other interests were formed, other dependencies, other connexions, other communications. The

24 ibid 144–145.
25 Ross JS Hoffman, *Edmund Burke, New York Agent: With His Letters to the New York Assembly and Intimate Correspondence with Charles O'Hara, 1761–1776* (The American Philosophical Society 1956).

> middle classes had swelled far beyond their former proportion. ... The spirit of ambition had taken possession of this class as violently as ever it had done of any other. The correspondence of the monied and the mercantile world, the literary intercourse of academies; but, above all, the press, of which they had in a manner, entire possession, make a kind of electrick communication every where. The press, in reality, has made every Government, in it's spirit, almost democratick.[26]

The same tone had been present in his opinions since 1791 about these same 'monied men, merchants, principal tradesmen, and men of letters' who led the French Revolution because they 'were electrified, and made to lose the natural spirit of their situation'.[27] There is of course a scientific and a cultural context for Burke's feelings concerning electricity, and he was by no means alone in associating radical politics and this new scientific phenomenon, as Mary Fairclough in particular has described.[28] For many political thinkers of the period (see Samantha Wesner for a thorough survey),[29] electricity's mysterious, vitalist, even contagious characteristics meant that it could stand for intangible processes through which ideas could spread, crowds could form and become animated and, to put it in terms that Douzinas and others use, *constituent power* could start to emerge.[30]

Electricity becomes a potent political metaphor in this period because it is something that seems both to join us together into new political bodies, and it separates us from each other by sundering the natural, hierarchical ties of tradition. If it is a *techne* that would eventually go on to develop us as having individual rights to electricity, does it come at the expense of constituent rights? Or is it something that upends hierarchies and social stratifications, in the process forcing us into community with others? Certainly the off-grid fantasy of the modern prepper micro-community grows out of a kind of anti-communitarian zeal that is well described by Allison Ford as a 'double

26 Edmund Burke, *The Writings and Speeches of Edmund Burke*, vol IX (RB McDowell ed, OUP 1991) 291–292.

27 Edmund Burke, *The Writings and Speeches of Edmund Burke*, vol VIII (LG Mitchell ed, OUP 1989) 346.

28 Mary Fairclough, *The Romantic Crowd: Sympathy, Controversy and Print Culture* (University of Cambridge Press 2013); Mary Fairclough, *Literature, Electricity and Politics 1740–1840: Electrick Communication Every Where* (Palgrave Macmillan 2017).

29 Samantha Wesner, 'Revolutionary Electricity in 1790: Shock, Consensus, and the Birth of a Political Metaphor' (2021) 54 *The British Journal for the History of Science* 259–261.

30 Antonio Negri, *Insurgencies: Constituent Power and the Modern State* (University of Minnesota Press 2009); Illan Rua Wall, *Human Rights and Constituent Power: Without Model or Warranty* (Routledge 2013).

bind of reliance and distrust'[31] (see also Patrice Flichy).[32] Similarly, in a well-known anthropology of Californian electricity customers, Wilk and Wilhite found in the 1980s that 'all public utilities ... are seen by homeowners as intrusions into private space that carry unnamed dangers. ... Utility lines connect the intimate world to the welter of unknown powers that inhabit a world of commerce and government'.[33] This social alienation then in turn provides a basis for a political interpretation of infrastructure. Burke's usefulness is in the way that he expresses how the modern technology of electricity, which cannot exist in isolation but must move from point to point, person to person, is regarded from the outset as an extreme social force.

50,000,000 Lightbulbs

The Goelro electrification plan, which was launched by Lenin in 1920 and reached relative completion over ten years later, was a highly ambitious attempt to create a generation and distribution grid across Russia. The existing system was very undeveloped, so the scale of the project was enormous, as Lenin outlined at the start:

> [I]n three years we expect to have 50,000,000 lightbulbs burning in Russia. There are 70,000,000 in the United States, I believe, but in a land where electricity is in its infancy more than two-thirds of that number is a very high figure to achieve. Electrification is to my mind the most momentous of the great tasks that confront us.[34]

There is no doubt as to the utopian ardour and optimism with which Lenin pursued the electrification plan. The emphasis in his speeches and interviews in the period of the launch of Goelro is as much on electrification as a project to be pursued, as it is on having an electricity supply in place. That is, he regards the process of building the system as a momentous project in itself. The mobilising drive towards communism was as important as the final destination, or at least more politically meaningful because it is the process of becoming communist that is the liberation offered by the Soviets (whose

31 Allison Ford, 'The Self-Sufficient Citizen: Ecological Habitus and Changing Environmental Practices' (2019) 62 *Sociological Perspectives* 627.

32 Patrice Flichy, *Understanding Technological Innovation: A Socio-Technical Approach* (Edward Elgar 2007).

33 Richard Wilk, 'Bottled Water: The Pure Commodity in the Age of Branding' (2006) 6 *Journal of Consumer Culture* 311. See also H Wilhite and R Wilk, 'Household Energy Conservation Decision-Making in Santa Cruz County, California' in BM Morrison and W Kempton (eds), *Families and Energy: Coping with Uncertainty* (Proceedings, Michigan State University, East Lansing 1983) 449–458.

34 Vladimir Lenin, *Collected Works* Vol 42 (Progress 1969) 180.

political future was far from certain in 1920). So for Lenin, infrastructure was both a good in itself and it was an organising concept for political management. What would become the cycle of Five Year Plans that characterised the Soviet economy in this period was set in motion by Goelro, both in terms of the affordances made available to the economy by electricity, and in terms of the political affordances of coordinated, centralised, utopian megaprojects that animated Soviet communism's self-conception.

Comparison with Burke is difficult, given the technological transformation that had taken place in the intervening period. But the late 18th-century attitude, typified by Burke, survives in a certain way in the communist project, in the sense that the physical characteristics of electricity are understood in political terms. That is, the lateral connectedness that leads to a form of corrupting social communication for Burke is for Lenin the thing that is to be pursued on the path towards communism. The technological utopianism of the early Soviet Union cannot be considered apart from its socio-political utopianism. The programme of electrification required years of self-liberation, self-realisation and self-establishment by the communist state-to-come.

In light of this, might it be the case that electrification is the constituent force of a becoming-state, i.e. may it be compared to the constituent violence of a revolution, which is then, as Douzinas makes clear in the '*Adikia*' essay, assimilated and disavowed? The answer may lie in our interpretation of Lenin's great, much-repeated slogan of this period, 'Communism is Soviet power plus the electrification of the whole country'. The phrase appears first somewhat buried in a November 1920 speech 'Our Foreign and Domestic Position and Party Tasks'[35] delivered to a conference on trade unions in Moscow. A month later, evidently having appreciated its rhetorical punch, Lenin uses it more prominently in a much more stirring speech, the 'Report on the Work of the Council of People's Commissars'.[36]

The slogan bears comparison, I suggest, to the opening words of the French Declaration of the Rights of Man and Citizen (1789), which Douzinas calls 'perhaps the greatest modern normative maxim':[37] 'All men are born and remain free and equal in rights'. The French statement achieves its normative force thanks to its hybrid of constative and illocutionary elements. That is, it establishes how things ought to be by combining plain description and implied intention; not all people are born free and equal, and the injustice of this is extinguished by asserting that they really are and/or will be. Lenin's maxim is a similar hybrid that, by aping a mathematical formula, seems to express

35 Vladimir Lenin, *Collected Works* Vol 31 (Progress 1966) 408–426.
36 ibid 513–518.
37 Douzinas (n 20) 82.

and establish a logical situation simultaneously. Communism, as ephemeral as human rights in the French case, exists and yet does not exist yet, at least not until the people combine two real things: Soviet power and electrification.

So what happens when electrification is complete? Lenin characterises the process, in the November 1920 speech, as a necessary step in terms of Marxist theory: 'trade unions must frankly admit the existence of a class struggle and its inevitability until the electrification of industry and agriculture is completed'.[38] The problem arises for the communist project as it does for any revolutionary movement: where does the political energy, the striving for justice, go when the old regime has been toppled? Does the dialectic of class struggle peter out once communism is achieved, as Lenin seems to foretell? Douzinas suggests that the normative demands for rights found in documents such as the French Declaration are transformed when they are adopted by the system they aspire to install, with the result that 'positive human rights ... become defence mechanisms against the possibility of resistance and revolution'.[39] Extrapolating from this, we might say that the politically exciting process of electrification, once complete, installs a system devoted to the suppression of political excitement.

Electricity and Its Discontents

The idea that modern infrastructural life is in fact a kind of prison-house is espoused clearly in this period by Lenin's near contemporary and ideological enemy, Carl Schmitt. As a conservative, he regards the modern devotion to infrastructural development (economics, science, technology) as a falling away from the safety of tradition, as a tragic preference for enlightened disenchantment. In 1923, when the Bolsheviks finally prevail in the Russian Civil War, and with Goelro underway, Schmitt looks on critically:

> The world-view of the modern capitalist is the same as that of the industrial proletarian, as if one were the twin brother of the other. Thus they are of one accord when they struggle side by side for economic thinking. Insofar as socialism has become the religion of the industrial proletariat of big cities it contraposes a fabulous mechanism to that of the capitalist world. ... The big industrialist has no other ideal than that of Lenin – an 'electrified earth'. They disagree essentially on the correct method of electrification.[40]

38 Lenin (n 34) 377.
39 Douzinas (n 20) 83.
40 Carl Schmitt, *Roman Catholicism and Political Form* (GL Ulmen tr, Greenwood 1996), 13.

This essay, 'Roman Catholicism and Political Form', is concerned with what he regards as the impossibility of coexistence between the Catholic Church in Germany and industrial capitalism. He identifies a metaphysical risk to the Church (as institution, and as building) of inhabiting the same city block as temples of pleasure:

> If and when all the sanctuary lamps fronting all Catholic altars are supplied by the same electricity company that supplies the theaters and dance halls of the city, then Catholicism will also become something instinctively and logically comprehensible to economic thinking, something accepted as a matter of course.[41]

Once again, we recognise a tendency to view the physical connectedness of the electrical system, and of the people who use it, in metaphysical terms. The threat for Schmitt is that the disruptive, unnatural light of electricity disenchants the relation of the Christian to the divine. Like a Promethean fire, electricity is transformative and destructive because it promotes the human to an inhuman position on the planet and because it removes us from the family of nature, from the natural order. Electricity repeatedly appears in Schmitt's later works, deployed to describe what was for him the inexorable connection between an epoch's metaphysical self-conception and its forms of political and infrastructural organisation.

In the late 1930s – at the peak of his Nazi involvement – he adopted the term 'Großraum' to describe the unwieldy and historically unprecedented claim to spatial dominance of the modern state. The entire substrate of the global European legal system had been destabilised by massive infrastructural expansion since the early part of the 20th century:

> The first steps in this development fall in the time around the turn of the century, when great power plants and energy distribution centers were built around 1900, when, already around 1913, the proprietary electrical works of small cities and communities were made obsolete. Shortly before the outbreak of the world war there began, too, the inexorable electrification of agricultural and thinly populated regions … [and by the mid-1920s] 'Großraum economy' became specifically clear as a word and fact for the first time, all as a result of the cooperation of distant electrical power and gas line networks stretching across great distances …[42]

41 ibid 16

42 Carl Schmitt, *Writings on War*, Timothy Nunan (ed) (Polity 2011) 78.

Also in the late 1930s, he traces even further back to what he describes as the original moment when the part-human, part-divine sovereign was conceptually displaced in political theory. This took place in the 17th century, and is most apparent in Thomas Hobbes's *Leviathan*. In *The Leviathan in the State Theory of Thomas Hobbes*, Schmitt homes in on the mechanical aspects of Hobbes's incarnation of the people-as-state, the Leviathan. Although Hobbes does not in fact use the terms 'machine' or 'mechanism', Schmitt places emphasis on Hobbes's references early in the work to the Leviathan as 'artificial' and 'automaton', and adduces the influence on Hobbes of Descartes's conception of the human as a mechanism.[43] At any rate, the birth of the modern state that took place in the 17th century set human political and infrastructural development onto its current path:

> The decisive metaphysical step in the construction of the theory of the state occurred with the conception of the state as a mechanism. All that followed – as, for example, the development from the clock mechanism to the steam engine, to the electric motor, to chemical or to biological processes – resulted in the further development of technology and scientific thinking, which did not need any new metaphysical determination.[44]

Problems of Change

The problem that faces revolutionaries and counter-revolutionaries alike is the problem of change. Dialectical thinking, as it appears in the citation at the start of this essay from Douzinas, promises a never-ending churn of attempts to achieve justice in the face of injustice, which itself is always in a state of becoming. The assertion that 'the other is part of the intimacy of a self' is a promise that political change never stops because the paradox is never resolvable. Highly integrated infrastructures seem to intensify this process, as they lock in systems (transport, electricity, Internet, democracy, bureaucracy) that make it impossible to dis-integrate oneself from others. And yet, there is no shortage of stories of the alienation and political isolation experienced by those who live under intense surveillance, in energy poverty, in social-media addiction, in urban wastelands, in disenfranchisement, without papers. When theorising infrastructure, it is important to highlight not just 'the democratic potential but the narrowness or paucity of the network as a political model', as Ruth A. Miller points out.[45] Being connected

43 Carl Schmitt, *The Leviathan in the State Theory of Thomas Hobbes: Meaning and Failure of a Political Symbol* (University of Chicago Press 2008) 32–37.
44 ibid 99
45 Ruth A Miller, *Snarl: In Defense of Stalled Traffic and Faulty Networks* (University of Michigan Press 2013) <https://doi.org/10.3998/mpub.5959928> Conclusion n.p.

in a non-hierarchical network is not a good in itself; Burke and Schmitt are keenly aware of this. And, indeed, so is Lenin, whose embrace of Russian electrification was highly conditional, i.e. it could only take place with the vital ingredient of 'Soviet power'.

The Greek example cited earlier, where supply to those who could not or would not pay was switched off and on, illustrates the dialectic of networked togetherness in action. The network can be manipulated by both sides for political ends. The infrastructural network is, in fact, the political interface itself. This is not to say that the Greek struggle of the last decade and a half is limited to this set of events. Rather, it is to illustrate that infrastructure is the mode through which political action is expressed and established simultaneously. In this light, the ongoing reorganisation of infrastructures, which shows no sign of slowing, may be viewed optimistically; there is always a connection, and it may always be broken.

14

FROM ANOMIE TO ANTIGONE

A Retrospective on the Right to Resistance in the Work of Costas Douzinas

Ceylan Begüm Yıldız

I met Costas Douzinas for the first time in the autumn of 2013 at Birkbeck College, right after the nationwide Gezi protests in Turkey. Soon after the introductions, it became clear that we shared a curiosity and excitement about the global wave of protests which began in 2010; the Arab Spring, the Occupy movement in the US, the anti-austerity protests in Europe, followed by Gezi protests in Turkey and free-fare protests in Brazil. From that moment on, we had many debates over the protests about what they revealed, where they led, and what needed to be done. While I was disheartened and felt defeated by how the protests gave birth to more oppressive and authoritarian regimes in my home country and around the globe, Douzinas, on the other hand, felt a sense of duty. He became a Member of Parliament (MP) in the Syriza government in Greece. Douzinas often mentioned the duty of an intellectual in his talks at the time. For him, the aftermath of the protests was a crucial moment to act – to give direction to the political energy that burst during the protests.[1]

Now, slightly more than a decade later, revisiting Douzinas' work on the right to resistance could illuminate our path at a crossroads of change. As humanity is facing a multi-layered existential crisis, a global climate crisis, complemented by global and local economic and political crises, military invasions and genocide, people voice their opinions and demand change through different forms of protests, which vary from planned mass demonstrations to impromptu road blockings and encampments. Although today's

1 Douzinas reflects on his time as an MP in his 2017 book, titled *Syriza in Power: Reflections of an Accidental Politician* (Polity Press 2017).

DOI: 10.4324/9781032622224-14

protests are diversified in tactics, they are fragmented compared to the 2010–2013 nationwide protests, which indicate the government's strategy to control and limit protests. Academics and human rights organisations highlight the alarming trend of militarisation of policing tactics in protests that is complemented by laws and regulations which expand policing powers and criminalise protests and protestors.[2]

One of the most recent examples of this practice is the new Public Order Act 2023 in England and Wales, which has extended the scope of existing controversial 'stop and search powers' and introduced a set of new crimes in response to tactics used by the climate protestors, such as 'locking on' or 'being equipped for locking on'.[3] To justify the need for adopting these measures, the government explicitly referred to the tactics used by environmental groups Extinction Rebellion, Just Stop Oil, HS2, and Insulate Britain and labelled them as 'highly disruptive' while noting that excessive amounts of public funds are used to police these protests.[4] Not only does this line of argument beg the question of how increasing policing measures would reduce the costs of policing at protests, but it should also be understood and scrutinised as a neo-liberal policy to curtail the right to resistance by presenting a false dichotomy between rights and public funds and services. Protest is a direct form of political participation; it is nothing but absurd to limit protests based on the neo-liberal calculation of cost-effectiveness. Protests are meant to be disruptive. Protests aim to raise the voice of public opinion when the governments refuse to listen, such as in the case of recent

2 As Amnesty International's global campaign 'Protect the Protest' demonstrates, restricting protest rights and militarisation of policing powers are globally concerning trends. See Amnesty International, 'Protect the Protest' (Amnesty 2023) <https://www.amnesty.org/en/what-we-do/freedom-of-expression/protest/> accessed 14 December 2023.

3 The Public Order Act 2023 has been in force since 3 May 2023. It has introduced new offences that especially criminalise tactics used by environmental activists, such as 'locking on', which stands for activists attaching themselves to objects or each other and being equipped for locking on (Part 1 (1)), in addition to causing serious disruption by tunnelling (Part 1(3–4)), obstructing major transport works (Part 1(6)) and interfering with key national infrastructure (Part 1(7)) while at the same time introducing expanded stop and search powers (Part 1(10–11)).

4 Home Office, *Public Order Bill: Factsheet* (Home Office 2023) < https://www.gov.uk/government/publications/public-order-bill-overarching-documents/public-order-bill-factsheet> accessed 31 August 2023. The UK government first attempted to expand policing powers at protests through the Police, Crime, Sentencing and Courts Act 2022. At the time, the government listed Black Lives Matter protests as one reason for extending policing powers. However, the government did not fully achieve its objectives as some measures were not passed by the House of Lords. See Home Office, '*Protest Powers: Police, Crime, Sentencing and Courts Act 2022 Factsheet*' (Home Office 2022) < https://www.gov.uk/government/publications/police-crime-sentencing-and-courts-bill-2021-factsheets/police-crime-sentencing-and-courts-bill-2021-protest-powers-factsheet> accessed 31 August 2023.

pro-Palestine protests. In weekly peaceful protests in London, people voice their dissatisfaction with the government's response and urge the government to increase its efforts for a peaceful solution.

In return, however, the UK government came up with a new definition of extremism that is even more vague than the previous one.[5] The government's on going attempt to ban the Palestine Action is an example of how it is understood and implemented. What is happening in Britain is just an example of a global trend. As I am writing this chapter, pro-Palestinian student protests in the US are facing violent mass arrests after police were called into campuses.[6] Instead of coming up with policies that respect people's demands from their elected representatives, governments around the globe deal with political, economic, social, environmental, and humanitarian crises and the urgent demand for change by criminalising protest tactics and rendering demands marginal and illegitimate.

Moreover, the global trend of limiting and criminalising protests and protestors indicates that the existing human rights-based formulations, i.e. freedom of speech and right to assembly, have run their course. Instead of discussing the limitations and erosion of existing definitions of human rights, this chapter elaborates on the right to resistance beyond the limitations of existing human rights concepts and mechanisms. With this aim, this chapter revisits Douzinas' work on the right to resistance through the lens of today's challenges. In so doing, it aims to contribute to the academic and activist attempts to protect and defend the acts of resistance while elaborating on its possible conceptual framework. In that regard, Douzinas's work presents an invaluable starting point, as his work on the right to resistance presents both a philosophical exploration and a reflection on its practice based on the 2011 anti-austerity protests in Greece. Following in his footsteps, this chapter first aims to understand the context that yields resistance, then traces

5 The new definition of extremism states that:

Extremism is the promotion or advancement of an ideology based on violence, hatred or intolerance, that aims to: 1. negate or destroy the fundamental rights and freedoms of others; or 2. undermine, overturn or replace the UK's system of liberal parliamentary democracy and democratic rights; or 3. intentionally create a permissive environment for others to achieve the results in (1) or (2).(New Definition of Extremism, 2024)

6 The protests began at Columbia University and quickly spread to other universities. Student-led protests set up encampments on the campuses, demanding universities cut ties with companies linked to Israel. The House of Congress pressured Columbia president Minouche Shafik over antisemitism, which led to ordering the New York Police Department to clear the encampment. Protests spread to other universities in the US following the arrests at Columbia. The protests are spreading globally following the mass arrests and police violence in the US universities. See L Aratani, 'Israel, Gaza and Divestment: Why Are Columbia Students Protesting?' (The *Guardian*, 22 April 2024) < https://www.theguardian.com/us-news/2024/apr/22/columbia-university-student-protests-israel-gaza > accessed 20 April 2024.

the philosophical foundations of the right to resistance in Douzinas' writings, and finally, it presents an analysis of the implications for the resisting subject.

Anomie: When Time Is Out of Joint

'The end of history and the dawn of a "new world order" was announced in 1989. If it was a "new" order, it was the shortest in history. It came to an abrupt end in 2010'.[7] Douzinas announced the upcoming new world order in these words in 2014. It is possible to argue that since the beginning of 2010, the world has been living in a global state of limbo between the old and the new. Humanity is held in suspense in what appears like an endless dialectical struggle between the old politico-legal structures and the new, which are yet to be formed. Being in suspense, however, does not imply passivity. Resistance occurs at this state of limbo, at the state of *anomie*.

In his book *Philosophy and Resistance in the Crisis*,[8] Douzinas offers a reading of the conditions that led to the 2011 anti-austerity protests in Greece through the notion of anomie. He writes, '*A-nomie* means the absence or lack of *nomos* law' and he adds, 'the [Greek] government chose law and legality as a favourable terrain for delegitimizing the resistance'.[9] Douzinas explains that the Greek government used the term to delegitimise the ones who either could not or refused to fulfil their financial obligations due to austerity measures. These acts varied from not paying public transport to not paying taxes or rent. Douzinas replies to the then Minister for Public Transport's warning that Greece is at risk of being associated with 'countries characterised by *anomie*', by stating that 'he was confusing civil disobedience with illegality and lawlessness'.[10] His response displays the parameters of his understanding of disobedience and resistance. Indeed, as it is discussed further in the following sections, Douzinas considers resistance as something integral to law, although he seeks its origins outside of law. This double placement of resistance, however, brings obstacles to its conceptualisation, which I aim to demonstrate in the following sections.

Governments, both with authoritarian or liberal tendencies, declare acts of disobedience and resistance as lawless in an attempt to marginalise these acts and their demands. However, is it necessary to claim otherwise to defend the right to resistance? As the word suggests, disobedience – either

7 Costas Douzinas, 'Philosophy and the Right to Resistance' in Costas Douzinas and Conor Gearty (eds), *The Meanings of Rights: The Philosophy and Social Theory of Human Rights* (CUP 2014) 85.
8 Costas Douzinas, *Philosophy and Resistance in the Crisis* (Polity Press 2013).
9 ibid 50.
10 ibid.

due to necessity or by choice – is disobeying the existing legal order. It is an act of nullifying the existing legal order by resisting its performance. Douzinas brings up the term 'negative performative act' elsewhere, unrelated to this discussion on *anomie*, which I propose to consider at the heart of it.[11] Douzinas mentions the term 'negative performative act' in reference to contract law's ability to nullify a former contract, in which law performs to annul the former legal performance.[12] I suggest cross-reading this term with the acts of individual disobedience and collective resistance. The term negative performative act could be helpful to describe the double movement of nullifying the existing legal order by performing its alternative, which is often the case in acts of disobedience and resistance. The occupied squares of the 2010–2013 protest exemplify this double performance; people resisted the existing laws and legal order by performing the alternative. In 2013, the Turkish government's project of demolishing Gezi Park to build a shopping mall with a neo-Ottoman aesthetic became a symbol of the government's violent neo-liberal policies with a neo-Ottoman ambition. In response, Gezi Park was transformed into a collective living ecosystem that consciously excluded money and police from its borders, challenging the legitimacy of neo-liberal policies by performing its alternative. In that regard, the Gezi Park occupation exposes a negative performative act, that on the one hand, nullified the legal order of demolishing the park, while performing an alternative new legal order. It is also possible to observe a similar negative performance in passive acts of disobedience. Indeed, what is left of law when it is not performed? In reference to *Bartleby*,[13] the story of a law copyist who simply refuses to reproduce the legal order with one simple sentence 'I would prefer not to', I ask what happens to law when an individual, or a collective, refuses to perform the law? On the contrary to critiques of passivity, I suggest that refusing to act according to written or unwritten law is a deliberate and active form of nullifying the law by rendering it unenforceable. As in the case of Greece in 2011, when people refused to fulfil their financial obligations, either out of necessity or as a reaction, this could be understood as a declaration of nullifying the existing legal order. *We would prefer not to pay our taxes*. The passive resistance of not performing the law exposes that the legal order is without force, and it can no longer be applied. In that regard, it is a suspension of the legal order, a state of *anomie*. That is a state between the old and the new legal order, a process in which disobedience and resistance eliminate laws that are no longer relevant or applicable.

11 Douzinas (n 7) 98.
12 ibid.
13 Herman Melville, *Bartleby, The Scrivener: A Story of Wall-street* (The Piazza Tales 1856).

Surely, it is possible to identify an Agambenian logic in my conceptualisation of *anomie*, as I am building upon my previous engagement with Giorgio Agamben's thought that I will not restate here.[14] In contrast, however, Douzinas adopts the Durkheimian approach to *anomie* to explain the conditions on which resistance arises, as he explains, 'Anomie emerges when systematic integration is eroded either as a result of disrupted group life or deficient social regulation. Systemic failure occurs when people become too remote from each other and relationships are "scattered"'.[15] To demonstrate that, Douzinas mentions increasing suicide rates and mental health issues in Greece and concludes that 'modernization and austerity have distorted social ethos'.[16] And thus, he offers a different meaning to the state of *anomie* as the erosion of social ethos, as he elaborates further:

> Anomie is precisely the cause and effect of the erosion of social ethos. It happens both at the macro and micro-social levels. A particularly acute type of anomie results from a substantial mismatch between the social ethos on the one hand and institutional strategies on the other. When social and economic policies and laws attack and undermine popular values, habits and understanding they create extensive disenchantment, fear and aggressiveness.[17]

For Douzinas, then, *anomie* occurs when laws and legal order do not reflect the social ethos. What Douzinas means by social ethos, however, is rather unclear. He suggests that '[s]ocial ethos has elements from both ethics and morality. It helps construct the identity and sense of belonging of individuals, groups and communities'.[18] While providing examples of social ethos, Douzinas wonders in his own childhood and refers to concepts such as 'family ethos' and 'national ethos'[19] in which unwritten and informal conventions are formed over time.[20] At the same time, for Douzinas, social ethos appears to be something integral to law and its operation; 'without such unwritten

14 Ceylan Begüm Yıldız, 'A State in *Anomie*: An Analysis of Modern Turkey's States of Exception', in CS. Cercel, G Fusco and S Lavis (eds), *States of Exception: Law, History, Theory* (Routledge 2021) 167–183.
15 Douzinas (n 8) 51.
16 ibid 51.
17 ibid.
18 ibid.
19 As Douzinas differentiates between morality and social ethos, he writes 'Unlike moral rules claiming universality, the social ethos is always situated in place, activity or nation' (ibid 53). However, this differentiation does not appear in his other writings where he situates the origins of the right to resistance in morality.
20 ibid 51–54.

conventions, the law, formal morality and social interaction misfire'.[21] This is a dangerous territory, as often claims of shared ethics lead to politics of exclusion by designing the subjectivity of its members, which I deliberate further in the final section through the figure of Antigone. At this point, Douzinas' concept of social ethos recalls Louis Althusser's formulation of ideology and *interpellation* of the subject.[22] Although Douzinas recognises the *interpellating* function of these unwritten conventions that 'are learned and reproduced in the family, the school, the neighbourhood and church' and that 'are passed from generation to generation',[23] nonetheless he attributes a positive meaning by suggesting social ethos is the force behind collective resistance. According to Douzinas, the anomic individual and social condition caused by the distortion of social ethos, in return, yields well-organised solidarity campaigns and cooperative initiatives. Douzinas reads this as the resistance of social ethos against 'radical atomisation'.[24] Thus, in Douzinas, the concept of *anomie* is a symptom of the severed social ethos and a condition of resistance in the name of preserving social ethos. Indeed, Douzinas suggests that the social ethos is the natural law that makes resistance possible, as he explains:

> The German philosopher of law Rudolph von Jhering argued that reality has a normative force that occasionally trumps the force of law. In our terms, this is the force of social ethos. It functions like a flexible and adjustable 'natural law' that keeps the place together.[25]

The quote above demonstrates Douzinas' objective in proposing the concept of social ethos. For Douzinas, social ethos stands for unwritten law, which could also be understood as natural law or morality, higher than state law. The legal order should represent the social ethos of a society. Anomie occurs when there is a discordance between the social ethos and the legal order. And when that happens, social ethos resists the state law. Douzinas grounds the right to resistance on social ethos to establish its foundation outside the limits of state law. In so doing, Douzinas frees resistance from the state law. Resistance can drive its legitimacy outside the boundaries of law, and thus, resistance becomes possible and legitimate even when it is restricted or criminalised by state law. Although Douzinas' aim to originate the legitimacy of the right to resistance outside of the law is understandable, I argue the notion

21 ibid 53.
22 Louis Althusser, 'Ideology and Ideological State Apparatuses' in Louis Althusser (ed), *On the Reproduction of Capitalism* (Verso 2014) 232–272.
23 Douzinas (n 8) 52.
24 ibid.
25 ibid 54.

of social ethos presents new problems. Who claims social ethos, and what happens when there are competing claims over social ethos? I argue that Douzinas' formulation of social ethos is reminiscent of Althusser's reading of ideology and, thus, holds similar problems in designing subjects and subjectivity. Before presenting this critique, however, it is necessary to unpack further the origins of the right to resistance to understand the origins of the social ethos and its operation. Douzinas offers a more in-depth analysis of the origins of the right to resistance in his search for the philosophical foundations of the right to resistance, which I present below.

The Right to Resistance

In the book chapter titled 'Philosophy and the Right to Resistance',[26] Douzinas presents a detailed analysis of the philosophical foundations of the right to resistance, which I trace in this section. To put it in his own words, the chapter 'examines philosophy's hesitant exploration of the link between revolution and right'.[27] In the chapter, Douzinas mainly limits his investigation of the notion of resistance to the works of John Locke, Immanuel Kant, and Georg Wilhelm Friedrich Hegel. Perhaps it is possible to explain Douzinas' disappointment with the philosophical formulations of resistance, or the lack thereof, with his direction. One can argue that Douzinas was looking for resistance in all the wrong places, and instead, he could have found more satisfactory formulations in feminist, queer, and critical race scholarship – which resist the authority of the Western classical canon and challenge the dominating neo-liberal politico-legal order that arises from it. Nonetheless, Douzinas' evaluation of Locke, Kant, and Hegel is crucial in discussing the parameters of the right to resistance and understanding how he formulates its origins. Similar to his conceptualisation of social ethos, in his elaboration, Douzinas searches for a higher law, a higher purpose to establish the right to resistance beyond the limits of the state legal order.

Before exploring his analysis, however, it is necessary to begin with a note for clarification. While offering his analysis on the lacks and gaps of the existing philosophical formulations on the right to resistance, Douzinas uses the terms resistance and revolution interchangeably. This usage results from the causal relationship between the two notions. Douzinas defines resistance as 'mass popular action, which rejects and challenges ideologies and structures of power supporting domination or oppression'.[28] Additionally, he explains the relationship between resistance and revolution, which guides us towards

26 Douzinas (n 7).
27 ibid 85.
28 ibid 86.

understanding how Douzinas relates the two notions; '[m]ost revolutions start with acts of individual disobedience, followed by collective resistance and insurrectional activities [...]'.[29] Although Douzinas acknowledges that the 'normative considerations rarely distinguish between the two',[30] nonetheless, he also does not distinguish between the two for the rest of the chapter. In that regard, the parameters of the right to resistance expand to the right to revolution; as he puts it, 'resistance precedes revolution'.[31] This expansion impacts the conceptual framework of the right to resistance, as it becomes something belonging to history, something that transcends time and space.

Douzinas begins his inquiry with Locke and finds Locke's formulation of the right to resistance insufficient due to its limited aim of protecting private property; 'Locke's right to revolution, which initially looked as a continuation of the medieval *jus resistentiae*, turns out to be a way for protecting property'.[32] For Douzinas, this excludes the masses from the right to resistance. Quoting from Illan Rua Wall, Douzinas explains, 'Locke's conception of the right to revolt is fundamentally prefigured by the question of property. This precondition sets property beyond the revolution'.[33] Although Locke conditioned the right to resistance to the protection of private property, I argue, it still holds a revolutionary potential. Examples such as Palestinian resistance to systematic land-grabbing and dispossession urge us to reconsider the significance of resistance for the purpose of protecting ownership over property and land.

In the chapter titled 'Of the Dissolution of Government' in the *Second Treatise of Government*,[34] Locke describes in which circumstances resistance is not only acceptable but also necessary. 'And thus the *community* perpetually *retains a supreme power* of saving themselves from the attempts and designs of any body, even of their legislators, whenever they shall be so foolish, or so wicked, as to lay and carry on designs against the liberties and properties of the subject'.[35] Surely, Locke's formulation is quite limited and appears to be an exclusive right given to the property-owning minority to strike a balance between property-owning citizens and the state. In today's world, however, Locke's conservative formulation of the right to resistance for the aim of protecting private property remains radical. From indigenous peoples' resistance against the neo-liberal land-grabbing to Palestinian

29 ibid.
30 ibid.
31 ibid.
32 ibid 87.
33 ibid.
34 John Locke, *Second Treatise of Government* (Hackett Publishing Company 1980).
35 ibid 78.

resistance to systematic land-grabbing through the settler policy of Israel, it provides a philosophical ground for the type of resistance that challenges the neo-liberal political and legal order in which land-grabbing and property confiscation have become legitimate for the purposes of capitalist and nationalist expansion.

Furthermore, it is possible to expand the meaning of private property, as Locke attributes a broader meaning to property that is not limited to material goods; 'By *property* I must be understood here, as in other places, to mean that property which men have in their persons as well as goods.[36] If his expanded understanding of property is combined with the significance of self-preservation, which he suggests is a 'fundamental, sacred, and unalterable law',[37] it is possible to conclude that Locke assigns a higher importance to the protection of private property than state law, and thus it constitutes the foundation of rightful resistance. In today's context, I suggest Locke's formulation could gain revolutionary meanings in response to neo-colonial expansion and neo-liberal confiscation of land and natural resources. However, Douzinas does not offer such a reading as he considers Locke's formulation of property and property ownership only in a material sense. In accordance with the canonised Marxist stance against private property, Douzinas relates property and revolution in opposition to one another; 'If for Locke revolution was invented in order to protect property, today revolution has been banned in order to keep it intact. This is why the right to resistance returns whenever wealth inequality and capitalist injustice come to the fore'.[38]

If Locke's formulation of the right to resistance is unsatisfactory due to its limited use to protect private property, in Kant and Hegel, Douzinas observes a rejection of the right to resistance in favour of legal and political order; 'a combination of philosophical idealism and legal positivism led the Germans to reject the right to revolution'.[39] However, for him, this does not imply a straightforward rejection of revolution, as both Kantian and Hegelian thought are built upon the notions of freedom, emancipation and historical progress. However, I suggest, what we rather observe in Kant and Hegel is a wish to make use of the emancipatory potential of resistance in a controlled manner for the purpose of achieving a gapless, ideal, omnipotent, and omnipresent legal and political order.

The emancipatory force of resistance is instrumental for Kant to reach his project of perpetual peace and for Hegel to reach *Sittlichkeit*; that is

36 ibid 90.
37 ibid 78.
38 Douzinas (n 7) 88.
39 ibid 89.

translated as 'the ethical life' or 'the ethical state'. That being said, there are notable differences between the Hegelian and Kantian approaches. While, in Hegel, the emancipatory force of resistance is external to law, in Kantian thought it is contained within the limits of legal order. In reference to Kant's favourable reception of the American and French revolutions, Douzinas writes, '[b]ut while Kant retained his enthusiasm for the revolution, he went to great lengths to dismiss disobedience and the idea of a "right to revolution"'.[40] It is possible to observe Kant's paradox, as Douzinas puts it, in his careful differentiation between public and private use of reason; 'The *public* use of man's reason must always be free, and it alone can bring about enlightenment among men; the *private use* of reason may quite often be very narrowly restricted, however, without undue hindrance to the process of enlightenment'.[41] While Kant expects people to obey the duties arising from private office or citizenship in favour of maintaining legal and political order, he emphasises the significance of critique as a public service which alone could lead to enlightenment and emancipation. To relate back to the example of people refusing to pay taxes due to austerity measures in Greece, Kant openly finds such an act of disobedience against the duty of the citizen and only accepts people to express their 'thoughts on the impropriety or even injustice of such fiscal measures'.[42] But who is the addressee of this critique? How could critique lead to emancipation? In Kantian thought, emancipation is conditioned to the grace and tolerance of the sovereign.

> a head of state who favours freedom in the arts and sciences extends even further, for he realises that there is no danger even to his *legislation* if he allows his subjects to make *public* use of their own reason and to put before the public their thoughts on better ways of drawing up laws, even if this entails forthright criticism of the current legislation.[43]

Limiting the emancipatory potential of resistance to public critique, however, poses a threat to the Kantian project of enlightenment, as his formulation requires an enlightened sovereign who would take critique into consideration on the condition of absolute obedience from his subjects. As he further writes:

> But only a ruler who is himself enlightened and has no fear of phantoms, yet who likewise has at hand a well-disciplined and numerous army to

40 ibid.
41 Immanuel Kant, *Political Writings* (HS Reiss ed, Cambridge University Press 1991) 55.
42 ibid 56.
43 ibid 59.

guarantee public security, may say what no republic would dare to say: *Argue as much as you like and about whatever you like, but obey!*[44]

In reference to Kant, Douzinas explains in detail how acknowledging the right to resistance in a constitutional order would challenge the sovereign authority of the political and legal order, 'A right to revolution would imply that the head of the state is not the supreme power; people could appeal to a higher authority'.[45] Nonetheless, Douzinas declares moral triumph over state law in reference to Kant's teleological conceptualisation of nature, which, in a nutshell, suggests that progress towards emancipation is inevitable since nature granted humans with reason, and thus human progress towards emancipation is nature's hidden plan.[46] When Kant's teleological understanding of nature is considered together with his quoted comments above on the necessity of public use of reason, it is possible to argue that his words imply a warning to the sovereigns; either accept the emancipatory progress of history or perish. However, it would be wrong to claim that Kant was on the side of resistance and revolution, as he clearly positions revolution against emancipation; 'Thus a public can only achieve enlightenment slowly. A revolution may well put an end to autocratic despotism and to rapacious or power-seeking oppression, but it will never produce a true reform in ways of thinking'.[47] For Kant, public use of reason contributes to the development of laws on the path towards an ideal political constitution.[48] Hence, it is possible to conclude Kant reduces the emancipatory potential of resistance to public criticism and utilises it for the purpose of achieving perfect legal order and unity.

If Douzinas finds 'a law beyond state law' in Kant's formulation of inevitable historical progress,[49] he recognises a force of resistance imbedded within the Hegelian dialectical process. Similar to Kant, Hegel too rejects the right to resistance. His understanding of history and historical progress overall coincides with the Kantian understanding of nature and its hidden plan. Nonetheless, Douzinas suggests in Hegelian thought 'history dictates the necessity of the revolution', and he concludes, 'The rejection of the legal right to resistance does not deter history's right to overthrow the whole legal order'.[50] In his ambitious project, *Philosophy of Right*, Hegel designs a historical process which proceeds dialectically starting from the

44 ibid.
45 Douzinas (n 7) 90.
46 Kant (41) 41–53.
47 ibid 55.
48 ibid 50.
49 Douzinas (n 7) 93.
50 ibid 94.

recognition of self-consciousness towards its actualisation in *Sittlichkeit*.[51] Douzinas observes 'a separation between legal right and historical necessity' in Hegelian dialectics.[52] At each stage, the separation between legal right and historical necessity gives birth to a new form, and hence, history progresses towards universal freedom in a dialectical manner. For Douzinas, this separation is what makes revolution possible. If, in Kantian thought, the process towards perpetual peace has to be carried out only within the limits of law, in Hegelian thought, actors who enact according to historical necessity could disobey the state laws. In that regard, in Hegelian thought, historical necessity appears as a law higher than the state law, which, for Douzinas, is the source of its revolutionary spirit. Douzinas continues demonstrating the revolutionary spirit of Hegelian thought by explaining the radicalness of Hegel's position on private property in comparison to Locke's. He writes:

> Hegel considers the right to property as an important first step in the struggle for recognition which leads to the emergence of identity of the autonomous person. But he rejects an absolute right, subordinating property to the political community. Locke had privileged property over life and considered theft and damage to property the vilest of crimes. [...] Hegel argues exactly the opposite. Limited freedoms, such as property, can be violated to prevent the total loss of rights.[53]

However, I argue, Hegel's approach to property and property ownership appears way more complex than Douzinas' reading. Property has a significant place in Hegelian dialectical process and plays a crucial role towards the path of *Sittlichkeit*. At the first stage, property is essential for the exercise of freedom. A subject, who is conscious of themselves, thus their own rights, has to exercise their will and rights over something external in order to actualise themselves. In so doing, abstract rights transform into freedom; 'A person must translate his freedom into an external sphere in order to exist as Idea'.[54] At each stage, consciousness consistently moves towards the external and actualises itself through appropriating and negating the external. Hence, *Sittlichkeit*, the final stage, represents the perfect unity of self-consciousness and the external world. In that regard, property and property ownership are the main building blocks as they constitute the first external expansion of consciousness. Furthermore, regarding the right to property, Hegel suggests

51 GWF Hegel, *Hegel's Philosophy of Right* (OUP 1967).
52 Douzinas (n 7) 93.
53 ibid 95.
54 Hegel (n 51) 40.

property belongs to the one who takes the property first and that this bars others from claiming ownership over that property; '[...] a second person cannot take into his possession what is already the property of another'.[55] What is significant in Hegel's approach, however, is that occupancy is also a condition for property ownership; 'Since property is the embodiment of personality, my inward idea and will that something is to be mine is not enough to make it my property; to secure this end occupancy is requisite'.[56] Hence, for Hegel, it is not enough to own property; one has to actualise oneself through appropriating the external object. Based on this formulation, at first glance, it appears as if Hegel is in favour of claiming property based on use and necessity, rather than an absolute right of ownership. However, he explicitly states otherwise; '[...] the owner's will, in accordance with which a thing is his, is the primary substantive basis of property; use is a further modification of property, secondary to that universal basis'.[57] The separation between ownership (realisation) and use (actualisation) of property, however, may result in alienation of property in which one may abandon or 'yield it to the will of another',[58] which brings out the concept of contract. Thus, in Hegel, the dialectical relationship between ownership and use constitutes the foundation of law through contract. Contractual relationship is significant for Hegel, as the successful completion of a contract manifests common will into existence. Finally, it is possible to observe a similar pattern based on property in Hegel's elaboration on family which constitutes the early beginnings of *Sittlichkeit*; as Hegel explains, 'The family, as a person, has its real external existence in property; and it is only when this property takes the form of capital that it becomes the embodiment of the substantial personality of the family'.[59]

In that regard, I argue, it is hard to claim the insignificance of private property in Hegelian thought. On the contrary, due to its significant role in the realisation and actualisation of self-consciousness towards *Sittlichkeit*, it could be argued that property ownership is as important to Hegel as it is for Locke, if not more. If, similar to Kant, Hegel too objects to the right to resistance and if private property has a notable role in achieving the ideal world order, how come Douzinas favours Hegelian thought in relation to the right to resistance over Locke and Kant? The answer may lie in the section where Hegel introduces the concept of morality. For Hegel, a dichotomy between crime and right arises from the possible failures of the

55 ibid 45.
56 ibid.
57 ibid 49.
58 ibid 52.
59 ibid 116.

contractual relationship, which in a dialectical fashion, yield the concept of morality.[60] At this point, Hegel mentions justice 'in the form of revenge' as an act that nullifies crime, and thus, morality appears as a concept 'not simply demanded; it has emerged in the course of this movement itself'.[61] For Hegel, revenge can be enacted by anyone, and he celebrates it as 'a positive action of a particular will' and 'a subjectivity becomes explicit in this way, is the principle of the moral standpoint'.[62] Hegel's formulation of justice in the form of revenge, that materialises as a negating force against crime, could be understood as an affirmation of resistance against injustice. In *Sittlichkeit*, however, as Douzinas summarises elsewhere, 'the modern state, morality and legality are finally reunited into an organic whole and become the state's institutional manifestation'.[63] I argue, even though as Douzinas suggests Hegelian dialectics progresses through overthrowing the existing order, in the final stage the revolutionary potential is dissolved, or to put it in Hegelian terms sublated, within the state and its legal order. In conclusion, I suggest, Hegel too attributes an instrumental significance to resistance that serves as a catalyst to historical progress towards a universal state and legal order.

It is evident that Douzinas seeks a philosophical ground beyond the limits of positive state law, which could claim its superiority in times of crisis and legitimise individual or collective acts of resistance. 'Resistance is both a fact and a right. The right does not derive from positive law, domestic state or international. The 'higher' law justifying resistance is both immanent and transcendent'.[64] Either it is called social ethos, nature's hidden plan, or consciousness' struggle for recognition; in Douzinas' work, morality appears as the legitimating ground for resistance, something beyond the limits of positive law, and thus higher than state law and legal order. Douzinas is right in suggesting that resistance, and the right to resistance, cannot be recognised within the limits of positive law. It also cannot be formulated within normative human rights discourse, as resistance exceeds the borders of such limited freedoms. Resistance originates beyond the borders of law and its practice cannot be captured by its operating logic. As a result, I argue, resistance is *anomos*. It is both a state of being outside of law, either individually or collectively, that escapes the legal order and a practice that challenges the legal order by performing its alternative. As Douzinas demonstrates, attempts to include the right to resistance within the legal order

60 ibid 73–74.
61 ibid 73.
62 ibid 73–74.
63 Costs Douzinas, 'Identity, Recognition, Rights: What can Hegel Teach Us About Human Rights?' (2002) 29(3) *Journal of Law and Society* 318.
64 Douzinas (n 8) 96.

would challenge the authority of law and sovereign political power. And thus, positive law cannot recognise resistance in its full potential. It is possible to observe this impossibility in two rights: freedom of expression and assembly, which are closely associated with acts of resistance. As it is stated in the European Convention of Human Rights, these rights can be restricted by law 'in the interest of national security or public safety, for the prevention of disorder or crime, for the protection of health or morals or for the protection of the rights and freedoms of others'.[65] The legal formulation of these rights, however, demonstrates law's claim over morality as the articles suggest these rights can be suspended or restricted by law on the grounds of public morality. Douzinas would not oppose this claim, as he argues laws should reflect social ethos or public morality, but morality overcomes state law when there is a discordance between the two, as state law loses its legitimacy in the eyes of the public. 'The duty to obey the law is absolute only when accompanied by a free judgment that the law is morally right and democratically legitimate'.[66] In that regard, for Douzinas, disobedience and resistance operate as a moral compass for the legal order. However, law's claim over morality poses a challenge; whose morality holds a higher power in times of crisis? In reference to Hegel and Kant, Douzinas argues for a universal moral command that is unnegotiable, which motivates the resisting subject and provides an undisputable legitimacy to resistance over state law, as he states:

> Against the idea of national salvation and unquestionable obedience to law, the destruction of whole generations and the humanitarian crisis give rise to non-negotiable moral principles [...] The excluded give rise to a universal moral command. As moral, the command is addressed at individuals not groups but can be realized only through political action. The moral imperative calls to a collective attack on the symptoms of social decay. This way, politics acquires a strong moral basis. This is not a moralization of politics but a politicization of morality.[67]

Although it is necessary to establish the legitimacy of the right to resistance beyond the borders of state law, a number of questions arise from the formulation based on morality. Morality is subjective and thus relative. Positive law, due to its claim of objectivity and universality, fails to contain the subjective nature of morality, which can be traced in relation to the crisis of justice, as what law delivers as justice often falls short of individual or

65 European Convention of Human Rights 1953, arts 10 and 11.
66 Douzinas (n 8) 96.
67 ibid 63.

collective demands of justice. It could be argued that the law's impossibility of capturing morality within its limits constitutes the possibility of resistance. However, as the right to resistance expands to the right to revolution, morality's subjective character transforms into a universal moral command. As morality gains a transcendental, universal meaning, the multiplicity of subjective morality is reduced to a singular higher command. However, where does it originate? Who holds the power to claim it? Moreover, how does the universal moral command force subjects to act in resistance? In other words, who is this moral subject, and how does morality shape the subjectivity of the resisting subject?

Antigone's Sacrifice

> From Antigone to campaigners for the vote and workers' rights, from suffragettes and conscientious objectors to civil rights and anti-Vietnam war militants, disobedience does not equal illegality and criminality [...] Disobedience is a sign of moral conscience and of political fidelity to principles of justice that stand higher than state law and policy.[68]

In his writings on resistance, Douzinas often mentions Antigone when he elaborates on the resisting subject. Aligning with her common reception in critical literature, in Douzinas' work, Antigone represents the devoted resisting subject. In the book chapter titled '*Adikia*: On Communism and Rights', Douzinas inquiries into the origins of this devotion. 'Yet Antigone's defiance, Paul's conversion, and Lenin's resoluteness did not emerge *ex nihilo*. The militants are partly prepared and supported by norms and beliefs pre-existing the dramatic act and leading to their abiding fidelity'.[69] Douzinas explains the force that leads subjects towards defiance through the dichotomy between *adikia* and *dike*. In reference to Heidegger and Derrida, Douzinas defines *adikia* as disjointure, dislocation and injustice; *dike*, on the other hand, is 'the response to enduring disorder and conflict' that is *adikia*.[70] Douzinas discloses a reciprocal relationship between *adikia* and *dike* similar to his reading of *anomie*, as he states that '*adikia* is the cause and effect of *dike*'.[71] In other words, for Douzinas, a crisis of injustice and conflict, either referred to as *adikia* or *anomie*, is the force that motivates the militants to act in defiance by shaping their subjectivity, 'each type of *adikia* creates its own subjectivity by inducing subjects who resist and radically transform it',

68 Douzinas (n 8) 89.
69 Costas Douzinas, *Adikia*: On Communism and Rights' in Costas Douzinas and Slavoj Žižek (eds), *The Idea of Communism* (Verso Books 2010) 86.
70 ibid 87.
71 ibid 88.

and he declares Antigone 'as the champion of *dike*'.[72] What makes Antigone the champion of justice? I suggest that her glorified reception reveals an expectation from the moral subject, exposing the connection between resistance and sacrifice.

To briefly recall, Sophocles' famous tragedy *Antigone* presents the aftermath of two brothers' deaths, Eteocles and Polynices, who lead opposite sides in Thebes's civil war and die fighting against each other. Creon, the ruler of Thebes, orders Eteocles to be honoured, while he publicly shames Polyneices by ordering him to be left unburied. Antigone, who is the sister of two brothers and the fiancé of Creon's son, Haemon, goes against the sovereign order of Creon and buries her brother Polynices despite knowing this act is punishable by being stoned to death. While Antigone's act of defiance brings her own death, the ruler Creon regrets his punishment, which, in the end, brings his ruin.[73] In literature, the tragedy of *Antigone* has a special place, and its significance revolves around the dichotomy represented by Antigone and Creon. For instance, Hegel provides a gendered reading of the tragedy as a clash between natural law and state law in which he attributes the former to womanhood and the latter to manhood. As Butler summarises, in *The Phenomenology of Spirit* 'Hegel claims that Antigone represents the law of the household gods [...] and that Creon represents the law of the state. He insists that the conflict between them is one in which kinship must give way to state authority as the final arbiter of justice'.[74] Hegel also writes about Antigone in *Aesthetics: Lectures on Fine Art Volume II*, in which he elaborates in a similar vein, 'in Antigone, the "spiritual power" of family piety is independently personified in her, while Creon is the independent personification of law and the state'.[75] In a dialectical manner, Hegel reads the tragedy as a struggle between the state and the family and sublates the dichotomy by emphasising the reciprocal duty they hold for each other. For Hegel, Antigone 'ought to pay obedience to the royal command', and Creon 'should have respected the sacred tie of blood and not ordered anything against its pious observance'.[76] Hegel's response to Antigone reiterates his formulation of *Sittlichkeit*, in which state law and morality are unified; however, he fails to offer any solution in times of crisis.

In literature, Antigone is often celebrated as a heroine, a martyr, and a speaker of the truth who selflessly acts against the sovereign and exposes his tyrannical laws. In *Antigone Interrupted*, Bonnie Honig summarises the

72 ibid 89.

73 Sophocles, *Antigone, Oedipus the King, and Electra* (Edith Hall ed, OUP 1994).

74 4–5.Judith Butler, *Antigone's Claim: Kinship Between Life and Death.* (Colombia University Press 2000).

75 GWF Hegel, *Aesthetics: Lectures on Fine Art* (Clarendon Press 1975) 1163 footnote 1.

76 ibid 1217.

canonised readings of Antigone, as 'heroic conscience objector who on political grounds violates an unjust law, challenges a powerful sovereign, and all by herself dares speak truth to power', 'humanist lamenter of the dead, grieving sister/mother/daughter', and 'monstrous creature of desire [...] even passionately eager, to die for her cause'.[77] Indeed, in Sophocles' tragedy, nothing can intervene between Antigone and her deadly fate, although she is interrupted several times on her path towards death. Honig, in her reading of Antigone, focuses on these interruptions to highlight Antigone's determination and her political agency, something, according to Honig, is disregarded in the canonical readings of Antigone. Neither her sister Ismene's cautionary words nor the son of Creon and her fiancé Haemon's attempts to reconcile between Antigone and Creon bear fruit. Creon, too, goes against his command and orders Antigone to be walled up in a cave rather than being stoned to death. When Haemon finally convinces his father to free Antigone, it is all too late. Despite all the interruptions which could have saved Antigone, she reaches her glorious death by taking her own life inside the stone vault where she is imprisoned.

Why must Antigone die? I suggest the tragedy insinuates that there is no other option for the devoted disobedient ones but death. Sophocles's tragedy teaches its audience that an act of disobedience always requires its actors to sacrifice themselves if they are truly committed to morality and justice. Indeed, any act of resistance brings risk to the lives of the resisting subject. However, I ask what makes the moral subject a devoted resisting subject. In 'Law's Birth and Antigone's Death', Douzinas suggests Antigone represents excess, a state of being beyond the reason of law that Creon represents. Douzinas asks, 'What are the fears of Law?' and responds, '"Woman", madness, anarchy, everything that cannot be translated to gain and utility'.[78] This juxtaposition places the resisting subject outside of reason and the acts of resistance against rational decision-making. The reason of law renders Antigone an irrational being, a mad woman who is displayed in her uninterrupted, persistent resistance towards her death. However, her madness towards self-sacrifice is glorified as Antigone becomes an embodiment of excess that challenges the limits of law. As Douzinas writes, 'In desiring unto death, Antigone challenges the symbolic order of state law and male authority and becomes a rebel in the name of desire'.[79] Thus, Antigone's mad desire for death makes her a champion of *dike*.

77 Bonnie Honig, *Antigone, Interrupted* (Cambridge University Press 2013) 7.

78 Costas Douzinas 'Law's Birth and Antigone's Death: On Ontological and Psychoanalytical Ethics' (1995) *16*(3–4) *Cardozo Law Review* 1340.

79 ibid 1348.

In Antigone, her devotion to the moral command is intertwined with her desire for her own death. I suggest that the figure of Antigone and her reception in critical literature exposes an interconnection between morality and self-sacrifice. Thus, I argue that although conceptualising the origins of resistance in morality frees resistance from the authority of law, this formulation conditions the resisting subject to their death. Being devoted to a higher moral law drives the resisting subject towards self-sacrifice, that is, self-sacrifice in the name of an imagined higher good, either referred to as 'social ethos' or 'the universal moral command'. In this formulation, similar to the violence of the state, the universal moral command, too, distributes death to those resisting. Even when resisting for a just future, death becomes an inescapable fate for the cursed ones, who are already subjected to the deadly policies of the state. Thus, it is necessary to pose the question: is it possible to conceptualise resistance without glorifying death? Is it possible to reimagine resistance that does not condemn the resisting subject to death? I argue that setting the foundations of resistance in morality fails to challenge the deadly fate that falls upon the resisting subject. The only future that is bestowed upon the devoted moral subject is being a martyr for the cause, a martyr of justice. I suggest it is time to break this deadly fate, in theory and in practice, that falls upon those who are resisting for a just future. In such times of crisis, when humanity is surrounded by death, it is time to reimagine resistance that prioritises life.

Conclusion: Reflections for the Future

On 17 December 2010, the 26-year-old street vendor, Mohamed Bouazizi, set himself on fire in Tunisia. Bouazizi became the flame that sparked the nationwide protests, which spread around the world in waves for three years. Banu Bargu reads Bouazizi's self-sacrificial protest as a performance of his agency.[80] For Bargu, necropolitical resistance is the last resort to resist the distribution of deadly fate by the existing order; 'the very destruction of the body is the weapon to assert the claim that a life without justice is not worth living'.[81] As Bargu explains, his self-killing is considered to be the beginning of resistance, 'Bouazizi was hailed as the "martyr of the revolution" soon after his death'.[82] His self-killing was glorified as an *event*[83] that

80 Banu Bargu, 'Why Did Bouazizi Burn Himself? The Politics of Fate and Fatal Politics' (2016) 23(1) *Constellations* 27–36.

81 ibid 33.

82 ibid 28.

83 Alan Badiou's mathematised exploration of the concepts of being and event, initially published in 1988, was translated into English in 2005 under the title *Being and Event*. In his book, Badiou describes an event as a situation that is always localised: 'An event is always

gained a transcendental meaning. Even though his act of self-killing could be understood as a resistance of his agency, it, nonetheless, did not break the curse of his deadly fate. I argue that the glorification of the devoted moral subject is a reductionist approach that fails to consider the historical factors that give birth to resistance and fails to account for the impact of systematic acts of defiance that are not sensationalist (heroic) and temporary but rational, stubborn, and persistent. Bargu also mentions that his self-sacrifice exposes desperation and solitude against the existing order that distributed injustice and oppression in his life.[84] In that regard, the resistance that could have broken the curse of Bouazizi's deadly fate is the type of resistance that prioritises life. Thus, I suggest it is time to free resistance from its moral chains. It is time to rethink resistance that does not condemn its actors to self-sacrifice. In these times, when the existing order distributes senseless death and destruction, it is time to recognise resistance as a rational choice. Indeed, what is more rational: neo-liberal destruction of the earth with everything living in it in the name of profit and nationalist ambitions or resisting for a new world order and way of living? This new form of resistance is already practised on the streets. Practices of chosen family, mutual aid, and collective solidarity open the path towards resistance for life; it is the duty of critical scholarship to follow their lead.

in a point of a situation, which means that it "concerns" a multiple presented in the situation' (178). Alain Badiou, *Being and Event* (Oliver Feltham tr Continuum 2005). He suggests an event is distinct from a fact as the criteria of a fact 'are global and historical' while the criterion of an event is local. After its English translation, Badiou's explorations of *being* and *event* had another life. The maxim he presents in the book's preface, 'A subject is nothing other than an active fidelity to the event of truth. This means that a subject is a militant of truth' (xiii) is commonly referenced in relation to the 2010–2013 global wave of protests. So much so that the concept of the event has become synonymous with resistance and revolt without any reference to Badiou's coinage. This is also evident in Costas Douzinas' article titled 'The "Right to the Event"', where Douzinas presents a reading of the legal foundations of revolution and resistance without referencing Badiou or providing any other explanation of his usage of *event*. See Costas Douzinas, 'The "Right to the Event" The Legality and Morality of Revolution and Resistance' (2014) 2(1) *Metodo. International Studies in Phenomenology and Philosophy* 151–167.

84 ibid.

15

A LEGEND

Oscar Guardiola-Rivera

Tall Tale

Legend has it that before Professor Costas Douzinas entered the territory controlled by the Revolutionary Armed Forces of Colombia (FARC) during a visit to Latin America in the early 2000s, his partner told him: 'If you are retained by the FARC, be sure to make yourself useful.' In other words, put your body where your revolutionary mouth is. We can imagine Professor Douzinas engaging in deep political and philosophical discussion with the rebels. What would be the subject? The likelihood of revolution? Perhaps the alleged complicity between certain conceptions of human rights advanced by interventionist governments in the West and their commitment to protect the interests of economic actors abroad, which 'turn them [human rights] into the perfect companion of neoliberalism?'[1]

Those would have been worthy subjects of discussion. No matter how controversial they might seem to today's culture warriors and mainstream academics, questions of non reformist reform, revolution, and the relation between the pessimist outlook of certain tenets of liberal or left theoretical practice and the rise of neoliberalism and neoconservatism are more practically relevant nowadays than they may have been back when we visited

1 'The predominantly negative meaning of freedom as the absence of external constraints – a euphemism for keeping state regulation of the economy at a minimum – has dominated the Western conception of human rights and turned them into the perfect companion of neoliberalism,' in Costas Douzinas, 'Seven Theses on Human Rights' *(Critical Legal Thinking,* 23 May 2013) https://criticallegalthinking.com/2013/05/23/seven-theses-on-human-rights-3-neoliberal-capitalism-voluntary-imperialism/ accessed 17 Jun 2025.

DOI: 10.4324/9781032622224-15

Colombia. Such is the starting point of this paper. A question: given we no longer have faith in the story that a politics of progress could serve as a blueprint towards guaranteed freedom and equality, are we fated to live between the purgatory of complacency and hellish dystopia?

It resonates with the question posited by Ernst Bloch at the end of his life. A formidable challenge to the prominent affect of contemporary history and philosophy: 'We owe to the grandest writer of expressionism, Schopenhauer, an exceptionally powerful image [of the world] which shows, at the same time his vital abulia and his sceptic, angry outlook, and denunciation of life.' He tells us that 'if we consider it from a moral point of view, the world is a den of evil thugs; and if we consider its intellectual orientation, a madhouse.' For Bloch, after Auschwitz and Majdanek, our moral image of the world has redescribed the old problem of evil for modern times.

The old problem of evil concerned the causes and justification of suffering. 'If God is benevolent, omnipotent and omniscient, why does He allow bad things to happen to good people?' Answers to this kind of question by philosophers and theologians often included a distinction between 'natural' evil—caused by nonhuman agency—and 'moral' evil, attributed to human will. The former set of answers makes it clear that the real problem concerns suffering. The latter set of answers is insufficient to explain suffering caused without human agency. When the latter is opposed to the former, it emphasizes and characterizes nature as an inert fact-based objectivity ruled by immutable laws and mostly or completely indifferent to human fate or effort.

The 'new' problem of evil (*neue*, in Bloch's parlance, connoting that a patina of innovation masks the staying power of old falsehoods) is different. We know there are no ultimate grounds for belief in evil, 'yet we find ourselves unable to give up acting *as if* we believe in it,' to quote Mark Fisher.[2]

The Kantian 'as if' in the quote marks the persistence of metaphysical and voluntaristic forms of thinking after Enlightenment science ought to have debunked them. We know we no longer believe in such easy dualisms as Good/Evil, but we dismiss, or more precisely, disavow that knowledge. Moreover, such disavowal is structural – a cognitive and social structure of ignorance. It operates by positing and imposing upon us a cognitive schema – a way of seeing and imaging that emphasizes the naturalized position of an observer distant from phenomena, looking at the phenomena arranged on a stage or plane from without – and elevating such schema to the status of a norm. Or a principle of the mind and thought affixed to individual identity as a viewpoint, which predisposes us to act as if we still believed in such

2 Mark Fisher, 'The New Problem of Evil' in Pascal Gielen and Niels Van Tomme (eds), *Aesthetic Justice. Intersecting Artistic and Moral Perspectives* (Valiz 2015) 50.

things as Good, Evil, Liberty or any number of abstract wholes or kinds that belong to the same constellation of timeless things such as Eternity and God. The implication is that the materials of this time-bound world are not fit to give birth to truly new social forms or temporal alterity (*novum*, in Bloch's parlance) without the aid of some kind of God-like agency from without, even if it is just a *deus ex machina*. In a world like this, without immanent forces operating in the process of becoming, with no 'interweaving process-connections between past, present, and future,' there is no room for 'real possibility.'[3]

Such a world would be a hopeless world. One unable to envision the growth of the genuinely new. It could only be described 'realistically.' That is, via the conventions of the staging perspective of melodrama. The problem is that modern history and philosophy reach an end point, a dead end, when they settle for this compromise between the uncoupling of morality from established religion and the conventional perspective of the apparent realism of melodramatic theatricality. Moreover, the pull of such a conventional perspective and narrative, descriptive structure upon the imagination has implications for ethics and politics that are, simply put, reactionary. For Bloch, this compromise is best made visible when mainstream modern philosophy and social theory are shown to operate within the trajectory exemplified more clearly through the prism of Arthur Schopenhauer, the Polish-Lithuanian philosopher representative of persisting metaphysical voluntarism and philosophical pessimism: 'The bloody abyss [of Auschwitz]... presupposes a new contribution to Schopenhauer's theory,' Bloch says,

> [It] connects... the dreadful myths of Hades with his reading of Dante's Divine Comedy...: 'Where could Dante take the matter to build his Hell if not out of our real world?' This way, he gave form to a true Hell. But when asked to describe Heaven and its joys he was confronted by an unsurmountable difficulty, simply because the actual world offers no material to orient such task.[4]

Notice that in the passage Bloch quotes from Schopenhauer's moral image of the world, the key terms come from a singular physics and metaphysics: Aristotle's. Or to be more precise, what Bloch himself distinguished and specified as right-wing Aristotelianism.

3 Ernst Bloch, *The Principle of Hope* Vol 1 (The MIT Press 1986) 198; Ernst Bloch, *Avicenna and the Aristotelian Left* (Columbia University Press 2019) xiii–xv.

4 Ernst Bloch, *Abschied von der Utopie?* (Suhrkamp Verlag 1980) 10; Ernst Bloch, *Despedida de la utopía?* (Sandra Santana Perez tr, A Machado Libros 2017) 11, citing Schopenhauer.

In it, matter is inert, void of dynamic volatility. Moreover, when Schopenhauer's moral image is interpreted in the wake of World War II, the concentration camps, and the gulag, the world appears lacking any novelty or changeability. *Privatio* would be the word to characterize such a world, in need of shaping or form. *Form* is here imperative, categorical, and substantial. But in performing its causal or structuring role, this conception of Form also maintains that morality, now understood as the right/wrong or good/evil binary arising from human ability to shape things freely with our hands and our individually exceptional minds, in the analogy with handiwork and the new problem of evil, is still dependent on strong will and belief in immortality, God, and God-given liberty. In the right-Aristotelian formulation, Actuality is the temporality of a world seen as *machina mundi*, the instrumental *energeia* of global trade and excess value, and the post-Kantian formulation of the 'as if.' Potentiality, in turn, becomes in this formula the structured and structuring or normalizing type leading matter from motion to final rest in place that Aristotle would have termed *kata to dynaton*. A term which Bloch renders as *Nach-Möchlichkeit-Sein* or, in English, 'Being-According-to-Possibility,' and more precisely, 'what-is-considered-possible.'[5] In accordance with the modern rendition of this formula, it may be the case that we know there are no longer firmer grounds to believe in mechanical laws or the causal power of evil, but, nevertheless, we are called upon to continue acting as if we believe in such things.

Practically speaking, this is demonstrated, on the one hand, by the strong compulsions of a call-out public culture on both the liberal and conservative poles of the political spectrum to blame systemic tendencies or historical injustices such as racism, patriarchy, or the appropriation of excess value on the villainous proclivities of a constantly renewing cast of individuals. That kind of publicity calls on us to envision collective agency on the model of individual agency alone.

On the other hand, this strong compulsion shows up in academic practice and in the practice of the social sciences in which the only proper comparison is said to be the one between already existing comparative points or alternative origins within the realm of what is considered possible or 'realistic.' This kind of comparativist perspective is often presented as realist, empirical, or 'non-ideal theory' as opposed to 'ideal theory.' Non-ideal theorists see themselves as using quantitative and qualitative data to make their comparisons within the frame of what just is (and is considered possible) and on that firm basis arrive at descriptive or purportedly firmer evaluative conclusions. And some of them relate the distinction between non-ideal and

5 Loren Goldman, 'Introduction' in Ernst Bloch (ed), *Avicenna and the Aristotelian Left* (n 2) xvii.

ideal theory to perspectives or theories of justice that distinguish between the optimum approach and the maximum approach to justice.

For example, Harvard scholar of human rights policy Kathryn Sikkink defines her non-ideal approach to progress in the history of human rights precisely in terms of the optimum approach that she finds in Amartya Sen's *The Idea of Justice* and, principally, in Albert O. Hirschman's possibilist account of hope-bias and progress in his developmentalist economic policy-making and international relations studies: 'that is, the best alternative compared to other existing alternatives within the realm of the possible, as opposed to the maximum ideal of justice.'[6] As Sikkink says, 'empirical comparisons are connected to the optimum approach, or alternatives within the realm of the possible.'[7] This is an approach she adapts to the field of human rights to argue for an optimum goal for human rights policy consistent with possibilism.

Specifically, she conceptualizes movement along the lines of and within a visuality framework termed a 'compliance continuum' for human rights. According to her, such graphing can empirically measure and 'detect both progress and retrogression' in a way that ideal theory cannot.[8] This informs, in turn, her criticism of human rights critical scholars like Samuel Moyn and Costas Douzinas. She sees them as negative critics engaged in purely ideal theorization related to maximalist theories of justice and accuses them of engaging in comparison to an ideal that often remains implicit, and/or combining such implicit idealist comparison with hidden causal statements about human rights policies somehow leading to or making possible neoliberal economic policies.

Regardless of whether her criticism of the analytical (in)distinction between human rights and neoliberalism's distinct focus on the individual hits the mark, methodologically speaking, whether or not Sikkink's reading of Sen's theory of justice is the only or the correct one, or why it seems to her it is fair to lump together the indeterminate negativism of law and economics theorists like Eric Posner with the determinate negation of existing negativity in critical theory, the real problem concerns the unexamined metaphysical assumptions of self-styled 'realist' or non-ideal approaches and

6 Kathryn Sikkink, *Evidence for Hope. Making Human Rights Work in the 21st Century* (Princeton University Press 2017) 32 referencing César Rodríguez-Garavito; Amartya Sen, *The Idea of Justice* (Cambridge, MA: Belknap Press of Harvard University Press 2009); Mathias Risse, 'World Societal and Pluralist Internationalism' (unpublished, August 1, 2015); Albert O. Hirschman, *Journeys Towards Progress: Studies of Economic Policy-Making in Latin America* (New York: Greenwood Press 1968) for Sikkink's conception of hope as progress along the lines of developmentalist policy paradigms designed in the USA for Latin America.

7 Sikkink (n 6) 32.

8 ibid 33–34.

possibilism. In a nutshell, my point here is that instead of being realist they turn out to have a much-reduced conception of reality that leaves no room for the unfinished nature of matter or events in time and the unfinished materiality or reality of time itself. Including the possibility of thorough material and historical transformation, changeability or the unprecedented.

If so, the causality that possibilist non-ideal (measuring, scientistic) approaches call for turns out to be a species of already apparent, originating (efficient or final) causes acting on given materials otherwise inert or passive in accordance with more or less mechanistic laws. If so, the seemingly neutral or 'centrist' position of this modern scientism in fact looks a lot like an old position, closer to the unexamined set of (right-wing) post-Aristotelian metaphysical assumptions. In other words, approaches like this speak or visualize history and nature in terms of a timeless spatial configuration or, at best, a block-spatial picture in which what is real is only the entire history of the world, from past to present, taken as one or compressed in what just is. In this picture, the past no longer announces a different future and the dead, not passing, relate to us in a profoundly melancholic way. There is no open future in this visualization of history, but a perception and representation of time in a graph, compressed in a figure of the present. This is known as 'presentism.' In this picture, according to such an image of the world, time tends to be treated as a dimension of and reducible to space, a plane or frame of reference that contains quantification of what is spatially perceptible, compressed. As it happens, for example, when the proposed method is deemed 'empirical' in that it calls upon us to compare what is possible in terms of 'contrasting what is actually happening to what has happened' in the same place 'in the past or to what is happening in other countries,' or places, 'at the same time.'[9]

Here, motion is frozen by graphing records of past observations or individual cases. Sikkink's 'compliance continuum' of 'types' of human rights violations, for instance, is precisely that: a continuum. A graphing visuality measuring 'progress' or 'retrogression' along a line that makes depth and proximity apparent, calling observers to take such appearances as if they were actual temporal patterns. In fact, this kind of imaginal figuration suggests already that the 'empirical' operates here much closer to aesthetic ideals or orientations than the empiricist theorist would like us to believe. But even then, the power of judgment, imagination, projective thinking and possibility are severely constrained by the freezing of motion and a moral image of the world parallel to the timeless configuration space of classical mechanics or the block-universe picture of spacetime.

9 ibid 31.

So, causation within time is replaced here by an effectively timeless modality of logical-quantitative (even if not necessarily probabilistic) inference and/or an account of what counts as evidence in which the axiomatic and the arbitrary go hand in hand. And if apparently going beyond classical mechanics this non-ideal approach grounded in possibilism speaks of change and histories evolving over time, this is qualitative change/time in the weaker sense of numerical/mathematical order only. Quantitative expression or simulating figuration taken as actual, complete temporal patterns stripped of the coming into being of unprecedented events.

Provocatively, let us speak of these as approaches in which time is not real. They are non-naturalist in the temporal sense. Which is perhaps why their ideal/non-ideal as well as optimum/maximum basic distinctions map so well onto posited conceptions of legality, developmental economics, and positivist social science. They all seem to labour under a common fallacy: the assumption that visualizing or narrating the state of a historical, social system from its initial conditions or its more and less diverse but in any case singular origins makes it predictable (as a 'type' not a 'bomb,' to paraphrase Bruno Latour) and that such paradigmatic assumption can be extended to make a theory or philosophy of history or the universe empirical, realist, able to detect progress and so on.

After Bloch, let's say that this is the result of the persistence of what he would call the physics and metaphysics of right-Aristotelianism in contemporary philosophy, history, and social science. Including the possibilism that social scientists like Sikkink adapt to the field of human rights. I believe Costas Douzinas would agree with such a diagnosis, especially given the turn of his most recent work on the philosophy and history of human rights towards hope and utopia in the explicit and determinate sense of Bloch's history, critical theory, and naturalism. This turn is most apparent in the chapter 'Human Rights in History' in the second part of his most recent book titled *States of Exception: Human Rights, Biopolitics, Utopia*.[10]

He might respond to the criticisms lodged by the likes of Kathryn Sikkink or Philip Alston by pointing out that: (a) he moves across case-by-case or empirical comparison, and beyond, towards comparison between what is lacking in what just is and fullness to come or not-yet, to avoid collapsing justice with what just is, by making explicit non-capitalist and anarchist ideals in the precise terms of aesthetic, normative ideas such as the hope-principle applied to the principle of precedent that is familiar to the operation of judges in the Common Law tradition and in human rights or constitutional jurisdictions in other legal traditions; and (b) this move involves revising

10 Costas Douzinas, *States of Exception. Human Rights, Biopolitics, Utopia* (Edward Elgar Publishing 2024) 132–148.

our presuppositions about what counts as evidence and causality in time, to go beyond teleology, univocity, and graphs or stories of origin if we want to reinsert the unprecedented, randomness, and determinate chance as well as elements of irreversibility, or the reality of time, in our histories and ontologies.

We must do so, among other reasons, because considering what is possible given the present worldly state of affairs, we can only see hell, as Schopenhauer did, or, at best, evidence of progress or retrogression within a timeless or block-universe configuration of spacetime leaving no room for true novelty. That would be the equivalent of a theory telling us that our efforts in the past-present to realize grander or maximal designs of historical justice in the present-future are fated to fail or remain more or less inconsequential. In such a world, justice is not an option. The result of such a theory is the eternal look *ad pessimum* that predominates among contemporary philosophers and so-called public intellectuals writing in the popular media, inspired by the Schopenhauerian negativity Bloch warns us against. Which is also the opposite of what liberal progressives like Sikkink tell us they desire. Crucially, however, if the future is genuinely open, at least in the sense that when there are no precedents there will be no prediction for how a system will behave or respond to measurement, then no such pessimistic theory is possible. Here, justice becomes an option.

This is the real import of Douzinas' lifework. Ditto, it becomes more apparent in the Blochian, hopeful and liberatory, left-Aristotelian shift that takes place in his most recent work.

Remember Freedom

In the previous section, we set out to answer a crucial question for our times: is there any place for hope in the wake of lost and last utopias? I suggested that Douzinas' emphasis on the high stakes of the methodological problems elucidated by the revisionist history of human rights advanced by Samuel Moyn and critics thereof held the key to answering such a question. Moreover, it was proposed that the apparent turn towards Blochian remembrance of utopia, his more capacious understandings of possibility and (temporal) naturalism greatly aided us in this endeavour. In what follows, let me stress-test the argument that Douzinas' critical lifework can be best read and interpreted as a fruitful response to this pressing question.

The question is pressing not only for theoretical but also practical reasons. Not least, the growing sense that after the 2008 economic meltdown, the re-emergence of quasi- or derivative fascism among conservatives and libertarians in at least three continents, and the humanitarian catastrophe unfolding in Gaza and elsewhere, we may be confronting the real end of the promise of international law and human rights that Douzinas and others seemed to prophesy in criticism and theory. Further, this may explain the new choreography that becomes apparent in Douzinas' more recent work: in one move, the ethical agency that can be understood as the element of human rights politics and practice which animates the other static, positivist legal element is now grounded in the dynamicity and vulnerability of matter; this is not only a move towards the corporeality of the ethical agent or 'ethical flesh riveted to history' but also, or rather, a move to the point at which the vulnerability of the other becomes mine to respond to.[11]

This move brings Douzinas' commitment to Continental Philosophy and European Critical Theory closer, as in a dance, with decolonizing approaches in ethics and the practice of international law and human rights called for by the likes of Enrique Dussel and Houda Abadi, among others. In another move, questions of periodization, the force of events of rupture and/or continuity in history, and what I have called temporal naturalism, bring specificity to the call for alternatives and projective thinking in the face of ongoing tendencies replacing hope for perfection with fear of apocalypse.

As we shall see, the dialogue with historians like Samuel Moyn and critics like Ernst Bloch helps pave the way across these two sides of fatalism. Furthermore, let me argue that they might take us beyond. Thus, I make explicit and propose a third move: a left-Aristotelian move, both to renew the Marxian formula of the relation between 'the poetry of the past' and 'the poetry of the future' and to avoid the perceived lack of specificity of certain decolonial and critical discourses that risk essentializing historically grounded responses (for instance indigenous vitalist materialism in colonial and post-colonial times, or Cold War liberal responses to the horrors of world war and nuclear build-up) thereby losing sight of the subversive potentialities of previous eras as orientations for the future.[12]

11 Amy Allen and Eduardo Mendieta (eds), *Decolonizing Ethics. The Critical Theory of Enrique Dussel* (The Pennsylvania State University Press 2021) 12–13.

12 Bloch, *Abschied von der Utopie?* (n 4) 22–25; Bloch, *Despedida de la utopía?* (n 4) 23–25, 39–51: 'Everything is before the world's creation,' he says citing the end of *The Principle of Hope*, 'or, to put it otherwise: "the true beginning cannot be found in the first chapters of the Bible, in the Book of Genesis, but at the end."' (51). Compare this statement to T. W. Adorno's dictum 'progress occurs where it ends,' taken as a motif in Amy Allen, *The End of Progress. Decolonizing the Normative Foundations of Critical Theory* (Columbia University Press, 2015) 204–230; Amy Allen, 'The Ethics and Politic of Progress: Dussel and the Frankfurt School', in *Decolonizing Ethics. The Critical Theory of Enrique Dussel* (n 11) 167–181, clarifying the distinction between 'geopolitics of progress' or developmentalism and 'ethics of progress' to avoid the twin perils of formalism (as in Habermasian discourse ethics) and positivist accounts of law and legal rationalism that end up appealing to the transhistorical claim that transitions between time periods can be understood on a model of sociocultural learning or accumulative development; Alexander Kluge, *Difference and Orientation: The Alexander Kluge Reader* (R. Langston ed, Cornell University Press 2019) 439.

A different kind of critique begins to emerge here. Investigative, detective-like, less indeterminate, associated with a general (as opposed to particular) jurisprudence that exercises not only the power of forensic judgment but also a hopeful, projective, aesthetic, or fantastic judgment capable of mobilizing the force of a new beginning from the interrupted orientations of the past into the future. If not in terms of proximity, then at least in terms of connectivity, liminal boundary, and super- or trans-position. This is a view of the not-yet. Not only what just is, but also justice.

Such is the way to reimagine today the kind of principle that Bloch described as a becoming-human before all of creation or nature, the environment we are part of, and at the same time a practice of radical humanization against all forms of de-humanization (not only discrimination). 'The seventh day hasn't arrived, not yet,' was his response to the pessimistic survivalism that indexed the previous generation's responses to the horrors of world war and the prospect of nuclear exchange between the USA and the USSR – the two countries that in the twentieth century embodied messianic, univocal, aggressive, or 'hot' utopias. Such a principled vision, which may be likened to a kind of dance move backwards looking forwards, can also inspire our response to this generation's affect vis-à-vis impending climate collapse. It is also the kind of move that defines the new choreographies of protest and rights-based activism we have witnessed in recent years as younger generations attempt to salvage and reinvent the politics and aesthetics of indigenous communities, Tricontinentalism, Afro-futurism, and the subversive 1970s to confront the challenges of financial and environmental violence at the local and international level.[13]

Decolonizing a Legend

Before we sketch a sequence of these moves to map them onto Douzinas' own choreography, let me wrap up our little anecdote about the trip of a group of legendary intellectuals into rebel-controlled Colombian territory in the early 2000s. When we were about to begin the day's proceedings

13 Oscar Guardiola-Rivera, *Story of a Death Foretold. The Coup d'état Against Salvador Allende. 11 September 1973* (Bloomsbury 2013–4); Anne Garland-Mahler, *From the Tricontinental to the Global South. Race, Radicalism, and Transnational Solidarity* (Duke University Press 2018); Kathryn Greenman, Anne Orford, Anna Saunders and Ntina Tzouvala (eds), *Revolutions in International Law. The Legacies of 1917* (Cambridge: Cambridge University Press 2021); Cristina Heatherton, *Arise! Global Radicalism in the Era of the Mexican Revolution* (University of California Press 2022); Michael Hardt, *The Subversive Seventies* (Oxford University Press 2023); Silvia Rivera Cusicanqui, *Sociología de la imagen. Miradas ch'ixi desde la historia andina* (Tinta Limón 2015); Ursula K Le Guin, 'A Non-Euclidean View of California as a Cold Place to Be' in *Thomas More's Utopia* (Verso 2016) 163–194.

at Universidad de Antioquia, a couple of guerrilleros stormed the stage. Upon reading a statement, they left. Not a word about the visiting professors. No retentions. No opportunity for tall tales or heroism. As it turned out, the FARC were not that interested in a bunch of political philosophers and legal academics flying high and fast. That might seem a bit of an anti-climax for our adventurous Western friends, but in fact, the FARC guerrillas knew more about Birkbeck College than many of the young students in the auditorium that day. Former President of Birkbeck College and renowned historian Eric Hobsbawm had once hosted members of the revolutionary group in Birkbeck's cafeteria in London.[14] In the statement, rebels called on the students to know more about the history and philosophy of Latin America rather than take the word of European intellectuals as if the Bible, and to speak up against the gross violations of human rights committed by US-trained state and state-sponsored paramilitary forces in the name of liberty against communism as well as law and order. They denounced Plan Colombia, an agreement between the USA and the Colombian government signed and executed in the early 2000s that effectively replaced the progressive rights-orientation and popular drive of the 1991 Constitution under the pretext of providing assistance for security, aid in the War on Drugs, and development or modernization, in terms that echoed our critical analyses.

The main target of our critique at the time was the teleological and telecratic 'geopolitics of knowledge' and progress that informed foreign policy and interventionist 'law and order' and economic development agreements such as Plan Colombia. This hijacked human rights and other universalist discourses to pass their own particular interests, conventional standards, and institutional stories of origin as global and originating designs representative of supposedly necessary law-like natural regularities or irrefutable premises valid for all times and spaces. The point we made, which we wanted to present to and discuss with Douzinas and our other Western-friendly visitors back then in Colombia, and which resonated with the experience of movements and communities of struggle in the country, was a simple one:

> We believe the work of critical theory... is to show the ways in which certain social *dispositifs* of knowledge production have been turned into veritable 'tribunals of reason' that manage and negatively judge... subaltern counter- or sub-cultures, and nowadays, ultimately, ways of life,

14 Joanna Bourke, *Birkbeck: 200 Years of Radical Learning for Working People* (OUP 2022) 364 citing Eric Hobsbawm, *Interesting Times: A Twentieth-Century Life* (Alen Lane, 2002) 381–382.

while elevating their particular standpoint to a place of hegemonic cultural centrality.[15]

Already in the late 1990s and early 2000s, we were putting forward a proposal to renew critical theory in the direction of critical ethics, law, biopolitics or the politics of life and death in the lands of our childhood and political economy, following the trail blazed before us by Fanon and Dussel, among others, in dialogue with Western colleagues such as Douzinas. But we felt it was not enough to simply exchange such knowledge with our networked colleagues in Europe or the USA. We wanted to make kin and form alliances between peoples in struggle and thinkers ready to see for themselves and be part of such contexts of conflict and struggle. Not to inspire sympathy or import their ideas into our 'local' contexts, but to challenge the celebratory histories of so-called 'central' nations as myths of origin based on metaphysics of form, final and efficient causes that allowed them to adjudge negatively the cultural products and practices of so-called peripheries as merely ornamental, inert matter in need of creative inspiration from without. To question such metaphysics and stories of origin by presenting other starting points and events as options to politically contest deep-seated conventions that represented the continent of knowledge and accumulated wealth created through extraction, securitization, and financialization as if it were an unclaimed territory, ready to hand, out there for the taking.

We were aiming not only to question and deconstruct such conventional notions and presuppositions but to create, to think and act together, to take a position, to change together the general intellect and force changes on the ways in which European intellectuals and other political actors imagined their centrality and managed this centrality. For it was in the management of this centrality that the stories of origin and ritual myths of superiority, hegemony, or exceptionality had emerged. This included the stories, ritual conventions, and presuppositions animating the moral image of ideological and crisis management that informed foreign policy agreements with normative, political and legal import such as Plan Colombia. For us, these policy constructions were exemplary of a 'traditional' way of thinking and observing that harked back to colonial and imperial perspectives on knowledge extractivism, instrumental manipulation, and military, political, and economic domination toying with normalizing binary concepts like modernity/tradition, public/hidden, or order/disorder, which had survived the end of formal colonialism and imperialism.

15 Santiago Castro-Gómez and Oscar Guardiola-Rivera, 'El Plan Colombia, o de cómo una historia global se convierte en diseño global' (Bogotá, September–October 2001) 175 *Revista Nueva Sociedad* 111–120 at 112; Costas Douzinas, *States of Exception* (n 10) 134–140.

This way, in dialogue with Douzinas and others, we opened the debates on what is now known worldwide as the 'Decolonial Turn.' Namely, whether coloniality is the key element of the definition of modernity. To change not only the sense of the question (of history and philosophy) but to change the sense of sense itself through considerations of meaning, significance, or development, and beyond such considerations towards sense as possibility, truly new orientations (in the Blochian sense of the *novum*), and alternative, altering, or reorienting figurations of the human away from 'common sense' philosophies and meta-normative presuppositions defining humanity in terms of homogeneity, business, and communication that relocated the metaphysics of handiwork, abstract form and inert matter in the space of global security stability and markets.[16]

For us, the result of the 'traditional' way of thinking and seeing has been the concealment of what is most eventful and truly transformative in historical experience and ethical-political experimentation. Namely, the practical paths through which the institutional and meta-normative presuppositions of the normative orderings of social life, its normative precedents and orders get established, invested upon, disinvested or decomposed and recomposed, changed, or remade in unprecedented ways. The ways in which old positions and problems are dissolved in wider practical fields and get resolved or reimagined in new positions or recomposed as bodies and timespaces in which the unpredictable and unprecedented can emerge. Often, from within states of exception or emergency.

In the absence of visibility or insight into this most crucial process of socio-political and historical study, we believe the vital, dynamic link between insight into what just is and imagination of what is but not yet (namely, the adjacent possibilities) is severed. History and philosophy as well as social science in general, and the history and philosophy of law and human rights in particular, degenerate afterwards into right-wing Hegelianism and/or right-Aristotelianism found in the politics of developmentalist progress. Also, in philosophies of history and 'realist' studies that retrospectively rationalize the world along the model provided by right-Hegelian philosophies of history or *The Phenomenology of Spirit*. Frameworks that hijack contextualized struggles for liberation and a more integral humanity, including uses of human rights discourses, to make them complicit with liberal and neoliberal globalization.[17]

16 Santiago Castro-Gómez and Oscar Guardiola-Rivera, 'El Plan Colombia, o de cómo una historia global se convierte en diseño global' (n 15) 114–116; Costas Douzinas, *States of Exception* (n 10) 135–138.

17 Santiago Castro-Gómez and Oscar Guardiola-Rivera, 'El Plan Colombia, o de cómo una historia global se convierte en diseño global' (n 15) 113.

That might explain why the far-right wing paramilitary, on the other hand, were far more concerned about our dialogue with academics like Costas during their visit to Colombia in the early 2000s. They were notorious for chastising human rights activists and scholars as guerrilla collaborators, and the field of human rights itself as a communist conceit. Among other reasons, this is because when neoliberalism emerged in Latin America sometime between the 1970s and 1990s, writers and intellectuals of the left like Julio Cortázar and Gabriel García Márquez, together with community activists and witnesses of the atrocities committed by US-supported governments in the name of law and constitutional sacrosanct rights to property as well as traditional individual roles within the family, often used the language of human rights to protest 'traumatic events such as those in Chile [that] had a continuous effect on social practices and institutions. Specifically, in the form of unjust gains by multinationals that continue to appreciate in time and would continue to do so even after the 'evil' of direct perpetrators... were recognised in verdicts of tribunals such as Russell II.'[18] They effectively denounced 'violations by authoritarian anti-communist regimes that were simultaneously implementing neoliberal economic policies.'[19]

Crucially, in their usage, the language of human rights was inseparable from an understanding of political action that was both decidedly realistic and livingly, lovingly utopian. Not only did these subversive 1970s intellectuals speak of human rights, cultural rights, and peoples' rights in ways that recovered and reinvented the legacies of such powerful intellectual and practical political trajectories as the Haitian Revolution of the nineteenth century and the Mexican Revolution of the twentieth century, a sequence that included such innovative normative advances as the 1804 Constitution of the Black Republic of Haiti and the Carranza Doctrine, which pioneered principles of equal application of basic rights and protections among nations, diplomacy for the establishment of universal confraternity, and avoidance of uses of force by powerful states to pressure or protect their interests in 'weaker' ones, incorporated into article 27 of the 1917 revolutionary Mexican Constitution. They also negotiated those languages and the legacies of these real, historical events while reimagining institutions from below such as the peoples' II Russel Tribunal.

18 Oscar Guardiola-Rivera, 'Attainable Utopias' in *Crime Fiction and the Law* (Maria Aristodemou, Fiona MacMillan and Patricia Tuitt eds, Routledge 2016) Ch. 6.

19 Kathryn Sikkink, *Evidence for Hope* (n 6) 40 citing Costas Douzinas, 'Seven Theses on Human Rights' (n 1) 38; Costas Douzinas, *States of* Exception (n 10) 181; Oscar Guardiola-Rivera, *Story of a Death Foretold. The Coup d'état Against Salvador Allende. 11 September 1973* (n 13) 329–402.

In doing so, these activists and intellectuals were risking injury while exercising their and the public's political imagination. Gatherings such as the II Russell Tribunal collected evidence from below challenging or creatively reinventing evidentiary rules that in the hands of the state served to silence, disqualify, or dehumanize indigenous, racialized, or gendered peoples. It included testimonials, storytelling, documentary traces, oral history, and other kinds of hard and harder evidentiary data. Meanwhile, they built republican trust and virtues of plebeian courage, and mobilized aesthetic and political imaginations to create new languages and media for publicizing human rights when the written-letter and court-like language of state law proved too dry, too forensic, or incapable of moving anyone. And they sought to transform the reality of their situation in the direction of such political and aesthetic ideals.

Such tribunals engaged in comparisons between really existing cases and contexts, differentiating and analysing what just is. But they also made comparisons between what was/is lacking in the present and fullness not-yet developed or yet to come. The terms of such comparison may seem formal, especially the latter. But if we dispense with such ungrounded grounds and positivities, we would be left with the distance between them. And isn't such distance what we call justice?

If we conceive such distance as an index of change, of points of historical inflection or events, which can be expressed imaginatively (even mathematically) in ways that yield new information deriving from changes (in underlying indexes) without the need for a common denominator, reductionist homogeneity, or a yardstick within the realm of what is considered possible, what we are left with is something similar to what sociologists and anthropologists call effervescence, charisma, second (potentiated) sight, or the force of the event. What Bloch termed the unstructured energy of 'what-may-become-possible,' mobilizing the ambiguity of matter's potentiality and the energetic force of open *entelechia* in Aristotle against the primacy of form that Aristotle himself implied and which colonial economic policy-makers in the Americas read into their denials of indigenous self-governance in natural law and early modern fetishizations of excess money and self-creating precious metals. Today's financial engineers also refer to this force. No longer as self-creating or vitalist but as gravitational-like when they create new investment vehicles through derivation based on changing prices and indexes. They call it volatility. And point out that what matters in our global markets is not the (univocal, finalist) direction of change but, precisely, its volatility.

The phenomenon of volatility may be akin to what anthropologists, political theorists and philosophers attentive to the rhetorical nature of the grounds and foundations of our societies understand as 'the moment of the ethical investment in the normative.' They refer thusly to the event that happens when a certain order comes to behave and be like something else, fulfilling the ordering function only because the changing environment affords it or makes it available and because even in periods of deep social crisis, which may seem to participants as apocalyptic, vast areas of society remain unshaken. Hence, they say, the need for constant negotiation and renegotiation of the relationship between the ethical element and the normative or legal element.[20]

Put otherwise, the relation between the ethical and the normative is one of investment and derivation. The investment of the ethical in the normative is radical because there is no guarantee of fixed return or arrival at a set destination. On the contrary, the investment is made in the absence of such guarantees of destination, return, final causes, or telos. Derivation comes to mean here something akin to the French *dérive*. It is a move to the realm of adjacent possibilities or the open future. This kind of rhetorical, imaginative move creates a shared space of what-if thinking or aesthetic ideas. This is an aspect of the power of judgment that, being publicly available, allows us to think collectively and to envision alternatives collectively. By exercising this aspect of our capacity for judgment we can give a distinct, precise shape to alternatives and possibilities, even to realize them. This is a different kind of precision. It is not like the praetorian, legalistic precision that subsumes an individual case to a given rule or precedent and comes to a final decision. Instead, it is a fantastic precision that dissolves the case or the problem by immersing it in the wider solution of possibilities. 'Fantastic' means here both a part of the imagination and a point of contact with real relations. Like the sideways or backwards moves of contemporary dance, situationist or post-surrealist poetics of revolt. Or like the clinamen from the straight line theorized by the early materialist philosophers that influenced Karl Marx.[21]

In other words, we are called to radically invest our ethical actions in existing normative orders or contexts without having complete knowledge of the situation. Our viewpoint here is closer to that of contemporary financial engineers than to the point of view of Renaissance painters drawing a line of the horizon and then proceeding to fugue or project everything reductively to that horizon, realm of possibility, or common denominator. What matters to us is not this kind of fixed or timeless geometrical vanishing point or direction, but volatility. This means that the gap between existing normative orders and (the act of) ordering cannot be rationally closed or foreclosed, because there is no 'real world'

20 Ernesto Laclau, 'Ethics, Normativity and the Heteronomy of Law' in *The Rhetorical Foundations of Society* (Verso 2014) 127–138.

21 Ernst Bloch, *On Marx* (J Mazwell tr, Verso 2018) 16–53.

of specifiable socio-legal norms applicable trans-historically. This is not because one advocates some kind of irrationalism but because such a gap is inherent to reality itself.

In other words, if the future is open, no given order can claim a monopoly of the ordering function. Just as no theory can claim that our protest will remain inconsequential or does not matter. There may be no universality of ordering from the standpoint of stories of origin or visualizations of starting conditions, but there is universalization or generalization. No static order by calculation but more and less hopeful pre-appearances, visions, derivations from changes in volatility accompanied by a thoroughly plebeian sense of courage to act and reanimate such visions.

This is no voluntarism, but something much humbler: the drive to persevere in one's existence; not just survival but survivance. Not progress towards achievement followed by stasis, which is the machine's mode, or rather, the mode of the *machina mundi* imagined under the premises of the Aristotelian right. Instead, this is an interactive, rhythmic, even unstable process in the sense that no guarantee of final rest in place is warranted. In this respect, to act for historical justice is not about amassing certain means towards an end, or tactics and strategy, but an end in itself. This is how hopeful vision or utopia can be best understood in Douzinas' reading of Blochian left-Aristotelianism. The practical corollary is that, if so, then the ability to win or lose from heightened volatility becomes the real, primary site of struggle. Isn't this the case of our concrete contexts of financialized, global, and neocolonial capitalism?

Perhaps. But this paper is intended as a humbler sketch, a sequence rather than a blueprint. So, for now, let us keep the idea that this means to say that what is common and fundamental to both the human rights activism of late twentieth-century or early twenty-first century actors/victims of historical injustice or gross rights violations (like the Latin American activists and intellectuals referred to above) and to the more recent critical human rights and jurisprudence scholarship of activist writers like Costas Douzinas is, to insist, that they put their vulnerable bodies where their mouth is. In other words, my argument here vis-à-vis the critical human rights and jurisprudence position that Douzinas has advanced in his more recent interventions, *The Radical Philosophy of Human Rights* (2019) and *States of Exception* (2024), is that a major shift was needed. And a major shift has taken place.

From the Other to History & Matter

On the one hand, what began negatively 'with the exhaustion of all attempts to ground action upon cognition and reason or some a priori stipulated conception of the good,'[22] has now moved on to become an affirmation: namely, that ethical agency, as an element of the human rights composite, is grounded in the vulnerability and injurability of ethical subjects that are historically indexed or constructed as a community of victims. Put otherwise, the Levinasian 'Other' of earlier critical interventions that sought to de-mystify or destroy legal formalism or ideology has not only gone through a first metamorphosis when transformed into the subject of legal construction. In the move to historical constructivism, the judgment of justice also changed. It was relocated both within the law, where it might risk becoming 'the mirror image and companion of the judge,' and outside it. Meaning that in the constructive, affirmative move towards the border between inside and outside, there begins to emerge a 'strong ethical position' mobilizing 'the quasi-transcendental... concept of the "Other" and the associate gambits of "incalculable justice"... and "democracy to come."'[23]

Ditto, this re-orientation toward changeability and historical alterity forms what-just-is, privileges the ordinary as the timespace when ongoing ethical-political action takes place: a move to the point at which the bodily vulnerability of the other becomes mine to respond to. This move implies an invocation of hope (for a just law and society) 'transferred into some unpredictable future and the contingency of the event.'[24]

On the other hand, however bold and transformative, the affirmation of a quasi-transcendental ethical conception risks sidelining politics, disavowing the need for socio-historical evidence or the grounding of ethical agency, and it also risks leaving implicit the comparison between what just is and the hopeful ideal of justice as well as some presumed affirmations of causality rooted in Greek classical philosophy. Thereby running the risk of falling into moralism or leaving itself open to the criticisms of ahistoricism, implicit idealism, or confusion between human rights, human rights movements from below, NGOs working with the aid-security global industry, and US or UK governmental human rights policies.[25]

In view of these risks and criticisms, my argument that a major shift has taken place in Douzinas' human rights philosophy and jurisprudence will be presented in the final sections of this paper as twofold. One side of my argument is that far from being either reducible to or incompatible with his initial deconstructive bent, this shift takes Douzinas across a left-Heideggerian trajectory. And beyond. Towards a neo-Marxian position that brings him in proximity to critical theoretical re-appraisals of the critique of political

22 Costas Douzinas and Ronnie Warrington, '"A Well-Founded Fear of Justice": Law and Ethics in Postmodernity' in *Law & Critique* Vol 2 (Springer, September 1991) 115–147.
23 Costas Douzinas, *States of Exception* (n 10) 7.
24 ibid.
25 Kathryn Sikkink, *Evidence for Hope* (n 6) 41n55 citing Costas Douzinas.

economy. Such as those present in the Law & Political Economy movement engaged by Samuel Moyn, among others, and, before them, by the theoretical practice of members of the Caribbean Philosophical Association like Enrique Dussel, Drucilla Cornell and I, who have also been associated with the Birkbeck Institute for the Humanities since its foundation by Douzinas. That theoretical practice has aimed to take the position of decolonial critical theory away from essentialism and in the direction of current debates concerning the importance of the socio-historical grounding of ethical principles in concrete contexts of political and economic struggle, the role of the imagination in such concrete political contexts, and materialism.[26]

Crucially, this entails a further move towards left-Aristotelianism in the debates concerning old and new materialisms. A move that, as I have suggested in this paper, maps onto the ontology of the not-yet developed by Frankfurt critical theorist Ernst Bloch. It can be best understood as a certain legal-political naturalism. Also, a temporal naturalism. It emerges out of our collective teaching of Bloch's *Natural Law and Human Dignity*, which I introduced in the History and Philosophy of Human Rights masters course that Douzinas and I have been co-teaching at Birkbeck College for years now, and most recently together with our colleague Kojo Koram. I argue that this ontology takes a protagonist role in Douzinas' *States of Exception.*

This is also a move towards the contemporary reinvention of natural philosophy, a deflationary and naturalistic view of mathematics, and the renewal of the history of humanity based on recent evidence highlighting the importance of projective imagination and visual systems in the history of humanity. It matters to observe how the latter moves approximate a series of dialogues that have taken place, in parallel, between law and the natural sciences (between physicist Lee Smolin and political philosopher Drucilla Cornell, for example, also between Smolin and Critical Legal Studies socio-legal theorist Roberto Mangabeira Unger in the Americas), legal historians and anthropologists such as Michael Taussig or David Graeber and David Wengrow, and with novel aesthetic and philosophy of mathematics or encryption approaches (Eyal Weizman, Fernando Zalamea, Ricardo Sanin-Restrepo inter alia).[27]

26 Samuel Moyn, 'Reconstructing Critical Legal Studies' (4 August 2023) 134 *Yale Law Journal* <https://papers.ssrn.com/sol3/papers.cfm?abstract_id=4531492>; 'Does LPE Need Theory?' 9 April 2023 <https://lpeproject.org/blog/does-lpe-need-theory/>

27 Bloch, *Avicenna and the Aristotelian Left* (n 2) xi; Slavoj Žižek, *The Privatization of Hope. Ernst Bloch and the Future of Utopia* (Duke University Press 2013) cited by Douzinas *States of Exception* (n 10) 247; Orlando Bentancor, *The Matter of Empire. Metaphysics and Mining in Colonial Peru* (University of Pittsburgh 2017) for the link between Aristotelian metaphysics, decolonial theories, and trajectories of natural law; Drucilla Cornell, *The Imaginary Domain* (Routledge 1995) 38 criticizing the right-Aristotelian metaphysical 'human' instrumentalism by which vulnerable bodies (of women,

The other side of my argument about the major shift that Douzinas' recent work has contributed to in the political philosophy and history of human rights and jurisprudence concerns three elements that have begun to emerge in response to perceived weaknesses, risks, or the critics. First, critical ethics require intersubjective and inter-temporal validity. This means that, if not consensus, then the validation of those affected by the application of forensic judgment or rules is required to justify and generalize such judgment and rules. Second, any *longue durée* historical approach to ethics and human rights must recover the traces, trajectories, and evidential lessons left by the victims of historical ethical/legal systems rendered illegitimate, invalid, or immoral by the critical agency of the victims themselves left unheard and made invisible by such systems. Third, to put it in terms that resonate with Enrique Dussel's critical ethics of liberation, 'ethical agency is grounded in the corporeality of the ethical agent... being-alive as a condition of the possibility of ethical agency. For this reason, we should think of ethical agency as ethical flesh... corporeality. But this flesh is thoroughly historical.'[28]

To fully unpack these elements would take us beyond the scope of this paper. So, for now, let us draft a final section in the guise of an invitation for further investigation rather than a definitive conclusion.

Conclusion: The Matter of Hope

Douzinas' understanding of human rights and jurisprudence was born of struggle. As he says, it 'developed during the 1967–74 Greek dictatorship.'[29] The dates are not inconsequential. On the one hand, they can be mapped onto the rejection of the 'politics of progress' or 'continuity' history and philosophy of law, human rights, and politics. Such rejection is best exemplified by the critical theory and historiographic work of people like Enrique

in the case of struggles over the right to abortion) are placed 'in the hands and imaginings of others' cited by Douzinas, *States of Exception* (n 10); Drucilla Cornell, 'Derrida's Negotiations as a Technique of Liberation' in *Discourse* 39.2, special edition *Photoelectric Technologies of Liberation* (O Guardiola-Rivera ed, Wayne University Press, Spring 2017) 195–215; Lee Smolin and Roberto Mangabeira Unger, *The Singular Universe and the Reality of Time* (Cambridge University Press 2015); Eyal Weizman and Matthew Fuller, *Investigative Aesthetics. Conflicts and Commons in the Politics of Truth* (Verso 2021) citing Fernando Zalamea, *Synthetic Philosophy of Contemporary Mathematics* (ZL Fraser tr, Urbanomic 2012) originally publ. as *Filosofía Sintética de las Matemáticas Contemporáneas* (Universidad Nacional de Colombia 2009); Oscar Guardiola-Rivera, *A Hopeful Political Imagination. Courage and Fantastic Critique in the Age of Meltdown* (Bloomsbury 2025) citing Fernando Zalamea, David Wengrow, Ricardo Sanin-Restrepo and Hans Lindahl.

28 Amy Allen and Eduardo Mendieta, 'Introduction' in *Decolonizing Ethics. The Critical Theory of Enrique Dussel* (n 11) 12.

29 Costas Douzinas, *States of Exception* (n 10) 9.

Dussel and Samuel Moyn in the Americas. On the other hand, the emphasis on rupture events during the 1970s, concretely exemplified by the Greek dictatorship or the coup d'état against Salvador Allende in Chile, is the link connecting the depoliticization of anti-capitalist or anti-colonial struggles around the world with the apotheosis of a specific law-form elevated to the status of a principle of the imagination and political action. That is, the elevation or sacredness of the 'human' in human rights as a legalistic form that produces itself and the centripetal, taming force of its perspective at the same time as the liquidity-form, disruptive and excessive, breaks through and globally displaces the other moments of global capitalist accumulation. In short, this is the process through which commodity production, colonial extraction and trade, or the commodity-form, gets displaced by the liquidity-form characteristic of the Big Bang of the financial moment of global capitalism. Which can be dated, roughly speaking, to the early 1970s.

As they are being used here, terms like 'continuity' and 'politics of progress' refer to 'the entanglement of ideas of progress, development, and modernity with the exclusion, domination, and exploitation of the victims of colonialism and imperialism' that continue to grab hold of our imagination and institutional practices even after the formal finalization of such regimes indexed under such prefixes as 'post' (for example, in post-colonialism or post-modernism) the abuse of which in the media and academia works to hide changing and persistent relations of domination and excess appropriation in the age of globalization and exclusion. As Dussel says, what is captured in such terms is 'the double movement that the global peripheries' of the world, including southern European countries such as modern Greece, are 'caught between: on the one hand, 'the supposed modernization occasioned by the formal globalization of finance capital... but, on the other hand, the increasing material, discursive, and formal exclusion of the victims of this purported civilising process.'[30]

This double movement resonates with the idea of two contrasting or, as Douzinas would have it, paradoxical paradigms of modernity also apparent as the paradoxes of human rights. First, the centripetal force of the Eurocentric (imperial or imperialist metropolitan) paradigm according to which the phenomenon of modernity, developing out of the late Middle Ages or the Renaissance and spreading to the rest of the world, can be explained in terms of its exceptional internal characteristics that allowed it to supersede through its rationality and hierarchically dominate all other bodies,

30 Enrique Dussel, *Ethics of Liberation: In the Age of Globalization and Exclusion* (E Mendieta, CB Perez, Y Angulo and N Maldonado-Torres tr, Duke University Press 2013) xxii, 24 cited by Amy Allen, 'The Ethics and Politics of Progress. Dussel and the Frankfurt School' in *Decolonizing Ethics. The Critical Theory of Enrique Dussel* (n 11) 170.

natural and cultural. This paradigm is contradicted by the second, or planetary paradigm of modernity. Here, Europe is not self-referential but merely part of the world system and its centrality not a function of the internal superiority or exceptionality of Europe (or parts of it) but an effect of conquest, colonization, and globalization even after the formal end of empires.

This is to say that, on the one hand, ruptural events like 1492 or 1973/4 give communities in struggle the inflection points of historical transformation: conflict, difference, dissent, motion, active imagination, and complexity. These stand in contrast (a contrast that is humorous and ironic, not melodramatic) with the demands of staid naturalistic or cultural 'authenticity' that both settler liberalism and a certain Heideggerianism place on individual or commonist experiences and claims subordinated to the rationalistic self-surety and apparent timelessness of the established, posited word and the set realm of possibilities. As legions of legal critics have put it, at least from Robert Cover onwards, such legal rationalism results in a paralysis of legal thought and action. Namely, the law's letter standing in the way of what cannot be understood, rationalized, or completely enunciated and finished. That is, history. The history of the ever-shifting relations between peoples, environs and institutions.

Samuel Moyn has 'offered a great service by indicating the political and professional flaws in mainstream historiography,' as Douzinas says, precisely by moving the idea of a human rights rupture to the 1970s. More concretely, to the gap created by the post-68 defeat of radicalism. A gap that liberals attempted to fill by (re)establishing human rights in a relationship of allegiance with international law and morality. In this newly set relation 'the emphasis on law,' posited law, 'weakens... their [human rights] usefulness for radical politics.'[31]

But to underline the force of events in history, for instance the history of human rights, also helps us to reject the idea of univocal or unidirectional causality and the finality of the limits of the possible that seems to inform 'continuity' historiographies and the 'politics of progress' so dear to liberal narratives. The latter worry that discourses about the tainted origins of human rights, such as Moyn's apparently, may either obscure their more diverse, polycentric, 'more complicated' origins and/or confuse their present sense and future destination.[32] In addition, these liberal critics focused on origins and destination complain that people like Moyn and Douzinas discuss the legitimacy and effectiveness of human rights by making comparisons to an ideal rather than engaging in empirical, non-ideal and, supposedly, more

31 Costas Douzinas, *States of Exception* (n 10) 134–135.
32 Kathryn Sikkink, *Evidence for Hope* (n 6) 29.

real comparisons limited 'within the realm of the possible.'[33] Douzinas, for example, is accused of using 'implicit comparison to the ideal with hidden causal statements' in his critical jurisprudence.[34]

While I tend to agree with the critique that we risk underestimating the connection between decolonization, previous political and intellectual trajectories, and rights-based struggles when insisting on relocating the human rights breakthrough point to the 1970s, more specifically to the espousal of human rights discourses by the US Carter administration, and that in following such a way revisionists like Moyn may lose 'the radical impulse of rights,' as Douzinas says,[35] what interests me the most is the melancholic attachment of liberal critics (and also less liberal ones) to questions of origins and destination. For this attachment reveals the metaphysical presuppositions left unexamined by supposedly realist, non-ideal, empirical approaches to human rights' progress. Namely, the metaphysical presuppositions of right-Aristotelianism.

Let us call the set of such right-Aristotelian presuppositions, still present in the purportedly realistic, modern, secular, and empirical endeavours of current socio-legal scholars of human rights of a more and less liberal persuasion, a teleocratic view of socio-political and human rights. It seems to remain implicit in these scholars' appeal to and concern for origins and destinations. The methodological stakes of this question are very high indeed, as Douzinas observes, given that 'stories of origin claim that historical phenomena have a starting point… [and] the political and cultural debates and concerns at that point influence their future development and iterations.'[36]

The question is less whether that point is singular or whether there are many, diverse points of origin. On the one hand, it is true, as Douzinas says, that 'all origins of a complex practice are arbitrary.'[37] Too often, such points are situated at either end of time. Whether it is the Adamic paradise of celebratory religious and national histories, the Sumerian myth of the golden age, or the post-apocalyptic, redemptive time of dystopian novels and the Andaman myth of future time, they tend to remove to an equally unattain-

33 ibid 32; see Drucilla Cornell, *Defending Ideals: War, Democracy, and Political Struggles* (Routledge 2004) 41–84; Drucilla Cornell, *Moral Images of Freedom. A Future for Critical Theory* (Rowman & Littlefield 2008) 27–37; Jane Ana Gordon, 'Introduction: Engaging Justice, Engaging Freedom' (2014) 41(1) *Philosophy and Social Criticism*, published 7 October 2014 <https://doi.org/10.1177/0191453714553497> for a contrasting interpretation of Sen and John Rawls that suggests reading their work in the direction of a more expansive notion of reality beyond what just is, and the more capacious role of the imagination

34 Kathryn Sikkink, *Evidence for Hope* (n 6) 38.

35 Costas Douzinas, *States of Exception* (n 10) 10.

36 ibid 135.

37 ibid 135–136.

able past or future the excess joys of a world in which one might keep to oneself and keep everything for oneself.

On the other hand, 'to gain without losing' and to 'enjoy without sharing' are, as Claude Lévi-Strauss had already observed, variations on the singular theme of the dream of a world without others. Without having to care for others. Without paying attention to the point at which their vulnerability becomes mine to respond to. Without having to care for 'the law of exchange' in reciprocity, as Lévi-Strauss put it.[38] The point made by Lévi-Strauss is the one to which Douzinas' shift is directed. It is also borne out by the evidence amassed by contemporary archaeology and anthropology. That most or all groups throughout history have felt the urge to resist the temptation of living in isolation and have accepted, according to various modalities that account for a flexible institutional and political imagination far wider and more attuned to environmental volatility than we thought possible, the need to live with others. This does not amount to a refusal of living in specific timespaces, with one's language, beliefs, rituals and so on. What we are concerned with here are social forms of production and reproduction and the basic freedoms that become apparent as we study the evidence and traces of such social forms.

These basic freedoms attest to relations and to generalizable values inherent to such relations that become concrete and can be perceived in the act of gift-giving that underpins, for example, rituals of exogamic marriage and what anthropologists call the incest prohibition. That is, the gift. Not just any gift, but the gift that is ritual, reciprocal, and public. Which is constructive of public body-spaces and of what we now call the public. Basic freedoms such as the freedom to move away, migrate or relocate from one's surroundings; the freedom to disobey commands issued by some central power or arché (an-'archism,' to borrow a felicitous term coined by James Martel); and the freedom to re-imagine, mimic, and shape or re-shape our bodies, locales, and social realities.[39]

The gift that animates and sustains these basic freedoms, which are 'basic' in the sense that they respond to the riddle of historical processes of value change and their justification-generalization based on mounting archaeological and anthropological evidence, entails and makes apparent an ontological element of alterity that is also most basic. As the requirement of any exchange or kinship relation, it is the outcome of a certain concrete position.

38 Claude Lévi-Strauss, *The Elementary Structures of Kinship* (J Harle Belle, tr, JR von Sturmer and R Needham, Beacon Press 1969) 496–497.

39 David Graeber and David Wengrow, *The Dawn of Everything. A New History of Humanity* (Allen Lane 2021) 503; David Wengrow, *On Historical Materialism and The Dawn of Everything*. I am quoting from a pre-proof version of a piece to appear in *Contemporary Political Theory* (2024) with thanks to the author for his generosity.

Or transposition, if we speak of exchange as involving change, going across and beyond, or involving thorough transformation. And it becomes a kind of value that propagates in all variegated, complex, behaviours, situations, and relationships. In short, this basic and concrete element of alterity composes extensive networks of value and of connotations in a wide variety of contexts in a way that is similar to the kinds of systems that archaeologists like David Wengrow call image-systems. Which they believe to be crucial in human history.[40]

This is the kind of alterity that is ignored or disavowed when one denies others the ability to respond, or when one abuses the means of exchange and communication to deny or limit others' time. For words and imaginals or techniques and their respective technologies are not merely neutral media of communication. Rather, they are bearers of value. They are offered to others as something that comes from us. They are precious or priceless, opposed to the useful exchange-value goods that we make with our hands out of supposedly inert matter and to the excess-value appropriation goods we create in the analogy between the accumulation of the portion of wealth due to the appreciation of pre-existing wealth and the occupation of some hitherto 'undiscovered' continent that is/was our final destination. What emerges here, in this genealogy of basic freedoms and so-called human rights, is an ontology that markedly differs from the right-Aristotelian physics and metaphysics underpinning the focus on origins and destination that still seems to predominate in mainstream socio-historical approaches to jurisprudence, economics, and rights which would like to imagine themselves realistic and empirical. It expands the horizon of possibility in the direction of the open future and the kind of temporal naturalism that Bloch sees as the gift of the Aristotelian Left. In short, the shift from left-Heideggerian to left-Hegelian, neo-Marxian and left-Aristotelian positions in Douzinas' trajectory emerges from within his critical study of states of emergency. In the boundary and connection between 'the desire called utopia' and realist human rights.

This expanded reality and realism are the gift of Douzinas' lifework. It is a precious gift. And we are grateful for it.

40 David Wengrow, 'On Image Systems in Human History' in D Wengrow (ed), *Image, Thought, and the Making of Social Worlds* (Propylaeum 2022) 3–18; Hans Joas, *The Sacredness of the Person: A New Genealogy of Human Rights* (Georgetown University Press 2013) 9–36 and 140–194.

16

'OCCUPY EVERYTHING'

The Critique of Human Rights Meets the Age of Resistance in Brazil

Moniza Rizzini Ansari

I heard about it for the first time in 2010. A murmuring caught my attention in the hallway of my workplace, the Rio de Janeiro State Secretariat for Human Rights building. While representatives of social movements deliberated in the main room what would then become Rio's state Human Rights Plan, a small group of activists was having a separate discussion outside. They were talking about the upcoming visit of Costas Douzinas to Brazil and making plans to attend his talks. One of them held a book – *The End of Human Rights* – and I remember being puzzled about it and taking note of the author, with the feeling that I was lagging behind something clearly important.

This scene stayed in my memory because it changed the course of my own activist journey. A new world opened to me when I later began reading his books. Moved by this new discovery, presented to me by activists, I started an academic journey in a Master's degree programme to learn more about Critical Legal scholarship. It was then, at the Federal University of Rio de Janeiro, where Costas later returned in 2014, that we got to meet in person. Before I knew it, I was in London pursuing a PhD under his supervision.

Most importantly, that scene in 2010 also says a lot about the reach of Costas Douzinas' work in Brazil. It was not from academics that I first heard about him; it was from members of social movements in a politically significant but very local event. This shows how his theoretical and political work resonates with social struggles in Latin America. At the time, his work was already focused on the new political unrests and tactics – what he termed the 'age of resistance' – inaugurated by a shift in global governance and by the

DOI: 10.4324/9781032622224-16

rise of new modes of resistance epitomised by the Occupy global wave.[1] In Brazil, however, he was launching the translation of his earlier work on the critique of human rights, which arrived around the same time as the potent news about protest occupations of Tahrir Square, Syntagma Square, Taksim Square... and Wall Street and the City of London of all places.

At the dawn of the 'Latin American spring',[2] such massive unrests that also took to the streets of Rio de Janeiro and São Paulo, among other Brazilian cities, Douzinas' critique found fertile ground in Brazil. In Rio, at least for certain progressive groups which took to the streets in the so-called 'June 2013 Journeys', the call for 'real democracy' and the critique of human rights combined into a big and productive agenda. Despite the critical approach to the mainstream international human rights framework, these groups identified with the umbrella term 'human rights movements' – *movimentos de direitos humanos* – a term still evoked by key political actors defending against proto-fascist attacks, which, in turn, gained strength from the conservative backlash of the 2010s uprisings leading to a parliamentary (as well as judicial, mediatic and corporate) coup d'état in 2016. Indeed, 'human rights' was (and still is) the proxy term for a progressive, leftist stance in the context of a political dispute that started in the streets and took over institutional politics.

This essay examines the recent transformations on the horizons of resistance from the perspective of the 'human rights movements' in Rio de Janeiro. Drawing from Douzina's analysis and involvement in both the street and the institutional politics,[3] it offers reflections on a distinctive feature of critical legal theory as praxis foregrounding the collaborative encounter between street protest and human rights activism in Brazil.

'Occupy and Resist': How the Occupation of Everything Gained Momentum

As mass protests erupted all over the world, the 'age of resistance' developed in a peculiar way in the Brazilian political landscape, reviving nostalgic experiences of massive street demonstrations that had determined the country's history but which had lost force and demobilized an entire generation of disillusioned youth.[4] Provocatively, '*the giant awoken*' became one of the

1 Costas Douzinas, *Philosophy and Resistance in the Crisis* (Polity Press 2013).
2 Bethania Assy, 'Insurgent Subjectivities and the Political Empowerment of the Streets: Notes on the Brazilian Protests' (2017) 7 *Post Filosofie Revista di Pratica Filosofica e Scienza Umane* 118–124.
3 Costas Douzinas, *Syriza in Power: Reflections of an Accidental Politician* (Polity Press 2017)
4 Anthony D'Andrea, '2013 Protests in Brazil: The Kite and the Byte in New Forms of Popular Mobilization' (2014) 87(3) *Anthropological Quarterly* 935–942.

watchwords of the time, in reference to a decades-long dormant discontentment and popular demobilization.

Other key slogans soon emerged – '*come to the street!*' and '*no flags!*' – calling individuals to join the multitude in an unprecedented disregard and contempt for parties, social movements, trade unions and institutions that traditionally, until then, mobilized political demonstrations. Members of such parties, movements and institutions, initially optimistic about the political revitalization and the expansion of indignation with the establishment, gradually noticed that those around them in the streets had new faces, in events that were increasingly more difficult to decipher. Rapidly, they faced violent reactions of the multitude to their banners, t-shirts and any other form of collective identification, opening the way to an increasingly more green-and-yellow nationalistic homogenization of the masses revealing that something much bigger and more alarming than 'the people' had awoken.

Unsuspiciously at first, these internal clashes foreshadowed drastic changes to Brazilian political stability since its re-democratization in the 1980s. Central to the analysis here, from the perspective of social movements, specifically human rights movements, the promising occupation of streets in the country's major urban centres and the rise of new forms of conservative mobilization that followed led to irreversible changes to their possibilities for action and their role in the Brazilian political scene. Below is a succinct way to retrace the unfolding of events in the age of resistance, referring to key commentators who examine their complexity in more depth:

- In 2011, with inspiration coming from the global wave of the Occupy trend,[5] various occupations of squares mushroomed in cities all over the country – 'Ocupa Cinelândia' in Rio, 'Ocupa Sampa' in São Paulo, 'Ocupe Estelita' in Recife, among many others.[6] Occupations, of course, were not a novel political method in Brazil. Urban social movements have been, for decades, occupying unused private and public properties, reclaiming housing and urban rights. Also, beyond cities, organized occupations of unproductive lands in rural Brazil are a world-renowned tactic influencing practices of social movements globally.[7] What was mainly new in 2011 occupations was, first, the crowd of protesters

5 Marlies Glasius and Geoffrey Pleyers, 'The Global Moment of 2011: Democracy, Social Justice and Dignity' (2013) 44(3) *Development and Change* 547–567.

6 E.g. Liliana Galindo Ramírez, 'The Network as Chronotope: Internet and Political Practices in the Colombian Student Movement mane and Occupy São Paulo' in C Feixa, C Leccardi and P Nilan (eds), *Youth, Space and Time: Agoras and Chronotopes in the Global City* (Brill 2016) 365–384.

7 Gabriel Ondetti, *Land, Protest, and Politics: The Landless Movement and the Struggle for Agrarian Reform in Brazil* (Pennsylvania University Press 2008).

involved (largely educated youth realizing or redefining their class position in times of financial capitalism, i.e. 'the 99%') and their broad demands (e.g. 'real democracy' and systemic changes to wealth inequality at large and the various forms of inequality that follow, such as employment, education, security, health, etc).[8] By camping in public squares and claiming space, protesters develop new ways of co-living, new social interactions and new imaginations of the future.[9] Another new aspect of these experiences was the media coverage, particularly of the violent police repression that succeeded their installation in public spaces – while the repression of more traditional occupation movements remains largely uncovered by the media to date – also due to their high levels of social media activity and the emergence of digital activism and journalism.

- In 2013, mass protest gained an entirely new dimension in what came to be referred to as the 'June Journeys' (*Jornadas de Junho*), which took place in hundreds of cities all over Brazil, beyond state capitals, and which lasted for months. In an unparalleled autonomist way of protest, millions of people took to the streets with novel tactics (including self-organized, anonymous and black bloc tactics) protesting the neoliberal and financialized socioeconomic policies, starting by contesting a rise in urban transport fares and the growing urban redevelopments in preparation for mega-events such as the forthcoming FIFA World Cup in 2014 and the Olympics in 2016.[10] The demonstrations were indeed massive and widespread, increasingly less connected to traditional forms of mobilizations and opening the way for a wide diversity of protesters disputing the streets.[11] Without meaning to indicate a direct causal link, it is notable that, with agonistic reverberations of contradictory indignations occurring until 2015, the waves of protest gradually transformed into massively divisive iterations and consolidated a sentiment particularly among the so-called 'new middle-class' (forged out of the country's own neodevelopmentist policies)[12] of rising rejection of the Brazilian Workers' Party (PT), in power since 2003, and gave way to growing calls for far-right and military intervention (thus revealing a

8 Slavoj Žižek, 'Remarks on Occupy Wall Street' (2012) 25 *Log* 118–120.

9 Jenny Pickerill and John Krinsky, 'Why Does Occupy Matter?' (2012) 11(3–4) *Social Movement Studies* 279–287.

10 Erick Omena de Melo, 'Just Because of 20 Cents? For a Genealogy of the Brazilian "Demonstrations Cup"' (2020) 12(1) *International Journal of Urban Sustainable Development* 103–118.

11 Guilherme Leite Gonçalves, 'Neoliberal Malaise, 2013 "June Journeys" and the Criminalization of the Protests in Brazil: A Re-reading Through Louis Althusser' (2023) 36 *International Journal of Politics, Culture and Society* 499–526.

12 Assy (n 2).

class-based nostalgia for the 21 years of military rule in Brazil which had been deposed only 28 years before).[13]

President Dilma Rousseff, the first woman elected president in Brazilian history, herself a former militant of the armed struggle against the dictatorship, tried to contain the crisis by proposing national pacts (for fiscal responsibility, social participation, health, transport and education as well as anticorruption measures) and signalling the convocation of a national referendum to establish an unprecedented constituent process aimed at political reform. Soon after, she also passed a Criminal Organisations Act and, a couple of years after, the Antiterror Law – which, by the way, is a requirement by FIFA and the International Olympic Committee for host countries[14] – thus strengthening the criminalization of protesters and social movements in the streets, particularly her administration's own supporters.

- In 2015 and 2016, with a series of other factors involved (including the late effects of the economic crisis, a neodevelopmentalist emphasis of government and a major anticorruption lawfare operation), millions of anti-PT protesters took to the streets in hundreds of cities calling for the government's deposition as well as, in increasingly smaller scale, supporting Rousseff and defending democracy (the latter promoted by traditional social movements and trade unions, in a way, taking back to their hands the mission to save democracy and call for progressive agendas). Rousseff was eventually impeached in 2016, in a legally legitimized parliamentary 'soft coup' with support from corporate, judicial and mainstream media sectors.[15] The interim government succeeded, led by Rousseff's former vice-president and allied to the forces leading to the coup, then became the object of various demonstrations against its lack of democratic legitimacy throughout 2017 and 2018 until the elections were called. The interim president, Michel Temer, led a conservative government programme, venturing a series of unpopular neoliberal measures, including pension and labour reforms and retrenchments to social policies and a public spending ceiling for the duration of 20 years (the so-called 'Evil' constitutional amendment).[16] Such measures consolidated

13 Alfredo Saad-Filho, 'Mass Protests under "Left Neoliberalism": Brazil, June–July 2013' (2013) 39(5) *Critical Sociology*, 657–669.

14 Adriano de Freixo and Vinicius Armele, 'The Brazilian Anti-Terrorism Bill and the International Circulation of Punitive Legal Regimes' (2021) 13(1) *Passagens Revista Internacional de História Política e Cultura Jurídica* 105–128.

15 André Singer, 'From a Rooseveltian Dream to the Nightmare of Parliamentary Coup' in V Puzone and LF Miguel (eds), *The Brazilian Left in the 21st Century: Marx, Engels, and Marxisms* (Palgrave Macmillan 2019).

16 Niels Søndergaard, 'Reforming in a Democratic Vacuum: The Authoritarian Neoliberalism of the Temer Administration from 2016 to 2018' (2021) 18(4) *Globalizations* 568–583.

the drastic shift in government from left to right-wing,[17] despite various forms of protests in the streets, social media and cultural events. This period was marked by a new wave of political occupations of strategic spaces, with the emergence of novel social mobilizations, namely the public secondary schools' occupation movement, which mobilized students from all over the country to rise up against the Secondary Education Reform, also joined by universities. Students began to occupy their schools, improving their infrastructure and pedagogic organization based on autonomy and horizontality.[18] The 'Occupy Everything' slogan became a reality when, for months, protesters took charge of school activities and received wide support from intellectual and cultural sectors. Differently from the dissipated effects of street protests, such occupations gained direct attention from government institutions, albeit at local level, in attempts to mediate demands.

- In 2018, by the time of the elections, the initial diversity of protesters' claims was already solidified in a simplified and populist polarization of the Brazilian population into left *vs* right, exacerbated by former president Lula's controversial arrest and the (until recently unanticipated) rise of 'bolsonarism'.[19] The street demonstrations became more and more oriented towards institutional politics and were used as an electoral campaign strategy. In other words, it could be suggested that institutional and electoral politics gained back their centrality, despite the new politics of the streets in the age of resistance. Women's anti-Bolsonaro marches were prevalent at that time, with the 'Not him' (*#EleNão*) slogan.[20] What followed from the electoral-based marches continued throughout the four years of Bolsonaro's administration, with opponents attempting to depose it, and supporters defending it, every step of the way.[21]
- In 2020, as if things were not incendiary enough, then came the COVID-19 pandemic's devastating toll on Brazil along with the full package of polarizations against and pro lockdown social distancing, vaccination,

17 Natália Sátyro, 'The Paradigmatic Radical Reform in Brazil's Social Policies: The Impact of the Temer Administration' in N Sátyro, E del Pino and C Midaglia (eds), *Latin American Social Policy Developments in the Twenty-First Century* (Palgrave Macmillan 2021).

18 Rosa Malena de Araújo Carvalho and Andreza Oliveira Berti, 'The time in Public Education: Essay Starting from the Movement "Occupy Everything"' (2018) 22(4) *Educação* 307–315.

19 Glenn Greenwald, *Securing Democracy: My Fight for Press Freedom and Justice in Bolsonaro's Brazil* (Haymarket Book 2021).

20 Karina Bárcenas Barajas, '#EleNão (Él no): tecnofeminismo interseccional en Brasil frente al ascenso del neoconservadurismo evangélico y el posfascismo' (2020) 30(59) *Alteridades* 43–56.

21 Paul Scott, 'Securing Democracy: My Fight for Press Freedom and Justice in Bolsonaro's Brazil' (2019) 42 *Galáxia* 5–22.

use of masks and so on and so forth. After a period of uncertainty and protesting from home (e.g. synchronized action from windows and balconies), public demonstrations were resumed, particularly in 2022 (another electoral year), from the part of those against exceptional and denialist measures in response to the pandemic that violated rights and revealed the face of sanitary and climate injustice.[22] On the other hand, a series of disruptive events unfolded after Lula's election defeating Bolsonaro, some of which applied familiar tactics of the 'age of resistance' albeit with clear connections to conspiracies attempting another coup d'état: families occupied public spaces of the Brazilian capital city with military aid; truck drivers blocked main national highways; mobs invaded and depredated the buildings of the three powers (Congress, Supreme Court and presidential palace) mirroring the 2021 insurrections at the US Capitol.

From this brief recompilation of events, one can see how the new age of resistance in Brazil unfolded in waves, each time opening the way for new possibilities of action which are not only unpredictable and often volatile, but also specific to contingent combinations of macro- and micro-political factors that make them extremely complex to comprehend. Hence, political commentators still grapple with how certain actors, tactics and confluences of agendas emerged on the left and on the right in contrast to what previously dominated the public arena. One thing is for sure, although spanning a wide ideological spectrum these collective protests are products of the same sociopolitical opening, proper to the new forms of organization seen worldwide in the 2010s.[23] Also, although initiated and 'multitudinous' (in terms of participants, agendas, ideologies, etc), it eventually led to increasingly more polarized disputes gravitating around institutional politics. Figure 16.1 illustrates this polarization and institutions-centred ordering of the multitudes.

Focusing on the progressive waves of innovative protest tactics – as opposed to bringing to the spotlight the serpent's egg of fascism that the left's political weakening incites[24] – it might also be productive to question

22 Tatiana Maia and Denise De Sordi, 'The Radicalness of Social Solidarity: Protests and Political Change in Contemporary Brazil' (2022) 29(50) *Esboços* 21–34.

23 Breno Bringel and Geoffrey Pleyers, 'June 2013, Five Years Later: Polarization, Reconfiguration of Activism, and Challenges for the Brazilian Left' in V Puzone and LF Miguel (eds), *The Brazilian Left in the 21st Century: Marx, Engels, and Marxisms* (Palgrave Macmillan 2019).

24 Vladmir Safatle, 'The day Brazil stopped for ten years' ['*O dia no qual o Brasil parou por dez anos*'] in Breno Altman and Maria Carlotto (eds), *Junho de 2013: a rebelião fantasma* (Boitempo 2023).

FIGURE 16.1 The crowd awaits, in front of Congress, the counting of votes in Rousseff's impeachment process with walls separating 'anti' (in red) and 'pro' (in green and yellow) protesters, Brasilia, 17/04/2016. Credit: Juca Varella/Agência Brasil (CC:BY 3.0 Brazil).

what it is that the multitude protested about after all. And this is not to highlight a lack of specific or concrete agendas from a leaderless movement.[25] In fact, it is about recognizing that this multitude is not demanding any specific rights as concessions from the state or the sovereign power, as liberal legal and political theories expect. The key aspect that differentiates this from other more traditional movements is that their interlocutor is not specifically the state and their resistance is not straightforwardly reactions to violations of their own liberties.

They operate at the biopolitical level.[26] The search for new ways to protest is to take politics into one's own hands, in prefiguring and building a different world. In other words, as Douzinas frequently reminds us, resistance is not merely reactive but also active.[27] It is about building new, dissident modes of living and resisting state-based capitulations, while knowing well that new assemblages are always subject to being captured by power in a continuous cycle of resisting, reinventing and reliving. On this point,

25 Milo Sweedler, 'Demanding the Impossible: The Truth of the Occupy Movement' in Amal Treacher Kabesh and James Arvanitakis (eds), *Revolt and Revolution: Reaching for the Possible* (Brill 2014) 15–24.

26 Costas Douzinas, *States of Exception: Human Rights, Biopolitics, Utopia* (Elgar 2023).

27 ibid.

a trendy wordplay of those effervescent years is particularly meaningful: where derivations of the word *resistência* are spelled as *re-existência* or *re-existir*, i.e. re-existence or to re-exist.

However, we have seen how the interlocution with institutional politics and the state is inescapable and, occasionally, encloses the crowd. In the case of the protest in Brazil, protesters very quickly went from a festive experience of direct democracy to a devastating nightmare of democratic instability, in having their indignation captured to fuel old, party-based and putschist disputes. It thus seems important to reflect on the paradoxical co-implication of these opposed registers of politics: the streets and the institutions. The participation of human rights movements in the events recounted above can offer interesting insight on this.

'No Violence!': the Brazilian Paradox of Human Rights Take the Streets

Despite different forms of organization and tactics observed throughout the years of street politics revitalization, one element that persistently accompanied the unfolding events, besides the persistent reactionary responses, was the violence of police repression. Certainly, the constant policing of mass protests was not equally performed in the same way across different sectors taking the streets. It was evident that there was a more permissive attitude to conservative demonstrations in which, as a matter of fact, protesters celebrated the police presence, as if joining their march in support of pro-gun agendas and the military at large. In fact, such demonstrators would typically applaud and take pictures with police officers supervising their events, in an atmosphere of mutual identification.[28]

On the other side of the political spectrum, as more traditionally occurs, the clash between protesters and the police was extremely violent, with many severely injured, illegally arrested and, eventually, killed.[29] This was certainly a major aspect discouraging adhesion of the wider population to the marches and demobilizing the crowds in periods of more intense repression. A key watchword for such circumstances in the streets was 'no violence!' ['*sem violência!*'], which the crowds would shout in chorus in an attempt to convince both the police forces and their own more incendiary segments to refrain from engaging in confrontations.

These unison cries for no violence soon gave clearer shape to the very purpose of the multitude occupying the cityscape. It became a matter of reclaiming one's basic liberty to protest. Hence, their resistance was about countering the police offensive and defending a general right to take the

28 Maia and De Sordi (n 22).
29 Saad Filho (n 13).

streets, that is, as a 'biopolitical right of the governed'.[30] Even if there's no posited right to resist, as a granted right from the state to its citizens, resistance rises in face of the injustice of police violence and abusive law enforcement. The right to resist entails the freedom (if not a duty) of subjects of rights to take an active stance and mobilize actions against legal, legitimized injustice.[31] Thus, new individual and collective insurgent subjectivities emerged in a resolute objection to institutional politics and representative democracy,[32] while also holding on to their fundamental right to not being brutalized by state violence.

Of course, this transcendent rights-based discussion of resistance has its own pitfalls, particularly in potentially opening the way to counterarguments legitimizing state-based self-preservation responses to alleged 'abuses of rights' from protesters.[33] However, what remains radically inspiring from the discussion above is how a new utopia, as imagination of the future, emerges in the abrupt interruption of oppression in the 'here and now' of acting together politically and in solidarity.[34] And, indeed, political solidarity from the movements oriented around human rights towards the multitude propitiated the formation of a unique, radical encounter in defence of street politics in the face of the violent responses of institutional politics.

Throughout the violent clashes, in moments of complete powerlessness of protesters before the war-like, militarized apparatus mobilized by law enforcement, the networks of 'human rights' played important roles both locally and nationally. Cases of police brutality or abuses in general were visibilized and circumstances of criminalization of protest were reported by the 'human rights movements', i.e., mostly groups of human rights defenders, rather than institutionalized organizations, which formed provisory collectives to work in shifts in all demonstrations to support victims. For example, in Rio de Janeiro, the organization *Instituto dos Defensores de Direitos Humanos* (DDH) formed groups of voluntary lawyers to observe and be on call in case of any legal aid emergency during marches.[35] In such kinds of initiatives, human rights defenders were simultaneously protesters,

30 Douzinas, *States of Exception* (n 26).

31 Costas Douzinas, *The Radical Philosophy of Rights* (Routledge 2019).

32 Costas Douzinas, 'Notes Towards an Analytics of Resistance' (2014) 83 *New Formations* 79–98.

33 Patricia Tuitt, 'Walter Benjamin, Race and the Critique of Rights' (2018) 27(4) *Griffith Law Review* 453–468.

34 Assy (n 2).

35 DDH also took on the defence case of Rafael Braga Vieira, the first and only person convicted (wrongfully sentenced to five years in prison) among the many arrested in the context of protests nationwide. Significantly, Braga was very different from the profile of protesters actually joining the marches, being a black, homeless man sleeping rough, incriminated for the possession of cleaning products, purportedly homemade explosive

observers and advocates, ready to take action when detecting misconducts. They had the experience that other protesters lacked, specifically knowledge of their rights, of what to do in case of brutality and illegality, of legal aid resources, of channels for reporting violations, of international protection pathways, etc. Moreover, as part of a wider network that includes allies and penetration in public institutions, nationally and internationally, they potentially held key connections to resolve matters more effectively.

Hence, human rights activists and movements facilitated the age of resistance in many steps along the way. This is a fundamentally democratic role that human rights defenders would keep up for the entire duration of the succeeding institutional shifts that led to Bolsonaro's administration.[36] Also because of that, they have been a constant target – increasingly antagonized and criminalized.[37] Moreover, they contribute to the preservation of the 'spirit' of insurgency that erupted and was revived on several occasions in the last ten years. When the dust settles, the multitudes are out of the streets, back to their everyday lives; the celebrated new subjectivities that momentarily emerged in the streets are back home, perhaps waiting for the next momentum to manifest again. Human rights movements, however, remain key actors permanently mediating street and institutional politics.[38]

It might be argued that a contributing factor to this permanent and democratic role of human rights movements throughout the ups and downs of the Brazilian age of resistance is, precisely, a distinctive feature of their own configuration merging 'human rights' and 'social movements'. This distinctive feature is critique. And that is because not only is the critical instrumentalization of human rights for social struggles their foundational act, but also because the 'critique of human rights' was already circulating vividly among defenders, which also set out to revise the terms and extent of that which they defended.[39]

Therefore, such movements were not naively proclaiming universal principles and the higher powers of fundamental rights in international declarations or the Brazilian constitution. They were highly aware of their Eurocentric grounds and imperialist expansion of Western values as well as

devices. See in Amnesty International, "*They use a Strategy of Fear": protecting the right to protest in Brazil* (Amnesty International 2014).

36 Ulisses Terto Neto, 'Bolsonaro, Populism and the Fascist Threat: The Role of Human Rights Defenders in Protecting Brazilian Democracy' (2020) 5(1) *Kairos: A Journal of Critical Symposium* 47–66.

37 Gabriela Quijiano and Mauro Kiithi Arima Junior, *Threats to environmental and human rights defenders in Brazil – Legal and policy gaps* (OECD Watch, FIDH, OBS, OMCT 2022).

38 Terto Neto (n 36).

39 Joseph Hoover and Marta Iñiguez De Heredia, 'Philosophers, Activists, and Radicals: A Story of Human Rights and Other Scandals' (2011) 12 *Human Rights Review* 191–220.

their paradoxical nature in how global biopolitical law transforms human rights into tools of control under the promise of freedom.[40] More accurately, human rights movements re-politicize human rights, putting them into practice, to the service of the new resisting subjectivities, to support radical change.[41] Most likely because of that, human rights militants became a target of the extreme right's offensive that followed.

'Call the Human Rights': How Human Rights Endure as a Proxy in the New Age of Resistance

There is a distinctive, invocative functionality to 'human rights' which is not only instrumentalized by a segment of social justice activists but also by conservative segments that admonish human rights, thus forming opposing fields. It is an invocative functionality in the sense of calling up the abstract powers of human rights as if it were an entity, rather than a legal-political framework or an institutional infrastructure. In fact, and this might also be the case elsewhere, but 'call the human rights' ('*chama os direitos humanos*'), is a typical expression used both by victims and, with derision, by perpetrators (or bystanders) of state and institutional violence. This derision from the latter is even materialized in allegorical objects of torture, such as batons that are engraved with the term 'human rights' – which can even be found for sale online.

Hence, despite critiques, 'human rights' is a long-lasting proxy of two significations which split two opposing camps. In the Brazilian age of resistance, it has been a clearly disputed term irrespective of its legal effectivity. The term highlights an ongoing political dispute (a dispute which, in reality, is made up of multiple, inner sub-disputes) beyond the original ethical consensus around human rights uniting ideological adversaries.[42]

Returning to the point, moving past conservative provocations, 'human rights' is the name given to many different things, including legal-procedural instruments, normative concepts, political capital, discursive resources, international frameworks and local circles gathering likeminded affiliations albeit without a conclusive and unified goal. It is, thus, less a matter of identifying the objective nature of human rights and more about the gathering of various intentions around something conventionally named as such. In other words, human rights are first and foremost a network, an epistemic-political

40 Costas Douzinas, *The End of Human Rights: Critical Legal Thought at the Turn of the Century* (Hart 2000).

41 Douzinas, *The Radical Philosophy* (n 31).

42 Costas Douzinas, 'Postmodern Just Wars and the New World Order' (2006) 5(3) *Journal of Human Rights* 355–375.

community.[43] A number of diverse actors, both individual and collective, local and international, participate on a daily basis in its construction and preservation, which might reflect or impact institutional arrangements. Their forms of articulation and mobilization have temporary specificities and institutional differences. They range from occasional meetings and collaborations, summoned work groups or collectives and formal organizations. Their practices also encompass a wide range of mundane actions leading to increasingly more institutionalized projects such as national or international strategic litigation; production of advocacy and ghost reports; policy influencing advancing the state's accountability in the realization of human rights; partaking in monitoring and participatory spaces; participation in international civil society committees and human rights 'systems'; and interlocution between traditional social movements and non-governmental organizations. Importantly, it is not just a network premised on demanding rights concessions from the state, but also to forge pathways to more radical politics.[44]

Certainly, the processes resulting from the 'everyday world', i.e. the sphere of daily life, impact, guide or even construct the 'institutional world'.[45] However, there is more to it, especially when one acknowledges the antagonistic and counterhegemonic activity of human rights as practice[46] – i.e., practised by social movements worldwide without identifying with their inherently liberal origination, universal pretension and ethical-ideological normative standards.[47] Not meaning to disregard how human rights also reinforce imperialist and capitalist oppression, there is space for critical thinking and praxis within diverse and mundane practices of human rights.

Hence, 'human rights movements' (more frequently the invoked 'entity' mentioned above in situations of violation) forge their struggles towards insurgent practices.[48] This seems to be particularly the case in the so-called 'global south', i.e. the former colonial world, which has been historically led to translate their post-colonial struggles into a non-belligerent international

43 Mark Goodale, 'Introduction Locating Rights, Envisioning Law between the Global and the Local' in Mark Goodale and Sally Engle Merry (eds), *The Practice of Human Rights: Tracking Law between the Global and the Local* (Cambridge University Press 2007) 1–38.

44 Douzinas, *The Radical Philosophy* (n 31).

45 On the institutional structures of human rights being constructed from the practices of social struggles, see Neil Stammers, *Human Rights and Social Movements* (Pluto Press 2009).

46 Kathryn McNeilly, 'After the Critique of Rights: For a Radical Democratic Theory and Practice of Human Rights' (2016) 27 *Law and Critique* 269–288.

47 Hoover and De Heredia (n 39).

48 Upendra Baxi, *The Future of Human Rights* (OUP 2006).

human rights and development frameworks[49] but which also turned these frameworks on their heads as potent tools for liberation beyond courts, offices and reports. For example, carrying on with the 'southern' revolutionary history, the assimilation and radicalization of human rights have supported transatlantic networks for liberation and anti-colonial politics.[50]

However, the point here is less about how movements skilfully deploy the language of human rights and more precisely on how human rights actors – individuals, groups, associations and organizations – form their own collaborative network to, bit by bit, as parts of a greater whole, press structural changes. Strictly speaking, human rights movements do not have a formal or cohesive existence on the scene of social movements. However, it is a broader collective that brings together activists, advocates, academics (as well as victims, survivors of human rights violations and their families[51]) that enact human rights and have the know-how to strategize and radicalize it as a political weapon. The connections between actors and movements in this network of human rights are formed transiently and incidentally, unified by a common cause of fighting injustice and rights violations.

Moreover, human rights movements have demonstrated a growing ability to infiltrate state structures – particularly in the context of the Latin American 'pink tide' – with significant occupation of public office by activists and union leaders, and members of social movements at large, including taking the chair as heads of state, as is the case of Lula in Brazil and Morales in Bolivia.[52] This is also how various members of parliaments, public defenders, prosecutors, public administrators and advisers are recognized as part of the human rights movement, forming their own articulated fronts of struggle and contesting the state from within.

Precisely because of their widespread presence in different sectors of society, the human rights movement managed to perform its key role during the events in the streets in the 2010s onwards. Protesters, members of social movements, legal aid societies, public prosecutors and attorneys, government officials, members of parliament, NGO workers and university scholars – each played a part in resisting and overturning the militarized

49 GK Bhambra and Robbie Shilliam, 'Introduction: "Silence" and Human Rights' in GK Bhambra and R Shilliam (eds), *Silencing Human Rights: Critical Engagements with a Contested Project* (Palgrave Macmillan 2009) 1–16.

50 Meredith Terretta, 'From Below and to the Left? Human Rights and Liberation Politics in Africa's Postcolonial Age' (2013) 24(2) *Journal of World History* 389–416.

51 E.g. Wanda C Krause, 'The Role and Example of Chilean and Argentinian Mothers in Democratisation' (2004) 14(3) *Development in Practice* 366–380.

52 Daniel M. Goldstein, 'Human Rights as Culprit, Human Rights as Victim: Rights and Security in the State of Exception' in Mark Goodale and Sally Engle Merry (eds), *The Practice of Human Rights: Tracking Law between the Global and the Local* (Cambridge University Press 2007) 4–77.

measures of protest criminalization. They did so without having to renounce or negotiate critique but, indeed, enacting the utopian end of human rights, i.e., of fighting injustices. In fact, a critical stance is what allows for human rights movements to maintain their actual purpose and justification – that which is revealed in both the genuine and derisive gestures of 'calling' the human rights.

Building Global Networks of Resistance: Critical Legal Theory as Praxis

In the contingent occurrences of the age of resistance in Brazil, human rights movements demonstrated (if only briefly and momentarily) that the legitimization of biopolitical power by the proxy 'human rights' can be subverted to counterstrike the very powers that depoliticize and tame it. Hence, human rights endure, not in the name of universal emancipation, but as a network of global resistance that applies critical theory to practices worldwide.

With the post-pandemic 'global state of exception' affecting daily lives all over the world,[53] we are bound to see more events of resistance, in increasingly more globally combined indignations challenging the global-local established orders. To prepare for it, there might be something to learn and radicalize from the above recounted experience of convergence between street protests and human rights activism, albeit situated and contingent to the specific context of 2010–2020 Brazilian political landscape.

Notably, the lesson that stands out in the discussion above is that critical legal theory thrives as praxis, i.e. in being put to action toward radical change. This encompasses reflecting on the place of theory, against the 'academization' of radical politics as well as acknowledging the political worth of depoliticized frameworks when practised at the service of dissenters. Resistance arises from the indignation with injustice. It is not an idea, a concept, but a factual occurrence of coming together in a common place and time.[54] The part critique plays is to interrupt the inaccessible legal order, to challenge its foundations, to unveil its paradoxical ideals of justice when injustice is so clear and urgent.[55]

Moreover, critical thinking plays a part in enabling lines of escape (or indeed never-ending attempts to escape) by making visible or foreseeable the permanent risks of capitulation and of reactionary backlashes to resisting mobilizations. Critical legal theory, particularly, evidences law's accommodating force to de-escalate threats to order, significantly through the granting 'rights' that demobilize and depoliticize struggles. The history of rights

53 Douzinas, *States of Exception* (n 26).
54 Douzinas, *Philosophy and Resistance in the Crisis* (n 1).
55 ibid.

and legal theory demonstrates this and supports means of radical reappropriation.[56] Hence, the critical application of human rights to practice, closer to its own ends, is realized through resistant reappropriations and utopic (and provisory) reconstructions of a fairer world.

From this perspective, critical legal theory *is* praxis. In fact, praxis is at the origins of the Critical Legal Studies movement which counters the apolitical formalism in classic jurisprudence – dedicated to foundations of law and ideals of justice – with radical politics. As a pioneer in the field, Costas Douzinas himself set out to reconstitute the history of Critical Legal scholarship (in a periodization centred on the aesthetic, ethical and political turns).[57] While in the 1980s' 'epoch of aesthetics' the focus on rhetoric and semiotics allowed us to unpack traces of injustice and exploitation in the law, the 1990s' ethical turn prompted the critics to reimagine a legal order in which 'people are no longer despised or degraded, oppressed or dominated'.[58] In the 2010s, the 'age of resistance' set out to turn to politics and theorize on the right to resist, as discussed in this chapter. One could argue that the latter and current 'epoch' is the quintessential manifestation of critique as praxis – one which found, at least in the Latin American 'spring', situated ways to reconnect with its radical origins.

Indeed, the implications of human rights in Latin America are distinctively 'radical', in these terms. With a peculiar political tradition of social struggles in the region, the international discussion of rights has created a consistent legacy of instrumental application by social movements. Practices of strategic judicialization, legal activism, community justice and legal pluralism are some of the examples in which legal theory and practice have aligned politically in the region, with Latin American social movements contributing to (rather than being fed by) the formation of what is frequently termed an 'insurgent' critique of law.[59] It is, thus, not surprising that when the new waves of global resistance reached Brazil, a very productive theoretical-practical encounter between critiques emerged – i.e. the new forms of global resistance and the previous insurgent atmosphere in which human rights movements were forged – to reclaim a radical agenda.[60]

56 Douzinas, *The End of Human Rights* (n 40); Douzinas, *The Radical Philosophy of Rights* (n 31).

57 Costas Douzinas, 'A Short History of the British Critical Legal Conference or, the Responsibility of the Critic' (2014) 25 *Law and Critique* 187. see also Douzinas, *States of Exception* (n 26).

58 Douzinas, 'Notes Towards an Analytics of Resistance' (n 32) 193.

59 See Dossiê: Breno Bringel, Emiliano Maldonado and Renata VS Varella (eds), 'Introduction – *Latin American Critical Thinking, militant research and subversive perspectives of rights*' (2016) 7(13) *Direito e Praxis* 4–17.

60 Douzinas, *The Radical Philosophy of Rights* (n 31).

Without attempting to retrieve a liberation or emancipatory sense of rights within the political and legal system that concedes them, the point is to focus on how rights, resistance, radical politics and critique are acted on, as practices aimed at challenging established orders and/or creating new worlds. This is not a matter of evaluating their failures and successes. It is about recognizing that they will be continually practised, and that's a fact. Hence, in continually enacting 'resistant human rights',[61] one undoes (locally and momentarily) human rights' being an instrument of empire and creates commonality. In the situated and provisory coalition of human rights movements to resisting street politics, their being-together realizes a somewhat decolonial human rights.[62] After all, as Costas Douzinas has eloquently phrased it, 'politics combined with critique give rights their due'.[63]

61 Baxi (n 48).
62 Peter Fitzpatrick, 'The Revolutionary Past: Decolonizing Law and Human Rights' (2014) 2(1) *Metodo: International Studies in Phenomenology and Philosophy* 117–133.
63 Douzinas, *States of Exception* (n 26) 14.

17

THE RIGHT TO BURY THE DEAD

Alterity, Hope and Revolution

Marcus V. A. B. De Matos

In this chapter, I will argue that Douzinas' and Warrington's claim that justice must be associated with hope for a just society is the best response to abstract claims of neutral justice produced by *liberal jurisprudence* – a category that could include scholarship as diverse as John Rawls, Ronald Dworkin and Herbert Hart. Douzinas and Warrington have suggested that this hope can only be achieved through an emphasis on alterity. They have claimed that a just society presupposes our capacity to reject the world as it is and to develop hope – a hope that some agency might intervene and deliver justice to this society. And also that looking after and caring for the other is the way forward to deliver justice beyond the limits of the law – transgressing the borders of neoliberal aesthetics and authority.[1] To follow their steps and take their theory further, I want to claim *the right to bury the dead*. This is to question the results of abstract jurisprudence in producing liberal conceptions of human rights that are disembodied – and often destitute of relevance for those who suffer most. To find hope in justice after the dismissal of ethics in modern legal theory, I will look for theological archetypes of Christian texts and philosophical forms of Greek literature. This road will eventually take us through the emergence of modern state bureaucracy, and the exclusion of social and economic justice from contemporary conceptions of human rights. The right to bury the dead will help us deconstruct and

1 Costas Douzinas and Ronnie Warrington, 'The Face of Justice: A Jurisprudence of Alterity' (1994) 3(3) *Social & Legal Studies* 405–425 <https://doi.org/10.1177/096466399400300306>.

DOI: 10.4324/9781032622224-17

reclaim human rights as a secularized conception of justice that (re)emerges from one the most ancient rights.

Instead of starting with a conceptual and abstract definition of justice, I want to do what lawyers usually do: I want to start with a case. Something that challenged courts, judges and police officers in real life. Starting from the disappearance of the body of Juan de Moraes – an 11-year-old boy killed by police officers in 2011 in Rio de Janeiro, I want to reflect on the deliverance of bodies as a form of justice. To claim and deliver back lost bodies might be one of the oldest forms of justice deliverance in human history. Was justice done when the Trojan king Priam approached Achilles to take back his son's body? Is it possible to do justice to Juan? Douzinas and Warrington's work on the aesthetics and ethics of justice can help us find out.

The Right to Bury the Dead

In July 2011, two police officers invaded a slum during the evening. This was a poor community in the outskirts of Rio de Janeiro. They were supposedly searching for a thief who was reported as living in that area. However, once they invaded the slum, they did what police officers historically do since colonial times: they opened fire, unrestrictedly, against people living in the area. Those who were shot had committed no crime, except living in the same area and having the same skin colour as the burglar they were looking for. But after shooting an 18-year-old boy and a 15-year-old adolescent, they realized they had gone too far: they had also killed an 11-year-old boy.

We don't know, to this day, if Juan de Moraes died at the scene. What we know is that the 18-year-old boy lost a leg, but survived, along with the 15-year-old teenager. They saw the police officers put Juan's body into the back of their car. And both joined the Witness Protection programme that I used to coordinate in Rio de Janeiro back then.[2] This only happened, I need to say, after these kids were publicly accused by the same police officers of selling drugs and shooting back at them – something that further police investigation found out to be a baseless accusation. The police officers reported engaging in a shoot-out with several people, but there were absolutely no signs, no evidence and no witnesses that could confirm that this had happened. Juan's body disappeared. For 16 days, no one could find it.

Juan's body was found in a pig shed, amongst the animals. The police officers had tried to get rid of the body by taking it to a nearby city. They

2 To read a critical approach to human rights protection policies in that context, see: Marcus VAB De Matos and Andrea Sepúlveda, 'Human Rights in the Lion's Den: Law, Politics, Policy and Witness Protection in Rio de Janeiro' (November 2016) 4(1) *Birkbeck Law Review* 97.

thought that the starved pigs would make all evidence disappear. But the pigs did not complete their job. After several DNA tests, the scientific police – a rare species of police officers in the larger part of the world – confirmed that the human remains found in the area were what was left of Juan's body. This finding was only possible because of huge public pressure on the State authorities. There were several Human Rights movements and Members of Parliament who called for a solution to the case. Juan was shortly inserted in the long list of disappeared people in Brazil. But the public pressure that started as a small demonstration led by Juan's parents in their neighbourhood resonated in two strategic places: the Rio de Janeiro Human Rights State Council and the Church-based NGO, *Rio de Paz*.[3] These two places echoed the desperate cries of Juan's parents for justice, which could not be ignored.

On the 7th of July 2011, I organized the ceremony that buried Juan.[4] Both police officers accused of his killing were arrested. But I never really recovered from this injustice. I have tried to exorcise these memories, but I could never really turn this page.[5] Nothing seems to be enough to heal me from this damage – on which, I need to say, I am probably among those who suffered the least. I find this case to be a brutal injustice, but not only so: I think what happened in that small slum in the outskirts of Rio might shed some light on our understanding of justice. There are at least two issues that haunt me about the case that need some reflection, that we shall now turn to.

The first thing that strikes me when dealing with such a case is feeling powerless in the face of such pain. Justice, in our current understanding of the term, does not seem to be able to heal our pain. Modern justice is currently considered as something to be administered, legally, and separated from ethics. It does not seem to have the power to heal wounds. It is more likely that in dealing with the legal system, justice will hurt people further rather than heal them. Perhaps this is why justice does not have a face, nor looks at people: the image of justice that emerged after the Enlightened revolutions keeps its eyes shut so it won't see the damage it doeswhen

3 Clayton Guerreiro, 'Os protestos dos protestantes. Produção de legitimidade e performances da ONG Rio de Paz' (24 June 2016) *Ponto Urbe. Revista do núcleo de antropologia urbana da USP* No 18 <https://doi.org/10.4000/pontourbe.3010>.

4 RJTV, *Corpo do menino Juan é enterrado na Baixada Fluminense, no RJ* (Rio de Janeiro, 7 July 2011) <http://g1.globo.com/rio-de-janeiro/noticia/2011/07/corpo-do-menino-juan-e-enterrado-na-baixada-fluminense-no-rj.html>.

5 For a detailed case study on this, see: Marcus VAB Matos, 'Onde está Juan? Um estudo de caso sobre o PPCAAM na proteção de crianças ameaçadas no Brasil' in Mário Luiz Ramidoff, Marcela Carvalho Bocayuva and Viviane Coêlho de Séllos-Knoerr (eds), *ECA 30 Anos: Emancipação Subjetiva, Mudança Cultural e Responsabilidade Social* (Instituto Memória 2020) 717.

justice is supposedly delivered, or the Goddess of justice is satisfied[6] – perhaps by the sacrifice of children's bodies.

The second issue that emerges from this case is that in reclaiming lost bodies, we might be dealing with a foundational aspect of so-called Western civilization. The right to bury our dead, the right to cry upon those we lost, is probably one of the first human feelings about injustice, the injustice that we all feel when facing death – or the death of those we love. Death supposedly leaves us with bodies to cry upon. But as the legal case of Juan's disappearance reveals, even this right, the right to cry for those we lost, cannot be something we take for granted.

In the Trojan War, we see, perhaps for the first time, this kind of pain. King Priam loses his first-born son: Prince Hector is killed by the warrior Achilles who drags away Hector's body and keeps it for himself.[7] The pain that King Priam felt is perhaps similar to the one that afflicted Juan's parents. And while King Priam went directly to Achilles to reclaim his son's body, Juan's parents organized a demonstration in the slum where they lived, claiming the exact same right: the right to bury their dead.[8] But this right is often denied to those that are not even recognized as enemies, or those who are not considered as human beings. When there is no reciprocity in the image of those who are opposed, or engaged in war, this ancient right has been denied.

This is usually the case in history when vengeance was executed without any limits. It happened when all-out war was unleashed and people fought each other without recognizing themselves in the pain they inflicted upon their enemies. This is what the Greeks did to the Trojans after they mischievously got inside their city: the murder and extermination of all citizens, servants and slaves in Troy, without any consideration for their deeds, responsibility or innocence. This practice, that we now have a name for – *genocide*, is something profoundly attached to human history, especially in recent colonial times. Although genocide is a fairly new legal term, something that was born alongside our current notion of human rights, the practice it represents was already described in the Old Testament and in other sacred texts.

However displaced in time and space these practices might seem to be, in places like Brazil, India, South Africa and the United States, we often hear about targeted killings against minorities, of actions that remind us of genocides. These are often violent practices that can take many forms: mass

6 *Construindo Memória: Seminários Direito e Cinema* (Rio de Janeiro: Faculdade Nacional de Direito : CNPq 2009).

7 Homer, *Homer's Iliad* (G Routledge 1887).

8 Lucía Eilbaum and Flavia Medeiros, "'Onde está Juan?': moralidades e sensos de justiça na administração judicial de conflitos no Rio de Janeiro" (1 July 2016) *Anuário Antropológico* No I 9–33. https://doi.org/10.4000/aa.1530.

murder, lynching, burning of people and buildings, public executions, etc. They all follow traces of recent colonialism: when the colonizers exercised unlimited violence against certain ethnic groups. But I want to follow the traces of injustice here as a police investigator would do when following a lead from a crime scene.[9] I believe the patterns that are foundational to this kind of injustice – some of which we see in Juan's case – are those that involve a degree of fake evidence, biased trials, execution, torture and the destruction or disappearance of bodies.

The founding case of what we now call genocide – and which partially defines our current understanding of human rights – is possibly what happened when the German State targeted its own citizens, a minority of Germans who were Jews.[10] The Holocaust that happened in Nazi Germany was the leading case for the emergence of the concept of genocide and its supposed antidote: the notion of human rights as we have it today. But important as these definitions might be historically and legally, two issues must be noted. The first is that these conceptions do not apply to violations of human rights that are regularly perpetrated by the state or state agents on the national level. They also do not account for most colonial state actions and the concept of genocide is repeatedly denied application for institutional practices that follow legal procedures – such as police violence against minorities on a daily basis.[11] Secondly, it is necessary to note that these are negative conceptions of justice.

Perhaps there is another major foundation to these kinds of injustice that determines the right to bury the dead. Most definitions of justice and injustice available today have some influence from Christian theology – which overlaps with Natural Law and Ethics in many aspects. Perhaps the biggest foundation of injustice in Western societies is the Crucifixion: the negative theological incident where one could see an absolute expression of injustice. Crucifixion defines a pattern we still see today in many parts of the world: an innocent is arrested, subject to a biased trial (or no trial at all), tortured, executed and her or his body disappears. This is perhaps the Western foundation of injustice. And here we see the first challenge to a legal conception of law that could include ethics. In the Christian narrative, the only hope for their theological perspective is resurrection. There is no living ethics for Christians without the resurrection of the body.

Losing the body, in Walter Benjamin's words, is also losing the memory of history.[12] Resisting this loss is an act of resistance to claim memory over

9 Carlo Ginzburg, *Clues, Myths, and the Historical Method* (Baltimore: JHU Press 2013).
10 Samuel Moyn, *The Last Utopia* (Harvard University Press 2010).
11 BBC News, *Black Brazilians Protest against Racism and Police Violence* (Latin America & Caribbean, 14 May 2021) <https://www.bbc.com/news/world-latin-america-57112382>.
12 Walter Benjamin, *The Arcades Project* (Harvard University Press 1999).

tradition: an act not to conform to defeat when the victory of the enemy threatens the very existence of the dead.[13] But secularly speaking, *the right to bury the dead* is fundamental to building an ethics of law that does not abandon justice. It occupies a position in historical materialism where the right to memory is associated with the moment of danger – in a Benjaminian sense. Perhaps the right to the lost body is the most fundamental right – or the real foundation of human rights we could find today.

21st Century Bodies: Human Rights as a New Foundation of Justice

What we now call human rights is more than a concept; it is also a movement. It is an international movement of nation states, international courts, civil society organizations and individuals. Human rights are a notion that, according to Samuel Moyn, have two recent foundations: one in 1948 and another in 1968.[14] They were partially formulated after the Second World War and defined that state agents cannot justify their brutality by claiming adherence to their own legislation alone. Just following law and order is not enough to do justice – and is certainly no excuse to promote or let injustice happen unchallenged.[15] When any state agent is performing his/her duty, they need to ask if they will inflict a brutal injustice upon someone else. But its second origins are more troublesome to current neoliberal politics.[16]

By the end of the 1970s, the modern notion of human rights encountered a paradox that had been previously challenged by ancient conceptions of Natural Law.[17] Douzinas explains this as a shift in the very conception of what it means to be human, and the contradictions in extending universal rights to all people, while sometimes paradoxically denying them basic fundamental rights.[18] And here I am talking about the emergence of a Human Rights global movement that shaped an international civil society movement revolving around the idea of Human rights. Those were times of political unrest in many parts of the world. What happened then was a kind of

13 Ibid.
14 Moyn (n 10).
15 Lon L Fuller, 'Positivism and Fidelity to Law: A Reply to Professor Hart' (1958) 71(4) *Harvard Law Review* 630–672 <https://doi.org/10.2307/1338226>.
16 David Harvey, *A Brief History of Neoliberalism* (OUP 2005).
17 I refer here to the theological and legal debate about the rights of Amerindian peoples, which considered the question of whether native people had a 'soul' and, as such, if they could be considered as persons and bearers of Natural Rights. See: Bartolomé de Las Casas, 'Princípios para defender a justiça dos índios' in Carlos Frederico Marés de Souza Filho (ed), *Textos clássicos sobre o direito e os povos indígenas*, 1a ed. (Curitiba: Juruá & Núcleo de Direitos Indígenas 1992) 13.
18 Costas Douzinas, *The End of Human Rights: Critical Legal Thought at the Turn of the Century* (Hart Pubisher 2000) 108–110.

awakening: several minorities and interest groups realized that, although they were not necessarily being exterminated by the state, they were, nevertheless, being treated as non-humans, or second-class citizens. Their suffering resulted from extreme poverty, segregation, racial and gender discrimination, political and religious persecution – which in many cases were legally achieved by the dominant classes. These people were being denied their freedom and basic rights. They were denied human rights.[19] To resist these situations, this was a powerful discourse. It connected people globally. In the USA, this human rights discourse turned the Civil Rights Movement into a beacon. In South Africa, it fuelled the anti-apartheid struggle and it also ignited many liberation and anti-colonial movements worldwide.

But when something is a success like this, it doesn't take long before it becomes a propaganda tool of some politician or a bureaucratic heartless policy for certain capitalist state actors and their market supporters. In the 1980s, several international conflicts revolved around human rights. The most significant perhaps was the fall of the Berlin Wall and the dismantling of the Soviet Union. The 1990s brought in a different approach to human rights, now branded by the winners of the Cold War as a discourse embedded in fancy diplomatic dinners and military interventions – some of them clearly pretending to be humanitarian wars. This is what we entered the 21st century with: wars that were supposedly waged for defending human rights.[20]

The invasion of Iraq, Afghanistan and the terrible civil wars in Libya and Syria are tragic examples of what happens when human rights are used as an excuse for military interventions. It is what happens when Western leaders believe they can export democracy and human rights using armies and bombs, instead of schools and books. It must be said, though, that these discourses are not too different from Russia's excuse to 'denazify' Ukraine as a justification for its military invasion in both 2014 and 2021.[21] However hypocritical these propositions might sound, they should not shade the central role human rights have played in the moral discourse of international conflict.

This discourse that took over human rights on the international level was less subtle than what happened at the national state level: the complete association of human rights and neoliberal politics. This produced a soft, dehydrated notion of human rights in liberal democracies that persistently tried to make them compatible with permanent social inequality and deep

19 ibid 109.

20 ibid.

21 Daniel Pick, *Brainwashed: A New History of Thought Control*, main ed. (Wellcome Collection 2022) viii.

structural racism. It added evidence to the 'paradox of human rights,' as critical legal theory formulates it: the more human rights are legally accepted the greater the possibility that they will be violated or not fulfilled.[22] If Human Rights can be understood as a movement, as Moyn suggests, this movement urgently needs to produce a critique of the neoliberal notions of human rights that are compatible with brutal social inequality, structural racism and military interventions disguised as *humanitarian* actions. We shall now turn to examine the relationship between human rights and ethics – and hope to find a notion of justice to reclaim lost bodies and bury the dead.

Injustice Is Materially Seen, But Justice Is Something We Can Only Hope For

Justice is a concept that is historically very hard to define. The most ambitious definitions we can find today are old and were devised before the invention of the modern state. Some of these definitions take us back to Aristotle and to the ancient pre-Socratic philosophers, who defended justice as the sum of all virtues. Most importantly for the argument here, justice is usually defined in the negative, in the form of a denial. Douzinas and Warrington claim that this is the case, for example, in most of Greek philosophy, as well as in the Old Testament.[23] The problem we face when defining justice – and I propose, also in defining human rights, is that most definitions are in the negative, in the form of a denial or an absence: such as the absence of a body.

This is possibly the result of an idea of justice that is completely disembodied or, as Ronald Dworkin puts it, is understood as 'the most abstract political concept of all.'[24] The modern idea of justice is built upon the creation of the subject of the law as a rational and abstract being: an individual built in the logic of modern institutions and with no regard for class, ethnic or gender differences – almost as a *persona*, a fictional character or, as Douzinas suggests, someone using a mask.[25] This conceptual abstraction and disembodiment of justice is perhaps a relevant clue to search for an ethics of law capable of delivering justice – and to search for an ethics that is capable of recovering lost bodies.

Terry Eagleton challenges these abstract conceptions of justice on two claims. First, there can be no state authority – and for the same reason,

22 Costas Douzinas, 'The Paradoxes of Human Rights' (1 March 2013) 20(1) *Constellations* 51–67 <https://doi.org/10.1111/cons.12021>.

23 Douzinas and Warrington (n 1)

24 Ronald Dworkin, 'Hart's Postscript and the Character of Political Philosophy' (2004) 24(1) *Oxford Journal of Legal Studies* 1–37 <https://doi.org/10.1093/ojls/24.1.1>.

25 Costas Douzinas, 'The Legality of the Image' (2000) 63(6) *The Modern Law Review* 813 <https://doi.org/10.1111/1468-2230.00296>.

authorized law – independent from ethical values. Secondly, there can be no Marxist ethics capable of criticizing injustice from outside Western ethics and Christian theology. Eagleton's striking propositions can be summarized as such: if our idea of justice is not capable of ethically recognizing evil, then we are bound to let the Red Kimmer escape from the same hook where they have impaled young children.[26] These disturbing propositions lead us back to the historical difficulties in building up a theory of justice – or a concept of law – in the classical jurisprudential debate. Should we accept restrictive notions of justice that are limited to the possibilities of the liberal, secular state and its positive law? Or should we step aside from these political and philosophical traditions, towards ethical ideas – both substantive and procedural?

The modern, bourgeois state was supposedly built on Enlightened notions of reason and rationality. To make this possible, it was necessary to separate all ancient values, divine or metaphysical, from the *praxis* of power. This is why the modern capitalist state was created after a separation between religion and authority, which was followed by the divorce between law and ethics. A series of *differentiations* would follow these two separations: legality and morality; validity and value; form and substance.[27] These would eventually lead to the foundation of judicial institutions that were completely separated from ethics and morality. Perhaps the greatest expression of this kind of development was Hans Kelsen's defence of justice as a moral concept, alien to any positive law and legislation. Kelsen developed a notion of positive law whose validity is completely independent from any idea of justice.[28]

After Legal Positivism, in all its different trends, the 'dominant'[29] legal theory would now stand as a claim that law's validity was independent from its results. Justice was to be seen as something external to the legal system, and not to be considered on issues of legality. The only relevant issue for the legal system and the judiciary power was from now on related to the application of the law – if the law was correctly and justly applied, and not if justice was done. Even those who broadly opposed this idea – such as Lon Fuller – would do so claiming that the most important issue for justice was related to procedure.[30] This was a move towards finding a procedural concept of justice. Justice was now a matter of legal procedures that needed to be administered.

26 Terry Eagleton, *On Evil* (Yale University Press 2010).
27 Niklas Luhmann, *Law as a Social System* (OUP 2004).
28 Hans Kelsen, *O problema da justiça* (Martins Fontes 1998).
29 Ronald Dworkin, *Levando os Direitos a Sério* (WMF Martins Fontes 2007).
30 Lon L Fuller, *The Morality of Law*, rev. ed., Storrs Lectures on Jurisprudence (Yale University Press 1969) 33–41.

This jurisprudential move was crucial for the consolidation of the bureaucratic modern state that was built by the end of the 19th century. It would exceed the aims of this paper to discuss if Max Weber explained or created modern bureaucracy. But his rationale provided the modern state under the new ruling class – the bourgeoisie – with a rational tool to exercise and legitimate its power.[31] This bureaucratic-power arrangement would then find new forms and concepts of justice, and develop new ways to exercise power and violence – such as those in Legal Positivism and Process Jurisprudence. But such changes would not escape some collateral damage – including political and juridical ones that would cripple the 20th century emerging notion of human rights.

The adoption of a neutral and formal concept of justice, valid to all, inadvertently impacted the moral concept of responsibility – which is now to be determined by administrative courts or judicial review. This move consolidated the separation between institutional politics and individual responsibility. Justice became an issue to be applied to rights and property alone, and ethics was to be concealed in the individual consciousness. This is the change that would make possible the emergence of a notion of human rights completely focused on the individual, and not concerned with social justice, class division, racial discrimination or economic conditions. It is no coincidence, then, that some of the most shocking atrocities against humanity in the 20th century were committed by bureaucrats who, in their own defence, argued for the neutrality of ethics in fulfilling their legal duty and administrative responsibility.

Nevertheless, the new modern bureaucracy with its red-tape power and black-letter law also has a disturbing theological archetype.[32] I am referring here to those bodies of sadistic people who enjoy exercising small bureaucratic powers. We know them: those who delight in asking for an additional form to be handed in, or who have pleasure (almost of a sexual nature) in hiding and retaining information, writing Hansard or checking if the regulations were all fulfilled. But they are not new in history. The most striking archetype of the modern bureaucrat are those people portrayed in the New Testament, in several dialogues with Jesus. In these passages of the Christian Bible, they attempted to trick Jesus by challenging the legality of using his

31 Luiz Werneck Vianna, 'Weber e a interpretação do Brasil' (1999) No 53 *Novos Estudos CEBRAP* 33.

32 My use of Carl Jung's notion of archetype here is strategic. For a full discussion please see: C G Jung, *The Archetypes and the Collective Unconscious* (Routledge 2014). And also: Marcus VAB De Matos, 'O cavaleiro negro em Tropa de Elite: arquétipos, dispositivos e imaginários / The Dark Knight in Elite Squad: archetypes, apparatus and the imaginary' (8 December 2021) 12(4) Revista Direito e Práxis 2847.

ability to help people in need. They are those who ask: 'Is it lawful to heal on the Sabbath?'[33]

When justice is completely separated from ethics, what then? What is the result of this differentiation? The result is the liberal bureaucratic exercise of power. In the ancient regime, authority was based on divine or traditional models. The absolute power of the prince was once a justification of the means by the ends. The liberal and capitalist modern state authority, however, is justified and made legitimate by the choice of its (legal) subjects. In these conditions, where justice and authority are dependent on individual subjects alone, there are no ends: it is a state where the means are independent of the ends. Justice has abandoned any substantive idea of value: there is only process, procedure and form(s) to be administered.

Conclusion

Justice has to be understood as hope, and this hope is the Ethics of alterity – such as proposed by Douzinas and Warrington. As we have noted, there are two aspects of this justice. First of all, both are heavily dependent on Christian theology archetypes and ethics. The fundamental paradigm for injustice in Western society is crucifixion – when all injustice becomes a narrative about Western law and power. From a secular perspective, crucifixion lays down a pattern that repeats itself to this day: an innocent person is unjustly confronted by police authorities, arrested, subject to a biased or exceptional trial, tortured, executed and his or her body disappears. Western society, in all its Nation-State forms – including post-colonial states – is a society of disappearing bodies. This is the foundation of injustice as we know it today.

But what about hope? The second aspect of this justice is finding hope. For the Christian, there is no hope without resurrection. As such, the secularized version of this claim is that there should be no hope without revolution. Douzinas and Warrington have claimed that there is a material demand in the world for a just society and fulfilling this demand depends upon the rejection of the world as it is, and hoping that some agency – either human or divine – could intervene and change society.[34] To find hope we need to think of justice as an 'ethics of response to the concrete person,'[35] where modern law and abstract jurisprudence are not the last authority – and do not have the last word. This ethics of alterity could lead us to a notion of justice of equivalence, comparison and attribution that would be just in

33 *The Bible*, Matthew 12:-9–10.
34 Douzinas and Warrington (n 1) 406.
35 ibid 424.

recognizing the impossibility of abandoning the other – of passing by and ignoring suffering.

These propositions also have a theological archetype. This can be found in the road to Jericho when the (good) Samaritan raises up and helps a completely unknown and unidentified person who has fallen on the road. To produce a better kind of justice, we would need to raise the falling bodies that we find in the road, but also to go further – and reclaim the collective aspects of human rights that have been abandoned by western conceptions of individual rights. Martin Luther King Jr. commented on this passage the day before he was murdered, the 3rd of April 1968: if we notice that people are always assaulted on the road to Jericho, shouldn't we raise awareness that something might be wrong with that road?[36] It is dangerous to claim that Human Rights should include social justice. We need to pursue justice that is permeated by a redeeming hope and revolutionary love for the other. The right to reclaim lost bodies and bury the dead might help us bring ethics closer to justice, and deliver human rights claims that accommodate social and economic justice. The Samaritan who helps those he finds fallen on the road to Jericho has found the way to Emmaus.

36 'American Rhetoric: Martin Luther King, Jr. – I've Been to the Mountaintop (3 April 1968) <https://www.americanrhetoric.com/speeches/mlkivebeentothemountaintop.htm> accessed 24 August 2023.

18

INTERVIEW WITH COSTAS DOUZINAS

Critical Legal Studies, Resistance and the Crisis

Daniel Matthews

Daniel Matthews (DM): You have been a key figure in developing a distinctive "British" critical legal studies movement that has turned to contemporary continental philosophy and critical theory in order to explore aesthetic, ethical and political concerns within legal scholarship. Can you say something about the genesis of this movement? How, for example, does this movement differ from the American CLS of the 1960s and 1970s?[1]

Costas Douzinas (CD): If you look at the Western tradition from the Old Testament to Plato, from the Romans all the way to the modern philosophy of Kant, Hegel and Marx – even contemporary philosophers like Habermas and Luhmann – you realise that thinking about law is absolutely central to understanding how society works. Most major philosophers throughout Western thought have either studied the law or used the law as a case study in an attempt to understand how body and soul come together and how the individual connects with others and social power. That kind of approach to the law was lost in legal pedagogy from the 19th century onwards as the result of the vocational turn in legal scholarship and education. Law schools became sites for skills training; they became finishing schools for lawyers that created minor bureaucrats and technocrats of power. When I started my career as a lawyer in 1981, the only reason that an academic in the humanities or social sciences would want to know anything about the law was if they were buying a house or getting a divorce. There was no interest whatsoever in what legal scholarship had to offer.

1 Editors' Note: this interview was conducted on 28 March 2013 by Dan Matthews and is published here for the first time.

DOI: 10.4324/9781032622224-18

In a sense, what the critical legal studies movement has done over the last 30 or so years has been to re-inscribe thinking about the law into the heart of the academy and wider culture. And the success of this movement in producing theoretical and socio-scientific perspectives for the study of law has been quite immense. I remember, in 1984, I sent an article with my friend and co-author Ronnie Warrington to a well-known law journal that was rejected on the basis that it included at least ten words that did not exist in the Oxford English Dictionary. This included words like "deconstruction" and "logocentrism". Of course now, you don't get an article in the top legal journals if you don't mention deconstruction or some such.

The critical legal studies movement that has developed in Britain emerged in the late 1970s and 1980s from a group of people that came from the political left. We came from a generation that had participated in the great counter-cultural movements: the anti-Vietnam war movement, May 1968, etc. These were people who belonged to political parties or movements but also happened to be legal academics. I think what struck us at the time was that some of the traditional theoretical and philosophical approaches used by radical lawyers and legal theory – particularly the kind of legal theory associated with the early American CLS movement – were not necessarily appropriate for continuing a theoretical and radical movement in law. What I have in mind, in particular, is that the American CLS, which was really a continuation of legal realism, had developed a certain attitude towards law which suggested that if you could show that a particular development in legal doctrine was internally contradictory or indeterminate and did not follow a clear and coherent line of argumentation, logic or precedent then the legitimacy of law would suffer or even collapse. That was the key idea: that at the heart of the legal system a fundamental contradiction decides or determines how the law works and this contradiction makes the surface of the legal text indeterminate. So you had a number of American critical legal scholars trying to discover the fundamental contradiction in the law of contract, company law or constitutional law. It struck us in Britain that this focus on legal ideology, particularly the legal ideology as seen by legal professionals, by judges and academics and lawyers, told only part of the story. We wanted to inquire into the ways in which the legal system operated within society and helped produce class, race and gender domination, how bodies became controlled and disciplined by the law, how next to legal ideology, the force of law made people conform. We argued that social being – the way society operates and organises its main constituencies – *precedes* social consciousness and if any change was to happen it would have to be at the level of social being, at the level, in other words, of radically changing political relations and eventually the relations of production.

Obviously we were very much influenced by the Americans from the beginning, but the British movement had a stronger Marxist sense in terms of the political economy of law, but also a stronger philosophical understanding of law as an aesthetic of form that appeared in the organisation of the legal person and rights, as well as in the legal text. Following the work of Jacques Derrida and other deconstructionists, we saw law as a series of textual and interpretative strategies. Our task, then, was not to show the indeterminacy and internal incoherencies in the law – actually, it is easy to show that in the law of contract or constitutional law there are a number of decisions that, despite a surface coherence, are actually incoherent. For us, the problem was precisely the opposite. We wanted to know how it was that that coherence and the semblance of a harmony of argumentation had been turned into such a major aspect of legal ideology while it was palpably not there. So the task was to discover the strategies and tactics used both within and without the law in order to present the law in this seemingly coherent way. Most people don't see past this edifice of coherence: people talk about law or about judges with a huge amount of respect and obedience and so on, and that was problematic. But the problem was not that this was false – it created results – but to understand how that kind of domination was being reproduced.

DM: You have recently written about a turn in contemporary critical legal scholarship away from ethics and aesthetics to explicitly political concerns. From what you've said, however, it seems that the movement has been overtly political from its inception.

CD: Well, all classifications and periodisation are problematic; often, things are much more plastic and open than they might seem. But at the early stages of the movement – when the Critical Legal Conference was created in 1984 and the journal *Law and Critique* was established – it was certainly true that a concern with the textuality of law had become central. The deconstructive approach helped us escape both the nightmare of positivism and the "noble dream" of Dworkin's legal interpretivism that dominated legal scholarship at this time. It seemed to us that both positivism and interpretivism ignored the forceful character of the legal system. Derrida's "The Force of Law" – his famous intervention at the Cardozo Law School in 1989 – managed to capture, and give us new tools to deal with, something that we already well understood: of course the law is about values, but those values are always contested and force, legal force, is always involved. So rather than claim, as interpretive jurisprudence did, that somehow only good values exist in the law, we argued that in every interpretative act certain alternative value positions will be involved. You cannot interpret without values. And those values for us, at a textual level, had to be pinpointed and unravelled on the text of law. We thought that by focusing on the text of law, by emphasising its rhetorical organisation, its figures of speech, its different elisions and omissions, we could indicate whether there is racism or sexism or whether there is a certain class bias within law. We argued that if racism, sexism and class domination exist in society, this would be reflected in the legal text. But also, following a more classical Marxist line, we wanted to work out precisely how the law works forcefully. Once the work of interpretation came to an end and a judgment was passed, then the life of the law for most people is one of pain, domination, torture and imprisonment. So those two things dominated our thinking: firstly, an emphasis on the textual organisation of the legal institution (which we suggested was much richer and more open to alternative readings than existing jurisprudence credited); and secondly, an emphasis on law as a social phenomenon which enforces and confirms a certain distribution of power.

From this point many of us began focusing on ethics. You have to remember that this was the early 1990s: we had just seen the collapse of the Soviet Union and with it the defeat of every leftist position – the strange thing being that those that were most defeated in the West were those that had been critical of the Soviet Union and the Stalinist regimes. In the wake of this collapse there emerged a mainstream narrative of globalisation with an emphasis on universal moral values, expressed primarily in human rights. In an effort to counter this narrative, we hoped to discover ethical resources, ethical theories, which confronted this idea of a universal morality. This was the period in which many people moved towards alternative ethical ideas from Levinas and Buber, to the late Derrida, Nancy, Benjamin or Bloch. Of course not everyone was doing this but there was a clear sense that if morality had become such a major site of contestation we should be there trying to develop an alternative approach. And of course, as you say, more recently politics has taken centre stage replacing aesthetics and ethics. But only in a Hegelian sense: there has been a kind of sublation where both aesthetic and textual approaches remain but they have been, in a sense, taken up at a level that focuses on the politics of law.

DM: It appears to be common consensus that CLS in the US has died (and died a while ago). Do you remain optimistic about critical legal scholarship in Britain?

CD: Yes. And I think this is because the critical legal studies movement here has not become obsessed with institutional politics. Of course, in proper Foucauldian micro-political terms, politics takes place in institutions but within the movement there has always been a consciousness of the politics that takes place in the wider social setting: be it within party politics at the state level or within social movements, local initiatives or international networks. The split that happened in the US between the old Marxists and the new social movements did not happen in the same way in Britain. Our own critical legal studies movement and conference takes the form of an "inoperative community" to use Nancy's term – it is a conference "always to come". We meet for three days in the first weekend in September and at the end of the third day we decide where we will go next year and from then on the conference and the movement continues in our own fields, in our own scholarship and teaching and, of course, in all the other political activities in which we are involved.

We never bought the idea that we were somehow going to take over Oxford and Cambridge and the London School of Economics and turn legal education into critical legal education. This has helped us retain a certain modesty but also maintain and reproduce the movement because we have not been fixated on simply taking over law schools and squabbling about who is going to become the Dean. Even though the movement has remained marginal, it has garnered a large amount of respect and recognition for the contribution it has made towards re-situating legal scholarship from a totally barren field, which was of no interest to anyone except a few sad people who had to teach jurisprudence and their long-suffering students, back into the heart of the wider academy.

DM: Turning to your work specifically, anyone who has read your books and articles will be struck by the breadth of your interests and references. You have written on law and images, jurisprudence and the philosophy of law, radical politics, as well as – and perhaps most famously – on human rights. You draw on a diverse canon: from Lacanian psychoanalysis to Derridian deconstruction, from Ancient Greek philosophy and tragedy to Hegel and Marx. When you reflect on your work today, do you see an overriding concern that connects these seemingly disparate legal and theoretical interests?

CD: The reason I have so many references is primarily down to old age. I've done all this reading and writing and I can't get rid of it – whatever antibiotics or drugs I'm given. Looking back – and of course we all always create, retrospectively, our own history – I think the two key themes or concepts in my work are resistance and justice. In the last few years I have been thinking systematically about resistance. Resistance, for me, is a law of being: wherever there is power there is resistance; resistance is something immanent to every power system. It seems to me that we need to go back to that, the idea of resistance as an immanent force, as a force that in the first instance is negative, refuting existing distributions of power, but in the second instance is positive and reconstructive. It becomes reconstructive through an analysis or deconstruction of the way in which power operates, breaking power into basic building blocks and then reassembling these blocks in a different way. This, it seems, is how great new theory works, through the analysis and breaking down of systems of thought and then putting them back together again. Resistance is a theoretical strategy which is always involved in a condition of struggle. Resistance will always take place in a position of confrontation or antagonism. We cannot occupy some kind of neutral position somehow outside the theoretical or social and political field and then from that Archimedean point have a global or rounded view. We need to see ourselves as always being involved in struggle and always involved in this business of demolishing and then building again. As far as justice is concerned, my abiding principle is that we don't know what justice is but we know rather we feel injustice and then we react, we resist, we fight.

DM: Thinking, then, of the wider question of politics and resistance, what connections, if any, do you see between the number of resistances and movements – from Athens to Cairo, Tunis to New York – that have emerged since the 2008 crash and what has this season of discontent told us about the state of late capitalism?

CD: There was a knock-on effect that started in Tunisia and moved to Egypt and then to Spain and then to Greece and then towards a global occupy movement. Paul Mason, the British commentator and writer, suggests that in the movements of 2011 we can see the beginnings of a worldwide insurrection. He claims that a former director of the British Intelligence Service thought at the time that what was happening in 2011 was pretty close to what happened in 1848 or 1914. But on the left, we had some unusual responses. Badiou published a book called *The Rebirth of History* – it's a good title, but he says that this rebirth did not really happen. And Žižek published a book called *The Year of Dreaming Dangerously*, not *being* or *acting* dangerously, only dreaming dangerously. I think that perhaps the British intelligence agent was closer to the truth than Badiou or Žižek.

These events that unfolded in 2011 do have a number of common characteristics. However, I should say immediately that resistance is always situated; it always takes place in relation to the specific circumstances in which you find yourself, and to this extent, each act of resistance in 2011 took a different form depending on the context. So you can't say that Tahrir Square was the same as Puerta del Sol or even the same as the uprising in Tunisia. These events took place in relation to specific, local tensions and concerns. Having said that, there are certain similarities in the conditions that gave rise to these resistances. In late capitalism, we have seen a move towards an immaterial type of labour and, significantly, a much greater reliance on flexible work. For most young people, the idea of a permanent job – a job for life – that enables you to plan life and make decisions has disappeared. And this occurred over a period of 20–30 years, a period in which most capitalist societies were telling people that if you get the right qualifications, you've got a guaranteed job at the end. I see this change as being structural and not simply the side-effect of a cyclical move within capitalism. As we know from Marx, capitalism relies on "a reserve army" of unemployed people in order to drive wages down. It seems to me that with the process of globalisation, which has seen the transfer of primary and secondary sectors of the economy from Europe to the developing world, as well as the increasing reliance on technology and robotics, many more workers than the traditional "reserve army" have become dispensable. A younger generation, as well as an older generation close to retirement, have become increasingly superfluous or they only have precarious, part-time and temporary jobs. President Eisenhower said in the 1950s, when America was growing hugely, if you can guarantee that two thirds of the population will have their living standards improve or be stable, then you will have no political problems; people will accept the overall organisation of the system. Now, in many countries where these occupations and actions have been taking place, that part of the population that has fallen behind – that one third that Eisenhower speaks of – has become more than half. And this gives rise to serious problems and serious responses.

As I have said – rather jokingly – 1,000 unemployed lawyers, architects and doctors are, in theory, much more revolutionary than 1,000 unskilled workers. They are more resistant to the propaganda of power and they have skills that can be transferred from the professional environment to resistance, particularly when they have been told over a period of time that if you train and get a good education then you will get a good job. And it was mostly young people like this who thought that they had good prospects who led the actions in the squares and the occupy movements.

One of the standard criticisms of these occupations and protests was the lack of a common ideology, the lack of political parties, concrete demands, a united voice, etc. But for me, this was precisely its strength. The importance of these events lies in the effect they have had on political subjectivity. There has been a certain conception of subjectivity created over the last 30 or 40 years whereby the individual has become integrated into the circuit of financial services and control of consumer capitalism. These recent events have seen a process of what we might call "political baptism". The subject starts to become de-subjectivised from that circuit of desire where satisfaction is produced through debt and consumption. Many of these occupations, especially when they began to acquire a political character, started to de-articulate people from their existing sense of subjectivity. The idea of a subject presents a sharply paradoxical situation. As a subject, you are *subjected* but also the subject, the bearer of freedom – according to our Modernist metaphysics. It seems to me that in late capitalism, the move towards a popular capitalism, where we are all told we are all free to have choices, we have personal responsibility, we are micro-capitalists of ourselves; all that works to conceal that the subject is in fact *subjected*. As lawyers, this is something well understood; a legal person – and person (*persona*) as a mask – exists because the law recognises certain positions, rights and duties. We have been told over the last 30 or so years that subjection no longer makes up part of our political and legal personality, as if all this has gone away and been replaced by individual freedom, as if we are all free subjects.

There has been this sense that the early modern promise of the West – expressed in the American Declaration of Independence as life, liberty and the pursuit of happiness – was going to be completed in late capitalism. We were told that the question of life and property, the question of freedom – as freedom of consumer choice – has more or less been resolved. Now all we need is to figure out the pursuit of happiness bit. The idea that late capitalism was going to allow us to achieve this happiness came to an end in 2008 when the money ran out. These rallies and protests and occupations that we have seen since 2008 have begun to put a stop to this narrative. Not through any clever ideas – don't forget it doesn't matter what you think, you can be an anarchist, or a Trotskyite, a Maoist or whatever, so long as your conduct follows certain protocols of integration within the labour force and within the system of circulation – but through changing how we understand ourselves and how we act. Not because some clever guy like Žižek has told us some smart ideas but through the movement of the body, through the coming together and the touching of bodies, through the abandonment of atomisation in an expression of being together. These occupations proved the idea that if you stop behaving in a way that integrates you into a particular system of production and consumption then possibilities open.

So these occupations and so on have led to a certain sense of de-subjectivisation, perhaps not a *re*-subjectivisation yet, but in these activities there is a sense that selves have become different in terms of conduct, comportment and affect and this is where certain possibilities lie. And let's not forget that this is only three years or so since a number of resistances emerged after the crash and this is three short years coming on the back of 30 or 40 years in which a certain conception of subjectivity, of comportment and obedience has been created.

DM: Are there specific tactics or practices that you see as being particularly important in creating and reproducing the conception of subjectivity that these occupations appear to be resisting?

CD: The first and most important is the function of debt. Following the work of Maurizio Lazzarato, debt – before being an economic relationship between creditor and debtor – is a moral and social relationship. It is a moral relationship because the indebted person always feels guilty, feels that there is something wrong with them, that they have to repent and that they have to change their behaviour. It is a social relationship of great importance because the debtor feels much more bound and acts in a much more obedient, pliant way towards the creditor than the employee towards the employer. The employee has a contract and if she doesn't like the job she can get out. When you're in debt, and of course nowadays most people are indebted for life, you can't get out. Debt determines the behaviour of the indebted person to a huge extent because, of course, if you're in debt you have to do certain things in order to repay. So on top of the moral guilt and the feeling that you have failed as a person because you have got into debt, there is this deep element of control. The employer controls your work for the seven or eight hours of the day you work for them, the rest of the day you are free to do what you want. The indebted person is in debt endlessly. Debt, for me, has become the central controlling mechanism of late capitalism.

I see these occupations we talked of before as being partly a resistance to this mechanism of control. And, I would add that it is in this light that we should understand the English riots of 2011. The people involved were people who have been told every day that what matters in life – the only thing that matters in life – is having the latest pair of trainers or the latest gadget, so no wonder they went out and shoplifted. Hegel analyses a similar situation in his own time. Hegel tells us that the poor, who are given the formal right to property, are treated, in legal terms, as equal in dignity and respect to everyone else. But the poor do not have the material means to realise their formal right to property: they feel a huge internal conflict, and according to Hegel, they are justified in going to steal food and the basic stuff for life. Hegel was very radical. I think that this analysis can apply to the unrest we saw in England, France and elsewhere. Of course, these people were stealing trainers, not bread. But in the UK, the basic stuff of life is not in short supply. For Hegel, though, the key thing is the mismatch between the formal respect and dignity that the political or legal system gives you and the reality of the inability to have the material preconditions that enable you to access that respect and dignity. This, I think, is precisely the same mismatch that we saw in the riots.

Another interesting thing that has been reproducing this conception of subjectivity over the last 20 or 30 years has been the way the subject has become integrated into the financial system through stocks and shares. People have been encouraged to take their savings out from under their mattress or from their deposit account and invest them in stocks and shares. And so you have a strange situation in countries like Greece and Spain, where there is crippling austerity; ordinary working people will often have some stocks and shares. So, as a working person, you are obviously against austerity, especially if you have lost your job, but as an investor (even if it is a pretty meagre investment of €3,000 or €4,000), you want the stock exchange to do well and the Euro to succeed. This is why a majority of the Greek people are against austerity but want to stay in the Euro. So Thatcher's idea of turning society into popular capitalism, where we give even the poorest in society a stake in the way the capitalist system works, has, in a sense, succeeded. This is why you see this contradiction. In Greece, many people want the radical Syriza party in power because it has good ideas, but on the other hand, people still want someone with a safe pair of hands who will look after their investments.

DM: Perhaps we see this paradox most acutely in Britain, where there has been some resistance to austerity, but there are so many people invested in the system, both financially and ideologically, that radical change seems much less likely than in Greece or Italy or Spain.

CD: Let's not forget that the British working people have a very strong tradition of resistance. This is why Britain developed one of the first welfare states. Free education, the National Health Service and social care were the result of campaigns and struggles led by the working class and the trade unions. But Britain was also the first and most advanced site of neoliberal rearrangement in Europe. Mrs Thatcher had a grand plan – she was a proper revolutionary – and she set about reorganising the system along neoliberal lines. For the socialists in Britain, what has remained is a pretty conservative position: always trying to preserve and defend what was fought for and is now being lost. You're right, people have been integrated into the system who actually appear to be completely outside of the system. It is a difficult situation. There is still a strong trade union movement but there is probably the most advanced atomisation of society in western Europe. So many people feel that they are just out for themselves and their family.

Now, there is still a strong moral sense; people contribute to humanitarian causes to help people suffering in Africa and so on, but there isn't such a strong concern for the guy next door who has lost his job or may be unemployed. This move towards a purely moral concern and dispensation actually acts as a kind of alibi. If I give some money to Action Aid or Bob Geldof or Bono, I feel like I'm really doing the right thing, but at the same time, this has produced an utter indifference to what's happening on my doorstep. When I came here in the 1970s, there was the winter of discontent, and you could see the social democratic experiment starting to dissolve, but there was still a very strong sense of community, solidarity, of doing things together. And over the last 40 years, this has been gradually undermined and has even decayed internally.

DM: Let's turn to Greece where resistance to austerity has been pronounced – you have written and spoken about this situation a great deal recently. In 2009, Syriza got just over 4% of the vote and in the second elections of 2012 got 27% of the vote and is now the main opposition party in Greece and the only radical left party to have broken into the mainstream political debate since the crash of 2008. What do you put this radical change of fortunes for the left in Greece down to?

CD: What we saw in Greece was the coming together of two movements from the left that have tended to be, certainly not friendly, and in some cases, actually antagonistic: the anarchists and post-anarchist tradition on the one hand and the more traditional socialist, communist or other radical left parties on the other. These were groups that had organised themselves according to opposing internal organisational principles and differed in terms of their approach to strategic questions. More traditional parties of the left had hung on to the idea of strong party discipline – democratic centralism as it was rather euphemistically called, euphemistically because there was lots of centralism but not much democracy. These parties retained the view that the state is the key site of political contestation and in order to effect change at the level of the state, a strong party was needed. In the anarchist movements, by contrast, which are made up of a number of different groupings and individuals, the internal organisation always depended on horizontality or direct democracy. The external strategy differed too. Anarchist groups often exhibited a disinterest in the state and state organisations, focusing, rather, on smaller initiatives and local concerns: squats, occupations, social movements and community activism. This would often involve a "subtraction" (as Badiou calls it) from state politics with the intention of creating open and free zones. In the occupations of the squares in Greece these two ideas came together.

Crucially, Syriza, whose members participated fully in the resistance and occupations, never tried to direct or impose a particular line; they accepted the wider idea that there was no common party ideology, no party banners, etc. And because members of Syriza had been involved in the anti-globalisation movements and major protests in Genoa and Seattle and so forth, when these things started happening in Greece, they found themselves in a pretty natural environment. So these ideas of direct democracy, decisions being made by the multitude and by consensus, which came out of the anarchist movements and had been taken on and developed in these other movements, came to the fore in the occupations of the squares. But the nature of the problems made it clear that the movement could not "subtract" from the state; subtracting from the state would be a suicidal policy. You can make a few more open zones and have a few more squats and occupations, but when you're unemployed and not likely to get a job, when your parents and relatives have had their income slashed by about half, when your universities do not work, when your hospitals have no medicines, clearly you cannot withdraw from the state. The logic of assembling in Syntagma Square and confronting the Parliament opposite is clearly different from the logic of creating some free and open zone. It became clear that in order to confront the state, not only did you need horizontal organisation but also a vertical organisation; you needed some kind of party that could take that struggle to the people, to Parliament and eventually to government: not as the be all and end all, not as the only method and way in which radical politics can be developed, but as a necessary component.

It was at this point that Syriza was adopted by the people as the party of change. In Syriza, we see a happy marriage between an extremely important tradition of direct democracy and an equally important, though until now failed, tradition of socialist and left party politics that concentrates its efforts on the state. And hopefully, this marriage will continue.

DM: Syriza has a real chance of winning the next election. This prospect perhaps returns us to the question of what happens the day after the elections or "the day after the revolution", as Žižek puts it. Has what has happened in Greece with the anti-austerity movement and the occupations of the squares and so on done enough to prepare Syriza and the left for the day after the elections?

CD: In relation to Žižek's point, and I have said it many times but I can only repeat it: what happens after the revolution is exactly what happened the day before. The Greek democratic left is trying to develop a double strategy of both hegemony (by contesting for elections, developing policies and so on that represent the majority of the people) and conflict (by defending a certain ideological position and fighting the dominant groups and classes). Now, this is what we are doing the day before the elections and this is exactly what we will do the day after the elections. Žižek's point, I think, is a bit silly. Socialism isn't going to happen by some group taking over the Winter Palace and then the next setting out about changing the whole of society. It happens – if it happens – through the deepening of democracy, through incremental moves. And it is impossible to declare "socialism has arrived". Socialism is like the horizon; as you get closer, it recedes. Democratic socialism is the endless road towards the ideal. You do exactly the same the day after as you did the day before. The problem in our struggle is to make the day before work well and then the day after will have already taken care of itself.

This brings the original interview to a close. But to finish off the volume, the editors asked Costas one more question: after 13 years, what is your reaction to the 2013 interview?

What strikes me today, reading this 2013 interview, is its optimism, this desire for radical change, a desire we can call utopia. The wave of resistances around the world, which did not utilise human rights but social justice expressed in the "We are the 99%" slogan, and the expected victory of Syriza in Greece gave me the sense that perhaps we were at a historical turning point. The first part of the hope was frustrated: the end of Arab Spring and the return of dictatorships throughout the region, the gradual decline of resistances in the West, the return of neoliberalism which had been the main cause of the global economic and political emergency. These reversals lead to a provisional first conclusion. Resistance is fragile if it is not complemented by social movements and political parties that will continue the struggle after the multitude that creates the explosive event, the utopian moment (occupations, strikes, disturbance of the state or the market) goes home. This brought resistances to an end in advanced capitalist states such as the US and the UK. In places where the ancient regime controls an authoritarian state and its extensive repressive apparatus, its reaction pushes back the mass but peaceful resistances and insurrections. The restoration becomes a vindictive and more extreme version of the old. This was the case in the sad end of the Arab Spring and resistances in Turkey. If the insurrection does not aim or does not succeed in overturning the government, the best hope for radical change depends on the existence of a mobilising entity (political party, social movement or other organisation) that helps turn the "multitude" into a "people" and involves it in institutional politics. This was the case in Spain with the creation of Podemos and in Portugal with the Left Bloco which continued resisting and institutional politics after the end of the occupations.

The most successful instance of this continuity over time and partial transfer of the street into institutional politics was Greece and Syriza. It was a party with a long history. It is a transubstantiation over several steps of the old Eurocommunist party that broke with the Soviet Union and adopted the democratic road to socialism. It was well placed both to support the resistance and to represent it in institutional fora including Parliament. Representation is antithetical to the direct democracy of the occupations. A compromise is necessary when the streets empty and Syriza was able to make the transition. So, the second part of my 2013 hope came true, with the electoral victory of Syriza in January 2015. The election of the first radical left government in Greece created a new hope in the country and a new vista for the European left. It also radically transformed my life. I was elected Member of Parliament and became an "accidental politician". I have recorded my contradictory experience in politics and my frustrations with the "really existing" left in various books.[2] Here I want to say a few words about my legal experience. After a lifetime in London and the University, I found myself in Athens and politics. More importantly, after a lifetime as a critic of the law, I found myself a lawmaker.

What are the lessons for the critical lawyer from this strange reversal of roles? Could CLS help develop legal strategies? Yes, and no. The first conclusion is that critical law has to think more about legislation. We have developed powerful critiques of the case law, the common law and the judiciary but have not deliberated much about what it means to make law if you, rarely, have the chance. What strategies and tactics can be developed and used to start the slow, gradual and hard road towards democratic socialism? This involves greater understanding and co-operation with socio-legal studies. I found myself reading sociological treatises of law more than I had ever done before. My greatest input into law-making was during the process of constitutional amendment in 2018. I had the huge honour to be involved in the planning of the reform and was the deputy proposer in Parliament. It gave me the chance to inscribe critical legal studies and the names of people like Derrida, Nancy, Benjamin, Rancière, and Laclau in the Greek Hansard. The reforms we proposed were modest: a deepening of popular and democratic participation in political decision-making and the strengthening of the badly wounded social state with constitutional guarantees for socio-economic rights. We soon realised that the defences the constitution had devised to prevent radical change would frustrate the modest changes. The Constitution is particularly "hard": under the amendment process two consecutive parliaments should approve the proposed changes, one with a two thirds majority. We managed a simple majority only for our proposals, which were exhaustively debated in a special parliamentary committee and then the floor of the House, in 2019. As soon as the right-wing government won the elections in July 2019, it unceremoniously and without much debate rejected all important constitutional amendments we had passed with a simple majority. The dominant political powers have inserted a strong insurance policy in the constitution and the law against even modest change. The legal establishment and the organic intellectuals sided with the right-wing

2 Costas Douzinas, *Syriza in Power: Reflections of an Accidental Politician* (Polity 2017); *The Radical Philosophy of Rights* (Routledge 2019); *From the University Chair to the Parliament's Benches* (in Greek); *States of Exception* (Elgar 2023).

opposition first and government later and stopped the attempt to insert a popular component and a modicum of social justice into the constitution. The overall experience was even worse however. The failure and the defeat of the Syriza government was primarily the work of the diktat by the European Union and the International Monetary Fund assisted by the domestic establishment. They were not prepared to accept that a small country and a small democratic socialist party with strong popular approval could challenge the neoliberal orthodoxy and There Is No Alternative's demand that left ideas be eliminated. It seems that the global and European institutional and legal environment does not accept left governments and will undermine progressive forces.

The second lesson is that in this exceptional situation of a first radical government in the country, the superior courts became the most effective opposition. It was a highly successful instance of "lawfare", the use of law to frustrate, marginalise and criminalise the left. Most important legislative acts of the Syriza government were declared unconstitutional or unlawful by the Conseil d'Etat and the Areios Pagos (the supreme public and civil courts). Policies that had been key parts of the Syriza manifesto and had wide popular support were annulled by the courts; members of the Syriza government were prosecuted later by the right-wing government for pursuing these policies. I have detailed how lawfare was extensively used against the left in my book "The State of Judges" published in Greek this year. I hope to publish soon an English version of "Critical Legal Studies goes Greek". It became clear that ordinary law and the courts are much more important in the defence of the political power of elites and the economic dominance of big capital than the constitution, the democratic mandate or the popular desire for change.

The final lesson is the primacy of politics over law. We cannot depend exclusively on law and rights as defences against the abuses of power, nor is there a legal road to socialism. Rights won through resistance and struggle can be easily reversed. The ability to make modest constitutional and legal amendments was won politically and electorally by the Greek left. They were lost in the courtrooms. The right to abortion, antidiscrimination policies and the rights of transgender people were won politically in the US and Britain but are being lost in the law courts. A critical legal strategy must combine the deconstruction of the legal text with the political struggle for change. The critical lawyer must be both in and against the law, criticising it when it does not deliver what it promises and fighting for its wholesale reform when it frustrates the struggle for social justice. Trump's attack on critical race theory, critical legal studies and DEI policies shows that the critical movement has succeeded and has influenced policy making in many areas. While this is a period of defeat and defence, we should not forget that we are starting from a much stronger position than our predecessors in the 1960s.

I should add that my answer to Žižek about the "day after" was wrong and, in any case, it was not followed by the government. The Syriza government did not continue the road that brought it to power. The party cadres moved to governmental positions, the organisation and the members were abandoned, the social movements became immobile and did not put the necessary pressure on the government to apply its more radical proposals. At this point of the global rise of the extreme right, it is not clear what is left of the left. Walter Benjamin said that fascism is the result of the failure of the revolution. Today, the rise of the extreme right is the result of the political failures of the left. We have to go back to the drawing board. As far as critical legal studies is concerned, the lesson is clear: critique of law works in conjunction with the struggle for another law.

INDEX

For Product Safety Concerns and Information please contact our EU representative GPSR@taylorandfrancis.com Taylor & Francis Verlag GmbH, Kaufingerstraße 24, 80331 München, Germany